WHISPERING CITY

WHISPERING CITY

———— ✳ ————

MODERN ROME AND ITS HISTORIES

R.J.B. BOSWORTH

YALE UNIVERSITY PRESS
NEW HAVEN AND LONDON

For information about this and other Yale University Press publications, please contact:
U.S. Office: sales.press@yale.edu   www.yalebooks.com
Europe Office: sales@yaleup.co.uk   www.yaleup.co.uk

Set in Minion Pro by IDSUK (DataConnection) Ltd
Printed in Great Britain by TJ International Ltd, Padstow, Cornwall

Library of Congress Cataloging-in-Publication Data

Bosworth, R.J.B.
   Whispering city : modern Rome and its histories/R.J.B. Bosworth.
      p. cm.
Includes bibliographical references.
ISBN 978–0–300–11471–3 (cloth:alk. paper)
1. Rome (Italy)—History. 2. Rome (Italy)—Historiography.
3. Memory—Social aspects—Italy–Rome. 4. Historic sites—Italy—Rome.
5. Historic buildings—Italy—Rome. 6. Architecture—Italy—Rome. 7. Rome
(Italy)—Description and travel. 8. Rome (Italy)—Buildings, structures,
etc. I. Title.
   DG809.B67 2011
   945'.632—dc22
                                                          2010033495

A catalogue record for this book is available from the British Library.

10 9 8 7 6 5 4 3 2 1

For Edmund, Mary and their Romes

Today the age
Of the private patron is over; Maecenas and Co.
Have no successors. . . .
What about writers of history? Do all their labours
Bring them a bigger return or merely consume
More midnight oil? With unrestricted licence
They pile up their thousand pages – and an enormous
Stationery bill: the vast extent of the theme,
Plus their professional conscience, makes this inevitable.
But what will the harvest yield, what fruit will all your grubbing
Bring you? Does any historian pull down a newsreader's wage?

Juvenal, *The sixteen satires* (Harmondsworth: Penguin, 1974), p. 166.

Rome 'is not simply a collection of dwellings; it is the history of the world, represented by different symbols and portrayed in different forms'.

G. de Stael, *Corinne or Italy* (ed. S. Raphael), Oxford University Press, 1998), p. 82.

CONTENTS

———— ✳ ————

ILLUSTRATIONS

———— ✳ ————

MAPS

———— ✳ ————

PREFACE

———— ✳ ————

At a distance of twenty-five years, I can neither forget nor express the strong emotions which agitated my mind as I first approached and entered the *eternal city*. After a sleepless night, I trod, with a lofty step, the ruins of the Forum; each memorable spot where Romulus *stood*, or Tully spoke, or Caesar fell, was at once present to my eye; and several days of intoxication were lost or enjoyed before I could descend to a cool and minute investigation . . . . [And] it was at Rome, on the 15th of October, 1764, as I sat musing amidst the ruins of the Capitol, while the barefoot friars were singing vespers in the Temple of Jupiter, that the idea of writing the decline and fall of the city first started to my mind.[1]

So the celebrated phrases from the autobiography of Edward Gibbon roll on. A contemporary historian can scarcely hope to imitate their Augustan majesty. Certainly my motivation for writing a study of the city of Rome over the last two centuries, with particular attention to the ways in which history has been represented and debated there, is less exalted than that of my great predecessor. It is now more than forty years since I first visited Rome and, unlike Gibbon, my initial stay has been followed by many others. If early moments from this trip or that were sleepless, then my insomnia reflected the ordeal of the Australia-based academic with global interests whose body and mind were still adapting to having been imprisoned in a Qantas tourist class seat for twenty-four hours while the 20,000 kilometres that separate Rome and my other life were traversed. Intoxication there may on occasion have been, but my emotional ties to the city that I secretly and anxiously claim as 'mine' are complex in their fragility and contrivance. In deciding on this topic, I heard the chant of no barefoot friars (even if modern critics are a little unsure whether Gibbon's memory was itself not tinctured by artifice).[2] The sirens who sang to me a challenge to write about Rome may have had a classical frame of a sort, but I remain a contemporary historian, unable and unwilling fully to separate my past, present and future, glad, rather, that they bounce around in my mind like atoms in endless movement and frequent collision, just as grander pasts, presents and futures, multiple and conflicted histories and not a single agreed history, shall be seen in the following pages to do in Rome. The Eternal City, we shall find, is a place where, perhaps more so than in any other site of human memory, the meanings of history have always been debated. To any who will stop and listen, Rome whispers with many pasts.

In my own special memory, two experiences teased me towards this opening of my ears and mind to Rome's messages. There was the day that I had spent virtuously in the garb of what Joseph Stalin, with the menacing sarcasm of a man who knew all the answers (and all the questions) and so thought that he possessed the final solution to the dilemmas of present, future and past, called the 'archive rat', the historian at labour. I had been poring over the papers of Mussolini's dictatorship in Italy, material conserved at the Archivio centrale dello stato (national archives), situated at the Fascist model suburb of EUR (Esposizione Universale di Roma: Universal Rome Exhibition). My day's work done, I caught the underground or Metropolitana back to central Rome, where I had found sanctuary in the house of the Spanish Sisters of the Holy Conception which, with some uneasy historical resonance (in the way of the Rome to be explored in this book), was situated in the Via Nino Bixio near the central station. Bixio, a defrocked priest, had made a historical name as a determined and brutal lieutenant to Giuseppe Garibaldi in the campaigns that brought Sicily and Naples into unification with Italy in 1860–1.

To regain my room, the most convenient place to alight from the crowded train was at the *Colosseo* or Colosseum station. So I stumbled out into what I remember as the heat of a Roman early evening and trudged up the stairs, my inner voice running over the stories that I had dug out of the archives about little people who had fallen victim to Benito Mussolini's secret police. As I was about to debouch into the busy street that runs past the remains of the Emperor Vespasian's great stadium, I looked absent-mindedly to my left where there was a station bar. In that place, sipping their restorative coffees and at least as sweaty as I, sat two Roman legionaries, in what looked like leather uniforms, with sheathed swords by their hips. They seemed at home and happy as they chatted to each other, perhaps tallying the number of blonde female tourists whose mobile phone numbers they had managed to scribble down on that Rome tourist day among many. When I retreated from the station up the Esquiline Hill and past the Emperor Nero's pharaonic Domus Aurea or Golden House, I cogitated about the contemporary significance of legionaries and reflected on the jangling histories that clamour to be acknowledged in the Rome of the third millennium after Christ.

The second trigger for this book was located not so far away from the *Colosseo* station bar and its modern coffee-drinking legionaries. It is perhaps the least celebrated triumphal arch that survives in the city from the time of the Empire of the Caesars. Between the recently restored Piazza Vittorio Emanuele (named for Italy's first king, Victor Emmanuel II 1861–78), architectural heart of the Esquiline Hill, and Santa Maria Maggiore, one of the four major Catholic basilicas in Rome, can be found the fourth-century church dedicated to Saints Vito, Modesto and Crescenzia (roughly restored for Holy Year or *Anno Santo* in 1900 but given much more sympathetic historical sprucing in the 1990s). Sagging a little and propped up by the church on one side and an undistinguished-looking modern building on the other is the 'Arch of Gallienus', emperor of Rome 253–268 CE. This Arch does not cry out for attention and is most unlikely to be thronged by camera-pointing tourists. Rather the Via San Vito smells of those Roman cats that will scuttle away when a human stops and concentrates on the surroundings. If the visitor then consults a guidebook, it will become clear that the Arch is something of a fake since it was adapted from a triple structure erected under Augustus that itself owed its origins to what was once a gate in the so-called Servian Wall, a city limit going back to the era of the kings who ruled the city in the decades following its alleged foundation in 753 BCE by Romulus. Over time, any imperial history ascribed to the structure became clouded, and, through the Middle Ages, ordinary Romans saw instead what they called the 'Arch of St Vitus'.[3]

Yet, when passing (literate) citizens looked up, on the architrave of the Arch they could read a striking dedication: GALLIENO CLEMENTISSIMO PRINCIPI CUIUS INVICTA VIRTUS SOLA PIETATE SUPERACTA EST SALONINAE SANCTISSIMAE AUGUSTAE AURELIUS VICTOR V[IR] E[GREGIUS] DICTATTISSIMUS NUMINI MAIESTATISQUE EORUM (To Gallienus, the most clement chief, whose unconquerable virtue is matched by his piety, and to Salonina, the most revered Augusta, Aurelius Victor, a man of distinction, [this is dedicated] in utter devotion to their divine majesty).

Of the many historical ghosts who stalk the streets of Rome and whose tread will resound through this book and will duly be recorded, Publius Licinius Egnatius Gallienus is not the most renowned. In the cast of thousands of 'historical Romans', he has few obvious claims to stand forward on a historian's stage. Yet he does so appropriately at the start of this book. Admittedly, Gallienus was the unlucky emperor who assumed the purple at the time of the 'Thirty Tyrants', each one trying to seize his throne. His father, Valerian, scion of a traditional Roman senatorial family, had seized the empire after a long and distinguished career as a magistrate and soldier. Thereafter, he raised his son to be his partner in government, launched a war against the Persians, lost, was captured and humiliated, and died. Gallienus, more circumspectly, lingered in Rome until he was ill advised enough to travel north, win a battle and, in the flush of victory, be murdered by his lieutenant.

1. Pious and ingratiating slogan on Arch of Gallienus.

Over the next seventeen hundred and fifty years, history seldom treated his rule kindly. Gibbon polished sardonic phrases on him, and the Victorians used him as a model for schoolchildren to illustrate the wages of debauchery. True, history being the discipline it is, Gallienus has, more recently, been an object of 'revisionism', there even being a literature about an alleged 'Gallienic Renaissance'.[4] Perhaps, then, Gallienus is not yet securely buried? Certainly, when, in my capacity as a present-day fan, I search Rome for his traces, I find that quite a bit survives, from busts of him and his wife in the Capitoline Museum to other records of their rule kept at the Montemartini Museum, opened in 1997 on the Via Ostiense. An estate, complete with a family tomb, can be traced on the Via Appia, near where it merges into what are today the distant outskirts of Rome. Much of the Esquiline Hill, converted into a city suburb after 1870, was in the mid-third century devoted to the Horti Liciniani or the garden of Gallienus, a place of such loveliness that one present-day aesthete argues that it offers final justification for the Emperor's 'complete rehabilitation'.[5]

In sum, although disputes about this embattled man do not lie at the heart of efforts over the last two centuries (or the fifteen before that) to find continuing historical lessons in Rome, Gallienus cannot altogether be silenced. To be sure, the meaning of his past may need decoding. The 'clemency' and 'virtue' that his dutiful subject recorded on the Arch may only have been weakness; the grovelling inscription may best be read as a warning against believing political puffery. History must remain true to its democratic ambition to preserve, as its 'first duty', 'criticism, criticism, again criticism and criticism once more'.[6] It must preserve a commitment to reading between the lines rather than simply believing surviving texts of whatever type. Yet the spectre of Gallienus still walks abroad in the expectation that fortune will grant him another historic moment, and, even when shoved aside by more celebrated and significant Romans, calls for attention. The failed emperor's body may have long mouldered in its grave but his soul goes marching or, perhaps better, plodding on.

'Rome is like that,' I hear myself concluding, remembering the advice that I received from an unknown Jewish stranger with whom I entered conversation one evening in 1970 when I was strolling near the Colosseum. I confessed to being then on only my third visit to the city. 'Ah,' said my interlocutor, 'I have come every year since Fascism fell. Each time I come, I see something old that is new to my eyes,' my brief friend counselled before we went our separate ways. So it has been for me, as I shall try to describe and explain in the pages that follow in a book designed to represent to its readers the interplay of very many Romes and very many histories, filtered through the irony of my own sensibility as a writer and historian.

The task is great; my powers may be little. But in a preface it is appropriate to remember that, in exploring Rome and its histories, I have been comforted and counselled by many people in the splendid global community of scholarship. I took the idea to Clare Alexander, agent extraordinaire, who passed it on to Robert Baldock, Heather McCallum, Rachael Lonsdale, Tami Halliday, Beth Humphries and their colleagues at Yale University Press. They remained patient with me when the ambitions of the book expanded. My wonderfully encouraging team of friend-readers and commentators as ever offered the appropriate blend of correction and encouragement. In this regard, I must especially salute the late Roger Absalom and the late Nick Atkin, Dani Baratieri, Gianfranco Cresciani, Christopher Duggan, Giuseppe Finaldi, Rebecca Rist, Rob Stuart and Mark Thompson. Samantha Quinn assiduously tracked down lost information. Wasim patrolled my house and home. Felix Lim cleverly designed the maps which should allow readers to place my descriptions into the Roman streetscape. I must also thank the vice-chancellors of the University of Western Australia and of Reading in the UK, who have generously endorsed the five-year plan that will end my academic employment, and so fostered what have thereby become my expanded network of colleagues in those two institutions.

Throughout my dealings with Rome, I have generally been accompanied by, and always had purpose and meaning attached to my scholarly activities in the city by the presence of my life partner, Michal (family photographer of the city), and, when they were younger, by Edmund and Mary. We Bosworths cherish our own special Roman history. How fortunate we have been to be, thereby, Australian Romans/romanised Australians of a kind! May readers of this book be equally blessed in finding justification in its pages and in other parts of their lives to find and invent new and old Romes for themselves, again and again there to go, to see, to cogitate and to argue.

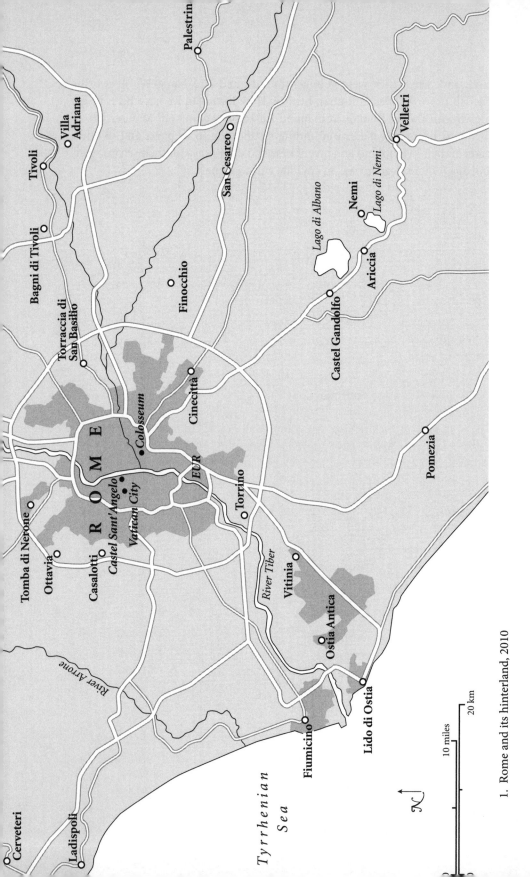

1. Rome and its hinterland, 2010

INTRODUCTION

———— ✳ ————

'What gives a city its special character is not just its topography or its buildings, but rather the sum total of every chance encounter, every memory, letter, colour and image jostling its inhabitants' crowded memories.'[1] So the Nobel Prize-winning novelist Orhan Pamuk explained as he ventured into his own magical portrait of Istanbul/Constantinople and those pasts and presents that had made him. Similarly, this combined image of the permanent and the fleeting was what Mark Mazower noticed at the beginning of his subtle exploration of Thessaloniki/Salonika, a place of 'more than two thousand years of urban life' and 'a city of ghosts', he wrote, where, nonetheless, 'change' has been 'the essence', since 'no successful city remains a museum to its own past'.[2] What happens, then, if Rome, the capital of Italy only since 1870 but possessed as it is of an even longer and more kaleidoscopic set of histories than the modern Turkish and Greek cities, is, with Pamuk's and Mazower's advice in mind, examined for historical messages and import from the past?

One typical approach has been to read the place as a palimpsest, wherein, peering through the accumulated debris of the years, a present observer can find much to learn from those remnants that somehow have not been buried for ever but instead resurface in reality or imagination. Certainly, in the historic centre of the 'Eternal City' (it was accorded that soubriquet by the poet Tibullus in 19 BCE), it is easy to detect layers of settlement and life across a vast span of time. A recent account has even penetrated further down to advise that the geological setting 'strongly influenced Roman architecture' and to alert historians to the new explanatory role being assumed by the city's 'urban speleologists'.[3] Almost every major current building in the city is constructed on something that was erected in an earlier era and Rome, since the burgeoning of modern excavation in the Enlightenment, has been the delight of archaeologists, Italian and foreign. Significantly, the enduringly cosmopolitan character of the work has meant that continuing archaeological labour has reinforced a broader meaning for Rome than was, by the nineteenth century, the norm for other places. Then, increasingly nationalised research on great cities made it common to channel their lessons into being merely for their nations.[4] Rome, by contrast, despite being smaller in population and industrial product than most and destined to be the capital of national Italy, remained by definition of universal appeal.

A good place for a visitor today to meditate on the accumulated dust of ages that so delights archaeologists is the Belvedere Monte Tarpeo or lookout from the Tarpeian Rock. Here in classical times malefactors were flung over a precipice to their certain death. Today the ground lies not so far below and anyone who was pushed from there, cushioned literally by the remnants of time, can be imagined picking themselves up with a shrug and sprinting off to safety. So shallow is the fall that some commentators insist that the 'real' site must be elsewhere.

Most celebrated among those who have probed the certainly piled-up and perhaps stratified character of Rome's soil is the 'father of psychoanalysis', Sigmund Freud. One for whom physical visits to the place came well after his detection in his mind of significant pasts there, Freud urged in his *Civilisation and its discontents* (1930) that Rome be comprehended as

> not a human dwelling place but a mental entity with just as long and varied a past history; that is, in which nothing once constructed had perished, and all the earlier stages of development had survived alongside the latest. This would mean that in Rome the palaces of the Caesars were still standing on the Palatine and the Septizonium of Septimius Severus was still towering to its old height; that the beautiful statues were still standing in the colonnades of Castel Sant'Angelo, as they were up to its siege by the Goths . . . . Where the Colosseum stands now, we could at the same time admire Nero's Golden House; on the Piazza of the Pantheon we should find not only the Pantheon of today as bequeathed to us by Hadrian, but on the same site also Agrippa's original edifice . . . . And the observer would need merely to shift the focus of his eyes, perhaps, or change his position, in order to call up a view of either the one or the other.[5]

The layering that Freud perceived in Rome had earlier proffered him a metaphor to help interpret the unconscious. Dreams and daytime fantasies, he mused, 'stand in much the same relation to the childhood memories from which they are derived as do some of the Baroque palaces of Rome to the ancient ruins whose pavements and columns have provided the material for the more recent structures'.[6] The far-off past, that which was in many senses 'deeper down', particularly the 'grandeur that was Rome'[7] when governed by the Caesars, was, he implied, still a crucial guide to his times, an indispensable aide-mémoire for those who strove to map the future.

Ironically, in this pondering on a past, Freud was indulging in unconscious omissions as significant as his conscious imaginings. Here was a person who believed in the Big History of the Caesars as the summation of the city's best lessons; the little histories of the people or even of political chiefs in less renowned ages and especially the rule of the popes were not worthy of his reflection. For all his fame, Freud was constructing history as a period piece. It is as revelatory of its author, his society, culture and era as it is of any 'real' Rome.

Nonetheless the idea that Rome is well understood as an accumulation of pasts, that can be teased apart and arranged in a hierarchy of significance, remains powerful and was, for example, given vivid cinematic presentation in Federico Fellini's *Roma* (1972). As the renowned director put it: 'What do I think of when I hear the name Rome? . . . I think of a ruddy face, brown, muddy ground; of a vast tattered sky, like an opera backdrop, with tones of violet, black, and silver. Funereal colours, but all things considered it is a comforting sight. Comforting because Rome, a horizontal city, stretched out, is the ideal platform for fantastic vertical flights.' Fellini's film portrayal, which was rather better appreciated outside Italy than within the country, strove to mix 'memory, documentary, and fantasy'.[8] As one analyst has put it (reinvoking Freud): 'Fellini's Rome is artificial and constructed – it is also spectacular, and dream-like. It is flooded with memories both personal and collective. It is difficult to find cohesive routes and vistas through it – and it is difficult to distinguish past, present, and future – let alone fact and fiction.'[9]

Fellini's audience was often composed of men and women who had visited or who hoped to visit Rome. The city's drawing power in that regard may have assisted what Dean MacCannell, a leading theoretician of contemporary tourism, has declared to be visitors' curious and always partially unsuccessful search for 'reality and authenticity'. As he adds wryly, 'the best indication of the final triumph of modernity over other sociocultural arrangements is not the disappearance of the non-modern world, but its artificial preservation and reconstruction'.[10] The present city, with its plentiful archaeological sites, rich galleries and museums, as well as its coffee-sipping legionaries, is, in this view, achieving a sleight of hand as it offers itself to be consumed as a 'real' history, an 'authentic' heritage site.

In recent times, this contemporary fascination with heritage has been solemnly accorded bureaucratic rules and yardsticks for the measurement of relative achievement in conserving or resuscitating the past. The Gubbio Charter, signed in September 1960, pledges to 'safeguard and refurbish historic centres', and that now seemingly automatic term only entered familiar discourse thereafter.[11] Soon UNESCO took charge of examining efforts that the nations made to keep their histories alive. Over the next decades, the list of places allegedly vibrant with a presently worthy past expanded to embrace 890 sites, with Italy always being the country acknowledged as possessing the primacy in global terms. So unconfined was 'Italian' history that, whereas for lesser countries UNESCO might bless a special building or natural setting, quite a few cities in the peninsula were simply admitted as a whole. The entry for Rome therefore describes it as 'the Historic Centre of Rome, the Properties of the Holy See in that City Enjoying Extraterritorial Rights and San Paolo Fuori le Mura'.[12]

This triumph of the heritage business is not without paradox and David Lowenthal has been the wittiest critic of those whose self-interest leads them to be 'possessed by the past' and whose tarnished product is an ever greater 'heritage glut'.[13] In Rome, after all, the year of the Gubbio Charter (as will be seen later in this book, it was also marked by the Rome Olympic Games and the centenary of the foundation of the modern Italian nation) saw the opening for business of Restauri centro storico spa (Restoring Historic Centre Inc.), an agency designed to bring profit to a major local real estate company. As one commentator, with his own ironical separation of the insertion of pasts into the present, has sadly assessed the result:

> shops and boutiques tended to occupy the medieval and more 'character-istic' parts of the city, once devoted to artisan manufacturing. Sumptuous baroque and neoclassical buildings tended to host banking and financial services. The new middle class, replacing the old nobility and reclaiming political control of the *comune* [local government], positioned itself in the Renaissance quarters. While piazzas and public squares became parking lots of the ubiquitous car, social services . . . and areas of common usage (parks and recreational areas) were cast out of the 'center'.[14]

For any sceptical of contemporary campaigns to buy and flaunt marketised histories, the victorious campaigns of heritage merchants often seem to blight serious understanding of the past. Heritage, Lowenthal laments, is the binary opposite of real history. Heritage, in his view,

> is not a testable or even a reasonably plausible account of some past, but a *declaration of faith* in that past. Critics castigate heritage as a travesty of history. But heritage is not history, even when it mimics history. It uses historical traces and tells historical tales, but these tales and traces are stitched into fables that are open neither to critical analysis nor to compara-tive scrutiny. Heritage and history rely on antithetical modes of persuasion. History seeks to convince by truth and succumbs to falsehood. Heritage exaggerates and omits, candidly invents and frankly forgets, and thrives on ignorance and error.[15]

Yet, if it can be agreed that the rhetoric of the heritage trade has a modern air and is dreadfully vulnerable to crass nationalist boasting and fakery, Rome has survived as a tourist site for millennia. Trade in the allure of the past there is scarcely a modern invention. Take, for example, the account by the historian Ammianus Marcellinus of the visit in 357 CE of the Emperor Constantius, son of that Constantine who had christianised his realm and moved its capital to Byzantium. 'As soon as he entered Rome, the home of empire and of all perfection', Ammianus reports, Constantius, as star-struck by the place and its inhabitants as is the most guileless modern tourist, 'went to the Rostra and looked with amazement at the Forum, that sublime monument of pristine power; wherever he turned he was dazzled by the concentration of wonderful sights'. And it was not the buildings alone that won him over but rather Rome's more general civility. 'On several occasions, when he held races in the Circus, he was amused by the witty sallies of the people, who kept their traditional freedom of speech without any loss of respect.' More subtle in his reaction was a Persian prince, Hormsidas, who had accompanied Constantius. According to Ammianus, on 'being asked what he thought of Rome, [he] replied that only one thing about it gave him pleasure, the discovery that there, too, men were mortal'.[16]

During the following centuries, there would scarcely be a time when visitors were not inscribing their own comprehension of Rome somewhere into their minds and being helped in the process by accommodating locals, who were themselves vending their own sense of the city. For two thousand years history has been on sale in Rome.

While 'heritage', at least according to some of its analysts, has been misleading the public, the term 'memory' has, during the last two decades, become one of the great drivers of historical research and been clothed in sumptuous intellectual prestige. From 1984 Pierre Nora has won many converts in his urging that 'memory' is code for a people's history more real, alive and 'truthful' than academic research. History, he charged, was 'how hopelessly forgetful modern societies, propelled by change, organise the past'. His present, he feared, was seeing the 'conquest and eradication of memory by history'. Memory was 'a perpetually actual phenomenon, a bond tying us to the eternal present'. History, by contrast, had as its arid purpose 'not to exalt but to annihilate what has in reality taken place'.[17]

Nora, in other words, was setting up another binary opposite where the minds of ordinary people, especially when anchored by a special place or a special day, were the richest current repositories of living, breathing and so creative survival from the past. Much fine work has been stimulated by Nora's insights, although, curiously, Rome has rarely been its preoccupation.[18] In the standard Italian account of memory there, Alberto Caracciolo has merely perceived an end of history in the modern city. 'In those four letters of the alphabet [ROMA]', he complained, 'nothing can be found to divert hurried and anxious modern man from his pursuit of the near at hand or of low horizons.'[19]

The more acute explorers of memory were, however, finding unsurprisingly that, in fact, recollection is 'never shaped in a vacuum; the motives of memory are never pure'.[20] Nor is memory guaranteed to arrive strictly from below. Its summoning is always likely to be contaminated by the numerous forces, led by the modern nation state, given to dabbling in the past for current purposes. As far as monuments and anniversaries are concerned, those with power have more authority and success in imprinting memory on them than do ordinary individuals. Men and women treasure their birthdays, name days and other special times of life's passage, including political trauma, as a way of recalling a past (often with advantages), but so does every institution and certainly all whose lives are somehow framed by Rome.

Indeed, as will be repeatedly seen in this book, the three thousand years of Rome's history have automatically made the city an opulent source of sites and dates that can trigger, or be haled into, alleged significance for contemporary commemoration. The Catholic Church, for example, is possessed of a memory that is deep and wide, all the more since both saints and divine providence are, by definition, prime bearers of the lessons of the pasts. Seldom does a pope make a present pronouncement without legitimising it through some claimed precedent. Helpful whispers from the past are regularly broadcast anew. In its similar recurrent and often obsessive search for a long and falsely united history, what is termed a 'usable past', the nation state, whether it be ruled by a totalitarian dictator or by liberal democrats, is no different (despite the common Italian complaint, revived in recent years, that their nation, afflicted by treacherously 'divided memory', is too weakly armoured with an agreed and approved single national history).[21] Memory-mongering is as habitual an activity in our present as is the sales spiel of the heritage trade. At the same time, neither can be written off as the complete opposite of history. Rather, each is better viewed as another passage into the past, flawed in its ability to express a vision of the truth except through a glass darkly. Yet neither is radically superior or inferior to the more conventional discipline of historians as, made respectable through their university careers, they have, since the Enlightenment, pursued the 'illusion of objectivity'.[22]

One effect of the evident multiplicity of the meanings being re/presented or commemorated in Rome has been to enhance the view, common in any case among postmodernists, that the city heaves with difference. Rather than accepting Freud's identification of a palimpsest where the 'most authentic' lies deepest among the ruins of the Great Buildings of Great Men, maybe Rome is most fruitfully conceived as a 'set of over-lapping cities', each needing its own specific map and each as worthy as any other.[23] Seeming to follow this lead, contemporary scholars in a variety of fields have endorsed current preoccupations with the same innocent alacrity as did Freud. For an expert on fine art, Rome has proved 'a dictionary of [visual] quotations, a shifting and allusive text which could puzzle or even alienate'.[24] For a film historian, the 'myth' of the classical city has held special power and durability, its images having 'permeated our civilization as a whole, our art, music, drama, cinema and even our notions of history itself'.[25] A classicist has agreed that Rome has a 'boundless capacity for multiple, indeed conflicting signification'; knowledge of the city can thereby helpfully destabilise 'history, politics, identity, memory and desire', and will always be both viscerally 'familiar' and viscerally 'other'.[26] Any who gaze into the past through reading, we are told, place themselves at the junction of the synchronic and the diachronic, where they confront and enjoy 'a concatenation of diverse elements, of different histories, advancing at different rates and subject to varying conditions'.[27] Rome, most recent scholarship seems to say, constitutes not a static palimpsest with separate layers that are as clear as day and as lasting as time. Instead, it is shifting and multidimensional, a place where historical currents flow, meet, fuse and disperse, with greater or lesser dynamic thrust, sometimes visible, sometimes not, but always giving propulsive charge of some sort to the present as contemporaries seek a path to the future.

Very likely. By its title, this book demonstrates its concern with multiple pasts and not with a single and set history. Moreover, so many Romes can be explored that, whenever reflection settles on the special past of a certain segment of the city, it is always tempting and often illuminating to look across the street or river, go around a corner, glance up instead of down, and find another history or another historical dispute there awaiting portrait or explication. Equally, just like space, time is a messy business in Rome where it may be hard reliably to separate one past from another. Each chapter of this book will focus on a certain period of Rome's history and the pages move from the Enlightenment to our own times. However, accepting that pasts interpenetrate, I shall not avoid circling back to an earlier era or on to the future when analysis makes it necessary.

I shall also be anxious not to slip into an absolute relativism, where all is always for the best in the best of all possible worlds. No doubt the first premise of this book is that democratic freedom is dependent on an acceptance that we are charged and informed by histories and not by history, and that these histories wax and wane in an argument (almost) without end. Yet, in what may appear a cheerful postmodernist celebration of diversity, politics and power must not be forgotten. The representation achieved through myth and memory, heritage and urban planning – in other words, history by one definition or another – is always sponsored more from above than below. The pasts that are most commonly made to matter are less innocent and more purposeful, and are very rarely merely 'speaking for themselves'. Fundamental to this book is therefore the concept of 'history wars'. Here I am not endorsing the neoconservative view that liberal democracies are beset by a culture or history war, a two-sided tussle between 'good guys' (themselves) and their deluded 'liberal' (in the American meaning of the word) opponents. My position is the reverse since, to my mind, a binary contest always traduces the actual complexity and nuance of humankind. A positive free play of ideas must occur in battles fought on many fronts and sometimes to the bitter end between rival claimants, each passionate and committed, yet all willing to admit that they do not possess the formula that will cure humankind. In such struggles over meaning, the contestants will, where need be, summon in their cause myths, monuments, anniversaries and other sites of memory, including the trinkets of heritage, as well as professional historical scholarship. They will use history wherever and whenever they can find it appropriate.

These confrontations over living pasts occur wherever humans gather. But Rome's longevity and the significance that has been inscribed onto it for so many centuries have made it an ideal post from which to reflect on recurrent efforts to win the past and in successive presents build an empire over time that will last into the future. The Catholic Church, ruler of Rome before 1870, and the Italian nation state which thereafter made the place its capital city (whether as a liberal monarchy, with lesser or greater imperial ambition, or as a Fascist and 'totalitarian' dictatorship or a liberal or Christian or social democratic or marketised republic since 1946) have naturally been the first in the field in claiming the past. But, throughout the centuries, they were joined or opposed by aristocrats and their servants, cardinals, priests and beggars, Jews and Muslims, immigrants and other foreign residents, tourists and gypsies, and the innumerable individuals who anywhere thought about Rome. All rejoiced in their own (often fluctuating) comprehension of what mattered in Rome's track through time; all crafted histories that will need to be charted in the pages that follow.

Before I embark on this task, it is worth reflecting on a recent manifestation of the deployment of histories in Rome. The occasion was June 2009 when the Libyan dictator, Mu'ammar Gaddafi, added himself to the endless tally of those who have visited Rome. Like every visitor, he brought quite a bit of his personal history with him, setting up a tent as his favoured accommodation in the gardens of the Villa Doria Pamphilj, the city's most extensive park. There he was guarded by what the Italian press, with classical reference somewhat syncretically ready to hand, insisted were '500 amazons'. But Gaddafi bore more specific histories, too, when he effusively praised his 'friend', Italian Prime Minister Silvio Berlusconi, who, in return, courteously called his visitor a great and wise leader of the Libyan people.

In the previous year, Berlusconi had suddenly apologised for Italian imperial rule in Libya from 1911 to 1943, pledging the Libyan regime five billion dollars compensation for it. Now to parade his nation's status as a virtuous victim, Gaddafi appeared in public with a photo of Omar al-Mukhtar pinned on his right breast. Under Fascism, Omar had been the Libyan Resistance chief, brutally executed by the Italian dictatorship in public in 1931; indeed the photo displayed him after his capture and just before he was killed. The image was, however, meant to finish a history, not revive it. With Fascist crimes exposed, admitted and compensated for, Gaddafi was ready to acknowledge 'closure' in regard to the imperial story of the 'Third Italy' in his country. As he told the Italian President, ex-communist Giorgio Napolitano, 'the page of the past has been turned over and a new page of friendship stands open'. So fine was the country now, it seemed, that Gaddafi announced that Italy should be accorded a permanent seat on the Security Council of the United Nations; at last, in other words, again to be hailed as a Great Power.[28]

But Gaddafi's history lesson was not confined to the contemporary. Having shed one past, he anxiously donned another. If 'Mussolini's Roman Empire' was now surpassed, Gaddafi was hopeful of winning lustre from the lingering fame of classical times for himself. He, too, he told the Italian parliament, was a Roman of some kind, the lineal heir of Septimius Severus, harsh and successful ruler of the empire from 193 to 211 CE and sometimes known as the 'African Emperor' (he may have been of Phoenician descent and was possibly born at Leptis Magna, present-day Libya's most remunerative ancient tourist site).[29] Now, when the Libyan dictator was ushered to an official ceremony at the Capitol, he could see that Septimius Severus had left his mark on Rome. Just below the Capitoline Hill at the western end of the Forum stands the grand triple arch commemorating this emperor.[30] Moreover, it was in his reign in 199 CE that Rome proclaimed itself the ruler over Mesopotamia, the borders of which largely coincide with present-day Iraq (and in an echo, Gaddafi took the occasion again to berate the USA for its 'terrorist' attack on Saddam Hussein's rule there).[31] Certainly, as far as Gaddafi was concerned, the most important history lesson for his hosts, those back home and what he hoped was an astonished and grateful world – predictably a nationalised history, if also a personalised one to fit a dictator's image – was that the present ruler of his country was the greatest 'Libyan' since Septimius Severus.

It may well be, it should at once be acknowledged, that no one who mattered was listening, and the flurry of historical evocations that occurred in those hot June days have quickly proved ephemeral. After all, a purist expert in ancient history might ask whether Gaddafi should have ignored his possible bond with the less alluring figure of Philip 'the Arab', a short-lived, embattled, emperor from 244 until his murder in 249, celebrated mainly for being in tenure when Games were held marking Rome's first millennium. Yet the Libyan dictator's days in Rome did add another tale to the city's pasts and to their use or exploitation. As a man who sought to arm himself with more than one potent and meaningful Rome, Gaddafi may have been crude and absurd. As will be seen, however, he was scarcely original.

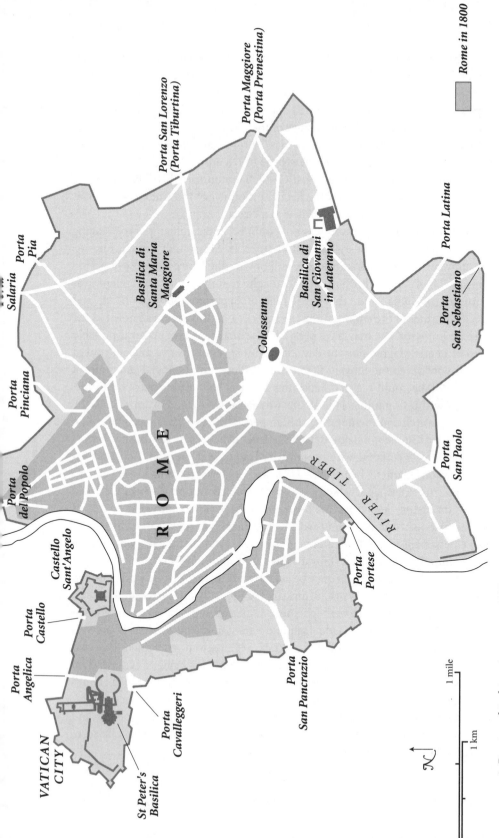

VATICAN CITY

St Peter's Basilica

Porta Angelica

Porta Castello

Castello Sant'Angelo

Porta Cavalleggeri

Porta del Popolo

Porta Pinciana

Porta Salaria

Porta Pia

Porta San Lorenzo (Porta Tiburtina)

Porta Maggiore (Porta Prenestina)

Basilica di Santa Maria Maggiore

R O M E

Colosseum

Basilica di San Giovanni in Laterano

Porta Latina

Porta San Sebastiano

Porta San Paolo

Porta San Pancrazio

Porta Portese

RIVER TIBER

Rome in 1800

N

1 mile

1 km

2. Rome and its historic centre, c.1800

1

---— ✳ ---—

ROME AND THE ROMES ACROSS TIME

Could a historiographer drive on his history, as a muleteer drives on his mule, – straightforward; – for instance, from *Rome* all the way to *Loretto*, without ever once turning his head aside either to the right hand or to the left, – he might venture to foretell you to an hour when he should get to his journey's end; – but the thing is, morally speaking, impossible: For, if he is the man of the least spirit, he will have fifty deviations from a straight line to make with this or that party as he goes along, which he can no ways avoid. He will have views and prospects to himself perpetually soliciting his eye, which he can no more help standing still to look at than to fly; he will moreover have various

Accounts to reconcile:

Anecdotes to pick up:

Inscriptions to make out:

Stories to weave in:

Traditions to sift:

Personages to call upon:

Panegyricks to paste up at this door:

Pasquinades at that: – All which both the man and his mule are quite exempt from. To sum up all; there are archives at every stage to be look'd into, and rolls, records, documents, and endless genealogies, which justice ever and anon calls him back to stay the reading of: – In short there is no end of it.[1]

If accounts, anecdotes, inscriptions, stories, traditions, personages, 'panegyricks' and pasquinades, archives, rolls, records, documents and genealogies, views and prospects, in short the panoply of evidence about the past, are to be sought by visitors to Rome, then there is no need for them to follow Tristram Shandy on the road north-east to Loreto. No doubt this small town boasts of being the sacred site of the 'Virgin's House', which, according to the faithful, miraculously arrived by air from Nazareth in the thirteenth century after being saved in a ruined state from invading Muslims.[2] Yet Rome has ruins, miracles, holy places and a sufficiency of histories to whet any reasonable appetite. It is time to savour them and identify those that have mattered most over the last two centuries and to whom they have mattered.

Still unavoidable as the starting point is the classical realm. Its tiny beginning is conventionally set with incredible exactitude on 21 April 753 BCE. Over the following millennium, Rome, first as monarchy, then republic, then Empire of the Caesars, expanded its control over present-day Italy, Europe, North Africa and Asia Minor and the rest of the Middle East. Its legacy is not yet ended. Over and over again, commentators have found meaning in this tale of rise and fall, one of the latest being Stanley Bing, an American eager to translate old news into the parlance of the contemporary business school: this Rome, Bing states, was 'the first great multinational corporation'. It was founded by two brothers, Romulus and Remus, 'who battled over where to put corporate headquarters'. But Romulus took the initiative and became the first king of the Eternal City. 'In killing his brother so that constructive work could go on, Romulus,' we are informed by the poker-faced author, 'was displaying all the elements of the true executive personality and establishing the corporate culture at the same time.'[3]

No doubt the more academic of my readers are thinking this comparison is 'odorous', and there is no need to pursue it too far. Yet everyone who arrives in Rome rapidly runs into the shards of classical times; they are present across the city's widest geographical bounds. So, as their plane descends to Fiumicino airport, visitors, when they glimpse from their windows the Tiber estuary, may discern south across the river the remains of Ostia antica. This port was allegedly founded by Rome's fourth king, Ancus Marcius, in the seventh century BCE. It prospered to become the entrepôt of empire, although much trade eventually was shipped from a new harbour at Portus, a few kilometres to the north. Ostia's remains are extensive and, as a result of modern archaeological labour, can be explored at length. For less studious visitors or those with more immediate needs, hunger can be satisfied near the entry to the ancient site at a modern restaurant euphoniously named Allo sbarco di Enea (The Landing Place of Aeneas). Its website promises a heritage that goes back before Romulus and the other six kings to the arrival of Aeneas from Troy (having abandoned the sorrowing Queen Dido in Carthage). The menu, we are assured, is based on 'a historic and fused culinary tradition', although its comprehension of Trojan and Carthaginian cuisine may be disputable.[4] For those with more humble tastes, next door to the restaurant stands the 'Domus Pizza' (Pizza as a Roman Mother Made), an outlet where the staff wear 'evocative tunics' to add authenticity to their fare.[5] If the sceptical historian detects the 'invention of tradition' in these offerings, Allo sbarco di Enea is a good place to admit that the forging of meaningful pasts is scarcely a modern habit

2. 'Historic' restaurant in Ostia, brings the past to your table.

alone.[6] After all, Virgil, the author of the *Aeneid* (composed *c.* 20 BCE), was working at the behest of the Emperor Augustus and manufacturing a foundation myth for his empire. Virgil's history of Aeneas and his heirs was fake, a power-laden and durable fake in which the senior God, Jupiter, proclaimed 'to Romans I set no boundary in space and time. I have granted them dominion, and it has no end'.[7] The *Aeneid* may make the most grandiose claim for a society and polity to control the passage of time but, in his wrenching of Rome's history to serve a cause, Virgil had many successors.

Hints at Ostia of turns to the left and to the right in the transfer of the Roman past to the present are not confined to words. They can also be located in the physical remains of the old port. The current set of ruined shops, houses, temples and more practical installations may have actually existed in ancient times, but they are also marked by history since then. They have both survived and been 'restored'. Centuries of decay shrivelled a town, beset by malaria and the silting up of its anchorages; by the early nineteenth century, all an English traveller found there was 'a miserable fortified village, containing scarcely fifty sickly inhabitants. Such is the badness of the air, real or supposed,' he added, 'none but malefactors and banditti will inhabit it.'[8] Revival came only with a new consciousness of historical importance demonstrated in the commencement of scholarly excavation under Pope Pius IX in 1854. That process went very slowly

and brought change as well as continuity in its train. The employment of immigrants from Ravenna in drainage and other heavy labour, for example, was
greeted with hostility by old inhabitants as entailing the penetration to the
outskirts of Rome of new 'barbarians'.[9] Only with the twentieth century did Ostia
antica begin to prosper as a tourist site, with the greatest impulse to archaeology
occurring in 1938–42 under the strenuously Fascist Guido Calza. Even today,
work continues haltingly at a 'historic site' whose appeal is conditioned and
checked by the rise from the 1950s of Ostia nuova and Fiumicino as popular
beach resorts, places where bodily pleasures can surpass those of the mind.

Yet Ostia is just one among a number of classical sites located on the edge of
Rome. On the opposite side of the city stands the celebrated Villa Adriana, the
villa built to accommodate the wandering, artistic and bearded emperor,
Hadrian (ruled 117 to 138 CE).[10] The placing of this emperor's estate on an
unlovely and insalubrious plain when the hills of Tivoli rise close by has always
puzzled observers. However, from the Renaissance onwards, rich hoards of statuary and other ornamentation had been unearthed in the ruins of the place and
many were reinstalled in Tivoli's coolly graceful Villa d'Este, delight of Cardinal
Ippolito d'Este from 1550. Thereafter digging and removal at the Villa Adriana
accelerated under succeeding popes. Such exploitation did not fully cease until
the land and buildings were taken over by the Italian state once it had seized
Rome on 20 September 1870. Archaeological work then fell under the more
scrupulous or scientific charge of the leading Liberal archaeologist, Rodolfo
Lanciani, and Hadrian's villa was confirmed as a place for the better instructed
to see on a visit to Rome. One to draw inspiration was the celebrated French
modernist architect Charles-Édouard Jeanneret-Gris (known as Le Corbusier),
who in 1911 concluded that the villa made manifest 'the creative transformation of the past'. From such ruins, he thought, 'one can meditate [productively]
. . . on the greatness of Rome. There they really planned.'[11]

It must be conceded that, until recent times, positive historical messages were
harder to draw from the immediate natural surrounds of Rome, despite the presence there of many classical ruins, given that malaria had taken deep hold on the
so-called Campagna.[12] These notoriously flat and marshy lands spread from the
city's walls to the Alban hills and the coast. Early in the twentieth century, critical
Italians compared the brutalised and disease-stricken peasants and shepherds
who eked out life there to 'Ethiopian tribesmen and women'. In the mind of the
time, such poor people were dispossessed of the vital force that even 'barbarians'
had possessed, 'dwelling in straw huts . . . deprived of water, education and a
single stone structure'.[13] Perhaps a positive spin could be put on the matter? In
1927 a polite British archaeologist underlined that 'there is no city which one can
so quickly and easily leave behind as Rome', even as he rejoiced at the potential
excavations that could occur in so 'unspoilt' a place as the Campagna.[14] But in his
heart, he, too, admitted that it was inside the Aurelian walls that the ancient past

and its sites of memory most obviously resided and reside, and where their lessons won most fans.[15]

The Emperor Hadrian is well to the fore there, too, since his mausoleum, now known as Castel Sant'Angelo, sits beside the Tiber and guards entry to the so-called 'Leonine city', that is, the Vatican complex from where the world-ranging Catholic Church is practically and spiritually governed. Already at the beginning of the fifth century Hadrian's tomb had been converted into a fortress and integrated into the defensive bulwark of the city walls. As such it was sacked by invading Goths and Huns who obliterated most of its classical character. Following the empire's collapse, Pope Gregory I (the Great, ruled 590–604) allegedly gave the building its modern name after he miraculously saw an angel sheathing its sword to signify the cessation of a plague that was afflicting the city. From here on, Castel Sant'Angelo was a key site during almost every political occurrence in Rome, while also acting as a prison on occasion (a purpose that was said to have begun under Theodoric, first ruler of the city after the fall of the emperors, 474 to 526 CE). During the brutal sack of Rome in 1527 by imperial troops – enrolled in the service of the Catholic Holy Roman Emperor, Charles V, although many were German Protestants – Castel Sant'Angelo acted as the last redoubt of Pope Clement VII. This assault on the city was all the more shocking given that, as a (Eurocentric) contemporary historian has put it, Rome was then 'acknowledged to be the centre of civilization. Venetian diplomats still spoke of the "mother" or the "home of us all" when referring to the papal city.'[16] Once the

3. Late eighteenth-century romantic view of the Tiber with Castel Sant'Angelo and St Peter's in the background.

bastion was fully invested on 27 May, we are told, 'even an old woman carrying a gift of lettuces to the pope was arrested and strangled in full view of the watchers from the castle battlements'. The flight of the pope and final overwhelming of the city was the 'death blow of Renaissance Rome'. Eventually there might be an agonising and slow recovery, but Rome 'was no longer the home of art, of beauty and of free speculation'.[17]

Despite this seeming 'end of history', Castel Sant'Angelo had more to experience and record. As if to signal that another plague had ended, Pope Paul III who, in 1534, followed Clement VII to the throne, raised the statue of a marble angel at the summit of the edifice (it was replaced by a bronze one with a more visible sword and scabbard in the mid-eighteenth century). Thereafter the angel watched over papal Rome through many vicissitudes, including 'revolution' in 1798–9, French occupation from 1808 to 1814 and revolution again in 1848–9. After the overthrow of the Roman Republic by invading French troops marshalled by then President Louis Napoleon Bonaparte (soon to promote himself Emperor Napoleon III), between 1849 and 1870 Castel Sant'Angelo was garrisoned as the major redoubt in the French defence of Rome against the Italy which was unifying in the Risorgimento. When Liberal Italy took over the place after its conquest of Rome, Hadrian's one-time tomb again was reduced to being a barracks and prison (back in the 1590s the heretic or freethinker, Giordano Bruno, was pent up here for six years). Only in 1901 was Castel Sant'Angelo handed over to 'heritage', and restoration work began. It culminated under Mussolini's Fascist dictatorship in 1933–4, a time when much of classical Rome was 'cleansed' of later accretions, these deemed of less value by a modern ideology that proclaimed its spiritual fount in *romanità* (Roman-ness, the Roman spirit). During the following decades, the mausoleum-fortress-prison has been open as a museum and eclectic exhibition site. The pleasure of visiting it and contemplating the many histories that circle across its stones has been increased during the last decade by the closure of the Lungotevere Castello, the road that separates it from the river, with a consequent drop in noise and pollution.

Still more renowned as a piece of ancient architecture and bearing at least as many histories is the Pantheon, raised originally, as can still be read on the pediment of its pronaos, by Marcus Agrippa, son-in-law of the first emperor, Augustus, in 27 BCE. The building was designed as a temple celebrating Augustus's victory over Antony and Cleopatra at the naval battle of Actium. Many have enthused over the place, with Henry James remarking that its elegance rendered St Peter's 'absurdly vulgar' by comparison.[18] The claim to authenticity from the first days of the empire may be false, however, since the actual building dates either to the reign of Domitian (81–96) or to that of Hadrian, when urban authorities were forced into drastic restoration by a destructive fire. Further reworkings followed, while barbarian invasion and papal rule picked away at the edifice, a decay that was at least partially stemmed in 609 CE when Pope Boniface IV declared the Pantheon sanctified as a church devoted to Santa Maria and Martyres. Later it endured less hallowed use as a fortress contested between rival noble factions while the popes took refuge at Avignon between 1305 and 1378. Yet the building was never stripped of its aura of historic grandeur, with city 'senators' throughout the Middle Ages and Renaissance on appointment pledging to defend *Maria Rotonda* (round Mary), as the edifice was now familiarly named, against attack. Not all popes were respectful to the place, however, with Urban VIII Barberini adding two towers at the front, almost as though he preferred the building with ears. He was still more ruthless in melting the bronze ceiling of the portico to help forge the *baldacchino* in St Peter's, with leftover metal being re-forged into cannon stationed at Castel Sant'Angelo.

The next major change to the fabric of the Pantheon occurred with the Risorgimento. In the anti-clerical atmosphere of the moment, for a time Santa Maria and Martyres was decommissioned. Furthermore, in 1878 the Pantheon became the august burial site of King Victor Emmanuel II (the Piedmontese king who, under this paradoxical title, was the first monarch of Italy). Eventually other members of the Savoy dynasty were also interred here. They joined the Renaissance painter, Raffaello Sanzio (Raphael), who was placed in a grave near one of the altars after his death in 1520. Even under the Republic established following a referendum on the monarchy in June 1946, the Savoys are occasionally commemorated at the Pantheon. Ironically, the idea of deploying the building as a tomb of national heroes was borrowed less from the ancient Romans than the French (it was they who were borrowing from Augustus). The Panthéon of Paris, a dominant feature on the city's central skyline, was adapted to that end after 1789 by revolutionaries, who utilised for lay purposes a church whose restoration happened to be complete that year. In the early 1790s Mirabeau, Voltaire, Marat and Rousseau all had their remains deposited there. In any case, the generic use of the word 'pantheon' to mean 'a building in which the illustrious dead of a nation are buried, or have memorials erected to them' had entered the English language in 1713. Agrippa's Pantheon has taught lessons and transferred histories that belong to many people and not merely the Romans.

For manifold reasons, then, the classical structure, despite its erection two millennia ago, is an icon for all seasons, alive into the present. The same is true of the most extensive ruins of ancient Rome, those that run from the Capitoline Hill across the Forum to Nero's Golden House and the Colosseum and, from there, back up to the Palatine Hill and down again to the Circus Maximus. In this central space lies Rome's key *zona archeologica*. For most who scan its history, it is the prime memory site of ancient times in the city. Inevitably, therefore, it has been subject to adaptation, restoration and reinterpretation across the centuries.

From 509 BCE to the sixth century CE, the Capitoline Hill was crowned with a temple to Jupiter Optimus Maximus, chief of the Roman gods, a place of worship designed to be the sacred symbol of ancient government. Nearby, on the land now occupied by the church of Santa Maria Aracoeli, stood the *Arx* or citadel of the city. There were preserved the 'Sibylline books', a magic repository of the history that was to come (at least if read and understood accurately or fortunately). This combination of religious, military and political authority and official history continued down the ages, with urban governors persistently seeking legitimacy by holding ceremonies there (and redeploying such titles as 'consul' and 'senator' long after the empire's fall). One major example was Cola di Rienzo, a self-proclaimed resuscitated 'tribune of the people', who 're-established' a Roman Republic in 1347 and who died beside the Capitol seven years later while trying to defend his last citadel.

During the Renaissance, the popes gave more refined attention to the furnishing of the Capitoline Hill, employing Michelangelo to design Piazza del Campidoglio (work not finished until the seventeenth century) and erecting the statue of Marcus Aurelius (reigned 161–180 CE), the so-called 'philosophic emperor', there. The statue had survived through the Middle Ages because it was long believed to represent Constantine, the first Christian emperor. Already in the fifteenth century, choice sculptures and inscriptions that had been unearthed elsewhere in the city were preserved inside the Palazzo dei conservatori, while the first version of the present-day Capitoline Museum was opened to the public in 1734. In sum, the Capitol was both the epicentre of the succession of Roman presents and the key repository of the treasure of Roman pasts.

At the other end of this sector of Rome, the Circus Maximus (Circo Massimo) had the most curious fate running into the twentieth century. This dip between the Palatine and Aventine hills is said to have been used for athletic contest from the time of King Tarquinius Priscus in the seventh century BCE. By imperial times it could seat an audience of 250,000 or more who came to view chariot races, mock sea battles (after the flooding of the central area) and fights between wild beasts or gladiators, as well as public executions. It is thought still to have functioned as a venue for games, in however reduced a fashion, into the sixth century CE. Shortly thereafter, in another case of a version of Rome migrating outside the city, King Chilperic staged what he heralded as 'Roman games' in Paris. They were to be proof of the fact that the Frankish city was 'the heir to Rome'.[19] In recording this ambition, a contemporary historian has commented that 'part of the myth of Paris is that it has engendered so many myths about itself'.[20] That this situation is also true of Rome is a major theme of this book, even if I prefer the term 'history' to 'myth'. Certainly, by the Renaissance it was widely agreed that 'a city became important if it had a past', and none was so amply furnished in that regard as was Rome.[21]

As for the Circo Massimo, after King Totila's games of 549 CE, it decayed into little more than a wilderness, yet another part of the city within the Aurelian Walls that was studded with a few rough huts from which poor Romans scrabbled a living that was likely to be nasty, brutish and short. Tangled vines grew there, as did fields of artichokes. So abandoned was the zone by more genteel Romans that, in 1852, its terrain was occupied by the first modern gasworks in the city, the British-financed Società Anglo-Romana per l'illuminazione a gas. First photographs show extensive buildings augmented by at least three gaso-meters, while a few shanties nearby housed a workforce who were scantily paid and exposed to the polluting smoke belching from the factory chimneys.[22]

At the river end of the circus, a family bakery, owned by the Pantanellas, began to serve the city at much the same time. Under Italian rule during the 1870s and 1880s, the business expanded 'into a ten-furnace steam-powered mill, bakery and pasta factory, with a workforce comprising 500 families'.[23] Propped up with Vatican finance, the industrial concern survived until the late 1920s, when it was closed and largely removed as part of the Fascist effort to eliminate from the city all that was not rigorously 'Roman'. Soon, there were ambitious plans to surround the site with new buildings proclaiming the fused grandeur of Rome and the Fascist party. The relic of this ambition can be found at the south-eastern end of the Circo Massimo on what is now again the Viale Aventino (for a while renamed under the dictatorship the Viale Africa). There, since its completion in 1950, has been located the head office of the United Nations Food and Agriculture Organisation (FAO) in a building originally planned for the Ministero dell'Africa Italiana (Ministry for Italian Africa).[24] From 1937 at its front as a Fascist 'entry statement' was erected the Axum stele, stolen from Ethiopia by Italian invaders intent on blotting out that country's national or independent history by demol-ishing its holiest historic site. The post-Fascist Republic promised to return the column in 1947 but it was not delivered until 2005.

Meanwhile the value of the open space of the sometime grand arena remains doubtful in contemporary Rome, despite its daytime attraction to joggers. The occasional rock concert held there, as well as an assembly of a claimed 700,000 people to cheer Italy's World Cup victory in 2006, have had no permanent impact, and the recent fencing of a segment of land near the Viale Aventino for what seems desultory archaeological work adds to the depressed air of the place. Despite the ghosts of charioteers and gladiators, fans and spectators, gas merchants and workers, who may throng the Circo Massimo with significant memories, sporting Rome these days locates its preferred stadiums in other parts of the city.

As the Capitol and the Circo Massimo in their different ways indicate, ancient and modern imperial and other histories meet and mingle in many parts of the Rome's *zona archeologica*. The task of delineating and reviewing their fusion and pulling apart will continue to occupy this book. The grand sites, however, are never alone in reminding contemporaries of classical times. Indeed, one of the pleasures of the contemporary city is the way that a stroll through a quiet street will lead a visitor suddenly to stumble on a relic of ancient history. A humble but telling example is the Mausoleum of Lucilius

4. Axum stele imports Ethiopian history to Rome, 1939.

Peto, set well below the street level at the fork of the Via Salaria and the Via Po, outside the walls and not far from the Villa Borghese, the city's prime urban park. This Republican tumulus is apparently circular in shape. It was rediscovered in the mid-eighteenth century and commemorates a worthy Roman and his sister who lived under Augustus but were scarcely dominant figures in the empire of that era. Perhaps fitting this relatively modest origin, the remains of this mausoleum have long been 'under restoration' and are closed to a public who can only see a part of the tomb's marble facing as they pass by.

Equally modest is the so-called 'Auditorium of Maecenas', found just off the Via Merulana, a major road carrying traffic from one great basilica, Santa Maria Maggiore, to another, San Giovanni in Laterano, St John Lateran. The classical remains are thought to be a surviving part of the immense holding of Gaius Maecenas, a friend of Augustus and major patron of the arts, on the Esquiline Hill which covers the land to the north-east of the Via Merulana up to the city wall. The 'auditorium' was unearthed and interpreted as late as 1874, when Liberal Rome was expanding its housing in this part of the city. Some believe confidently that, nineteen hundred years earlier, it was 'a miniature theatre, where Maecenas' protégés would recite their latest works'. Less romantically, however, it may merely have been an 'ancient setting for dinner parties', cooled by a cascade cunningly designed to run through the place and so a precursor of the celebrated 'fountains of Rome'.[25]

These whispered rival messages from ancient times can be discerned in many sectors of Rome, as well as in such other parts of its environs as the celebrated Via Appia, a Roman road that reached the city at the Porta San Sebastiano, or in the surrounds of the next gate further to the west, the Porta San Paolo. Near this latter stands the Piramide or Pyramid of Gaius Cestius. This man was another to live and die under Augustus, like Lucilius Peto having pursued a conspicuous but not glittering political and administrative career. Behind the pyramid is located the shaded 'Protestant' cemetery or *Cimitero acattolico*, which was set aside for non-Catholic burial in the eighteenth century. It was needed because of the spreading popularity of the 'Grand Tour' that was carrying thousands from northern European countries to Rome. It is said that the first to be buried at this cemetery in 1738 was 'an Oxford graduate named Langton', whose remains were disturbed and uncovered in archaeological work in 1928.[26]

Both here and along the Via Appia, where lie the fourth-century church of San Sebastiano and its linked catacombs (more of these structures both Christian and Jewish have been mapped nearby), ancient urban histories encounter more recent ones of global span. It was somewhere on this road that, according to pious legend, Christ met St Peter, fleeing from crucifixion in Rome, and asked sadly and reproachfully 'Quo vadis?' (where are you going?)[27] In 1896 the Polish Catholic novelist, Henryk Sienkiewicz published a novel about the event that brought its author global fame and the Nobel Prize for Literature (1905). The story was transposed to the screen in at least three silent film versions, and two more recent mini-series (1985, 2001), as well as in the MGM Hollywood blockbuster of 1951 that starred Robert Taylor, Deborah Kerr and Peter Ustinov. This continuing attention has ensured that 'memory' of the 'Quo vadis' legend, and the trinkets that can be taken away as further reminders of it, are a significant part of Rome's 'lessons' to the present.[28]

In regard to the themes of this book, what is most evident along the Via Appia or around the Pyramid of Cestius is the ubiquitous intermeshing in the city of the stories of the classical empire with those of early Christianity, with the shuffling of the lives of the emperors into those of the popes of the Catholic Church. Naturally enough, the best site where this history and its representations can be pursued is St Peter's. There the most ancient history has been re-examined in modern times. With a studied avoidance of contemporary politics that carried its own message about their significance over time, between 1939 and 1943 Pope Pius XII ordered archaeological work under a pavement preserved from the fourth-century version of the church. Pius put the German Monsignor Ludwig Kaas in charge of the dig. Kaas had been a pivotal figure in the German Centre Party's accommodation with Nazism and a key negotiator of a concordat between the Vatican and Hitler's dictatorship in 1933. Thereafter he retreated to Rome and, despite the outbreak of the Second World War, laying contemporary ideological issues aside he uncovered bones, brought to light directly under the *baldacchino* of Gian Lorenzo Bernini, the church's most opulent baroque ornament. The remains appeared to have been treated with religious respect on their first interment and may date to the reign of Vespasian (69 to 79 CE): pious and scientific analysis has confirmed that they belonged to a man in his sixties. Neither Kaas nor Pius XII was fully convinced of an unerring identification with St Peter, however, and for a while the bones were hidden or lost.[29] However, they were rediscovered and further appraised in the 1960s. On 26 June 1968 Pope Paul VI formally announced that they indeed belonged to the saint and human founder of the Catholic Church (although a rival theory in the 1950s asserted that Simon Peter's skeletal traces had actually been authenticated in Jerusalem).

Whichever story is true (and maybe neither is), of all buildings in Rome, St Peter's is the most complex site of memory, myth, heritage and history. Legends linger of its foundation in the first or perhaps second century after the death of Christ. The name of St Peter was undoubtedly tied to it from very early days of the presence of the followers of Christ in Rome. Certainly, after the Emperor Constantine opted for Christianity as the religion of his personal victory and of imperial rule, a basilica was erected between 324 and 326 CE, that is, during the pontificate of Sylvester I (314–335). The building was imposing, even if it was only about half the size of the present structure. Over following centuries it was frequently repaired and further ornamented, while serving as a key political site; Charlemagne was crowned first Holy Roman Emperor here in 800 CE.[30] Although the building was plundered by Saracen raiders from the sea in 846 (one effect being the construction of the Leonine walls in 852), ravaged by the Norman, Robert Guiscard, in 1084 (he abducted much of the urban population as slaves, while his men, swords in hand, ran through the church seizing the offerings from the altars) and sacked along with the city in 1527, it is a repository of many sacred relics and treasures, proof, at least to Catholics, of the special holiness of the basilica and the city.[31] The sacred leavings include, for example, a piece of the true cross, accidentally revealed during restoration work by Pope Sergius I (687–701).[32] The power of St Peter's expression of history helped ensure that, by the eighth century, the Vatican complex that grew alongside and behind the basilica had ousted the Forum as the city centre and, in natural and necessary linkage, its most telling memory site.[33]

Pilgrims were readily impressed. A Frank in the seventh century reported that, if a pious visitor wanted to carry off 'some blessed memorial, he throws inside [St Peter's alleged shrine] a small handkerchief which has been carefully weighted and then, watching and fasting, he prays most fervently that the apostle may give a favourable answer to his devotion. Wonderful to say, if the man's faith prevails, the handkerchief when drawn up from the tomb is so filled with divine virtue that it weighs much more than it did before'.[34] Happy and contented, the pilgrim could then return home, bearing evidence of the weight of (one version of) Rome's history in his purse or pocket. What is regarded as the first modern tourist booklet, the *Mirabilia Urbis Romae*, dating from the 1140s but over the next two centuries regularly amplified, was equally certain that Constantine had himself dug St Peter's foundations, 'and in reverence of the twelve Apostles did carry thereout twelve baskets full of earth'. The anonymous first author of this pioneer guide, who may have been attached to the basilica, was also sure that St Peter himself had set up the first altar in that part of Rome 'whereof Saint Peter celebrated mass'.[35] More scandalously, the guide reported that near the Colosseum (erroneously identified as a temple to the Sun God) was located an image of a female pope with a boy child, an ill-omened site that (male) popes strictly avoided.[36]

Nonetheless, throughout the Middle Ages, the many mutations experienced by the city and St Peter's Church, notably during the papal withdrawal to Avignon for much of the fourteenth century, speeded natural decay and Pope Nicholas V (1447 to 1455) determined on its rebuilding. This undertaking moved slowly and erratically, and it was only on 18 November 1626 that Pope Urban VIII, finding legitimacy for his act in the claim that the date marked the 1,300th anniversary of the original blessing, consecrated the new basilica. Over the two centuries of the church's remaking, the greatest artists, sculptors and architects of the Renaissance, including Leon Battista Alberti, Raphael, Bramante and Michelangelo, stamped their aesthetic sense (and personal histories) on to parts of the building. However, the major work occurred in the seventeenth century especially through the efforts of Bernini and his baroque predecessor, Carlo Maderna. True, there have been complications and debate since that era, notably with the unification of a nation called Italy in 1861 and with its drift into Fascist dictatorship after the First World War, given that, then, the baroque was dismissed as a time of national subjection when Italy was not really Italy. Aesthetically attuned foreigners joined in, superciliously disparaging what they deemed the excessive fondness for ornamentation of the seventeenth century. Patrick White, the Australian Nobel Prize-winning novelist, visiting Rome as late as 1971, agreed with Henry James that baroque St Peter's was 'just about the most vulgar important building on earth: it wouldn't look out of place in Manly'.[37]

The massive size of the baroque St Peter's, with its plain and even truculent message that the Church was armed and ready for militant empire in the

Counter-Reformation and beyond, had also soon aroused uneasy fears in some observers of a contradiction between papal ambition and the reality of Rome. As early as the Middle Ages, Petrarch, the Tuscan-born writer and so-called 'father of humanism', had lamented that Romans 'were the least competent to understand their own past and the least sensible to its grandeur' of any of the inhabitants of the Italian peninsula.[38] Dante, too, had declared that Rome was 'at once the tragedy and the hope of the world'.[39] Each dismissive comment was regularly replayed by later commentators. As the sense of Italian nationality began to be forged, the thought that Romans were corrupt and soft (just the people who, by the seventeenth century, would be attracted to the baroque) became ingrained in many who believed that men and not churchmen should control the future through a more rigorous understanding of the past. As far as many Italian nationalists were concerned, the age of the baroque was summed up as that of 'Spanish Rome', and indeed it was true that, in the sixteenth century, some Spanish historians had dismissed Romulus and Remus as a myth, arguing instead that the city had been named for Romi, the daughter of a king of Spain named Atlante.[40]

Italians were not alone in bewailing Roman decadence. The Anglican John Evelyn, visiting Rome in 1645, found St Peter's a site of what contemporaries thought of as the black cruelty and fanaticism of Spain. 'On Good Friday, we went again to St Peter's, where the handkerchief, lance and cross were all exposed, and worshipped together,' he noted critically. 'All the confession-seats were filled with devout people, and at night was a procession of several who most lamentably whipped themselves till the blood stained their clothes, for some had shirts, others upon the bare back, having visors and masks on their faces; at every three or four steps dashing the knotted and ravelled whip-cord over their shoulders, as hard as they could lay it on; whilst some of the religious orders and fraternities sung in a dismal tone, the lights and crosses going before, making all together a horrible and indeed heathenish pomp.'[41] As the Counter-Reformation turned into the Enlightenment, for the growing band of anti-clericals and modernisers across Europe, St Peter's began to carry a third history beyond those of classical times and the Church, one by no means worshipful of Catholicism's continuing lessons to the present.

The story of St Peter's and its conservation of histories did not end with the baroque and after 1800 the great basilica continued to be architecturally adapted and refreshed. At the same time, the contest over the histories that resided within its walls, in the square outside and in the complex of museums that, from the early eighteenth century, began to fill part of the Vatican site, did not cease. Moreover, similar debates eddied through almost every one of what the latest tally reckons are more than 900 churches in the city. Especially renowned were the three other grand basilicas, Santa Maria Maggiore, San Giovanni in Laterano and San Paolo fuori le mura. Each claimed origins that went back to Constantine or earlier; each has been subject to natural and human disaster ranging from damage from earthquake and fire to military assault; each has endured more planned 'restoration'. Each conserves numberless religious and artistic treasures. Each embodies 'the triumph of the cross on the ruins of the capitol' and so bespeaks a natural and providentially guided passage from classical rule to that of the popes. None is so heavily altered by the tastes of the baroque as is St Peter's.

Less grandiose religious edifices of the city's historic centre are equally freighted with histories, a prime example being the Irish Dominican church of San Clemente, a couple of blocks from the Colosseum. Here a visitor today can travel down through three levels, from a twelfth-century building to one erected in the fourth century and restored in the eighth, to a first-century Roman tenement, with attached second- or third-century *Mithraeum* (a temple for Mithras). From this point beneath the modern city can be heard the rushing waters of the Cloaca Maxima, the main drain of the city of the Caesars, still in use; it runs into the Tiber behind the Palatine Hill. Similarly emblematic is the church known as Santa Maria sopra Minerva, set in the sometime Campus Martius or Field of Mars, the most heavily populated part of the classical city and at other times. As its name suggests, the church was raised on what had been a temple to Minerva, the ancient virgin goddess of wisdom, commerce and music, and an intrepid warrior to boot. Santa Maria sopra Minerva was reconstructed in the thirteenth century and is the city's only major example of the Gothic style (although restored in the nineteenth century). On the square outside stands a small Egyptian obelisk, dating to the sixth century BCE but rediscovered in 1655 in the ruins of a temple of Isis. It is ornamented with a cute elephant carved to Bernini's design in 1667 and utilised by the Taviani brothers in their film, *Good Morning Babilonia*, in 1987 to express what they deemed a timeless artistry transferred from their Italy to the New World of the USA and the modern cinema.

In representing the histories of Rome, churches are supplemented by the various chief palaces of the city, with the Vatican being the most emblematic. To some degree it is challenged by the Quirinale or Quirinal palace, since 1870 the official home of the Italian head of state, a king of the Savoy dynasty until the referendum of June 1946 (Victor Emmanuel II until 1878, Umberto I 1878–1900, Victor Emmanuel III 1900 to May 1946 and Umberto II May–June 1946). Since then it has become the capital city residence of the Italian President, theoretically at least a person of great respect above politics who has been elected by the votes of the two houses of parliament, the Chamber of Deputies and the Senate.

The Quirinale stands at the top of one of Rome's seven hills, with classical structures there including a temple to Mars dating back to the early empire or republic. The current palace is in the main baroque, however, built by Carlo Maderna and others for Urban VIII in the 1620s and extended by Bernini and his colleagues through the following decades. The Quirinale was used by the popes until 1870 as a summer residence, although its papal occupation coincided directly with the construction, again by Maderna, of another *palazzo*, more coolly set at Castel Gandolfo in the Alban hills. The kings of Italy after 1870 never altogether renounced their Piedmontese origins and used the Quirinal sparingly, although Adolf Hitler spent what he claimed were some of the most boring and irritating days of his life as a guest of Victor Emmanuel III, still in May 1938 constitutional head of state and so the Führer's official partner, when the German Chancellor was on a state visit to his fellow dictator, Benito Mussolini.[42]

The erection and use of Roman palaces inevitably depended on the economic fortunes and the demography of the city. By the eighteenth century, with the Enlightenment spreading across Europe from France and the Industrial Revolution from Britain, the city could scarcely match Paris or London (or Naples or Milan) in size or power. After all, in 1870 Rome still boasted a population of just 225,000 (up from 150,000 in 1800, a tally that shrank to 118,000 by 1815 as a result of the social and economic turmoil and devastating wars of the Napoleonic era but revived to 170,000 in 1850). This total was still many fewer than had lived in the ancient city, even after it required protection by the Aurelian Walls. The meagre numbers meant that, at the commencement of Italian occupation, swathes of the city were devoted to vines and other agricultural production, most of it in the ownership either of religious institutions or noble families. In the swift growth after 1870 – the population expanded to 463,000 by 1901, 542,000 by 1911, 692,000 by 1921 and passed a million in 1931 (a spurt in the first Fascist decade of 45 per cent), reaching 1.4 million a decade later – nostalgics bewailed the loss of elegance occasioned by the razing of monasteries and villas for serried rows of modern apartment blocks. Particularly regretted was the destruction of the Villa Ludovisi on the hill now crossed by the Via Veneto (ironically to become in the 1950s and 1960s symbol of the lush 'decadence' of the *dolce vita*). The villa's gardens were greatly admired. Augustus Hare, an English observer in the later nineteenth century, grew splenetic at their disappearance. 'With the fury against trees that characterises Italians,' he expostulated, 'all the magnificent ilexes and cypresses were cut down as soon as the land was secured [for modern development], and the plots of building-land rendered altogether hideous and undesirable' by the erection of modern housing.[43] Contemporary history, he feared, was wiping out the beauty of the past.

Luckier in its fate was the Villa Borghese, after 1902 owned by the state as a park, national gallery and monument. Between 1613 and 1616, the buildings and estate had been designed as a place of pleasure for Pope Paul V and his nephew, the young Cardinal Scipione Borghese. Vineyards 'were turned into picturesque or romantic gardens and parks, with lakes and woody recesses opening out into wide sunlit clearings; and herms, statues and sarcophagi lined all the avenues', quite a few fake in the sense of being mock classical 'reproductions'.[44] The palace was further spruced up in the eighteenth century and its collection of ancient and modern sculpture and art enriched, classical works being brought in from a recently excavated site outside Rome.[45] Some precious items were lost during the period of Prince Camillo Borghese, who was ready and eager to sell them to Paris. He was married to Napoleon's younger sister, Pauline, who between 1804 and 1808 was independent enough to have herself sculpted semi-nude by the neoclassicist Antonio Canova, with the somewhat specious claim that she was representing Venus Victrix. She would be quizzically viewed by Hitler in that capacity on his 1938 trip to Rome. Nonetheless, despite depredation in the revolutionary era, the Borghese gallery remains the repository of important paintings supplemented by a celebrated collection of statues on classical themes by Bernini (who died in 1698). Here, the artist luxuriantly and with palpable self-confidence expressed the triumph by his times of the 'moderns' over the 'ancients'.[46]

Bernini has frequently been held responsible for the design of the not so much baroque as rococo Trevi Fountain, begun in 1732 and another familiar heritage site in the city. In fact, however, it was built under the charge of architect Nicola Salvi and only completed thirty years later, a decade after Salvi's death. Its form has aroused critics' ire, with an early nineteenth-century Anglo-Saxon visitor carping about its 'pompous confusion of fable and fact, gods and ediles, aqueducts and sea monsters'.[47] At other times, planners who prided themselves on being rationalist, under Napoleonic rule or Fascism, have pondered major reconstruction of the narrow Piazza di Trevi. Their aim has been to make the urban setting match the grandiosity of the fountain. Yet the place is so girded with histories that it is probably wiser to leave its surrounds as they are. Certainly, the Fontana di Trevi is another segment of the city exhibiting the layers of pasts that have provided a necessary or inevitable context to its beauty.

Unsurprisingly, they start with classical times. The water that pours down into the pool facing the square comes through a modernised version of the Aqua Virgo aqueduct that first slaked the thirst of city dwellers at the command of Marcus Agrippa. This conduit was wrecked by Gothic invaders in the sixth century (a few years later, in 546, the city was allegedly entirely denuded of inhabitants for forty days at the order of Totila, king of the Ostrogoths). Pope Nicholas V, however, reopened the aqueduct in 1453 and hired Alberti to construct an elegant basin appropriately to greet the waters' outpouring into the city. Later popes further ornamented the setting, with Bernini ensuring that a fountain there would be visible from the Quirinal palace; it could thus cheer any popes who grew overheated in summer. Already, then, before Salvi's reworking, the fountain had won significance in the city and it was natural for the magnificent new structure to become 'the best known and most spectacular monument of eighteenth century Rome'.[48]

Yet, as so often in the city, the image of a palimpsest where a place is the summation of many pasts is inadequate to explain fame since the Trevi Fountain carries later histories, too. One is the romantic view that the climate and 'environment', sunshine and plashing waters, are deeply inscribed into the meaning of Rome, especially for its many visitors from grey climes to the north. Ironically, this image was confirmed musically by the patriotic and Bologna-born modern composer, Ottorino Respighi. His Roman trilogy (*The Fountains of Rome*, 1915–16, *The Pines of Rome*, 1923–4, and *Roman Festivals*, 1928) resounded with the idea that Rome and the Roman spirit were given momentum by the dynamic interaction of people and nature.

If musical history provides one frame for the present-day Trevi Fountain, film offers another. Whereas Fascist film-makers (and their liberal predecessors) sought to emphasise classical times and settings, with a message either of stern rigour or titivating decadence, in the 1950s the Fontana di Trevi gave the visual proof that Rome was better conceived as a city of indulgence and pleasure.[49] The Hollywood movie, *Three Coins in the Fountain*, supplemented by the song of the same title (especially when performed by the Italo-American, Dean Martin, as at the 1955 Oscar ceremony), set out the new or adapted image. It spread knowledge of an invented tradition which suggested that it was lucky to toss a coin into the fountain's waters, with the result to be either success in love or a return trip to Rome. This global fame also helps to explain why today scaled-down ersatz versions of the Trevi Fountain can be visited at Las Vegas or the Shenzhen theme park in China.

In the post-war era the resonance of the Trevi site was mightily reinforced by another film, Federico Fellini's *La dolce vita* (1960). The scene where Anita Ekberg and Marcello Mastroianni make (clothed) love in the fountain's waters, even if Mastroianni carefully or parsimoniously removes his shoes before entering the pool, is one of the most celebrated in movie history. It has established an indelible memory of the Trevi Fountain in particular and Rome in general as the prime site of the sweet life. *La dolce vita* grossed 2,000 million lire in 1960, its first year of screening in Italy, and was the nation's top box office draw, acting as an ironic comment on the Olympic Games then being held in Rome, as well as on the series of official ceremonies in Turin and other cities commemorating the centenary of national unification and inevitably offering a pompously patriotic reading of history.[50]

By 1960, more than a decade after the fall of Fascism, the end of the war and the removal of the Savoy monarchy, Rome was once again changing. Its population continued its upward acceleration, reaching 1.65 million by 1951, 2.188 million by 1961 (in the 1950s, a rise of 32.5 per cent) and 2.73 million by 1969, before stabilising or even shedding population. That loss was more than compensated by the continued expansion of communes on the urban periphery, not counted in Rome's numbers but usually drawing their economic and political and, less reliably, their cultural sustenance from the city. Rome was becoming a metropolis.

This expansion was largely the result of immigration into the city by 'foreigners' from further and further beyond the Aurelian Walls. Already under Fascism, that traditional boundary had been widely breached and now those who actually lived in the city's historic centre became an ever smaller minority of the population. The ramifications of this situation on the histories of these newcomers will need tracing in this book since each settler bore another past, another present and different hopes for the future into the city mix.

This complex weave of continuity and change in the make-up of the city's inhabitants was scarcely new. As Seneca noted when Nero was emperor, 'a large proportion of the population [of Rome] is immigrant'.[51] So it remained even as the empire declined and fell, and 'dark age' and medieval Rome was reduced to a population of a few thousand. In 1513, before the sack, the city was confined to 40,000 inhabitants, perhaps a twentieth or less than the population of imperial times. A hundred years later, it was back to 100,000.[52] Medieval and early modern cities were always dependent on new immigrants to replenish their populations. But the presence of a church with global care ensured that Rome was an unusually cosmopolitan place. As a result, for many centuries, much urban culture was 'foreign'. 'Art, music, literature, science, humanistic scholarship,' it is said, 'all had to be imported from abroad.'[53] Quite a few Romans were also transient, many being pilgrims or camp-followers of this or that pope or cardinal. Beggars, too (there were 10,000 of them in 1660), were not necessarily Roman born.[54] The power of the Church also affected the gender profile of the city, with there being three men for every two women in Rome in 1600.[55] In compensation, the city always housed numbers of prostitutes; they were estimated to account for 3 per cent of the population in the 1520s.[56] Many were immigrant.

Despite this flux, some Roman families did survive from one generation to the next and somehow cherish and record their family histories. Among them were various leading nobles; according to one recent analyst who seems to reflect his own marketised age, between 1300 and 1700 such aristocrats constructed 'the magnificent capital we know today. Extravagant characters, wild ambitions and sudden tragedies are built into the map of Rome', we are assured. 'The theatrical quality of Roman history is reflected in the theatrical design of the city, explicitly remade as it was, again and again, to tell a story.'[57]

Yet more humble stock also endured through the centuries, with the area of Trastevere, across the Tiber from the Campus Martius, being frequently depicted as the heart of a 'real', for which read popular, Rome. Similarly ever present were the city's Jews, 1,000 strong in 1200, 2 per cent of the sparse urban population. They were reported to pay no special punitive taxes and to be flourishing as a community.[58] The Counter-Reformation was much tougher for such religious dissidents, with Pope Paul IV in 1555 instituting confinement in a ghetto, punitively built on marshy land beside the river opposite Trastevere. Levels of tolerance varied over time, but life there was frequently precarious. When plague afflicted the city in 1656–7, almost 20 per cent of deaths were among the Jews.[59] Anti-Semitism could flourish both in the highest Church circles and among ordinary citizens. In Rome, *giudate* or playlets hostile to the Jews constituted 'an essential part of the traditional popular drama acted on ox-carts around the streets during carnival'.[60] With the Enlightenment and the opening of new disputes about ideal political identity, divisions over whether or not non-Catholics had a legitimate present, future and past in the city intensified, with Pope Pius VI commencing his pontificate in 1775 by forcing urban Jews to wear yellow as a distinguishing device that combined menace and humiliation.

It is clear, then, that wherever visitors turn in Rome, they will find heritage, myth and memory, histories without end, piled higgledy-piggledy on top of each other. In this city, every vista is kaleidoscopic. No doubt, on occasion, historical meaning, historical 'truth', the facts about one sector or other of the city can be established, but always and only by stopping the machine, as it were. So long and complex has the human habitation of this city been, so 'eternal' is it, that everything that matters here is in movement, prompting not an answer, a cheap conclusion, but prolonged and vivacious, life-giving, debate. It is this whirlpool of histories, as 'brought back to a present' since the Enlightenment, that it is my task to chart.

One final caution. It may be agreed that demography and economics, social behaviour, culture and identity, have never settled into a single pattern in this city. But government, too, has changed. At the end of the eighteenth century, Rome and its surrounding territories were ruled directly by the pope, with the justification being that this authority had been granted by Constantine to providential purpose. Yet religious governance would not survive the onset of modernity. Since 1789, it is necessary to remember, Rome has been successively administered by home-grown 'Jacobin' revolutionaries in 1798–9, by a restored Papacy, 1799–1808, by the satraps of Napoleon 1808–14, by the line of popes and their clerical aides back again between 1814 and 1848, by new revolutionaries led by the nationalist 'prophet', Giuseppe Mazzini, in a republic in 1849, by the once 'liberal' but now conservative pope, Pius IX, from 1849 to 1870, by the Liberal unifiers (and inventors) of a nation called Italy between 1870 and 1922, and by Mussolini's Fascist dictatorship on its own account between 1922 and 1943, briefly toughened by Nazi overlordship from September 1943 before liberation by the Anglo-Americans in June 1944. As has already been noted, two years later a referendum overturned the monarchy and from then Rome has been the capital of a national Republic of idiosyncratic cast. This last state was in some years as 'Christian' or 'social' as it was democratic, and, in 2010, is headed nationally by 'entrepreneurial' Prime Minister Silvio Berlusconi and locally in Rome by the 'post-Fascist' *sindaco* or mayor, Gianni Alemanno.

Despite Pius IX in 1870 proclaiming himself a 'prisoner in the Vatican' and a cold war between Church and State bubbling on until its political and financial resolution in the deal signed by Mussolini and Pope Pius XI on 11 February 1929 (the so-called 'Lateran Pacts' that gave legal basis to the tiny independent state of 'Vatican City'), the Church has never ceased to proclaim all Rome as its capital and has ruled a spiritual empire that spans the world. Still today, Rome is thus furnished with two heads of state, the pope and the President of Italy. Of necessity, then, the result is a 'history war'. It is after all notorious that nations legitimise themselves with long histories; the modern way of doing history, with its ambiguous pretensions to be both a 'science' and an 'art', is coterminous with the nation, both discipline and political form being aspects of that 'modernity' established after the Enlightenment.[61] There is certainly much ruthless 'invention of tradition' in the national history of Italian Rome, made yet more drastic after the milder liberal 'fathers of their nation' were replaced by militant and 'totalitarian' Fascist sons. Yet the Catholic Church is also inconceivable without its claim to comprehend, smooth and embody the passage of time. It, too, preaches a gospel about history or it is nothing.

It will be no surprise to learn that a battle between Church and nation state over the city's history and the lessons that can be drawn from past to present and future has never ended despite the formal establishment of two states in Rome following the Lateran accords. Yet this is only one of the arguments that has threaded and still threads through the search for meaning in Rome. Within the Italian nation, unity was never fully imposed, with the partisans of rival ideologies, Liberal, Fascist, Marxist, 'anti-Fascist' and neo-Fascist, all seeking the high historical ground. So, too, did the many foreign visitors who came to Rome as residents or tourists or for religious or commercial business. German, British, American, French and even Australian Romes exist alongside the Italian one. So do Romes of the peoples, be they what are claimed to be the long-standing Romans of Trastevere or the successive newcomers on the successive peripheries, men and women today likely to originate from the ample spaces of the developing world, all with their own special histories transported to the place in their minds along with their bodies. It is for this reason that I must delineate many Romes and many histories, their battles and accommodations, as I review the experience of the Eternal City and the changing location of historical purpose in it across the last two centuries.

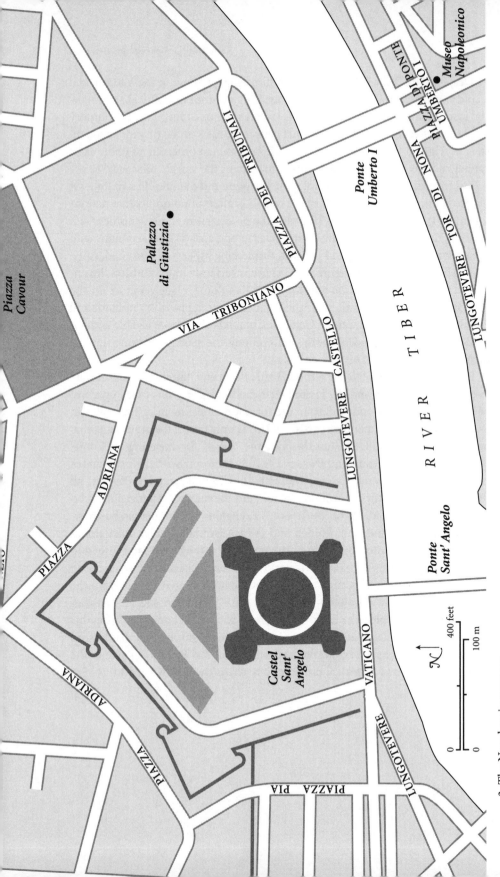

3. The Napoleonic museum

———— ✳ ————

2

ROME, REVOLUTION AND HISTORY

Amid the treasury of Roman tourist sites, the Museo Napoleonico, housed in the
Palazzo Primoli across the river from Castel Sant'Angelo, is not one of the city's
more celebrated buildings. Yet it is a place worth pondering by anyone investi-
gating how histories in the city make themselves heard, live, die or run together
at different times and with different needs and purposes. The current guidebook
to this place of memory of a Roman Napoleon relates proudly that it was
bequeathed to the Italian nation by Count Giuseppe Primoli on his death in
1927. Primoli was a great-grandson of Lucien Bonaparte, the next younger
brother in the numerous Bonaparte line to the 'great' Napoleon.[1] Inside the
museum, twelve rooms allow a devotee to pursue the history of the family from
the 'First Empire' to more modern times, with a concentration that is sometimes
on France but always with a bearing on Rome. A pious onlooker can examine
the tobacco boxes that Napoleon awarded to his kin and courtiers, and may draw
meaning from a portrait of Lucien clutching a book in a soulful manner.[2] The
fifth room highlights the Roman Republic of 1798–9, a time of revolution in
the city, and, with some eclecticism, the sixth the life of Pauline Bonaparte, who
married into the Borghese family of the Roman aristocracy. In the last two
rooms the pertinacious visitor can survey matters appertaining to 'the Roman
branch of the Bonapartes', including the family of the donor. The intended focus
may be a portrait of Primoli's great-aunt Carlotta, dressed in unlikely fashion 'as
a peasant', wearing rich and ornate clothes and toting a gilded basket of flowers
and greenery.

So much is pious display of the Emperor as grandiose heir of the French and
European revolution. But, as so often in Rome, time is not frozen in the era
between 1789 and 1815. The Museo Napoleonico was opened in 1927, five
years after Mussolini had been appointed Prime Minister. It marked a major
moment of the conversion of Fascist rule into what was called a totalitarian

QVESTO MVSEO NAPOLEONICO
IL CONTE GIVSEPPE NAPOLEONE PRIMOLI
PER DVPLICE DISCENDENZA PARENTE AI BONAPARTE
INSIEME COL FRATELLO LVIGI
LEGAVA ALLA CITTA DI ROMA
ESSENDONE GOVERNATORE
LVDOVICO SPADA POTENZIANI
CHE IL XXVIII OTTOBRE DEL MCMXXVII A·VI
NE PRENDEVA SOLENNEMENTE POSSESSO

VITTORIO EMANVELE III RE
BENITO MVSSOLINI DVCE

5. Napoleonic Museum plaque unites Emperor and Duce.

state. This process had begun on 3 January 1925, when Mussolini openly announced his approval of all Fascist violence since his movement's foundation in 1919, thereby endorsing a dictatorship and the ousting of a 'government' in favour of a 'regime'. At the end of 1925 the Duce named the next year the '*Anno Napoleonico*', a historic moment when no turning back from the imposition of Fascism on every Italian would be licit or possible.[3]

Nationalist Italian historians had long been accustomed to claim that Napoleon, born in a Corsica that, until 1768, had been ruled by Genoa, was 'really' Italian.[4] Now, under Fascism, it was as hard as ever in Rome to act without historical reflection. At least according to an English biographer, Mussolini, emulating a past hero for present purpose just as the 'Emperor' Napoleon had done with the Caesars, went further with the identification: 'he used to stand with legs astride, hands on hips, and with a slightly scowling face that some took to be self-consciously Napoleonic; or sometimes he would strike an attitude for the cameras with his hand inside his jacket – another Napoleonic affectation.'[5] Once his regime was established, the Fascist Duce found time to collaborate with the dramatist Giovacchino Forzano on a play about Napoleon that was translated into English by John Drinkwater and reached the stage of a number of European capitals. It focused on the Hundred Days before the Battle of Waterloo and was curiously pessimistic in nature, depicting a ruler troubled by illness, prevented by his sly police chief, Joseph Fouché, from assuming full dictatorial powers, and lamenting to his heroic mother that defamation, not glory, was what history would offer his shade.[6]

There were further occasions when the dictator wrestled with possible historical parallels between his ambitions and the ghost of Napoleon, anxiously measuring his 'greatness' against that of the Emperor. Ordinarily Fascism proclaimed itself destroyer of the ills allegedly resulting from the French Revolution. However, late in 1925, Mussolini acknowledged that, as far as Italy was concerned, the national unification and modernisation begun in the Risorgimento and to be brought to perfection by Fascism had been initiated by the Napoleonic invasions and the resultant overthrow of the *ancien régime* in Rome and the rest of the peninsula.[7] The dictator's cast on Napoleonic history explains the memorial stone affixed to the wall of the Museo Napoleonico, recalling that Primoli's gift was gratefully received by the *Governatore* or unelected, Fascist-appointed and aristocratic chief of Rome, Lodovico Spada Potenziani, on 28 October MCMXXVII, fifth anniversary of the March on Rome and therefore the herald of '*Anno VI*' in the 'revolutionary' Fascist calendar. As the inscription continues, these were the happy times when 'Victor Emmanuel III was king and Benito Mussolini Duce'.

However humble its part in a tourist itinerary of the contemporary city, the Museo Napoleonico is one of the innumerable sites where rival histories surface and blend, and where an alert onlooker can detect the spirit of individuals who, directly or indirectly, have amplified the modern Roman story. Many will find their place in this book as it reviews the last two centuries of city life and meaning. Certainly, the beginning of modernity with the Enlightenment and the revolutionary decades after 1789 quickly featured 'an ambiguous dialectic of the negation and recuperation of history' and so the self-conscious wiping out of some pasts and the privileging of others.[8] Commentators have agreed that, under Napoleon, ' "Rome" became a storehouse to be raided for new imperial conceits; in effect, a ruin to be scavenged for salvageable fragments which could be reinvented and located in evocatively new ideological frameworks'.[9] Yet this process was scarcely unusual. Rome always whispered, and whispers, with histories, and the Jacobins were not alone in selecting and adapting pasts to serve their cause. The Church, the 'people', the French invaders, those tourists who still reached Rome and who, after 1815, were to come in ever greater numbers, as well as the Roman revolutionaries, all summoned one past or other for future lesson and almost always did so with present intent.

No doubt, to most eyes, before the eighteenth century came to its bloody end in the French Revolution and the all but global war that resulted from it,

Rome seemed still a holy city, the sacred place from where the pope governed a universal Church, secure in a historic authority alleged to have been 'donated' by the Emperor Constantine to Pope (Saint) Sylvester I. The document that proclaimed this donation had been shown in the Renaissance to be an eighth-century forgery, but Church historians had still not altogether discountenanced it. Certainly the 'temporal power' of the Church and its right to rule Rome and its surrounding territory were held to be God-given. From its foundation by St Peter, the Church proclaimed a gospel that was, by definition, timeless. As a corollary, the meaning of papal Rome was also unchanging. Divine providence elevated the city to be supreme among the peoples, indeed Eternal Rome, a place possessed of and guided by one unchallengeable history.

Yet could Rome be merely holy? Could its dedication to Christ obscure that power of the Caesars which had given the city a famous empire? The fragments of classical Rome lay everywhere around and, as the eighteenth century wore on, became ever more important as a vehicle of the modern 'lessons of history', however defined. Already in 1347 Cola di Rienzo, a rebel against aristocratic rule, had inserted the classical past into his contemporary world as a living model when he proclaimed the 'restoration' of the 'Roman Republic' as the '*buono stato*', the ideal state. Thereafter, through Renaissance and Counter-Reformation and into the Enlightenment, Latin texts became an automatic part of every European education and Roman parallels naturally inspired thought and action. Popes themselves led the way. The warrior pontiff Julius II (1503–13) self-consciously donned the mantle of Julius Caesar, proclaiming the purpose of his wars to be an eventual Pax Romana.[10] Others were not behind-hand. At least according to the great nineteenth-century Swiss historian, Jacob Burckhardt, the Renaissance was nourished by a process through which Rome, 'the city of ruins', became the object of a new, rational, contemporary knowledge, where the pilgrim was ousted by the 'patriot and historian'.[11]

The words went naturally together because, during the Enlightenment, the nation was being invented as the dominant modern political form. Every 'new' nation grew dependent on 'invented tradition' to justify its present and guide its future.[12] In accompaniment, adepts of the discipline of history asserted a new scrupulousness and respectability. Soon Leopold von Ranke would be thought to have defined history's fundamental task as recounting 'what actually happened' in an irreproachably 'scientific' manner. As Gibbon had already demonstrated with his celebrated tally of more than 8,000 footnotes, modernising historians 'must not only tell stories but cite evidence'.[13] In previous centuries, people of all classes had been satisfied with 'incredible genealogies', tall tales and untrue from the misty past.[14] Now fact and fiction began to be viewed as opposite and irreconcilable matters. Ironically, Rome occupied a prominent place in this rise of the 'fact' because, in the subjective understanding of those beginning to seek the path to modernity, classical

Roman history, Christian and, ever more importantly, Republican and imperial history outweighed that of any other time.

To this end, the Grand Tour brought the best and the brightest of the countries beyond the Alps to the city, often, as Horace Walpole put it, with classical authors and their memorable 'facts' in hand.[15] The visitors gave glancing attention to the contemporary city, being filled with a sense that they were not so much exploring present Rome as having their knowledge of its past 'proved' and refreshed.[16] They arrived armed with a Roman history that was scarcely the Catholic one and left with their 'rationality' (Gibbon loved to hail its triumph over 'enthusiasm') confirmed.

They came, saw and considered because they had already decided that archaeology was the most fashionable and telling of 'scholarly' activities, and one that every educated layman could comprehend. Learning that contemporary urban habitation occupied only a small sector of the land guarded by the Aurelian Walls, visitors became all the surer that the ancient past was what mattered about the place. For these rich and influential foreigners, ruins were Rome. Indeed, according to one analyst of the Grand Tour, the half-uncovered sites 'gained much of their appeal for the degree to which past glory contrasted with a setting of present insignificance, poverty and backwardness'.[17] Classical Rome became a city of the mind whose spirit, whose 'historical lessons', could be purchased, packaged and carried home as another worthy and consoling portable memory. In the eighteenth century, 'Romes' of some sort spread far from the Seven Hills. Political leaders took to having themselves portrayed in 'Roman dress' or had their effigies preserved in busts that seemed in direct descent from those who had once been emperors. The Congress of the new American Republic was ornamented with fasces to claim the city of Washington as yet another new Rome.[18]

As men and women from confident rising northern societies flocked into the place, often staying from one year to the next (albeit with a cautious removal during the height of summer, given the deadly threat of malaria), Rome shifted a little to make room for them. The best surviving symbol of the process is the Protestant cemetery, where, at first, burials had to occur in secret and at night. Pilgrims today will find that the communist historian and philosopher, Antonio Gramsci, rests there along with those English and German residents, including Keats, Shelley and Julius Goethe, the only son of the poet, people who, over the passing decades, met their deaths in Rome.

Many of the Grand Tourists were the appreciative patrons of the work of Giovanni Battista Piranesi (1720–78), a Venetian who had moved to Rome and who pioneered a market in images of the city. Detecting what then mattered most about Rome's history, he gave a greater emphasis to classical than to religious sites. Soon another fan of the 'fact', he was involved in measuring ancient edifices more accurately than in the past.[19] Piranesi's images, with their combined representation of the power of the ancient and the crumbling decay of the present, reinforced foreign assumptions that 'their' Rome was a take-away product, a transportable site of memory, a literal 'souvenir'. Equally influential was Johann Joachim Winckelmann (1717–68). This German archaeologist and convert to Catholicism became the chief expert in charting what the century accepted as artistic beauty, praising the statuary and other material remains unearthed in Rome, whether 'Greek' or local in design, as peerless and timeless models.

With a combination of distinguished papal and foreign impulse – the sixth son of the English king, appropriately named Prince Augustus, worked on the excavation of a *mithraeum* at Ostia in 1793[20] – the city was gradually assuming a different aspect. Its history was now represented more self-consciously than in the past. With as yet little intimation that an Italian nation might be in the making, Rome's traditions were nonetheless being reinvented. Plans were sketched to overhaul the Forum, for example. Known as the Campo Vaccino or Cow Pasture, it was still trod by cattle waiting to be marketed for the city's consumption. Although two avenues of elm trees delineated a public promenade, many of the Forum's celebrated features were covered by the mud of centuries. The first superficial scratching of the soil, at the behest of the Swedish ambassador, Baron Carl Fredric of Fredenheim, commenced in 1788 in front of the church then called Santa Maria Liberatrice, the oldest Christian

6. Piranesi's view of the Campo Vaccino or Forum without galley slave labourers, 1772.

building in the area. Over the decades, this edifice was given further attention. In 1901–2, its relatively modern additions were demolished and it resumed the name of Santa Maria Antiqua, which it still possesses, following another major restoration.

The increasing importance of archaeology had not passed without notice by the Church. Could the past that its excavations brought into the light of day be reconciled with that of Catholicism? At the beginning of the eighteenth century, Pope Clement XI (1700–21), although direly unsuccessful in his high diplomacy and of little fame theologically (if vague about the detail, he did in 1708 make the feast of the Immaculate Conception obligatory throughout the Christian world on 8 December), set the tone for the following decades.[21] With the initial thrust of the Counter-Reformation losing intensity, Clement sought to reassert the centrality of Rome in the Christian story. Perhaps the urban 'reality' could uplift the spirit and enhance divine mystery; Clement's hope was not yet 'neoclassical' and factual; rather he, like his predecessors, hoped Church sponsorship of archaeology would enliven the city's Catholic holiness and ward off the Protestant enemy.[22]

The pope's technique was to cherish the city's alleged purity, as expressed in the extant, early churches, which were now restored – 60 centimetres of soil, the debris of many Tiber floods, had to be scraped away from the portal of Santa Maria in Cosmedin[23] – and in the patristic writings, to be consulted anew with pious but 'modern' scholarship. The Vatican Library must have its holdings increased from research ventures across the Mediterranean. A papal museum (Museo Ecclesiastico) should open and, as early as 1704, Clement issued a decree 'forbidding the transport or alteration of pictures, mosaics, inscriptions, and such without a special licence' from an official appointed to be *Presidente delle antichità* (Head of Antiquities).[24] Clement, in other words, looked to culture to shore up papal authority, contending that the history that lay so evidently around Rome was alive with religious possibility. The present, he believed, must be 'no simple custodian but an active participant in tradition'. Archaeological and historical research, and the carefully conserved museums resulting from it, must foster 're-presentations of the past in modern terms, not attempts to recreate a past indulged by the present'.[25] Roman history, a carefully crafted version of the new critical history, must defend and advance Catholicism.

Clement's successors continued this process of adapting the growing evidence of the classical past being unearthed by archaeology and newly punctilious philology to the papal cause. Christ and the early Church were to be placed at the centre of events that had mattered in classical Rome. In 1742 Benedict XIV (1740–58) created new chairs at the Collegio Romano in ecclesiastical history and in liturgy, with an assumption that the spreading devotion to historical accuracy could inform Catholic thought and practice.

In 1757 he added a Museo cristiano to what was becoming the Vatican complex.[26] Under Clement XIV (1769–74) and, especially, Pius VI (1775–99), this repository was expanded further in the Museo Pio-Clementino, a place that was as ready to house republican and imperial artefacts as overtly religious ones. For these popes, it was almost as if the lay and imperial 'permanence' of Rome made Catholicism permanent there and paradoxically swept from sight any recollection of pagan religion and later heresy or any challenge to papal succession.

Work advanced on many fronts. In 1803 Pope Pius VII (1800–23) ordered a 'general clearing of the Forum from the Arch of Septimius Severus to the Capitoline declivity', and, under the direction of Carlo Fea, his new *Commissario delle antichità* (Commissioner of Antiquities), the existing shops were purged from the Severan structure.[27] While papal rule survived, there were, from time to time, further digs in this heartland of the classical past. But progress was too limping for those whose imagination centred more on ancient Rome's imperial power than its holiness. In 1813 an English visitor found that 'a herdsman, seated on a pedestal while his oxen were drinking at the fountain, and a few pedestrians, moving at a distance in different directions, were the only human beings that disturbed the silence and the solitude that reigned around' the Forum. 'So far,' he philosophised, 'have the modern Romans forgotten the theatre of the glory and imperial power of their ancestors as to degrade it into a common market for cattle, and sink its name, illustrated by every page of Roman history, into the contemptible appellation of Campo Vaccino.'[28] Half a century later, the name, the elm trees and the promenades were still there, and a modern 'cleansing' had to await Liberal Italian governance after 1870.[29]

The Colosseum was also regarded with new attention and sensibility, especially after a lightning strike on 9 July 1776 dislodged a clatter of stones from the remaining structure.[30] Although the outer arches of the edifice continued to be used as a storage place for manure until 1811, both Pius VI and Pius VII sponsored restorative work on the place. By the 1780s annual reports were published about excavations occurring in the city or needed there. That of 1789 emphasised that the 'Flavian Ampitheatre, vulgarly called the Colosseum', 'once seen would never be forgotten'. Yet the paper remonstrated in words that would become familiar in the heritage trade, 'its collapse is happening so fast that, in a century's time, if it is not treated with particular care, the rest of its internal structure will be completely lost'.[31]

The warning was heeded and, under the next popes, restoration commenced, with greater or lesser ruthlessness, of what might be regarded as the building's original fabric. Those who pass by the Colosseum today can still locate plaques thanking Pius VII for his solicitude. His predecessor had been equally ready to be fascinated by the work initiated on Nero's 'Golden House', the Domus Aurea, while the tomb of the Scipios, identified in 1600 and then unaccountably lost, was rediscovered in 1780.[32] It, too, offered a mixture of pasts, given the presence of a third-century dwelling with imperial paintings and mosaics, and a Christian catacomb with linked chapel. During Pius VI's reign, three more Egyptian obelisks were discovered and raised in Roman squares.[33] Ennio Quirino Visconti, papal librarian from 1771, emerged as the lay figure most responsible for interpreting archaeological findings in the city and was destined to win lasting fame.[34]

To be sure, Pius VI was not altogether reliable in his commitment to saving and restoring the city's past. On occasion, this pope was happy to sell the products of archaeological effort in order to bolster sagging Church finances.[35] More suggestive of the gap between papal thought and the new ideas of liberty, equality and fraternity was the reversion to overt anti-Semitism that occurred under his aegis. There was some irony here since, in the twentieth century, Fascist Italy would be Nazi Germany's 'first ally' when that terrible regime endeavoured to achieve a modern (pseudo-)scientific and total 'solution' to the 'Jewish Question'. But the Counter-Reformation Church had sought in its way to tally and define its Jews with malign intent. From 1775 Pius VI restored various petty tyrannies that had slipped out of usage over the past decades, demanding limitations on clothing and behaviour that kept the city's ancient Jewish community locked in the ghetto in desperate material poverty and cultural deprivation. Such a revival of repression hinted at a papal anxiety about what times were doing to Church identity and so was not merely traditional but foreshadowed attitudes that were to become more murderous a century later.[36]

Certainly, despite efforts by succeeding popes to control history and time, the challenge to Catholic reading of Rome's present, future and past had not lessened as modernity advanced. One who asserted that the framing of Rome's meaning could not be left to the Vatican was the celebrated German writer J.W. Goethe, a giant of the Enlightenment and its version of liberal reform. In the months when, in France, the financial and governmental crisis that was to spark revolution in 1789 was boiling over, Goethe joined the respectable of his generation in an 'Italian journey'. At the centre of his imagined Italy stood Rome, 'the hub of the world', the 'First City', as he hailed it.[37] Rome was a place that occasioned diverse thoughts. For the worthy Protestant visitor, there was worry about 'the distorted baroque paganism' that ruled there and had stained the purer relics of the 'simple and innocent beginnings' of Christianity. Better were the classical ruins. Surveying the Colosseum led Goethe to the conclusion that, 'once one has seen it, everything else seems small. It is so huge that the mind cannot retain its image.' Similarly, the Pantheon, the Apollo Belvedere, the Sistine Chapel, each represented 'noble perfection'. 'The entire history of the world', Goethe mused, 'is linked up with this city, and I reckon my second life, a very re-birth, from the day when I entered Rome.'[38]

Yet irritations abounded. Goethe was not attracted by the other foreign visitors who congregated in Rome. They might seem like him but they lacked his seriousness. They lived perversely for the present and not, as he did, ethically for the past or future. Moreover, although he paid little attention to the humbler classes and their history, Goethe worried that it was 'a difficult and melancholy business, I must confess, separating the old Rome from the new'. Yet, despite these concerns, the message that the German writer drew from Rome was both positive and 'enlightened'. The virtuous past that he was sketching in his mind mattered. 'Here is an entity which has suffered so many drastic changes in the course of two thousand years, yet it is still the same soil, the same hill, often even the same column or the same wall, and in its people one still finds traces of their ancient character.' Crucial, Goethe reckoned, was to go beyond Catholicism in dealing with the place: 'It is history, above all, that one reads quite differently here from anywhere else in the world. Everywhere else one starts from the outside and works inward; here it seems to be the other way around. All history is encamped about us and all history sets forth again from us. This does not apply only to Roman history, but to the history of the whole world.'[39] Goethe conceived Rome and its history as of universal but not Catholic significance. In his attempt to adapt and use its traditions, Rome was too crucial a source of human understanding to be left to the Church, ordinary Romans or careless visitors of less than intellectual cast. It was the epitome of human (or European) brotherhood. It 'stood for' man's hope in perfectibility. Its history lesson illuminated a rational path to the future.

Less lofty visitors, however, read cruder messages from the place. For the sybaritic Venetian Giacomo Casanova, Rome scarcely taught high morality. Instead Casanova saw a place unequalled in the Catholic world for its laxity 'in matters of religion'. To make one's fortune there, he mused, a man, 'in this ancient capital of Italy must be a chameleon sensitive to all colours which the light casts on his surroundings. He must be flexible, insinuating, a great dissimulator, impenetrable, obliging, often base, ostensibly sincere, always pretending to know less than he does.'[40] For a man on the make, Casanova's recipe was a lasting one; a fawning cynicism was one way not to be forced to reckon with the actual complexities and multiplicities of Rome. Taking a different moral stance but equally damning were the Verri brothers, Lombard intellectuals, self-conscious in their hope in 'reform' and 'improvement'. For them, the inhabitants of Rome were the opposite of their fellows in bustling and modernising Milan. The southern city was 'the emblem of the degradation of the intellect, a desolate place where the poverty of the people, the obtuseness of the clergy and the silliness of writers predominated'.[41] Here, again, were views about Rome's past and present, its eternal corruption, the failure of its ordinary citizens to preserve their alleged ancient grandeur, and therefore Rome's inadequacy as a human springboard to the future, fated to survive and prosper. Maybe, such commentators suggested, the salutary meaning of the city's classical history was not its power and achievement but its decline and decadence. Maybe its major lesson to modern man was not what to do but what not to do.

It was after all evident that the common people of the city clung to a reading of the meaning and purpose of life as timeless as that of the Church. Staffing a booth that sold radishes in Nerva's Forum, offering a barber's service beneath the Arch of Septimius Severus, but gravely bowing to each of the daily religious parades and imbuing their lives with a popular Catholicism that needed no written texts to explain and defend it, men and women of the people lived as they thought men and women always had.[42] Both contemporary visitors and later historians have depicted a populace, still overwhelmingly illiterate, who did little to analyse their condition in an intellectual or modern manner. The project of 'scientific' archaeology to produce a more accurate record of the past left them cold. Rather, for them, the ruins re-emerging from the soil proved anew that their city was the capital of the world as it had always been. Ironically, they were as contemptuous of the place of their visitors in the flux of the centuries as the foreigners were of them. Any who arrived from outside its walls they deemed 'barbarians, people without history'.[43] The foreign, the Roman, and, indeed, humankind were, they thought, impervious to real change. As if in proof, the papal government disdained the modern reckoning of time, with a Roman day still measured from each sunrise rather than decreed automatically and 'rationally' by enlightening mathematics (Napoleon's 'best subject', along with history, when a schoolboy).[44]

The denizens of Trastevere, the suburb on the far side of the river from the remains of the Forum, people long thought to be the most 'authentic' of Romans, were said to have their pockets stuffed with a knife and a rosary: the use of either was viewed as an ordinary occurrence.[45] If newly scholarly priests throughout Christendom, consulting the works of the early fathers with a fresh and austere zeal, debated Jansenism or strove to decide whether the Jesuits remained a legitimate force in the world, the great majority of Romans avoided such pondering. 'While the practice of religion was a habit that was deeply engrained in the inmost soul of the people, they lived through their senses and an etherealized faith meant nothing to them. They had to hear and see and touch religion.'[46] Mass was not conducted in austere silence. Instead, 'men and women moved about freely, in and out, simple worshippers ejaculated, grieved, rocked to and fro, beat their breast or prayed their private prayers aloud, sometimes too loud'. Beside them, beggars and dogs sought attention and reward.[47]

Employment may have been precarious; in 1791 it was alleged that half the population lacked formal jobs.[48] Torture may have been common until 1831. Executions may have been public, with 251 taking place between 1700 and

1798; such criminals had their bodies exposed in public for some days after their deaths, before they were given ignominious burial in unmarked graves.[49] Typically they met their maker in Piazza del Popolo, before a jesting crowd and, during carnival, at the hands of an executioner dressed in a clown's clothes.[50] But such a fate, it was thought, had always been and would always be.

Religion or religiosity pervaded life. Monasteries, convents and other clerical-owned and administered places dominated the city's urban fabric (seventy-four churches were dedicated to the Madonna). Priests were marked by their special dress and privileges (for example, they paid no tax) in every sector of Roman life. As the French writer and *philosophe*, Montesquieu, put it, churches were good for 'divine service and homicide'; sanctuary remained normal practice under papal rule.[51] Charity was generous, and the average calorie intake of the city's inhabitants, even those on a 'minimum budget', was 2,515; the people of late eighteenth-century Paris made do on 1,669.[52] Festivals occupied 150 days each year; on the greatest occasions, St Peter's would be illuminated by 6,000 candles and would shine magically with what was then unexampled intensity. The streams of visiting foreigners arriving at the most prized religious destination of the Grand Tour added further to the prospect of remuneration, with one Frenchman commenting cynically that the locals looked 'after their ruins for the same reason that beggars look after their sores'.[53]

In the city, the meaning of 'foreign' was not yet nationalised, with Italians from outside Rome being thought alien to those who were born and raised within the Aurelian Walls. Did they not by definition lack Rome's history? The very churches were connected with this town or that – Santo Spirito was for Neapolitans and San Venanzio for those from Camerino, for example.[54] Clothing, too, acted as a marker of class, gender and region in a way that would disappear with homogenising modernity. As late as the 1820s, an onlooker described the sartorial variety of a congregation gathered to receive the blessing of the pope, given from the loggia of St Peter's. Then, 'the men are in their gayest attire, with blue or green velvet jackets, their hair gathered in a green silk net, with white stockings, and such silver buckles at their knee, and still more on the foot, that, if such articles had been discovered in an ancient tomb, and supposed to give a rule of proportion for the primeval wearer, they would have given the lie to the old proverb: *"Ex pede Herculem"* '. According to the same witness, women were still more brilliantly clad: 'the female attire on those occasions was, far more than now since the invasion of Manchester reached even Apennine villages, characteristically distinct. The peasants of Frascati and Albano, with immense gold earrings and necklaces, the silver skewer through their hair, under the snow-white flat kerchief with richly brocaded stomachers and showy silks looked almost poor beside the Oriental splendour of the costume, supposed to be Saracenic, of the dames from Nettuno. A veil of domestic texture of gold relieved by stripes of the richest colours framed the crown of a dress truly elegant and magnificent.'[55]

For these peasant visitors, drawn to the city for a festival, as for the *Trasteverini*, history, then, bore a double meaning. Rome itself was 'eternal'; the adjective was widely known and approved. Such eternity should, however, be best understood as the scenic backdrop to family histories, the only kind, apart from biblical or saints' tales and legends about the 'Satanic' Emperor Nero, that carried credible or significant echoes from the past. For the majority of Romans, for many decades yet, identity and its historical underpinning remained local and familial, impervious to the 'scientific' assumptions of the Enlightenment as well as to any prompting from the nation.

As the eighteenth century staggered to a violent close in revolution and war, the city of Rome may have seemed to sleep under Pius VI's flaccid rule. Yet its histories were alive and in contention, and were already fuelling passions that had been unleashed by the collapse of monarchical rule in France. Into this vortex would fall papal Rome, itself in 1798–9 swept by revolution.

What, then, did this revolution do to Rome's histories? The past could not be forgotten at this time of change but was, instead, summoned to justify every cause. In the second most renowned passage in his works, Karl Marx greeted the elevation in 1851 of Louis Napoleon, nephew of the 'great' Napoleon, to be the Emperor Napoleon III with the comment:

> Men make their own history, but not of their own free will; not under circumstances they themselves have chosen but under the given and inherited circumstances with which they are directly confronted. The tradition of the dead generations weighs like a nightmare on the minds of the living. And, just when they appear to be engaged in the revolutionary transformation of themselves and their material surroundings, in the creation of something which does not yet exist, precisely in such epochs of revolutionary crisis they timidly conjure up the spirits of the past to help them; they borrow their names, slogans and costumes so as to stage the new world-historical scene in this venerable disguise and borrowed language.

Typical, Marx continued, had been the way that the French Revolution of 1789 and after 'draped itself alternatively as the Roman republic and the Roman empire'.[56]

Certainly, between 1789 and 1815, the power of the myth of Rome was starkly apparent, both in the streets of Paris and in all those other places washed by the tsunami of revolution. The iconography of the time revived the *fascio littorio* (the bound rods of the lictor, with or without an axe), triumphal arches, the Phrygian cap of liberty and much else. Trajan's Column was hailed as the inspiration for new military commemorations and there was talk in France of buying it from the Romans so that it could be erected anew in the Place Vendôme in central Paris (after Napoleon's victory at Austerlitz an ersatz version would be raised there).[57] In an age congratulating itself on the death of tyrants, a list of French towns altered their names to work 'Brutus' into the title, with Monfort-l'Amaury becoming Monfort-le-Brutus, for example.[58] The most radical revolutionary, to fall to the guillotine in 1796 after leading an unsuccessful 'Conspiracy of Equals', called himself 'Gracchus' Babeuf, maintaining that the classical agrarian revolutionary was his model. Under the Directory during the second half of the 1790s, society women strove to have their hair cut in the style of the Emperors Titus or Caracalla.[59] The latter (ruled 211–217 CE) may have been a worrying choice for recollection, given his role in first murdering and then striving to eliminate the historical memory of his brother, Geta, with the attempted erasure still today visible on the arch erected in Rome to their father, Septimius Severus.

Napoleon's rise did nothing to eliminate the Roman references, both in his period as 'First Consul' (1799–1802) and when, in that last year, he elevated himself to emperor. This title was aimed at trumping the surviving *ancien régime* monarchies, among whom the Tsar of all the Russias and the Kaiser of Austria also by deliberate implication stood in historical descent from the Caesars. The dressage of Napoleon's regime took matters further, however, and official propaganda let it be known that the Corsican patriot, Pasquale Paoli, had hailed Napoleon in his youth with the words: 'You are an ancient Roman escaped from the stories told by Plutarch.'[60] With such words in the air, there was an inevitability in the elevation of Rome to 'the second city of the Empire' on 17 February 1810 and in the naming of Napoleon's infant son and heir as 'the King of Rome'. By then there was even talk of building new catacombs in Paris so that the city could be fully equipped for a sublime imperial destiny that could match that of Rome.[61] Napoleon also raised with the Austrian Foreign Minister, Clemens von Metternich, his most able diplomatic opponent, a project to transfer all Europe's archives to a fireproofed new building in Paris. There, the Emperor claimed, they could be read with 'safety and . . . science', although somewhere beneath such sentiments must have lain a grandiose imperial ambition, more totalitarian than any that occurred to Mussolini, to have all history made in his capital.[62]

Back in the 1790s, the zeal of the various factions in revolutionary France to annex the history and the memory of Rome to their cause was quickly exemplified in the terms and conditions imposed on the feeble papal forces by invading French armies. The armistice of May 1796 required the urgent shipment to Paris of a bronze bust of Lucius Junius Brutus and a marble head of Marcus Brutus, each deemed a worthy tyrannicide who carried the glory of his history into the present.[63] In the clauses of the Treaty of Tolentino (1797), the

Papacy was told that it must hand over one hundred works of art, ranging from the *Apollo Belvedere* and the *Dying Gaul* to Raphael's *Transfiguration* and Domenichino's *Last Communion of St Jerome*.[64] It would not be the last endeavour of the Vatican's enemies to wipe out its claims to Roman pasts by literally taking them away.

The French were all the more determined and vindictive in their zeal to seize Roman history for themselves and their cause because Pius VI had swiftly and publicly numbered himself among the foes of the revolutionary regime in Paris, ostentatiously turning the back of his Church to any novel view of the past and future. The pope's flirtations with some aspects of the modern world before 1789 had not persuaded him or his court to read the wicked *philosophes*. In the *Giornale ecclesiastico di Roma*, a paper established in 1785 to rebut the adversaries of Catholicism, the intellectual reformers were peremptorily dismissed as 'blowhards and buffoons, who fade into nothingness as soon as they are faced with those who are really wise and erudite'. Voltaire was written off as 'a literary juggler, lacking conscience or principles, allowing the most shameful passions to play, always racked by contradiction and the adversary of any who try in even a minimal way to dim his glory'.[65] In the papal mind the ideas of enlightened intellectuals were of no account in the great sweep of Catholic history.

By the early 1790s, papal officials were therefore predictably prominent in backing a 'crusade' by the *ancien régime* states against the Republic, with the *Giornale ecclesiastico* summing up the revolutionaries in familiar historical parallel as 'Huns, Goths, Vandals, Eruli, who [now] come not from the north nor the Black Sea but are found among us'.[66] In his clinging to reaction, Pius VI was joined by the common people of his city. News of the guillotining of Louis XVI in Paris was greeted in Rome with a popular assault on the ghetto.[67]

In June 1796, with French armies ranging across northern Italy, rumours spread of an assassination plot against the pope. The result in Rome was an outbreak of popular piety. It marked a summoning by the people of the history that they understood to act as a shield and buckler against the French and the threat of imponderable social and, especially, political and cultural change and any new, menacingly rational, past that might lie behind it. Through the summer of that year miraculous manifestations of the Madonna and of the crucified Christ multiplied in Rome and the rest of the Papal States. Stories revived of monstrous births and miracles, events that had always signalled a time of crisis and disaster. In the streets of the capital, men and women were reported tearing their hair, crying or whipping themselves while they grieved for their sins. 'Holy War', it was urged, should be unleashed against the sinful.[68] Giovanni Marchetti, one of the editorial team of the *Giornale ecclesiastico*, wrote that society had divided into the Good and the Bad as though for the Final Coming of Christ; taking the chance to inscribe a contemporary history for his cause, he blamed the revolution on a medley of Freemasons and Jansenists, and any who had doubted the eternity and truth of the pope's message.[69]

When, finally, in 1798–9, the revolution penetrated the gates of Rome, it is no surprise to find that a violent contest flamed over the relationship between past, present and future. The speed and unpredictability of events deepened the popular fear that these might be the last days, indeed 'the end of history'. On 28 December 1797 the French commander, General M.-L. Duphot, was murdered near the Porta Settimiana on the Vatican side of the Tiber, after a skirmish had broken out between papal guards and Romans who favoured the revolution. Duphot had only just left the presence of Joseph, oldest of the Bonaparte brothers, who was acting as the French Directory's ambassador to the Papacy. Joseph blamed the papal government for the death and, on 11 January, Napoleon ordered the Army of Italy to march on Rome and organise the foundation of a republic there, with the caution that the French should conceal their role in such a revolution.[70]

To marshal resistance, the pope, reliant more on historical than military strength, quickly fell back on the power of religious artefacts, held aloft in public. They included treasured relics conserved in the city, featuring 'the Sacred Image of the Most Holy Saviour from the *Sancta Sanctorum*, that of the Most Holy Virgin Mary from her church at the Campitelli, and the chains of St Peter, as conserved in San Pietro in vincoli'. A crowd of 100,000, almost the entire urban population, swollen by refugees from the disturbed countryside, followed the parade, crying out '*Viva Maria*' and 'Pardon us, O Lord God'.[71]

Such a holy past was, however, of scant immediate use. On 10 February 1798 papal troops evacuated Castel Sant'Angelo, the city's prime fortress, and that night Pius VI sent Louis-Alexandre Berthier, the French commander, an ingratiating gift of 'forty bottles of wine, a dressed calf and a whole sturgeon'.[72] Despite such blandishment of what the pope must have hoped was Berthier's gentlemanly side, on the 11th revolutionary troops formally occupied the city. One Catholic diarist mused that it amounted to 'Judgement Day'.[73] On 15 February the Republic was proclaimed in a ceremony at the Campo Vaccino. Five days later, Pius VI was hustled out of Rome, destined never to return. He was simultaneously deprived of his personal library of 60,000 books, the printed repository of his history. During the following months, the pope, old and ill, was harried from one prison to the next. He died in captivity on 29 August 1799, having taken the precaution of providing instructions about the procedure in a conclave when political excitation rendered papal election impossible in Rome.

Pius VII, acquiring the pallium in Venice on 14 March 1800, did not reach his capital until 3 July that year. Rome had by then lacked a papal ruler for twenty-seven tumultuous months. However, the Republic had scarcely been able securely to impose its own governance or, despite its strenuous efforts, an agreed new reading of the past. The world seemed raddled with instability. On 25 November 1798 the French, now commanded by General Jean-Antoine Championnet, having been besieged by an army under the Bourbon King Ferdinand IV of Naples-Sicily, agreed to evacuate the city. Their local Jacobin friends fled. Reactionary Neapolitan rule proved in its turn more brutal and short-lived than that of the revolutionaries. On 15 December the French army returned and the Neapolitans retreated, with their foes in pursuit. On 22 January 1799 the French entered Naples, where they proclaimed the Parthenopean Republic. This novel arrangement again did not last. The French forces pulled out of Naples on 7 May and left Rome on 26 September. Three days later, the vestiges of the Roman Republic were overwhelmed when a Neapolitan army took Rome once more.

How, then, in this breathless time of revolutionary power and its overthrow had the contesting forces dealt with the histories of Rome? What pasts mattered in the city during these stirring times?

The mixture was predictable enough: while revolution ruled, the classical past dislodged the Christian one. The revolutionary organisers of the ceremony of 15 February 1798, proclaiming the Republic, were as determined to establish historical justification for the new order as had been Pius VI when he processed to Santa Maria Maggiore or San Giovanni in Laterano, armed with his assortment of holy relics. Prominent in the ceremony was the new holy symbol of the 'Liberty Tree'. A painting of it in the green, white and red stripes that were being established as the Italian colours was carried to the Campidoglio, hailed as 'the most glorious of the hills of Rome'. The tricolour was there erected next to the statue of Marcus Aurelius, an emperor whose Stoic 'meditations' were thought to square with the Enlightenment.[74] On its pedestal were inscribed the hopes of the Revolution: 'Religion and Freedom; the Sovereignty of the People; Liberty and Equality'. Among the five 'consuls' now to assume administrative duties was Ennio Quirino Visconti. In his leadership role he was joined by a number of other doctors, lawyers and archaeologists.[75]

Back in the Forum, a doctor, Nicola Corona, told the crowd that the 'Roman People' were breaking free from a 'monstrous despotism' that had long oppressed them, although he also pledged that the Republic would avoid violence and defend religion, while, somewhat confusingly, this time unfurling a white, red and black tricolour. Later in the afternoon, the French chief, Berthier, spoke in approval of the Republic's assumption of 'the Government of ancient Rome' and promised 'the special protection of the French Army'. 'The shades of Pompey, Cato, Brutus, Cicero and Hortensius', his oration ran, 'here in the surrounds of the Campidoglio, now renewed, where so many times you defended the rights of the People, will receive the homage of the free French. The sons of the Gauls, carrying the olive branches of peace, now in this same place refresh the Altars of Liberty that the first Brutus raised.'[76] Here indeed were dead generations that, in their resurrection, were meant to arouse and not depress the minds of the living.

Present-day de-ideologised commentators are inclined to follow the leadership of François Furet in disillusion with the revolution and all its works, and so advise that there was no 'question here of native Italians drafting their own constitution. A commission of jurists was sent from Paris. They produced a structure full of ancient Roman terminology, with Consuls, a Senate, and a Tribunate, but modern and Parisian in form. . . . And nothing was to be enacted without the consent of the French commandant, who was for good measure authorized to make whatever laws he saw fit. Nothing could have stated more explicitly that the new Italian republics existed primarily for the convenience of the Great Nation [France]'.[77] Yet the revolutionaries were not the sole force left in Rome and not the only ones to gird themselves with a usable past. The common people had not forgotten their history and traditions. As if in proof of their rejection of revolutionary 'rationality' and using the excuse of the liberation of the ghetto on 17 February (the Jews had then erected a liberty tree at its gate),[78] on the 25th the *Trasteverini* rose with renewed evocation of the Madonna and revamped anti-Semitism. The rioters tried to hunt to death Jews and Jacobins, and throw any French occupiers who fell into their hands into the Tiber. In turn, they were energetically suppressed, twenty-two being publicly shot on the 27th in the Piazza del Popolo, renowned for pontifical execution but now experiencing for the first time a modern way of death, one that to a hostile onlooker suggested the return of the brutish age of the gladiators.[79]

The rigorous punishment of malefactors was only one part of the overall Enlightenment project to make the world more precise and scientific, and so open to accurate tabulation, a world where place and time were at last rational. Now, for the first time, Roman streets were given plaques with their names visible on them. A numbering system that had been developing for some decades was regularised; the returning Pius VII completed the project in 1800 and even promised street lighting, that most practical form of 'illumination'.[80] The Republic had also energetically engaged in amending the traditional names in the city: Piazza di Spagna, for example, was called Piazza della Libertà. The Colosseum was stripped of its cross and made the venue for worthy plays, inevitably most often evoking the heroes of classical Rome. Among the furniture given to the place was an ancient statue of Pompey, which, when transport proved difficult, had an arm sawn off and then inexpertly reattached in its new setting.[81]

The Republic pledged to conquer the city and forge its meaning in a new and drastic manner. Rome's familiar sectors or *rioni* were reduced from fourteen to twelve and each was given a classical appellation, with ancient history thereby trumping the papal past. In March 1798 an Altare della patria (Altar of the

Fatherland) was made to dominate St Peter's Square, with the civic religion that it expressed ostentatiously contesting the Church's tradition.[82] The revolutionary French calendar was imposed on 5 June, and Roman clocks made to chime with those of Paris.[83] Dress, too, altered; conservative Romans were appalled by the Jacobin fashion for women to wear thin silks and be rumoured (perhaps apocryphally) on occasion to have exposed their breasts to public view.[84] Democratic marriages were contracted not in church but in front of liberty trees.[85] Of more direct menace, three guillotines were set up in the city in the summer of 1799, and the pro-Jacobin *Monitore di Roma* enthused over them since liberty, it said, was 'only gained at the price of blood and through virtue'.[86] An allegedly wicked past was ceremoniously destroyed when the *Libro d'oro* (Golden Book) that confirmed aristocratic genealogy and the list of trials of the Holy Office or Inquisition was burned in a public square.[87] More generally, the new rulers, ruthlessly warring against popular history at a time when tourist income was minimal, pressed ahead with the abolition of the long list of traditional festivals and so promised the cancellation from memory of the pasts that they had celebrated.

Easy evocations of patriotism and sacrifice, propounded as the practice of the supremely virtuous classical Roman Republic with the reiterated line that 'the history of the past teaches the way to the future', were soon struggling with the negative practical effects of the radical changes being imposed.[88] A new history that claimed it was reviving classical times was widely perceived by ordinary Romans as destroying what they had treasured as familiar and timeless. Revolution arrived with little preparation or justification, except for the promise of 'national education'.[89] But reprogramming the popular mind is always a lengthy and difficult task, and 'reform' was not assisted by the effect of the revolution on everyday life. Inflation ran rampant. The food crisis deepened and, on 4 February 1799, the women of the city demonstrated against the lack of bread. The second period of Republican rule was proving even more troubled and insecure than the first, a situation poorly disguised by a formal procession, held on Christmas Eve, to transport the 'consuls' back through an illuminated city. Then, the restored rulers merged the old and the new by threatening 'national vendetta' against those guilty of conspiring with the counter-revolutionary forces, and issuing 'certificates of patriotism' to any in an official position. Anti-clerical measures became fiercer, with the 'traditional solemn *Te Deum*' banned on 31 December. The statue of the Archangel Michael, atop Castel Sant'Angelo, was painted in Republican colours and an announcement made that it was transmuted into 'the Genius of France, Liberator of Rome'; plainly rendered alien, it won few to the revolutionary cause.[90] At the same time, the French made little attempt to hide their determination to extract profit from the city, purloining its artworks, religious valuables and any cash they could find.[91] By January 1799 one commentator urged a friend to hurry to the place because, soon, the French would have stolen or wrecked even the ruins.[92] The death rate in the city rose 6 per cent per annum, with starvation being a leading cause.[93] Once again, in mutinous minds, parallels with the Goths and the Huns came to the fore.[94]

The first anniversary of the foundation of the Republic was marked on 14 February by another, perhaps desperate, effort to summon the ghosts of Rome's past behind the administration by historical display and the forging of public memory. At the ends of the Forum, the arches of Titus and Septimius Severus were garlanded with flowers in what was asserted to have been 'the ancient custom'. Busts were erected of Brutus and Cassius, while 'a boy, a youth and an old man, wearing the dress of the ancient Romans to represent the three ages of man, offered the consuls crowns of laurel, symbols of glory, as well as of oak leaves. Each then was given by the consuls a silver medal with an eagle printed on it with the inscription: *The Roman Republic*. On the other side was the epigraph: *One day of joy is worth many years of lament* and the date: 27 *piovoso*' (the Italian version of the month *Pluviôse* in the French revolutionary calendar).[95]

Apposite speeches followed. Thereupon, twenty-four maidens stepped forward, 'arrayed all in white . . . and with their heads bare in the ancient fashion' to present the consuls with 'laurel wreaths bound with tricolour ribbons'. In return, they were each handed a 'subsidy of forty *scudi*' and replaced by twenty-four young men, 'dressed in Roman clothes to mark their dedication to the Nation'. Before the ceremony was over, however, older women interrupted the pleasing classical evocations with strident cries: 'We want bread and We don't want the Republic!'

It was almost the last attempt to accord the Republic a winning history. Through the summer of 1799 the regime staggered chaotically to its collapse, evidently a failure in convincing Romans that the path from past to future must now follow the Jacobin track. When French occupation was replaced by Neapolitan on 29 September, counter-ceremonies were swiftly organised to restore a proper reading of history. Reactionary forces reasserted their control over past and present. On the prime site of the Campidoglio, the statue of Marcus Aurelius was hemmed in by a raised altar facing a tall cross with its Latin inscription warning against the false liberty and actual slavery imposed by the revolutionaries.[96]

After the entry into the city of the new pope the next summer, Rome returned to some sort of normality, although a conflict between Church and State smouldered. Pius VII tried to be virtuously accommodating at home and abroad, politely agreeing on 2 December 1804 to participate at Paris in Napoleon's (self-)coronation. In Rome itself, he did not renounce the classicising that had been so prominent during the Republic. Rather he issued a decree in 1802 banning 'the export of works of art whether public or private, sacred or profane', simultaneously deploring the French sack of the city and proclaiming that the city's past was his.[97] By no means hostile to scientific archaeological labour, in 1802 Pius VII appointed the distinguished and enlightened sculptor, Antonio Canova, as Inspector General of Archaeology and Fine Arts.

Yet the efforts of the new pope to cement a rapprochement between Caesar and Christ, and so to harness imperial Roman history directly in the Church's cause when he sought to persuade Napoleon that the ancient emperors had themselves instituted and defended the temporal power,[98] proved barren. The revolution, if now in its Napoleonic guise, was not finished with Rome. On 2 February 1808 French troops reoccupied the city in retribution for the pope's refusal to bow to imperial command. Fifteen months later, the residue of the Papal States was absorbed into the French empire. Pius refused to accept this temporal loss and, on 10 June, excommunicated 'the robbers of St Peter's patrimony'. In turn he was arrested and, like his predecessor, removed from Rome, by 1812 being imprisoned at Fontainebleau. In March 1814 he briefly returned to Rome: a formal entry ceremony was performed in traditionalist mode by the population prostrating themselves 'in silence and tears', although the setting of the recently extended Piazza del Popolo proved a novel 'amphitheatre' for such salutation.[99] Shortly after, however, Pius had to flee again during the Hundred Days. Just before Napoleon's defeat at Waterloo, the pope reclaimed his post on 7 June 1815.

The second period of French rule in the city saw renewed efforts to furnish it with a rational and modern past and present, with the latter to be guaranteed by the extension of the Napoleonic legal and commercial codes to the city in 1809. As for finding appropriate meaning in the past, Canova, who had been promised by Napoleon: 'I shall restore Rome', continued to work with Camille de Tournon, the French Prefect of the annexed city, in what has been called the first 'systematic excavation and restoration of the main classical remains'; in more ominous metaphor, its 'urban cleansing'.[100] Assisted by Giuseppe Valadier, the son of a local goldsmith, De Tournon drastically restructured Piazza del Popolo, for example demolishing existing buildings to convert the place into the vast, beautiful and welcoming square that it is today, its surface marked with geometrical designs as if in proof of the triumph of mathematically precise or Napoleonic modernity. On De Tournon's initiative, the Pincio, the hilly area that over looks the piazza and is said once to have been 'Caesar's own garden', was ordered into a public park and place of promenade.[101] Today, among its leafy walks studded with statues erected after 1870, stands an elegant restaurant called, perhaps appropriately, the Casino Valadier.

With an Enlightenment dedication to 'information', detail designed to make government more efficient and effective, De Tournon and his agents sponsored the collection of facts about Rome's past and present as never before.

They also dreamed of city 'beautification', with the establishment in 1811 of a commission to explore how this 'improvement' might be speeded. Thoughts ranged widely, including schemes brought to fruition much later of an archaeological zone to extend from the Colosseum to the Campidoglio, as well as a plan for the opening up of the Vatican with a road like the eventual Via della Conciliazione. More expressive of a grandiosity mocking hope that equality was to be achieved in modern times, Napoleon, although he never visited Rome, was said to have approved a local architect's grovelling project of a massive neo-imperial palace. It was to spread from Piazza Colonna to the Colosseum, thus outdoing Nero's Golden House, indeed a dictator's dream (and a citizen's nightmare). 'The Palazzo Venezia was to have been its administrative wing, the Aracoeli its chapel and the Forum its inner courtyard.'[102]

Although such a pharaonic structure was left on the drawing board, De Tournon was another for whom present reality in the city demeaned its past. He approved the complaint of an adviser that 'the Roman people were still of their own kind', unable to match the 'customs, habits, affections and opinions' of the French and modern times. Romans, he admitted, did possess 'a lively memory of their ancient grandeur', but it was 'an idea that filled their imagination without entering their soul'. Rather than being virtuously primed to conquer as their ancestors had been, Romans, he lamented, listlessly expected bread and circuses from their rulers.[103] De Tournon also continued to send artworks back to Paris. The theft of historical evidence proceeded more directly in the transfer to Paris in February 1810 of the voluminous archives of the Inquisition, a shipment that required 3,239 boxes.[104]

For an English commentator, anxious to damn the French and all their works, De Tournon's rule amounted to disaster: 'the French . . . have deprived Rome of its credit, its resources, its dignity, and its independence; they have robbed it of all that constitutes the prosperity and security of a state, and have thus caused it more real and permanent injury than the attacks of Genseric and Bourbon, or the transient fury of Odacer and Totila.'[105] This conclusion is much the same as that reached by contemporary historian Michael Broers in his analysis of French imperialism. The invaders, Broers maintains, believed that they could trust 'only the remote Italian past', while there 'was everything to guard against in the Italian present'. French rule was so alien and uncomprehending, he says, that it reinforced the practices of patronage, clientship and 'corruption' and 'taught the Italians to hate the state as never before', thus blighting their future for the next two centuries.[106]

It is a severe judgement and needs taking into account by those who see the revolutionary era as the happy prelude to a popular Risorgimento of the Italian nation and the effortless construction of an Italian Rome. Perhaps a final decision on the matter can be avoided in a book such as this and instead it can be noted that the violence, as well as the new and old imaginings that flourished during the era of revolutions, was added to the store of previous histories of the city. Whatever else it had done, revolutionary rigour had not obliterated Rome's multiple histories. Instead, this time of troubles, like many another, left its traces there to be absorbed into the city's historic fabric and, from 1927, to be given its formal (if inadequate and uncritical) site of memory in the Napoleonic Museum.

In 1815 peace broke out and thereafter Rome began to experience its version of the European Restoration. A welling up of romanticism set off a flood of enthusiasm for the Middle Ages, now for some a more important era than classical times, even though the Caesars were not forgotten. The new current pushed ahead both in clerical ranks and among those proto-nationalists who began to imagine a 'Third Italy'. History continued to matter urgently to both, but they disagreed over its meaning, just as their predecessors had done between 1789 and Napoleon's fall. History wars, old and new, were not stilled by the Congress of Vienna and diplomats' cheap talk about 'turning the clock back' to before 1789.

While the Emperor still strutted on the stage of history, Madame de Staël, a French liberal, critical of Napoleonic authoritarianism and military adventure, intervened aptly in her novel *Corinne, or Italy* (1807) to philosophise about visiting the Eternal City: 'You cannot take a step in Rome without bringing together the present and the past and the different pasts between them,' she wrote. 'But you learn to take the events of your own day calmly,' she added, 'when you see the ever-changing vicissitudes of human history. You are almost ashamed to be worried in the presence of so many centuries which have all overturned the work of their predecessors.'[107] Advocating such a serene reckoning with the multiple pasts (and futures) of Rome was one thing; achieving it was to prove another.

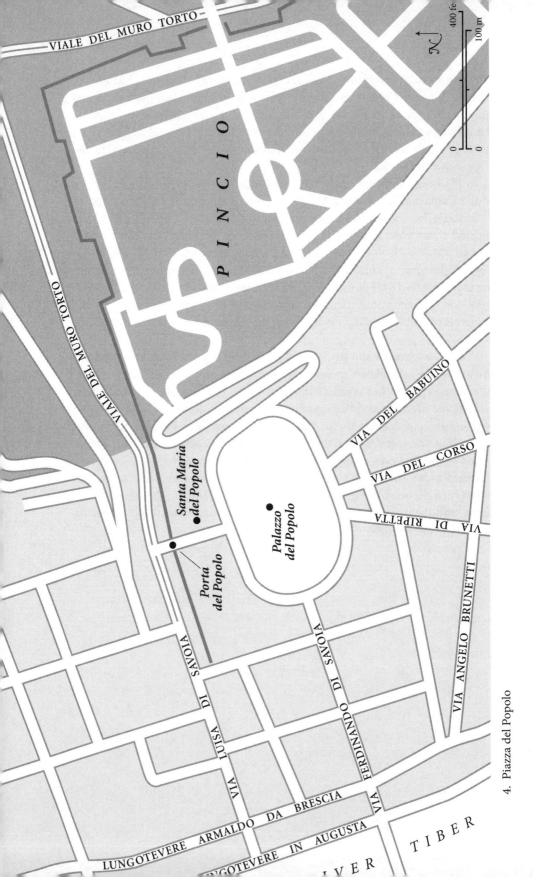

4. Piazza del Popolo

3

*

A HOLY CITY: ITS PAST AND
FUTURE RESTORED?

The harmonious Piazza del Popolo that De Tournon and Valadier planned but that was completed after 1815 under Pius VII is now usually thronged with tourists. It is yet another good place in Rome to consume history. The crowds may gaze at the Egyptian obelisk which stands at the centre of the square and is covered with hierogyphs celebrating the reigns of Pharaohs Rameses II and Merenptah from the thirteenth and twelfth centuries BCE. They may cool themselves from the spray of the lion fountains that guard the obelisk or from those at the middle of each hemicycle into which the square is divided, one evoking Neptune and the other the city of Rome as refreshed by the Anio (in Italian, Aniene) and Tiber (in Italian, Tevere) rivers. They may view the images of the Four Seasons, sculpted by Valadier himself. When the beauty of the square has been sufficiently absorbed into their memory banks, the more zealous pilgrims may enter the delightful church of Santa Maria del Popolo, erected at the end of the eleventh century to render propitious a spot earlier thought to have marked the grave of the Emperor Nero and to be haunted by demons. There they can identify a number of marvellous frescoes by Pintoricchio and two canvases by Caravaggio. Sated with art, they may leave the church to stroll up to the Pincio or turn down the Via di Ripetta to find other shops and monuments, or first take a coffee break at the celebrated bar positioned on the river side of the square. Or maybe they will decide to pass through the gate in the Aurelian Walls, the Porta del Popolo, on one side designed by Bernini and on the other by a follower of Michelangelo, and head down the Via Flaminia, ancient road leading north out of the city.

Here, then, in this one square is assembled in the Roman manner a set of artistic and architectural treasures and an array of histories that might fill the most worthy tourist notebook. Yet other pasts are present, too. If visitors descend the steps at the front of Santa Maria del Popolo and cross the narrow space leading to the gate, they can look up and see affixed to the wall confronting them an iron-grey commemorative plaque. At its top are two heads in bas-relief, each peering through a laurel wreath. Between their images is a set of fasces, those rods bound together and armed with threateningly sharp, single-headed, axes, which classical Roman lictors carried as the symbol of magisterial authority. What is this memorial's message? What past does it evoke as still bearing meaning in contemporary Rome?

The answer might seem most likely to be something to do with Mussolini's Fascist dictatorship. After all, Fascism gloried in what it called *romanità* and used the symbol of the rods and axes to underline its purpose of discipline and order. Yet the fasces above Piazza del Popolo are neither Fascist nor classical. The Phrygian cap – a bonnet that is brimless, limp and conical, with its top falling over to one side – that surmounts the fasces instead situates the plaque in a leftist revolutionary tradition. This headgear was worn with a dash in Paris in 1789 and for many decades after, whenever revolution revived.[1] It was donned in Rome in 1798–9 and 1848–9, even if, in that city, the cap's origin (it was a symbol of war for ancient Phrygians, but carried negative oriental connotations for Greeks and positive ones about freedom for Romans) added an eclecticism to the revolutionary assertion of classical antecedents.

To elucidate the meaning of this plaque, onlookers, it seems, must read further. When they do, they find that beneath the caps and the fasces is a stained cement slab, framed by the palm fronds of triumph. Its inscription explains in words rather than images the historical event that is being commemorated at the site – a guillotining of two members of a revolutionary secret society pledged to overthrow papal rule and unite Italy:

> To the memory of the *Carbonari*, Angelo Targhini and Leonida Montanari, who, on 23 November 1825, in this square, serenely confronted their condemnation to death, without proof or the chance to defend themselves, as ordered by the Pope. This stone was placed here by the Democratic Association G. Tavani at the admonishing will of the people, 2 June 1909.[2]

On this plaque, then, just as at the Napoleonic Museum noticed at the start of the previous chapter, pasts and their later interpretations intermingle. There, memory most directly addressed either the revolutionary era or Fascism. Here, however, it is the Restoration and Liberal Italy, the regime which replaced the popes in 1870 to rule a newly united nation, that come into play. In 1909 Rome was controlled by an anti-clerical and radical, patriotic, 'Mazzinian' administration headed by a Jewish *sindaco* or mayor, Ernesto Nathan. A Freemason, Nathan curbed his Republican antecedents respectfully to serve the Savoy dynasty but strove manfully to enhance the modernity and

7. Targhini–Montanari plaque, Piazza del Popolo.

the patriotism of his Rome, all the more since, in 1909, city and nation were gearing up to celebrate the coming fiftieth anniversary of a modern Italian state, 'reborn', it was said, in the Risorgimento.

The sacrifice of Targhini and Montanari was not one of the major events of the years of patriotic struggle that had preceded Italian unification. Indeed, according to Massimo D'Azeglio, the Piedmontese aristocrat and liberal who was more clear-eyed than many a nation-maker, the two *carbonari* were common murderers, exploiting revolutionary politics to nefarious ends.[3] Yet memory of the two men's deaths has not altogether vanished, as was evident in a film version of their story, directed by Luigi Magni in 1969 (readying for the centenary of an Italian Rome) and entitled *Nell'anno del Signore* (In the Year of Our Lord). It is not a great piece of cinema but rather an anachronistic romance where, providing the obligatory love interest, a clean, beautiful and well-fed Claudia Cardinale plays the part of a sassy maiden from the ghetto. Her character offers modish hints of 'Shoah business', given that the Swiss Guards speak German and may somehow be meant to represent 'eliminationist anti-Semitism'. But, despite the film's feebleness, one line in the text is evocative. It is a joke attributed to 'Pasquino', that anonymous satirist, indeed an ageless Roman, who, legend maintains, always has an acid pen poised to enlighten the city about human frailty: '*Santo Padre? Santo no, Padre sì*' (Holy Father? Holy no, Father yes).

The phrase is a reminder that, if Targhini and Montanari have faded into historical obscurity, Leo XII, the pope who ordered their public execution, was and remains a more significant figure. His history and his attempt to reimpose a wholly Catholic past on Rome and return it to being a holy city, his determination to make real the Restoration in his dominions, deserve notice. Leo XII was born Annibale Francesco Clemente Melchiore Girolamo Nicola della Genga, into the Umbrian nobility on 22 August 1760. The fifth son of a numerous family, he entered training for the priesthood at the age of thirteen. Favoured by Pope Pius VI, he rose quickly to high Church office, assuming important diplomatic roles at Cologne and Paris. After the death of Pius VII and in a contested conclave, he emerged as a compromise candidate to reign from 28 September 1823 until his death on 10 February 1829. By then 'he was profoundly unpopular', and his demise in the midst of Carnevale did nothing to alter his reputation as the ultimate killjoy.[4]

His has proved a durable unpopularity. For Luigi Pianciani, a patriot who saw himself as spokesman of the Roman people (although he, too, sprang from an Umbrian noble family) and was mayor of newly Italian Rome from 1872 to 1874, Leo XII incarnated all that was perverse about papal rule.[5] To a liberal filled with patriotic zeal to build a new and enlightened Italy, this pontiff was not just a Restoration villain, but a symbol of the durable evil and backwardness of the Church. According to Pianciani, the young priest owed his first promotion to his beauty, wantonly brought to the attention of the susceptible Pius VI. Created a bishop and then cardinal at a surprisingly young age, Della Genga was, Pianciani maintained, 'completely ignorant of anything to do with ecclesiastical issues', devoted rather to 'love and hunting . . . horses and balls'. In their adolescence, he and his brothers had committed rape and murder in their unbridled pursuit of peasant girls. As pontiff, Leo remained 'the very definition of ignorance', with his dim and unenlightened lament that books were the cause of all evil. In appropriate retribution for his sins, this pope 'died the victim of the shameful disease that he had caught as a bishop in the brothels of Paris'. His corpse decayed in so rapid and noisome a fashion that, during the funeral ceremonies at St Peter's, it had to be 'replaced by a puppet which was still kissed and adored by the faithful'. As a ruler, Leo was foolishly extravagant and skittishly given to undoing what he had just done. On his demise, papal administration lay in utter disorder, except that the Inquisition and the Jesuits had prospered, and spies had multiplied.[6] In Pianciani's keenly anti-clerical vision of the past, Leo XII was the very model of a stupid and pernicious pope, the incarnation of a history that had to die.

Few read Pianciani any more. Yet he is another whose whispers can still be heard in the modern city. As though still polishing his anti-clerical historical messages, Pianciani is rewarded in contemporary Rome by having a state school named after him. It stands at a corner of Piazza del Risorgimento, just down from the Vatican Museum and the walls of the Leonine city in a sector of the city formalised after Italian unification. In their naming, both square and school aggressively (and, in many ways, falsely) announce national victory in the history war between State and Church that Leo XII, Targhini and Montanari had disputed.

Leo XII's posthumous fate as a prime target of anti-clerical memory was appropriate because this pope, as the chief of the so-called *zelanti* (zealots), did, during his reign, preside over a forceful attempt to reclaim history, a transcendental, timeless and eternal history, for the Church and its governance over Rome. It was in his pontificate that the most robust efforts were made to cancel the legacy of the revolutionary and Napoleonic years. The special focus of this hope to cleanse minds of modern wickedness was the *Giubileo* or *Anno Santo* (Holy Year) of 1825 (late in which Targhini and Montanari met their deaths). Such jubilees have continued to feature in Roman history, the most recent being that celebrated in the pontificate of the arch-populist John Paul II in 2000. Every Holy Year has offered an occasion to revivify and re-justify the Catholic version of Rome's meaning. Despite what will be seen to be their not always regular succession, they signal the Church's hope that one true urban history will outlast and surpass its critics and enemies.

The first *Anno Santo* was held during the pontificate of Boniface VIII (1294–1303) in 1300. Like Leo XII, this pope endured posthumous travails, being damned by Dante to the third sector of the eighth circle of Hell, reserved for priestly simoniacs. The Jubilee, which was given its own redolent past as possessing Mosaic origins, was to be a time when the Church invited as many 'pilgrims' as possible to Rome, with the promise of plenary indulgences in return for their repentant worship at the various shrines and basilicas. Uniting the Old Testament and the New and, with its promise of an escape from sin, the *Giubileo* was, from its beginning, a celebration of religious control over past, present and future. It is said that Boniface VIII recognised the implicit claim to untrammelled power and control over time by dressing 'in imperial insignia, boasting that he was emperor no less than pope.'[7]

A further *Giubileo* was celebrated in 1350, when, despite the fact that Pope Clement VI had then taken sanctuary at Avignon, contemporaries claimed (with probable exaggeration) that over a million pilgrims were drawn to Rome.[8]

By the next century, jubilees, which had originally been thought of as centenary events, were occurring every twenty-five years, for example in 1450, 1475 and 1500.[9] This last event was presided over by the Borgia pope, Alexander VI, and it was this controversial pontiff who inaugurated the ceremony of opening and closing the Porta Santa or Holy Door, in normal times kept securely shut at St Peter's and at the other three great basilicas, San Giovanni in Laterano, Santa Maria Maggiore and San Paolo fuori le mura. These places became the venues of extra ceremonies replicating those in St Peter's but presided over by cardinals and not the pope, even though the pontiff processed to each at appropriate feasts that marked the passage of the year. It was now, too, that the title *Anno Santo* was attached to proceedings and the Borgia version was at least a short-term success. In 1500 a more accurate tally of 'pilgrims' than in the past reckoned their number at 200,000.[10] To be sure, this *Giubileo* was not without controversy since the funds then collected – and most Holy Years proved rich money-spinners for the Church – were said to have been passed straight to the pope's son, Cesare, to assist his bloody, aggressive and eventually unsuccessful military campaigns elsewhere in Italy.[11]

By now, however, a tradition had been successfully invented and *Anni Santi* won their regular niche in the papal calendar. As was seen in the last chapter, the eighteenth century, with the spread of enlightened scepticism and ration-ality, offered many challenges to the Catholic reading of history, while the rise of archaeology attracted throngs of non-religious visitors to the city every year. Nonetheless, the jubilees of 1725, 1750 and 1775 were heralded by Catholic leaders, with the pilgrims counted in their hundreds of thousands, quite a few from outside Italy.[12] During the *Anno Santo* of 1725, the habit of initiating major building projects at such times brought the erection of the grand stairway that connects Piazza di Spagna to Trinità dei Monti, there being some irony in the fact that traditionalist jubilees saw Rome grow above ground, while the modern attractions of archaeology focused on digging below.

The revolution, however, was to shatter the pattern of the years and chal-lenge the continuing expression of holy history in Rome. In 1800 the city was too disturbed and the position of the pope too contested for an *Anno Santo* to be celebrated. When the Restoration took over, could the loss ever be repaired and tradition revived, it was asked. As the year 1825 approached, the first issue for Leo XII to decide was whether the jubilees were a part of *ancien régime* history that should and could be re-presented in the era of Restoration. Could their traditions again be made unending, their lessons unerring?

The omens were bad. On the night of 15–16 July 1823, while Pius VII was on his deathbed, the basilica of San Paolo fuori le mura burned to the ground; rebuilding would not be complete until 1931. Could the great church's fiery end be a symbol of the victory of modern evil in Rome? Certainly, clericals were soon indiscriminately blaming *carbonari* or Jews for the conflagration (rationalist liberals instead condemned 'lazy Benedictines' and the incompetence of papal firemen for the loss).[13]

Pope Leo XII was elected on 28 September and, a month later, he made a pilgrimage to survey the charred remains of the basilica. His decision in regard to its restoration and to the holding of an *Anno Santo* (where the church of Santa Maria in Trastevere could substitute San Paolo) was not difficult to foresee. Even the relatively liberal Cardinal Consalvi, the loyal servant of the moderate Pius VII who was now dropped as Secretary of State, counselled in favour of a revival, urging it as a demonstration of papal independence, all the more because the Austrian Chancellor, Metternich, chief architect of the post-1815 world system, was said to be dubious about the idea.[14] In May 1824 Leo publicly announced the coming event and thereafter became busy in ensuring that his *Giubileo* made 'Rome spiritually attractive and spiritually only'.[15] Uprooting himself from the lavish surrounds of the Quirinal palace to the more austere and workaday Vatican, Leo plotted 'an authoritarian religious transformation of the city', when Catholic history would again be made integral with every aspect of Roman life.[16]

Few matters escaped the pope's attention. The public were counselled about appropriately pious demeanour if they walked the streets of the Holy City, with regulations affirming that 'no excrement, rubbish or other filth' should be dropped within 'four ordinary steps' of the wall of a religious building.[17] Women's clothing also preoccupied the pontiff who feared that females, 'when at first sight they seem covered up, by using close-fitting material that clings to their limbs and other bodily members, can maliciously foster lust'. Since, in his imagining, women were weaker vessels, the punishment of such erring sisters should be extended to their 'fathers, husbands, employers, or otherwise heads of their houses' and even to those tailors or seamstresses who so cunningly assisted their desire to sin.[18] According to Pianciani, Leo disguised himself in civilian dress, touring the streets to spy on any who infringed his decrees and whom he could deliver to the Inquisition.[19] Certainly, the English Cardinal Nicholas Wiseman remembered Swiss Guards being that year posted in every church to prevent infraction.[20]

In August and again in November and December 1824, the pope organised evangelising missions to the Roman people, formally blessing those who had assembled at Piazza Navona for the celebration of the feast of the Assumption. Once the Holy Door (Porta Santa) had been opened with a silver hammer in symbol of the commencement of the jubilee, religious processions occurred daily. To privilege the sacred, Leo rebuked human frailty with further bans. In pursuit of his neo-feudal utopia, the pontiff from March 1824 forbade the consumption of wine except with meals and, in 1825, all *osterie* or wine shops were closed (an ordinance that, in the memory of wayward papal severity preserved among the people, was recalled with disgust two or three generations later).[21] Even the sipping of coffee during missions was made illegal.[22] Card-playing drew papal anathema, no one could dance 'the highly obscene' waltz,[23] and the pope sought to mute any sound in the city that was not religious. The inaugural day of *Anno Santo*, 24 December, was to occur in holy silence. The playing of any musical instrument without spiritual purpose was specifically prohibited.[24]

Leo's ambitions to control the thriftless people (an ironical wish given that he and they shared many understandings that were being abandoned in more advanced European circles) spread from Rome into the rest of his dominion. From the beginning of his pontificate, Leo had devoted much energy to dealing militarily with those bandits who, for centuries, had beset the roads into Rome and were another social group with habits and histories of their own. Now they had multiplied during the social crisis resulting from the decades of war and revolution, and they regularly assaulted pilgrims trudging towards the Aurelian Walls. The method used against the bandits was one that would become familiar in later times when governments have sought to isolate peasant insurgents or other 'terrorists' by arresting their families and destroying their villages, even the deployment of violence by a ramshackle traditionalist administration like that of the Church could be brief and ineffectual. Bandits may have been easy to spot. They dressed in their own histories; according to Wiseman, such men, with deliberate provocation and proud to display the enduring traditions of their line of work, stood out from both the crowds and the priests in their attire of 'conical hats with hawks' feathers stuck in them, jackets, leggings or sandals, gay sashes, and carbines carried not on the back but in the hand, with a jaunty ease that showed an amicable readiness to let them off'.[25] One of the propaganda events of 1825 was the surrender on 23 September, following an amnesty, of the bandit 'Gasbaroni'. He was a figure who, through his extraordinarily long life, became a celebrity of a thrillingly menacing kind, exhibited to visiting milords from abroad and the author of ghosted memoirs.[26]

Bandits were still most likely to be peasants, a social group who, clinging firmly to their familial histories, long remained hostile to those urban dissidents who thought of themselves as revolutionaries, Freemasons and *carbonari* seeking to make the nation. Among these last, Targhini and Montanari were not the only 'patriots' to feel papal wrath when Holy Year gave opportunity for more vigorous action than was usual in papal government. At Ravenna, on the northern edge of the Papal States, for example, Cardinal Rivarola marked the Jubilee by publicly executing seven *carbonari* and exposing their bodies on the scaffold for a day thereafter as a spectacle of state terror.

But physical repression always remained secondary to spiritual control, spurred by a restored and stiffened past. In a fundamental, even fundamentalist sense, the pope sought to be master of the word. Leo's horror at any hint of national spirit extended to language, with his insistence that Latin be the only tolerated tongue both in writing and speech within papal law courts and universities.[27] His rejection of difference similarly ensured that he revived the anti-Semitism of his original patron, Pius VI, making harsher the ordinary life of Rome's Jews, yet again rigorously imprisoned in the ghetto and excluded from most remuneration.[28] Leo XII's understanding of universality was a narrow one.

Yet, despite his best efforts, Leo had not found a way of damming the stream of history. Rather, this papal endeavour at 'compulsory beatification' and at strictly confining the passage of time into a Catholic channel was neither a financial nor a moral success.[29] Numbers attending this Jubilee were well down compared with similar events in the eighteenth century, allegedly only 556 Germans and Austrians, 236 Swiss, 77 French, 29 Spaniards, one converted Turkish Jew, three Swedes, one Englishman, one Scot and one person from Ireland.[30] Perhaps these paltry figures lent credibility to the claim of Leo's supporters that he personally welcomed each arriving pilgrim. At most of the festivals during the year, the great majority of the congregations were Romans, who could not escape papal urging to worship.[31] The only royals to appear were from the minor dynasties uneasily ensconced in Naples, Lucca and Turin.

In staging his Holy Year on his own historic terms, Leo XII was proving himself fundamentally out of step with Europe, even while it was ruled by proponents of the Restoration.[32] In Protestant countries, Holy Year was viewed in a decidedly sardonic manner. The London *Times* led the way with tart commentary on the beatification that year of a Spanish Franciscan: 'Among the numberless miracles attributed to this holy monk', the paper informed its chuckling readers, 'is one of having resuscitated several couple of half-roasted fowl which, at his command, took wing from the spit, and flew away with miraculous velocity.'[33] Such credulity was old hat, the paper concluded in its review of the year for rational modern Britishers: 'The sale of indulgences is now past. Few people now believe in purgatory and still less have any faith in the power of the pope to relieve any soul in that place or remove them from it.' Only hope of entertainment or 'plunder', it maintained coldly, had drawn a drab and meagre parade of pilgrims to Rome.[34]

The event had been all the more disappointing given that, from the point of view of the Church, Rome in 1825 was meant to be reaffirmed as harbouring a holiness that was both universal and transcendental, indeed eternal, an unconquerable historic fortress against the modern evils of liberalism and nationalism. As the news-sheet *Diario di Roma* phrased it, Rome was 'the city where no one, particularly no Catholic, is foreign. It is the *patria* of *everyone*, the place where *everyone* finds sanctuary, protection and defence under the sceptre of the common Father.'[35] Leo himself almost sounded as though he had been reading Herder or was prefiguring Heidegger's notions of blood and soil when he asserted that, 'in this city, the very aspect of the soil, of the walls, of the churches, of the altars, of the tombs of the martyrs, of everything that is offered to our actual gaze, impresses something sacred into the soul'.[36]

Throughout his pontificate, Leo XII doubtless scaled the pinnacle of reaction, forging a special place for himself in Roman memory as a Canute-like figure absurdly trying to check the flow of history. He did, after all, reject science along with the rest, banning inoculation on the grounds that it unhealthily confused the animal and human conditions. Yet, at the heart of Leo's comprehension of Rome lay an interpretation of the fate and purpose of the past that still survives in Catholic circles and has never altogether been renounced by his papal successors. It is an 'integral' history that claims the supremacy of the religious over the profane and of the perpetual over change, necessary spiritual victory over what is viewed as the trumpery and interim, the 'merely' human. In the Church's reading of Rome, past, present and future may, for short-term and transient purposes, be acknowledged as separate and different. But, in the final analysis, all time is the same, providentially wrapped within a divine purpose that may seem inscrutable on occasion but will inevitably culminate in what has always been, the rule of God and the triumph of the blessed. For Catholic true believers, even in the twenty-first century, the spirit of Leo XII has not vanished from the city.

Leo XII's pontificate was a brief one. Neither his predecessor, Pius VII, nor his successors, Pius VIII (1829–30) and Gregory XVI (1831–46), were as drastic as he was in controlling history. Pius VII, in particular, had been ready to concede that the recent impact of revolution might not be easy wholly to amend. This pope did not always stand four-square against modern change. Perhaps Pius, whose own life had been so tumultuous, half shared the belief or fear of ordinary Romans that, sooner or later, war would return to the city and, with it, Napoleon and some version of the revolution.[37] While it was true that, immediately in 1815, feudal jurisdictions were restored, reasserting the eternal verities of papal government was not to prove a straightforward and universally convincing process.[38] The pope himself, by now old and often ill (he turned eighty in April 1822), had never been a complete reactionary and the most active figure in his administration, Consalvi, pressed ahead with the modernising town-planning innovations begun in Piazza del Popolo, the Pincio gardens and the Belvedere under French rule. It was under his guidance that the square in front of the Pantheon was purged, as modern fastidiousness required, of ' "ignoble huts" and [a] fish market', edifices that were defined as corrupt accretions, with the implication that, after their removal, the classical (and religious) history of the great building could shine through without contamination from more mundane medieval and baroque pasts. The Arch of Titus was another classical residue now 'restored to its ancient form'.[39]

In 1816 Pius VII approved the revival of the Pontificia Accademia Romana di Archeologia and briefly reappointed the great neoclassical sculptor, Antonio

Canova as its president, despite his equivocal record of having happily worked with the French rulers of Rome. This organisation had been established by an ex-Jacobin in 1810. Its leadership had moved quickly to advocate and achieve the isolation of the Temple of Vesta between the Aventine Hill and the Tiber, and to begin planning a shady (and didactic) walk, a 'historical tour', around the Palatine. Too lay and rational a figure to be fully at home in the Restoration, Canova only lasted in office until 1817 when he was replaced by a scholarly priest, Monsignore N.M. Nicolai. Nonetheless, the Academy embodied a continuity between the Napoleonic and Restoration periods, promising that papal support for archaeological 'science' would not cease and continuing to imply that the rationality and linearity of classical design and thought could well instruct the present.[40]

Nor was the rest of the city's artistic patrimony to be viewed too narrowly. From 1817 the Vatican Museum was given a new wing, the Braccio Nuovo, to provide sanctuary for the numerous classical statues that had been abducted by the French and were now returned to Rome in convoys. Under Pius VII's rule, Caesar came back to the city at least as evidently as did the early Church fathers. The arrival of the carts laden with the art of ages was painted by Francesco Hayez, an artist eventually destined to make the Risorgimento his own, and filled lunettes in the Chiaramonte corridors (named after Pius VII) in the Vatican Museum.[41] The Hayez series was designed to exhibit a papal favouring of culture, with the settings evoking classical Rome (and so illustrating yet again how hard it was to escape some apposite reference to that time of grandeur).[42] Elsewhere in the city with what might also seem secular purpose, the Pinacoteca Capitolina was initiated as the first public portrait gallery in Europe. By the 1820s museums were open with some reliability twice each week (on Mondays and Thursdays).[43] More directly hinting at a fresh approach to government owing something to revolutionary ideas about order and efficiency was the erection of a barracks for *carabinieri* on the site of a religious house beside Santa Maria del Popolo. It was directly opposite the spot where a guillotine would sever the heads of Targhini, Montanari and other convicted criminals from their bodies. Papal *carabinieri* took over policing from the more amateur *sbirri* in 1816.

Yet, even at the city's most celebrated sites, papal modernity was at best halfhearted. At the Colosseum, for example, the stations of the cross first erected under Benedict XIV were now restored, and the rationalist or revolutionary prescription that, in order to allow an efficient modern line of sight, the whole edifice should be purged of vegetable growth, was not pursued. Although the great Flavian structure demanded and received further shoring up under all the next popes (in 1845 seven of the building's arches were rebuilt), Richard Deakin, a studious English naturalist, in 1873 was still able to publish a detailed survey of the 'flora of the Coliseum', listing hundreds of different

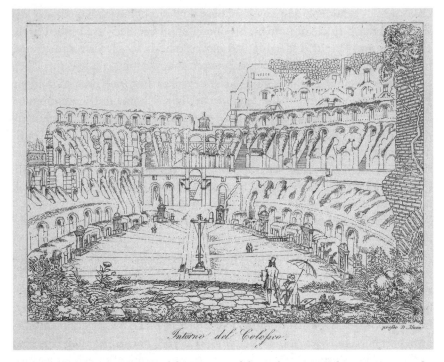

Interno del Colosseo.

8. Nineteenth-century image of the interior of the Colosseum with vegetation – only missing the odour of garlic.

species, including fig and olive trees and 'common garlic'. This last, he noted disapprovingly, expressing the common foreign fear that modern Romans lacked the personal discipline of the advancing peoples of the north,

> when taken into the stomach, . . . acts as a strong stimulant, diffusing its offensive alliaceous odour throughout the whole system, not only tainting the breath, but the perspiration and all the excretions of the body. It is a very favourable article of consumption with the lower orders of people in most parts of the continent; and the odour which they exhale, even to a person passing at a moderate distance, is very disagreeable; but, where a number of people are congregated together in a room, it is more so than can be conceived.[44]

Despite its formal re-consecration, the Colosseum had, then, while papal rule lasted, not been won again to religious purpose alone. Its histories remained multiple and contested. Other ruins retained a use that was scarcely sacralised and where the spirit of the city remained as popular as it was religious. The Augusteo, the tomb of the Emperor Augustus, for example, was cheerfully used until 1829 for bullfights or 'jousts between hunchbacks and Jews', and only

thereafter restricted to more decorous concerts and plays.[45] Despite archaeological excavation progressing in the Forum (to the scandal of visiting foreign
liberals because the labour was performed by shackled galley slaves), the place
remained a cattle market.

This ongoing cohabitation of people and popes, the cheerful intermeshing
of the sacred and profane, might be viewed as proof that history had indeed
not passed a turning point in Rome, despite the years of revolutionary agita-
tion. Was this medley of humdrum histories a better summary of the meaning
of Restoration than the purity aspired to by Leo XII? Certainly, during the relatively extended pontificate of Gregory XVI, the city slept peacefully if not
always comfortably. Its greatness again seemed securely confined to the past,
its history cocooned by the Church, its 'backwardness' accepted with apparent
content and without challenge by its people. Suggestive of a shrugging before
cruel destiny that was becoming unacceptable in the industrialising north,
malaria continued to cut down Romans who dwelled within the walls and,
more implacably, those unlucky enough to live in the Campagna. An epidemic
of that pre-modern scourge, cholera, further exposed the precariousness of
urban life when the city's population dwindled from 166,000 to 155,000, while
one Easter turned into the next in 1837–8.[46] Rome, it was plain, had not yet
opted for 'progress' and 'science'.

Indeed, despite the evident inadequacy of his government's welfare policies,
Gregory ignored suggestions of reform, rejecting intervention by the five Great
Powers – Austria, Britain, France, Russia and Prussia – whose ministers, in
May 1831, urged him to update the administrative practice in his state.[47] The
bathetic emblem of Gregory's determination to lie doggo became his refusal to
permit the penetration of that icon of the Industrial Revolution, the railway,
running on its tracks of steely rationality, into papal territory. Trains, the
pontiff remarked with sublime incomprehension of modernity, led only to
Hell. So adamant was he on the matter that his aides were too timid to pass on
to him a lavish toy train set 'in beautifully worked silver' that canny entrepreneurs had hoped would win him over to their scheme.[48] This pope was so loyal
to his version of the past that nothing would make him board the 'locomotive
of history'.

Although Gregory presided over the opening of an Etruscan segment of the
Vatican Museum (1837) – to be the basis of the present Museo Gregoriano
profano – and then an Egyptian one (1839), and also patronised new scientific
research into the city's catacomb complex, his Rome was designed to retain a
traditional mixture of the holy and the humdrum.[49] Every street carried religious symbols – images of the Madonna and other holy icons – and, as before
1789, Catholic rituals remained a customary activity, invading 'every nook of
private and communal life'. The populist dialect poet and satirist, Giuseppe
Gioachino ('G.G.') Belli, depicted a place where the cross adorned each edifice

no matter how humble, solemnly including Rome's urinals, or so he claimed.[50] SPQR, the ancient acronym of Roman government and short for 'the Senate and the Roman people', Belli stated sardonically, actually stood for '*Solo Preti Qui Rregnano: e ssilenzio*' (Priests only rule here; and silence).[51]

In Belli's portrayal, the largely illiterate people were not hostile to Gregory XVI's reactionary spirit but instead shared and seconded it, remaining comfortingly impervious to the rival currents of history that, in the sensibility of their betters, swirled around Rome. Nothing in their minds was as yet modernised and nationalised. In popular opinion, Belli maintained, now as in the previous century, archaeologists were viewed as macabre 'grave-robbers', exotic and alien lordly foreigners who extracted meaningless labour from those who dug at the various sites. As a recent analyst has put it: 'Living in a city whose ruins represent two millennia of historical change, Belli's characters have no conception of history. For them the city of Rome has always existed in its present form . . . since the day it was built by Romulus and Remus. . . . This comically foreshortened view of Roman history caricatured the basic papal claim of the continuity of the "two Romes".'[52] Romans, in other words, still clung to as unchanging a view of the past and future as did their priestly counsellors, but their comprehension of history was more practical than religious. As Belli imagined it cynically:

> Che me ne preme un cazzo de l'istoria.
> A me me piace de vive a la broccola . . .
> Bast'a ssapé c'oggni donna è pputtana
> E l'ommini una manica de ladri,
> Ecco imparata l'istoria romana.[53]

(Why should I give a shit about history? I'm perfectly happy to live on greens. . . . It's enough to know that women are all whores and men a gang of thieves. There we are – all of Roman history mastered.)

It is not difficult for a contemporary tourist to locate Belli's ghost in the city. The poet's reward for his recording of a popular philosophy of life is a statue at the entry point into Trastevere. Its twisting of history is unapologetic. The statue, carved by Michele Tripisciano, was erected in 1913 at the end of the radical Nathan administration, and the artist did not forget to adorn the plinth with images of the god of the nearby Tiber, as well as of Romulus and Remus, suckled by their she-wolf foster-mother. The inscription on the monument hails Belli as the 'poet of the Roman people', but he is also given a top hat and frock coat. This bourgeois dress adapts him for the new era of a Liberal nation and hides his actual loyalty to papal rule, and his and the Roman people's long refusal to accept the forging of national history that would gird this regime's rule over Rome and Italy.[54]

9. Monument to G.G. Belli, 1913, Trastevere.

Under the Restoration, proponents of liberal and national change, men and women who hoped that the revolutionary era was not yet over but rather had potentially switched the course of history on to a new track, were rarely at the forefront of Roman life. But they did exist and by the 1840s began to mount a major challenge to the political and cultural basis of papal rule. Eventually, the times were destined to witness the birth of an Italian nation state, which, from 1870, would place its capital in Rome and sacralise the process of unification as the 'Risorgimento' or rising again of the nation. The novelty of this building of a 'Third Italy' was to be disguised by the claim that it had, in reality, existed for eternity or at least for the 'three thousand years' that had elapsed since Romulus founded Rome. With quickening impulse, at least among some Italians and some foreigners, after 1815 a 'nationalised' Rome, whether teaching positive or negative lessons, became another competitor in debates about the present and future of the past.

One Italian nationalist with his own take on Rome was Massimo D'Azeglio, a liberal who became Prime Minister of Piedmont (1849–52) just as that state took on the role of being the major political driver towards Italian nationhood. In 1825 D'Azeglio had been a youthful spectator of Leo XII's effort to ensure that change was avoided, complaining that the *Anno Santo* was a time of 'gloom and hypocrisy', as might be expected of an event supervised by a pope around whom 'sinister rumours' of private sin circulated.[55] When it came to charting a better way forward, D'Azeglio pronounced, his generation required what in later times would be called a cultural revolution. They needed to become modern. They must redefine their relationship with history. 'Italy', he complained, 'is the ancient land of *Doubt*. . . . It is in our nature not to believe more than the priests believe, and the priests of Rome gave every indication of believing in very little indeed.'[56] The Catholic version of the past, he was implying, whether sincere in its spiritual claims and traditions or not, needed to be replaced by a lay and national one. Its history was dead.

What might a newly enlivening national past be? Did Rome offer some model in that regard? Certainly, when, shortly after the end of the Napoleonic era, D'Azeglio was brought by his diplomat father to the Eternal City, he was given an exhaustive tour of the classical sites by a relative of the leading archaeologist, E.Q. Visconti. 'We had the whole stock-in-trade, without leaving out a single brick', he recalled disconsolately, 'and we had to swallow with the faith of Moslems, Romulus, Clelia, Scaevola, Horace and the Pons Sublicius: the entire cast of that ancient drama'. 'Antiquarianism', he acknowledged, was 'one of the few subjects possible under priestly rule' that could wriggle free from their beliefs and offer a glimpse of a diverse past. This version of history failed to convince him, however. 'It was novelty I loved, not antiquity.'[57]

Then and thereafter, D'Azeglio's liberal scepticism prevented him from locating in the Caesars or Republic the lessons from the past that might best propel the future. When he sought historical insight into the 'happiness of mankind', he could discern few answers in the Rome of the Caesars. D'Azeglio could not see a hopeful future in classical rationality. The ancient empire was, he remarked acerbically, a place not so much of glory as of 'the killing, blood, tears, sorrow, suffering, exterminations, and desolation, which was the price the mass of humanity had to pay for the pleasure of having presented to their eyes and ears for centuries the great Roman phantasmagoria of victories and triumphs'. Rome's real message, one that had lasted fourteen centuries and should now be buried, he muttered, was 'the consecrated glorification of force against right; a sad legacy indeed!'[58] Undermined by this cruel inheritance and the equally pernicious one of the Church, the common people of Rome were, D'Azeglio complained, 'the most colossal mass of *canaille* known to history'. Similarly, the city's parasitic nobility were unlike his good Piedmontese self and lived 'in a complete nothingness, between the hammer and the anvil of the dominating clerical caste and the populace beneath'.[59] Rome, he admitted, through its pasts retained an aura of power; it was the 'Eternal City'. 'Rome, whether you are a believer or not, has existed and still exists, fascinating the hearts and imaginations of mankind.'[60] But, he urged, the place should not be allowed to drive a national Risorgimento. The flow of its history into a new Italian life was best confined to a trickle and romantic heroes for the nation should be located in the Middle Ages and elsewhere on the peninsula.[61]

D'Azeglio, then and later, was possessed of an unusual independence of mind but, more generally, among Europe's best and brightest, the decades after 1815 were the time of the flourishing of romanticism. Now ancient ruins did not signify past models of heroism and achievement and present prompts to their rational replication so much as a stimulus to individual melancholy, only deepened by the *Sturm und Drang* of the nature that grew over these pathetic shards of a lost past. The complexity of the Gothic was preferred to the simplicity of the classical. The blood and soil of the countryside offered a more telling legacy than the (sham) civilisation of the city. Now poets, artists, architects, political commentators and even the Papacy found their best past inspiration in the Middle Ages. The Restored Church was more ready to enthuse over such medieval philosophers as St Thomas Aquinas (*c.* 1225–74) than to invoke those early fathers who had been applauded in the eighteenth century. The reputation of Aquinas kept rising until he was declared by Pope Leo XIII in an encyclical in 1879 to have provided the definitive exposition of Catholic doctrine.

But what part might Rome play in this historical fashion, this reworking of tradition? Was it merely dead? One who half suggested that it was a cemetery of human dreams was the French writer, François-René de Chateaubriand, whose politics were staunchly anti-revolutionary. Chateaubriand was sent to Rome as ambassador in the aftermath of Leo XII's pontificate and found a 'sad and beautiful city', a place pervaded by melancholy where 'I pray. I love to pray on my knees; like that my heart is nearer to the dust and to the peace of eternity; I draw closer to the grave'. 'He has not seen Rome who has not walked through the streets of its suburbs,' Chateaubriand mused,

> streets interspersed with empty spaces, with gardens full of ruins, with enclosures planted with trees and vines, and with cloisters where palm-trees and cypresses stand, the former looking like women of the East, the latter like nuns in mourning. . . . Death seems to have been born in Rome. There are more tombs than dead in this city. I imagine that the deceased, when they feel too warm in their marble resting-place, slip into another which has remained empty. . . . One can almost hear the skeletons passing during the night from coffin to coffin.[62]

Yet, less common than Chateaubriand's macabre moralising about Roman soil was a search for romantic meaning beyond the city's gates. Aquinas, for one, after all, had had few direct contacts with the place, having been born in the Kingdom of Naples and having made his intellectual imprint at Paris, where he long resided. So, too, in the lay world, the novelist, Walter Scott, for many and especially in Italy, possessed the key to contemporary historical understanding and sensibility. He was the most saleable romantic. Yet Scott placed none of his novels in Rome, by implication denying the place romantic power.

One way Scott's ideas reached Italians was through that readily romantic musical form, the opera, throughout the peninsula a popular medium to convey messages about past and present.[63] The great Italian composers of the era, Gaetano Donizetti, Vincenzo Bellini and Giuseppe Verdi, used Scott with enthusiasm as a source of their plots, but, as though replicating their master's mistrust of Rome, rarely set their operas there. To be sure Donizetti wrote one piece about the Byzantine conqueror, Belisarius, while his *Poliuto* (1838), depicted derring-do in Roman Armenia during the anti-Christian persecutions of the Emperor Decius (249–251). This rarely staged opera ends flamboyantly with the hero and heroine led off in chains to be devoured by the lions. However, Verdi, whose work was most closely linked to the politics of the Risorgimento, avoided Roman settings and his most celebrated nationalist piece, the 'Va' pensiero' chorus from *Nabucco* (1842), with much irony given twentieth-century developments, depicted a persecuted Jewish nation struggling free from its Babylonian captivity. Verdi may have talked of being willing to act as a 'tribune' rather than a soldier of the revolutionary cause in Rome in 1848,[64] but, apart from the unsuccessful *Attila* (1846), he continued to compose operas that drew no direct inspiration from the city of Caesars.

The major exception to this rule that romance and Rome were musical antitheses was the young German composer, Richard Wagner, with his opera, *Rienzi* (1842). Wagner himself would soon dismiss this work as juvenilia but it remained popular, both in the German states as they approached unification in 1870 and elsewhere in Europe. The opera's plot recounts in heavily romantic vein the story of Cola di Rienzo (or di Rienzi), the Roman 'tribune' of the people who, as was noted earlier, established a Republic in the city in 1347. Wagner portrayed his hero as 'a grand and tragic superman, a leader who devoted his life to the peace and unity of Italy'. Di Rienzo's politics came down to a choice between victory and death, with the latter inevitably and romantically triumphant. Then 'the building [of the Senator's Palace] – and the hopes of a new Roman Reich – collapse into ashes and arias all around'.[65] Di Rienzo dies in the arms of the beautiful Irene, stoned by the populace and with the city ablaze. His last words are, 'as long as the Seven Hills of Rome are standing, as long as the Eternal City does not perish, you will see Rienzi return!'

Wagnerian history might not seem very serious but Cola di Rienzo was destined to live on in successive representations as the most important character from the city's Middle Ages, capable of carrying messages to the present. He became the chief emblem from the Roman past of what were sometimes claimed to be the medieval origins of an Italian nation. His alleged class position as a warrior against a violent and corrupt aristocracy of the sort thought by 1850 to have disappeared into the mists of the past, and his adroit combination of formal respect for the pope and studied intellectual independence made him a useful historical aide for those favouring a liberal Italian nation.

Di Rienzo received his reward in Rome once national unification was won. In the 1870s a street named for him was symbolically made to run across the burgeoning suburb of the Prati into Piazza del Risorgimento, athwart the Vatican. He was also awarded a site of memory at the centre of historic Rome, the Capitol from where he had once proclaimed his *buon governo* and Republic. In 1887 a statue, with Di Rienzo's face hidden by a cloth and his hand pointing accusingly towards the Vatican, was erected and still stands guarding the stairway to the Capitoline Hill. Following where Wagner had led, foreigners added Cola di Rienzo to their list of known Romans. He was lauded by the English novelist Edward Bulwer-Lytton, whose *Rienzi* was rushed out in a second edition in 1848 for readers seeking background to the exciting news about revolution in Rome, while another edition was printed in 1911 to coincide with the lavish patriotic celebrations of Italy's fiftieth anniversary.[66] Shortly after 1848 the German historian and Rome resident, Ferdinand Gregorovius, claimed Di Rienzo was 'the prophet of the Latin renascence'.[67] More critically, after the Second World War, an émigré German historian drew Di Rienzo as a medieval Hitler, a mad demagogue misleading the people.[68]

Italians, too, continued to reflect on Di Rienzo's career.[69] As if answering the charge that he may have been a proto-Nazi of deep menace, the witty, conservative and, in his time, Fascist, journalist, Luigi Barzini junior, writing to amuse, attract and appease his country's post-war American friends and in so doing picking up some of the themes of Casanova in his lucubrations on Rome and Romans, painted the medieval rebel as the archetypal Italian.[70] Cola di Rienzo, Barzini wrote, was the man who personified 'the national reliance on make-believe as an instrument of policy', no Hitler but perhaps a proto-Mussolini, sufficiently given to levity to be forgiven his sins. As Barzini explained with heavy contemporary reference, Cola di Rienzo possessed:

all the typical [national] attributes in their utmost purity. These are: literary, artistic, vague and contradictory ideas, practically unrelated to the contemporary world; the vast ambition to dominate all Italy, to re-establish the Empire and, in the end, to dominate the rest of Europe; the dream of building a 'new State', inspired by ancient history, in which peace, law and virtue would prevail; a genuine love for his people, his country and their glorious past, a love so intense it could be confused with self-love, as if he identified himself with Italy and the Italians; and the desire to avenge his people's ruin and humiliation, which he attributes solely to the wickedness of others. This man recklessly flung challenges to all the great powers of the day, tried to awaken his countrymen to a new sense of their mission, and dragged them reluctantly into wars neither he nor they were prepared to fight.[71]

In Barzini's portrait, Di Rienzo was not so much a medieval Roman as a nationalised Italian man for all seasons. Cola di Rienzo, it is plain, is another of those characters from the Roman past who has been pushed out again and again on to the historical stage to teach changing lessons to successive presents.

Yet, for all Di Rienzo's presence during or after the Risorgimento and despite the general flourishing of romantic ideals through the first half of the nineteenth century, the Roman Middle Ages could never obscure the ancient history of the city and outdo its legacies. In this regard, the naming of roads in the Prati is ironical proof to any strolling modern tourist or shopper of the power of the classics over most competitors. The Via Cola di Rienzo may be an important avenue from the Tiber to Piazza del Risorgimento. However, running parallel to it are the Via dei Gracchi, the Via Germanico, Via Pompeo Magno, the Via degli Scipioni and the Viale Giulio Cesare. By the 1880s the town planners of the city, when they selected what they intended as meaningful street names for an expanding city, were greater devotees of the classics than of the Middle Ages.

Two generations earlier, a romantic like Lord Byron might have viewed Rome as a 'marble wilderness'. His words did not, however, imply a reduction of the city to a mere trigger for melancholy contemplation of the death of kings. Instead, Byron was only one among many European intellectuals who took up the cause of Italian 'revival' as his own. He did so not by hailing a medieval past but by measuring a decline from classical grandeur and by demanding that modern Europe rally to the cause of restoring Rome to modern greatness. As his Childe Harold expressed it:

> Rome – Rome imperial bows her to the storm
> In the same dust and blackness, and we pass
> The skeleton of her Titanic form
> Wrecks of another world, whose ashes still are warm. . . .

> Europe, repentant of her parricide,
> Shall yet redeem thee, and, all backward driven,
> Roll the barbarian tide and sue to be forgiven.[72]

Similarly ready to preach stirring anti-clerical political messages based on the contrast between the tawdry present and the glory that was ancient Rome was the French writer, Henri-Marie Beyle, better known as Stendhal. Although plagiarising much of the period reality of his *Promenades dans Rome* from a compliant cousin who actually went there in 1828, Stendhal drew from his visits, real and imagined, the insistent message that papal rulers were too mired in an unworthy and dead medieval past to last for ever:

The pope's government is a pure despotism. . . . You have read Mill, Ricardo, Malthus, and all the other authors of political economy. Imagine the contrary of the rules of administration that they recommend; these are the ones observed in Rome, but often with the best intentions in the world. Here, as in France in the fifteenth century, the same matter may be decided by two or three different ministries; the amusing thing is that the various ministries keep no record of their decisions, there are only dossiers, and what is easier than to remove an important document from a forgotten file?[73]

Yet, 'Stendhal' maintained, Rome, permanently elevated in human thought by the grandeur of the Colosseum, the Pantheon and the Via del Corso, 'the most beautiful street in the universe' (if 'the smell of rotten cabbage' and the sight of 'rags' on too many people there could be blocked out), demanded recognition.[74] It was intolerable for it to be relegated to being a museum of anti-Enlightenment. The lingering power of the city's imperial past required that 'Europe' not forget Rome and, sooner or later, 'Stendhal' contended, it would have to 'improve' it.

In instance after instance, then, even if the leading English guide to the city still noted complacently that 'all that remains in Italy is outdone by England',[75] the classical sites, and the tourist trade that brought visitors to them, the foreign reading of Roman history, accorded Rome a higher profile in European culture than might be justified by its small size, 'backward' populace and antique economy. Ironically, for all its actual sleepiness, with every passing year of the nineteenth century, that age of 'new European empire', Rome, as the most evident bearer of the history of old empire, loomed larger. The battle to own its past became fiercer and was contested on fronts that ranged across the world.[76]

With a liberal imperial and global future beginning to loom on the horizon, during the 1840s clubs and societies multiplied in the various Italian states, and intellectuals debated ever more openly and fervently what might be the best path to a Risorgimento. Compared with the militarily efficient Piedmontese monarchy, modernising Milan or liberal Florence, contemporary Rome, under its palsied papal governance, offered few grounds for optimism to those who plotted change. Yet was there to be an unexpected chance of the Church shifting direction? On 1 June 1846 Gregory XVI died, to be rapidly replaced as pontiff by the fifty-four-year-old Cardinal Giovanni Maria Mastai-Ferretti of Imola in the Romagna, who took the title of Pius IX. He was reputed to be a liberal of some description – Gregory XVI had complained that, at Imola, even Cardinal Mastai's cat was a Freemason. Certainly Pius was anxious to end the grosser petty tyrannies of his predecessor's rule.[77]

The new pope also held ambitions to open some of the windows on ideas that Gregory had kept shut. Immediately after his elevation to the pontificate, on 16 July 1846 Pius decreed an amnesty for prisoners, quite a few of them 'political'. According to one English account, the news was greeted 'with a wild frenzy of delight' by the Roman people, belying, briefly at least, their reputation for political passivity and intolerance of change. At least for the moment, the human appeal of freedom held sway in every heart. 'Men wept and embraced in the streets, and the people of Rome, moved by an irresistible and unanimous impulse, marched as one man towards the Quirinal – one great convergent mass of emotional Italian humanity, vibrating with gratitude and affection.'[78]

Italian sources have different phrasing but do not paint a dissimilar picture. Whereas, in 1847, the people commemorated the first anniversary of the death of the grossly overweight and bibulous Gregory XVI with playfully public *maccheroni* dinners, Pius was saluted with more seriously didactic festivals from one week to the next.[79] In such events, history, the hope to draw convincing lessons from the past, was never far away. Frequently the recurrent festivities sought to be 'historical', either by illuminating key religious edifices in the city or through the construction of triumphal arches, uniting the living Pius with such 'good' dead emperors as Titus and Constantine. The ghosts of the Caesars were back in business and the Forum, the Campidoglio and the Baths of Diocletian were favoured sites for celebrations, flag-waving and lengthy speeches, full of claims that a good past was helpfully alive again.[80] To what extent Pius actually was a liberal or had understood the modernising world remains a conundrum, and it was not probed deeply in the first months after his succession, when Church, people and nationalist intellectuals all had reason to be joyful about the new pontiff and not ask too rigorously why and with what implication.

Instructive of the moment was a celebration on 21 April 1847, alleged to be the natal day of the city of Romulus and hailed since 1834 on the first initiative of the Pontificia Accademia Romana di Archeologia. Under the new pope, the determination to rework history through this anniversary was displayed in a grand public banquet held amid the ruins of the Baths of Titus in the shadow of the Colosseum. Decorations included the busts of Romulus and Numa, as well as the predictable she-wolf. Bands played, hymns were composed, while poems saluted the 'eternity' of Rome and its permanent destiny to lead the world.[81]

Foreigners were as likely to give hearing to such events as were Romans. The American radical republican onlooker, Margaret Fuller, was cheered by the general 'intoxication of hope and pleasure expressed across the classes', applauding Pius IX as a pope committed to a new beginning, destined to be 'the founder of another State'. Armed with their special memories of Rome, foreign liberals were readily enthralled by the prospect of a reforming Papacy; in Britain throughout the 1840s four books were published each year refreshing readers' memories of Roman sites and their meaning, and now quite a few Protestants believed that the world was about to see a Catholic Church cleansed of its historic corruption and superstition and a Roman people cured of the maleficent influence of superstition and reborn to national glory.[82]

Even after Pius IX had taken over, hopes could still be dashed, however. Fuller, for one, was not long persuaded by a happy alliance between pope and people or by the potential marriage of Church and classical history. 'Rome', she insisted, 'to resume her glory, must cease to be an ecclesiastical Capital; must renounce all this gorgeous mummery, whose poetry, whose picture, charms no one more than myself, but whose meaning is all of the Past and finds no echo in the Future.'[83] To her mind and that of many of her fellows, Catholic history had run its course. Now change was hammering at the gates of Rome. It must overwhelm what was bad about the past. It was no time for half-measures.

By January–February 1848 news came through, first from unlikely Palermo and then from Paris and almost every other continental European city, that 'Revolution' was back. Metternich and King Louis-Philippe of France were both driven into exile and the monarchs who survived were everywhere being forced to grant liberal constitutions and to meet the 'people'. Italy was astir. How, then, became the insistent query, might Rome choose from among its histories apposite pasts to serve the revolutionary cause? Was it realistically imaginable that the Papacy and a liberal nation could be united through history?

One key figure who, in the 1840s, had sought to map such a path to the future while surveying the past for its lessons was the abbé Vincenzo Gioberti. This Piedmontese priest had earned fame in 1843 with the publication of *On the moral and civil primacy of Italians*, an exposition of Italian historical 'primacy' across time. Pius IX was said to have taken a copy of the book with him to the conclave that elected him in 1846.[84] Heading a movement that, romantically recalling battles of the Middle Ages, was labelled neo-Guelph (when pro-Papal forces were Guelph and their opponents Ghibelline), Gioberti looked to a Risorgimento that would, through some form of federalism, win the approval of the Papacy and be led by it. By 1846–7, therefore, he seemed a prophet of a 'liberal pope' and the man who had best detected what would now prove the ideal path from past to future.

'History', Gioberti maintained, had demonstrated that 'religion is the progenitor of nations and of all their civilisation' and of no country was this truer than Italy. At one and the same time, as Gioberti argued that Tacitus had understood, 'Italy was always, both in civil and religious terms, the most cosmopolitan of nations' and 'the eternal centre of the inhabited world'.[85] Given this automatic fusion of the universal and the local, the pope was the 'natural' national head of state. Federalism constituted the clear way forward, a process that would not insult the past. A new Italy of this design would revive the Roman mission of opposing 'barbarism' and entrenching 'civilisation'.[86] It would seize and cement the real history of Rome.

In a later work attacking Jesuit obscurantism, Gioberti again drew comfort from the 'beautiful, great and sublime' Rome: 'the idea of a Rome both sacred and civilised is even grander and more lovely than Rome's pictures and monuments,' he contended. The city's populace had once been the epitome of sensibility, hard work and magnanimity, and traces of these inheritances survived, notably in Trastevere.[87] The popes had, through their museums, libraries and archaeological works, kept an ideal Rome alive, as had been made manifest in the city's refusal to bow to that 'man drunk with glory and power' – Napoleon. 'My Rome', Gioberti explained, which was also the 'real Rome', 'finally understands through the past and the present the nature of the future'. Destiny girded it with the power to 'legislate for, to unify and to redeem Italy, Europe and the world'. Naturally mastering history and time, Rome possessed a special dispensation to ignore and surpass the travails of the centuries. Both its classical Republic and its empire 'live still and will live for ever', positively conditioning every 'tongue, law, writing, art, habit'. Rome, in other words, was not bound by time as other, lesser, cities were. Rome was 'immortal, because its destiny is intermeshed with the preservation, diffusion and triumph of divine truth and with the ends of humankind'.[88] In Gioberti's 'neo-Guelph' vision, history ensured that a national Rome could and should remain a universal and Catholic one. An easy peace could end any apparent history war.

Yet, whatever the power or the fervour of his rhetoric and however briefly high his reputation as a seer, Gioberti had not sketched the model destined to triumph in the Risorgimento. Rather, it became ever more apparent as the revolutions of 1848–9 unfolded that a lay, modernising and liberal history could not cohabit with the Church as Gioberti and the neo-Guelphs wished. Now, especially in the words of 'national prophet' Giuseppe Mazzini, soon to be 'Triumvir' of a Roman Republic, the nation demanded all history for its own cause. It could not share with the Church. In Mazzini's utopian mind, the nation stood for totality; it had as its chief purpose the construction of a lay religion that would expel from Italian minds the degenerate gospel of the popes and shake off their now irrelevant past. From 1814 to 1846 it may have been true that Rome, both in reality and in imagining, had remained effectively in the hands of the Church and that, for some decades, Italian nationalists drew their greatest impulse from histories that were not Roman. Yet the Catholic ambition, decoded by Pianciani as cunningly crafted 'to proffer you a cheap past so that you will leave [the Papacy] be for the moment and concentrate your hopes in the future', was in 1848–9 to be radically attacked.[89] While revolution returned and plans to 'make Italy' revived, Rome, despite its small population and its dire lack of modern industry, proved inescapable as a fulcrum of political and cultural meaning and purpose. Soon, Mazzini and his associates were to trial on the streets of Rome a national Italian reading of the Eternal City, one allegedly expressing the past, present and future of the 'Rome of the people'.[90] Under liberal and nationalist aegis, the renewed revolution must cast aside the shackles of a Catholic past and find instead an Italian history. What, the revolutionaries of 1848–9 had forcibly and even obsessively begun to ask, might that be? What might this history do to Rome and what might Rome do to it?

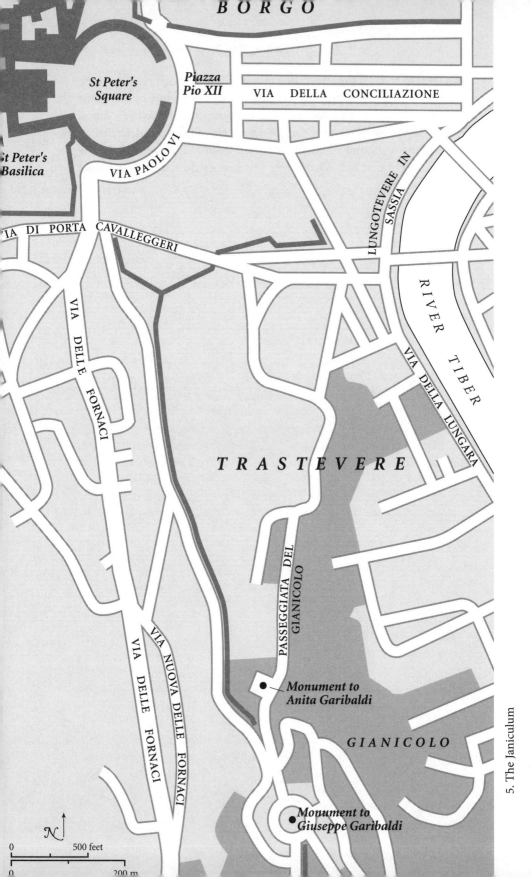

5. The Janiculum

4

---- ✳ ----

ROMAN REVOLUTION, NATIONAL
REVOLUTION

The Janiculum Hill, running from Trastevere to the edge of the Vatican, rises steeply some 100 metres above the Tiber and acts as the western frame of Rome's historic centre. It is a delightful place from which to survey the city and the sometimes snow-covered Apennines to the east. The hill has also on occasion acted as Rome's last natural military bulwark, for example in 1849, when French troops moved against the revolutionaries, headed by Mazzini, and their Republic. Then control of the San Pancrazio gate was bitterly contested, with the peerless 'hero' of the Risorgimento, Giuseppe Garibaldi, offering defence in a battle that took the life of young Goffredo Mameli, the author of *Fratelli d'Italia* (Italian brothers), a patriotic hymn, destined after 1946, when Italy itself became a Republic, to be accepted as the national anthem (despite its evident sexism).

One who stood on the heights of the Janiculum and cogitated was the English historian G.M. Trevelyan, an optimistic liberal or 'Whig' believer in progress. He wrote down his reflections in a trilogy about Garibaldi that he published between 1907 and 1911, that is, just as the Italian nation was celebrating the fiftieth anniversary of its unification and while the national capital was governed by Ernesto Nathan's reforming local administration. Like many of his predecessors and successors, Trevelyan, in his commentary on events in Rome, detected deep meaning in past and prospect. From the hill, he remarked, any could 'look back across the Tiber at the city spread beneath our feet, in all its mellow tints of white, and red, and brown, broken here and there by masses of dark green pine and cypress, and by shining cupolas raised to the sun'. The sweep over the city was special. The Rome whose course into becoming Italy's national capital Trevelyan was narrating carried a universal and permanent message: 'There it all lies beneath us, the heart of Europe and the living chronicle of man's long march to civilization. . . . As we look down we feel the presence of all the centuries of European history, a score of civiliza-tions dead and lying in state one beside the other; and in the midst of their eternal monuments mankind still swarms and labours, after all its strange and varied experience, still intent to live, still busily weaving the remote future out of the immemorial past.'[1] Italy, he was proclaiming, may have been made a nation and taken Rome as its capital. Yet decoding and representing the meaning of that site, he implied, was too important to be left to Italians alone. Although no Catholic, Trevelyan found now Liberal Rome still a place that carried a universal message.

The ironies in Trevelyan's commentary, and in what will be seen to be that of the many foreigners who sought to elucidate a grand historical purpose in the Risorgimento, did not end there. As he essayed his description of the 1848–9 revolution, its tragic defeat and glorious resolution in national and liberal unification, Trevelyan did not add to his rolling prose the point that Garibaldi, his hero of heroes, the man whom he portrayed as leading 'the most romantic life that history records', had, since 1895, been staring out at the same view.[2] There on the Janiculum, a visitor, even today, may salute the Hero, wearing his poncho and 'Hungarian' cap, 'outlandish' clothing that had been fashioned into his myth even in his own lifetime (and often at his own behest), and bestriding a subdued horse. Garibaldi's head is slightly bowed towards the north and is often thought to be glaring a challenge to the Vatican.[3] The statue had taken its sculptor, Emilio Gallori, a decade to complete and, weighing many tons, was said to be the heaviest in Europe. It marks another Roman site replete with histories, be they of the Risorgimento, of Liberal Italy, of Fascism or of the post-1946 Republic.

It was on 20 September 1895, exactly twenty-five years after Italian troops had broken through the Aurelian Walls, expelled the papal rulers and claimed Rome for the nation, that the statue was inaugurated on the Janiculum. The unveiling ceremony was transformed into a festival, one among a number in these years propagandising the ambition of the once radical and now ever more conservative Prime Minister, Francesco Crispi, to nationalise the Italian masses and give a modern thrust to the 'Third Rome'. More than 20,000 came to cheer, perhaps having read the opinion of *La Riforma*, a newspaper favourable to the Prime Minister, that the statue faced down the Vatican, while simultane-ously watching over 'that ill-starred northern way, along which the barbarian descended, and along which some new enemy could descend to strike at the heart of the fatherland'. Tailored to the occasion, Crispi's speech preached the gospel of anti-clericalism and of a new-style nationalism, harnessing an eclectic mix of Rome's histories to the *patria*. Papal rule over Rome, Crispi proclaimed, had once been 'the fulfilment of God's will'; now the Deity as surely sponsored a 'restored' Italian unity. Hereafter, 20 September could be affirmed as a national holiday, a lay *festa* to surpass and render redundant those saints' days

10. Giuseppe Garibaldi statue on the Janiculum, heroically overlooking the Vatican
*c.*1900.

that, regrettably, still drew the credulous and unmodern faithful to church. To make it clearer that Italy was unashamed of its assault on the Vatican and now directed the reading of history in the city, that afternoon Crispi opened a second monument, this time a classical column surmounted by a statue of Victory in front of the Porta Pia (the Holy Gate; designed by Michelangelo, it lies at the east of the historic centre) through which Italian troops had stormed in 1870.[4]

A decade and more later, there were further additions to Garibaldi's monument and an accompanying amplification of its message, fitting the purpose of the then ruling radical administration in the city. At the bottom of the massive stone plinth, panels were set alternately portraying olive wreaths and fasces until reaching the dedications that, on one side, pronounce 'To

Giuseppe Garibaldi' and, on the other, the slogan: 'Rome or Death' (implying the centrality of the acquisition of the Eternal City rather than the political or social unification of Italy as the Hero's mission). Set in front of this last slogan were the symbols of Freemasonry,[5] plus an iron coronet and laurel wreath, and a caption reading 'Giuseppe Garibaldi on the centenary of his birth, 2660 A.V.C.' (After the Foundation of the City), that is 1907.

At the next level up the monument there are four further statues, two recording heroic scenes from Garibaldi's life at Rome in 1849 and in Sicily in 1860, while the others represent Europe and America, thereby reminding onlookers of the vast arenas that welcomed the adventures and triumphs of 'the Hero of Two Worlds', maker of his nation but not merely that. In his time Garibaldi fought in civil campaigns in Uruguay and Brazil, as well as leading volunteers to the French side in the war against Prussian-made Germany in 1870. Beneath these global images are the trophies of battle, replicating in bas-relief those depicted on classical statuary, and guarded by the she-wolf with her infant twins since, even in the twentieth century, ancient history was automatically assumed to add legitimacy to recent events. The international theme is pursued further down the Janiculum, where, at the wish of Argentina, by then a New World society with many immigrants from Italy, a lighthouse had been positioned in 1900, the thirtieth anniversary of Rome being made Italy's capital. In March 2006 the place was given an extra message with a plaque deploring the military coup in Argentina in 1976, with the slogan 'Nunca Mas! Mai più!' (Never again).

So much might seem a story of international and domestic amity and the happy and durable triumph of an outward-looking liberal and fraternal nation, the country that Trevelyan was so warmly saluting on its fiftieth birthday. But it does not take long in Rome to find other sites, bearing other histories and displaying the complexity and divisions of the Risorgimento as much as its unity. Ironically, in 1895, Garibaldi was not the only proponent of Roman and Italian politics between 1848 and 1870 to be raised in some form of posthumous triumph in the national capital. So, on 22 September, in a ceremony just two days after the one on the Janiculum, Camillo Benso di Cavour, first national Prime Minister, no military hero but the cunning Piedmontese artificer of diplomatic victory in the 1850s, had his statue inaugurated in the square named after him. The aristocratic Cavour stands in a frock coat, a waist-coat doubtfully holding in his paunch, every inch a (fake) bourgeois, a statesman or politician slyly squinting at his surroundings (in the absence of his usual pince-nez). Rather than aggressively confronting papal backwardness as the Garibaldi statue does, this parliamentary maker of the nation looks out over the Palazzo di Giustizia, housing the Ministry of Justice, an ostensibly proper focus for a liberal. Yet in 1895 this building was already one of the more controversial in the city, derided by its critics as the *palazzaccio* (ugly, horrible, palace). Its construction took decades and was dogged by allegations of corruption (and injustice), charges that have rarely been absent from Roman real estate developments since.[6] To many, the Ministry of Justice stood for not the triumphs of Liberal Italy, but its limitations; not for its virtue but its vice.

The *palazzaccio* was not the only hint of the uneasy relationship between liberal theory and practice. Whereas Garibaldi's statue was unveiled to cheering crowds, the Cavour inauguration was attended mainly by notables, worthy in their class but few in number. By 1895 respectful memory of Cavour may have been a minority taste. But the third of what an author like Trevelyan was given to hailing as the 'trinity' of national unification, Giuseppe Mazzini – not the politician, not the hero but the 'prophet' of Italy's 'rebirth' – faced a more troubled fate in finding commemoration in Rome. As far as many in the Liberal leadership were concerned, Mazzini was too dangerously democratic and threateningly republican a figure to be conceded a revered place in the city's patriotic statuary.[7] To the comfortable classes of the new Italy, this Risorgimento ideologue was what is today damned as a terrorist.

True, a seated statue of him was commissioned in 1890 and completed in 1909 by sculptor Ettore Ferrari, a Mazzinian and sometime Grand Master of the Grande Oriente d'Italia, the more radical faction of the nation's Freemasons. Yet, even though, in 1909, Rome was in the charge of Nathan, who came from the family in whose house Mazzini had died, and who was a fellow Freemason, the statue was not erected until 1949, for what was then the centenary of the Roman Republic. The memorial is set above the Circo Massimo at an entry-point of the Aventine Hill, there allying the spirit of the Risorgimento and of classical times in a way that recalls in stone Mazzini's proclamation of the era of a 'Third Rome' and a 'Third Italy', as glorious as those of classical times and the Renaissance. It bears the simple slogan, 'Giuseppe Mazzini. *La Patria*' and carries at the back an admission of its belated installation.

A further instance of the multiple facets of the memorialisation of the Risorgimento in Rome, and the debates unleashed by its history, can be found by returning to the Janiculum, there to discover that Garibaldi is not the only member of his family to be commemorated. The city's monuments rarely address the gender order but, a visitor in the twenty-first century might take pleasure in noting, the Garibaldi memorial does. Slightly down the hill and lacking her husband's splendid view, Garibaldi's first wife, Anita (Ana Maria de Jesus Ribeiro da Silva), claims her own site of memory. This Brazilian of Azorean-Portuguese descent had eloped with the Hero while a teenager. They were (bigamously) married three years later. As every Italian schoolboy and girl is meant to know, Anita died in Giuseppe's arms outside Ravenna in August 1849. Although her illiteracy ensures that few direct sources on her life survive, she is still the target of romantic biographers.[8]

11. Anita Garibaldi demurely rides side-saddle on her statue's plinth, 1932.

On the Janiculum, the figure of Anita is mounted on a rearing horse. Intrepidly she carries a baby in one hand and packs a pistol in the other. Modestly she rides side-saddle, a way of managing her steed that is repeated in a bas-relief on the plinth, which shows her guiding her husband at the head of some trudging troops. Anita's sculptor was Mario Rutelli, born in Palermo in 1859 and sire of a family that would retain fame in Rome. Mario Rutelli died, full of years, in 1941. His celebration of the Garibaldi myth dates not to anti-clerical and Freemasonic Liberal Italy but to the Fascist dictatorship. Given that this regime, however committed to nationalising its masses and controlling their comprehension of history more aggressively than had the Liberals, was firm in its sexist view that women were best restricted to being 'exemplary wives and mothers', what history is the statue of Anita meant to convey?

The answer is complex. Anita's remains were translated from her previous place of burial at Genoa on 2 June 1932, for the fiftieth anniversary of her husband's death. A solemn inauguration of the statue occurred two days later in the presence of the Duce. It proved to be an event brimming with histories, some replete with the dictator's intention, some not. Mussolini had announced the construction of the statue in 1929, shortly after he had signed the Lateran Pacts in accommodation with the Church, and its first message underlined that, despite the yielding to the Church of the sovereign territory that composes 'Vatican City', the dictator had not made a complete surrender of the Fascist version of national history to the clerical interpretation of the past and future. No doubt the dictator had accepted that, from 1930, 20 September must be cancelled as a national holiday, to be replaced by 11 February, which would record the happy day when he and Pope Pius XI pledged their agreement. But, even as he abandoned one part of Crispi's legacy and terminated the war between Church and State that had smouldered since the Risorgimento, Mussolini stood resolute against intimations from the papal authorities that the monument to Garibaldi should be demolished or, at a minimum, moved from its symbolic overlooking of the Vatican.[9] Rather than backing away from the anti-clericalism that had featured so prominently during the process of national unification, the dictatorship, in celebrating Anita, was expanding the place of a Garibaldinian history in Rome.

The interpretation there to be affirmed was important enough for the dictator to intervene directly in the casting of the monument. Mussolini ostentatiously countered the initial flowing design sketched by sculptor Antonio Sciortino, an artist chosen for the task by Ezio Garibaldi, the Hero's youngest grandson. This Garibaldi had been a general in the First World War and was pro-Fascist, but his legacy in bearing the name of the dead Hero threatened danger for the jealous Duce, alert to rivals of his charisma, even dead ones.[10] So Mussolini transferred the commission to the more established Rutelli and advised further on the statue's character. With an attention to detail that some have found portentous but was mainly designed to express his own importance and might by now be viewed as petty, the Duce demanded that a baby (the Garibaldis' eldest son, Menotti) appear cradled in Anita's left arm (the infant had been wrapped into her bosom in Sciortino's design).[11] *Capitolium*, the semi-official journal of the Rome City Council, may have announced that the monument made manifest how 'the first Black Shirt in Italy is in ideal terms also a Red Shirt', yet, with his determined supervision of the detail, Mussolini was asserting a dictator's right to read history to his people.[12] In his view, the Garibaldis and their place in national unification only mattered in so far as they could be made Fascist. They must accept a posthumous alteration of their shirt colour.

As will be seen time and again to be true in Rome, an aspiration to a 'totalitarian' Fascist sway over the past was one thing, its achievement another. In his speech at the inauguration ceremony, Mussolini hinted at his pessimism about his ability to change the course of history by reminding his audience that Garibaldi had to endure 'the little, demeaning things that inevitably accompany action – polemics, ingratitude, abandon'.[13] This same pessimism had intruded into his lucubrations on Napoleon. Furthermore, in sacking Sciortino for Rutelli, Mussolini was not being as original or domineering as he thought he was. The melodramatic and even clichéd image of Anita that Rutelli produced fitted well not just with Mussolini's historical vision but also with that of the liberal capitalist world, whose messages were now reaching Rome and Italy, and were being expressed in the Hollywood film portrayal of Heroes, Heroines and the West. The galloping and pistol-packing Anita squared uneasily with the ideal Fascist (and Catholic) depiction of demure womanhood. Perhaps Rutelli had endeavoured to sculpt an exemplary woman of the frontier and so, by implication, one who, when her foes, whether 'Indians' or not, were beaten off, would settle down to a decorous and subordinate female role at the hearth. But, despite the infant and the side-saddle, the 'Anita' on the Janiculum potentially conveyed rousing feminist histories to come, ones that eventually dislodged the repressive masculine fixations of the Fascist years.

It is therefore no surprise to find that, once the bright Fascist show of 'total-itarianism' in the parades of June 1932 was over, historical debate about the meaning of the Garibaldis in Rome resumed. It is not yet stilled. After 1943 the communists gloried in the name 'Garibaldi brigades' to define their partisan forces. When anti-Fascist victory was won but led to further contest, in 1948 the communists went to the polls in crucial 'Cold War' elections with Garibaldi as their symbol, even if the news that he shared a first name with the 'Great Stalin' was underlined with different interpretations of the implications by friends on the left and enemies on the right. The conflict over a Garibaldi memory was again evident in 1982 during the centenary events of the Hero's death, disputed between communists, socialists and republicans. Garibaldi was still condemned by the Church, but now had to endure further criticism by the burgeoning forces of the Lega Nord and by other Italians willing to wonder out loud whether the entire Risorgimento, and especially the acquisition of the south, had been a mistake.[14] In the new millennium, *leghisti* were to put Garibaldi on mock trial and find him guilty of outrage to the *patria* of Naples-Sicily. In 2007 his bicentenary saw a seminar on him in the Sala della Lupa (Room of the She-Wolf) of the Italian Chamber of Deputies broken up by demonstrators, who distributed anti-Garibaldi leaflets. The sometime Hero was now interpreted as a villain in the long story that backers of the Lega were composing about the historical 'error' of national unification. Then, they argue, Italy had not so much been made as pushed in a false direction, dislodged from better, more federalist, historical tracks and corrupted by its dependence on Rome.

It is clear, then, that the statues of the Garibaldis on the Janiculum and those of their allies or rivals elsewhere in the city readily indicate that the search for the public meaning of the Risorgimento remains contested. This division should not dismay, since between 1848 and 1870 the unfolding of events was accompanied and justified by a rivalry over the messages of the past, among revolutionaries, Catholics and foreign observers, as well as the Roman people. As was noted at the end of the last chapter, the joyful harmony on the eleva-tion of a 'liberal pope' in 1846 had not lasted long. In what sense, it began to be asked, was Pius IX really a liberal or a nationalist? Could the ancient hierarchy of the Church be reconciled with excited and novel talk about democracy? How far could a Roman and Catholic pontiff go in backing demands for an Italian nation? Despite Gioberti's confident fervour, could Catholic history really be reconciled with that of the nation?

These and other questions began to arouse debate about which pasts in the city should now be regarded as exemplary. As early as June 1847 papal authorities were openly afraid that the festive atmosphere had grown too riotous. They tried, ineffectually, to ban the demonstrations of crowds who were given to hailing Pope Pius and Italy as though nation and Church were natural partners, and were as ready to sing national songs as to kneel and receive benediction in a *Te Deum*.[15] On 2 January 1848, for example, the throng under the popular leader 'Ciceruacchio' (Angelo Brunetti; his soubriquet curiously demonstrated how the oratory of Cicero had never been quite forgotten in the city), surrounded the papal carriage as it drove down the Corso. Ciceruacchio leaped on board to unfurl a banner that read: 'HOLY FATHER. TRUST IN THE PEOPLE'.[16] Pius was thought to have nodded his assent but, a diarist warned, his favourable response prompted cries of delight worryingly mixed with loud 'attacks on reactionaries, damning of the ministers, and imprecations against the police'.[17]

Despite such possibly menacing activism, for the moment the papal government survived in Rome. However, as one revolution followed another in the cities of Europe, Pius IX was being impelled to deny that there could be an alliance between Church, nation and liberal democracy. On 29 April the pope delivered a secret allocution to his cardinals, admitting that he could not be a participant in the military campaign being launched by the revolutionaries to eject Austrian forces from the Italian peninsula. By definition and throughout history, Pius observed, 'we reach to, and embrace, all kindreds, peoples, and nations, with equal solicitude of paternal affection'. A Church at war, he stressed, could not defend peace, as was its divine and permanent duty. Moreover, he added, now it was time to deny and reject neo-Guelph schemes for an Italian papacy: 'We cannot refrain from repudiating, before the face of all nations, the treacherous advice . . . of those who would have the Roman Pontiff to be the head and to preside over the formation of some sort of novel republic of the whole Italian people'.[18] The Roman Church, Pius had concluded, must not reduce itself to being Italian. Its historic universality could not be renounced. Its Rome was greater than any imaginable Italy.

But was it possible in this feverish atmosphere to back-pedal from the national cause? No doubt the Church could still summon some familiar histories that might retain influence. In March–April 1848 the news spread that a 'sacrilegious hand' had stolen the head of the apostle, St Andrew, preserved in the city since it had been wondrously saved from the sack of Constantinople. The relic was soon relocated, and, between 1 and 5 April, Rome, as so often in the past, was threaded with pious processions. Bells rang and the great churches were illuminated. The celebrations culminated in a parade that wound its way to St Peter's, attended by gorgeously dressed cardinals and more soberly clad civilians, seconded by the Papal Guard. The pope marched with them, escorted by the papal nobility, each man clutching a guttering torch. In the great basilica, the reliquary of St Andrew was solemnly given sanctuary on the high altar.[19]

Yet the excitement in the city was not calmed by such pious celebration of well-worn history. On 3 August a throng assembled outside the Quirinal palace, crying 'Death to the cardinals, death to the priests' and cheering for a provisional and lay government.[20] Political division widened, with a popular anti-Semitism again bubbling menacingly to the surface. Just as they had been in 1798–9, some Romans were unhappy with the demolition of the gates of the ghetto on 17 April and the subsequent elevation of three Jews to the municipal council.[21] More evident for the moment, however, was a social radicalism, heightened by the negative effects of revolution on Rome's economy. The considerable foreign presence in the city of fans of political change could not adequately replace the financial advantage provided in normal times by Catholic pilgrims. Demands for the urgent institution of more generous welfare spread, and they were not appeased when, in September, Pius appointed as his Chief Minister, Pellegrino Rossi, a liberal no doubt but one who preferred efficiency to revolution and who began to stiffen the police presence in the city and evince his determination to suppress the more exalted democrats. On 15 November outside the Palazzo della Cancelleria where a Council of Deputies now assembled, Rossi was stabbed to death by Luigi Brunetti, son of Ciceruacchio. Scarcely a week later, the pope fled his city by night in disguise to take refuge at Gaeta, the fortress port on the other side of the border of the Papal States with the Kingdom of Naples–Sicily. At least according to one diarist, the departure was greeted with indifference in the city, 'the shops open as usual, the cafes busy, everything tranquil'.[22] Yet, with the pope's departure and its signal of a historic break between old Church and new state in the making, the revolution would have to stand on its own. The problem of working out what it meant and how it could build a credible relationship between past, present and future was still to be resolved.

If the papal version of ancient monarchy had lost its lustre, then a fresh constitution must be framed and so it was, helped by the arrival of Garibaldi in Rome in mid-December. The Hero, who previously had been to the city for just a few days as a boy, would in his memoirs look to history to explain why he was attracted there. The killing of Rossi, he wrote, meant that Rome, 'the ancient metropolis of the world, [had] showed itself worthy of its illustrious past. A young Roman had wielded anew the sword of Brutus and drowned the marble steps of the Capitol with the tyrant's blood!'[23] Thus armed with lessons from classical times, Garibaldi over the next weeks pushed for further radical steps, while he billeted what he called his 'Legionaries' in various centres of the Papal States, readying them militarily to block any attempt to restore Pius IX.

Within Rome, the debate over the constitution was enlivened with more festivals, no longer of the old religious kind but lay ones preaching the religion of the nation and involving illumination of the city's main squares and buildings, the public display of tapestries and flags, the resounding of patriotic songs and airs, and the assertion of connections with an ideal past, especially a classical one. Typical was a ceremony on the Capitol in January 1849, where the statue of Marcus Aurelius was garlanded with a tricolour, while a caption explained: 'O Marcus Aurelius, because you are wise, hold aloft the tricolour . . . and be Roman or, rather, Italian.'[24] A priest from Venice, one of the many non-Roman Italians who had gathered to advance the revolutionary cause, read out the draft constitution, explaining that its phrases were 'those of the Gospel, as spoken by Our Lord, and not the language of tyrants'.[25]

Could a path be smoothed from the Roman past to an Italian future? Could Italy *farà da sè* (progress of its own accord)? Some revolutionaries thought the answer was yes. On 5 February the newly elected members of a Constituent Assembly were told by Garibaldi that 'the Roman people have no need to follow the examples of those who were once their disciples, be they English or French or anyone else. The Roman people have their own examples and they have models in their own history.'[26] Now, the Hero urged, a Republic must be 'restored', with the implication that the modern political form was as old as it was revolutionary. With more confused historical reference, Giuseppe Verdi's studiously romantic *La battaglia di Legnano*, whose lyrics depicted an affray fought in northern Italy in 1176, was successfully premiered at the Argentina Theatre that evening, although the composer, who, while in Rome late in 1848, had composed a battle hymn for Mazzini, had by then judiciously withdrawn to Paris.[27] For the moment Verdi's canny retreat was not remarked (and he was to retain a place in the nationalist pantheon as a progenitor of his nation). Exciting events had intervened. In Rome, on 9 February 1849, a Republic was formally proclaimed, with its key clauses stating that 'the form of government in the Roman state will be pure democracy, and will assume the glorious name of the Roman Republic. The Roman Republic will establish relations with the rest of Italy that will express our common nationality.'[28]

It took another four weeks for Giuseppe Mazzini, the prophet of these ideas about the natural unity of liberty and the nation, to reach Rome, a city where he had never before been (except in his mind when it ranged over Roman pasts; as a boy in school at Genoa, he had, for example, learned to 'worship Brutus').[29] It was now, with predictable re-evocation of classical terminology, that he was appointed 'Triumvir'. Mazzini's rhetoric was heavy with further similar reference, invoking a history that was as mystically lasting in character as was that of the Church or, rather, that sought to be even more enduring and complete. The Mazzinian nation, too, was to be eternal and universal, the natural, inevitable and godly fruit of history.[30]

> I have found in the ruins of Roman grandeur, and also in the pontifical tradition the miraculous and curative [*taumaturga*] idea. Romans, be great! I bless you in the Roman manner to become Italians. You conquer the world with the eagle [the imperial bird was swiftly added to the Republic's flag]; you conquer souls with the *labarum* [the Christian symbol adopted by Constantine]. Here are the eagle and the *labarum*. They stand for God and People. Rome is the centre and head of Italy. This city, that was created to be eternal and is predestined to be the fount of global unity, is rising again, and both Italy and Europe know it.[31]

Lest he be mistaken, in his first speech to the Rome Chamber of Deputies on 6 March, Mazzini added: 'After the Rome that worked through the conquest of arms and the Rome that worked through the conquest of words will come . . . the Rome that works through the virtue of example. After the Rome of Emperors and the Rome of Popes, now is coming the Rome of the People.'[32] 'I tell myself', he explained, 'it is impossible for a city which alone in the world has had two great lives . . . not to have a third.'[33]

These ringing words were backed up by festivals, such as those of Easter in Piazza San Pietro, where, with blatant 'invention of tradition', papal ceremony was reworked to fit the republican cause. On Good Friday the cross on the basilica's cupola was lit up, but now in the colours of the national tricolour, green, white and red. Three days later, Christ's resurrection was marked with a mass where the Holy Sacrament was carried to the crowd surrounded by Republican flags and with a revolutionary priest proclaiming that 'the Vicar of Christ is absent but not through our fault. With him gone, God and the People remain.'[34] To the plaudits of the throng, Mazzini himself appeared on the loggia where popes had been, and would be, accustomed to give their blessings.

But a lasting Third Rome or Third Italy was not to be forged by this Republic. Its history was not to prove sacred for long. Rather, the events in Rome amounted to the last throw for a revolution that mingled nationalist, liberal and democratic purpose with what would soon seem utopian ease. Even while the revolutionaries readied themselves for another festival commemorating, on 21 April, the anniversary of the foundation of the city by Romulus, the European powers began to move against the final redoubt of radicalism.[35] At the end of the month, Rome was surrounded by Neapolitan and Spanish forces to the south and a French army that had been landed at Civitavecchia to the north-west on the 24th. France, by now, was governed by President Louis Napoleon Bonaparte, that sometime *carbonaro* who was not yet Emperor Napoleon III.

Neither Mazzini's ideological purism nor Garibaldi's courage – typically he chafed under Mazzini's rule, petitioning either to be made 'dictator' or to serve the cause as an ordinary soldier – nor the passage of radical social legislation along with a calming defence of the rights of property could prevent the Republic's fall.[36] By early June the French were in control of the outskirts of the Janiculum, with the assault led by Garibaldi to drive the invaders from the Porta San Pancrazio ending on the 3rd after desperate and bloody battle. Even if the French did not enter the city for another month, Rome was lost. According to one diarist, some more fanatical Mazzinians contemplated exiting in dramatic style by blowing up St Peter's and the Vatican, a project to blast away Church history in what is now called the 'terrorist' style.[37] In practice, however, Mazzini, accustomed to defeat and perhaps preferring it, moved quickly to lock into the record his interpretation of the Republic's rule. The Republic, he had urged on 29 May, must leave its history in the city as a monumental 'deposit', although from exile, he would soon see his foes doing their best to stamp out all memory of the Republic.[38]

In Mazzini's intended process of seizing the moral high ground as much in defeat as in victory, as much in history as in current events, he was seconded by such foreign admirers as Margaret Fuller, who, on 21 June, reported to her friends in the USA that 'the French, who pretend to be the advance guard of civilization, are bombarding Rome. They dare take the risk of destroying the richest bequests made to man by the great Past.' To be sure, not all Romans won her over; maybe they were no more than fair-weather republicans and nationalists. 'I do not love them much,' she confessed, 'the women not at all; they are too low for me; it will be centuries before they emerge from a merely animal life.'[39] Yet romance could always return. When, in early July, she watched Garibaldi's retreat with his men (and with Anita, unknowingly moving towards her death), she added: 'I longed for Sir Walter Scott to be on earth again. . . . Never have I seen a sight so beautiful, so romantic and so sad.'[40] Mazzini himself found a predictably fulsome religious expression to summarise his hopes in defeat for his disciples. 'We are', he said on 22 June, 'consecrated victims.'[41] In this fate, he pronounced, the revolutionaries had seized the history of the city for their cause and, even as the Republic was being ploughed under, were planting the seeds of a lay religion of the nation. Their gospel was destined to replace the Catholic one. As if in demonstration of the market potential of the memory trade, the new skill of photography almost immediately added the military sites of the Janiculum to the other remains of the city, with the image merchants cheerfully defining them as 'new ruins'.[42]

Similarly illustrating that they feared Rome's past had been seized by Mazzini and Garibaldi, the successful counter-revolutionaries were soon worrying that their victory might not be permanent. Certainly they moved even more rapidly than had their fellows in 1799 or 1815 to wipe out the visible legacies of the Republic. The French commander, Nicolas Oudinot, and a junta of three

cardinals who, in the continued absence of Pius IX, took over the city's government, denied legitimacy to the Republic's rule. Oudinot at once ordered the
demolition of leftover Republican images as dreadful signs 'of anarchy and
terror'.[43] On 2 August 1849 all legislation passed since 16 November 1848 was
officially annulled, copies of the wicked decrees being publicly burned.[44]

Was such a purging of recent history sufficient? After all, social instability
lingered in the city, with martial law continuing into 1850 and so rendering
impossible the hope that a Holy Year might be instituted as was due. Pius IX
only came back to Rome on 12 April 1850, being greeted with a parade that
was ominously protected by well-armed French soldiers. The pope by now
was, as even a friendly biographer admits, 'a sadder and a wiser man'.[45] Could
he find a means to save the Church and its Rome from the political change
that, in spite of the Republic's overthrow, seemed likely to result from the
economic and social pressure of encroaching modernity? Did the Vatican still
possess a credible past? Could it underpin the present? Could 'revolution', the
nation, liberty and democracy be purged from Roman memory?

Perhaps they could since, although the 'people' may have clamoured for
change under Ciceruacchio or Mazzini, their lives remained for the most part
traditional, their families the heart of individuals' identities. Rome was still an
early modern city where the shops lacked glass windows and display, and where
almost anything could be found for sale. Many goods were marketed in the old
ambulatory fashion; among common traders were scrap meat and watermelon
sellers, coffee roasters, water carriers and those who heaved customers around
the streets in sedan chairs. A cholera epidemic struck Rome in 1854, while
public executions stained city life as late as 1868. No matter what the atmosphere, tourists continued to arrive and they were the main customers of Rome's
1,500 jewellers, 30 hotels and 31 *trattorie* (upmarket restaurants). Ordinary
Romans were more likely to enjoy the 712 *osterie* (pubs) and 217 coffee outlets.[46]
The ethnic allegiance of these people remained diverse and anything but nationalised, with pub-keepers being reported as likely to be Genoese, bakers from
Friuli, chestnut roasters from the Spoleto hills, cake-makers Swiss, horse-
cabmen from the Abruzzi, builders' labourers from Sardinia and hat-makers
from the Marche.[47] Those born in the city still knew that they were not like
them; history separated them.

Yet, despite these powerful traditions, some of the technological change
sweeping Europe intruded into Rome when, in 1851, the first papal postage
stamps were issued. In 1853, under French prompting, gas lighting was introduced in some streets, in 1854 a telegraph line was opened to Terracina on the
Papal States' southern border and, in 1856, Rome was joined by railway to
Frascati in the Alban hills.[48] During the next decade, the city became attached
to a railway system that crossed the peninsula and helped forge a nation, at
least for travellers. As a result, after the proclamation of an Italian state in 1860,

its citizens casually took to visiting Rome in greater numbers than non-Romans had in the past.[49] Running water could be obtained in hotels and some city apartments, and not just in the celebrated fountains, from 1867. Whatever might be the political future, papal Rome began to reflect contemporary scientific progress.

Maybe such modernity could be absorbed and the trick could be played of uniting eternal holiness with economic advance. Certainly the Vatican's official posture became that Pius IX stood at the head of a Church that could manage the different currents of past and present, just as it always had done. Cardinal Wiseman, for example, took pains to argue that Rome was fundamentally both modern and ancient: 'The one as warlike, factious, fiery, and full of indomitable purpose, the boiling vortex, which itself agitated and restless, pushes waves of irresistible conquests to every shore; the other, calmly intrepid, exercising a pacific spiritual rule over a still wider religious empire'. Underpinning this fusion, he believed, was a historic compromise:

Ancient Rome lives yet in modern Rome, so as to appear indestructible; and modern Rome is so interlaced with ancient Rome, as justly to seem primeval. They resemble two noble figures placed side by side, with the one form of old Tiber, crowned with sedges and pouring out his urn, at their feet; the one clothed in panoply and seated on the fragments of her ruined temples, pensive and repentant: the other standing over her, mild and majestic and warding off from her broken treasures the jealous stroke of time. The marble halls of the Vatican have offered an asylum to the choicest remains of heathen art, and the Capitol bears on its summit the symbol of the Christians' triumph. It would be difficult, therefore, to treat of Rome otherwise than as one . . . ,

Wiseman concluded with apparent confidence and conviction. Only Church rule could guarantee to preserve and embody such composite history without a collapse into sin and anarchy.[50]

In 1857 a parade to celebrate Pius IX's return to his city from a tour of the surviving papal provinces tried to display visible proof of such claims by representing both the pontiff's lay achievements (the telegraph, the railway, gas lighting and some new manufacturing industry) and his religious activities, notably the rebuilding of the basilica of San Lorenzo (where his tomb would eventually be lodged) and his proclamation on 8 December 1854 of the dogma of the Immaculate Conception.[51] This last act, in the pope's view, guaranteed his trumping of Mazzini and the revolutionaries. Typically it was an assertion of a Catholic history that was eternal and universal, and so by implication unmatchable by enthusiasts for the Italian nation.

Although discussion about the special qualities of the Virgin had long been a fixation of Church fathers, the decision of the pope and his Jesuit advisers to

12. Medal cast by Giuseppe Bianchi of Pius IX's ceremonial enunciation of the dogma of the Immaculate Conception in St Peter's, 8 December 1854. The Pope is being watched over by the Blessed Virgin, perched above him in the clouds.

issue a constitution entitled *Ineffabilis Deus* was prompted by the Republic's violation of Rome's holiness and by the continuing threat of a Risorgimento. It was, after all, on 8 December 1849, the day traditionally linked to Mary, the Mother of God, that Pius, still in exile, had damned the revolutionaries as slaves to 'the evil new systems of socialism and communism'.[52] On this and other occasions, the Virgin's uniqueness, and the understanding of Her history that the Church alone possessed, were invoked to illustrate that 'the pope's authority to command the beliefs of Christendom had not been shattered by the philosophical and political turmoil of the age of scepticism'. Those who accepted the dogma of the Immaculate Conception, with its mystery that surpassed science, were asked to bow to the ineffable power of Catholic Rome, and so proclaim anew an eternal historical role for the Church that had not been undermined by revolution.[53] The claim was quickly imprinted on Rome's streetscape, with the erection of a monument to the Immaculate Conception outside the Collegio di Propaganda Fide, centre of the Church's missionary work and records, in 1857. It can still be viewed and consists of a classical column, topped with a statue of Mary, her arms spread in charity to humanity, designed by Luigi Poletti, a neoclassical architect from the north.

Pius may have dreamed of religious revival, but the continuing presence of foreigners – 400 Americans were recorded as living in Rome through the winter of 1859–60 – offered the most obvious diverse readings of the city's meaning from those being proclaimed with revived ardour by the pope. These foreign residents were no longer the revolutionary fellow travellers of 1848–9. But, through their artistic, literary and historical works, they gave form and influence to German, American, British and other Romes, not identical with the Catholic one, if also not necessarily reliably locked into the cause of the Italian nation. After all, through the political vicissitudes, archaeology went on regardless, or almost so, with digging in the classical sites continuing through the summer of 1849, despite the approach of the French Army and its bombardment of the city.[54] From 1850 labour on the Via Appia converted the place to something like its present character, ending local landowners' belief that its prime purpose was to be a quarry.[55] One of the paradoxes of the decade before 1870 when French forces, stationed in Rome, constituted the major military barrier against Italian occupation was that, in 1861, Napoleon III had bought the Palatine Hill from its previous owners, the royal family of Naples-Sicily. The French Emperor patronised major archaeological work there, while endeavouring to write a lengthy biography of Julius Caesar (the first two volumes appeared in 1865–6). Its aim naturally was to make 'Napoleon the little' into the great Roman's obvious successor.[56] With a sense of modern publicity that Napoleon shared with Pius IX, the excavations were opened for public visits on Thursdays, with tickets available at the French embassy. The great German historians of ancient and medieval Rome, Theodor Mommsen and Ferdinand Gregorovius, were among early tourists to the site. The pope himself came on a surprise visit over Christmas 1863.[57]

One writer who drew less inspiration from 'scientific' archaeology than from romance was the American, Nathaniel Hawthorne. His novel, *The Marble Faun*, appeared in 1860, a coincidence with the events of the Risorgimento outside Rome that helped sales. Hawthorne's extravagant story was taken so seriously by contemporaries that an early publisher made available an interleaved edition, which 'enabled purchasers to personalise their copies, and to participate in the aesthetic experience of Romance, by pasting in photographs of themselves taken at locations described in the story'.[58]

In his preface, Hawthorne explained that he had sought a 'poetic or fairy precinct' wherein to set his tale, since 'Romance and poetry, like ivy, lichens, and wall-flowers, need Ruin to make them grow'.[59] Heir still to the romantic view that history was best placed in a dream-time, Hawthorne found in Rome a past that mattered but was detached from the city's present in what might seem an ideal recipe for the tourist, glorying in his irresponsibility for the alien world around him. Rome, Hawthorne wrote, elicited 'a vague sense of ponderous remembrances; a perception of such weight and density in a by-gone life, of which this spot was the centre, that the present moment is pressed down or crowded out, and our individual affairs and interests are but half as real here, as elsewhere. . . . Side by side with the massiveness of the Roman Past, all matters that we handle or dream of, now-a-days, look evanescent and visionary alike'.[60]

After all, Hawthorne knew, death ruled in the city and its environs:

The final charm is bestowed by the Malaria. There is a piercing, thrilling, delicious kind of regret in the idea of so much beauty thrown away, or only enjoyable at its half-development, in winter and early spring, and never to be dwelt amongst, as the home scenery of any human being. For, if you come hither in summer and stray through these glades [in the Villa Borghese] in the golden sunset, Fever walks arm and arm with you, and Death awaits you at the end of the dim vista. Thus the scene is like Eden in its loveliness; like Eden, too, in the fatal spell that removes it beyond the scope of man's actual possession.[61]

Like Chateaubriand, for him the city was a cemetery or yawning grave. Yet Hawthorne did not follow the French romantic in drawing from Rome a lesson of eternal loyalty to the popes. Rather, for a Protestant and a modern American man, Catholicism was as wasting a disease spiritually and intellectually as malaria was physically. Only the classics and their ruins offered firmer ground, fostering perhaps feeble hope for a modern future and not the tomb. 'Rome, as it now exists, has grown up under the Popes, and seems like nothing but a heap of broken rubbish, thrown into the great chasm between our own days and the Empire, merely to fill it up; and, for the better part of two thousand years, its annals of obscure policies, and wars, and continually recurrent misfortunes, seem also but broken rubbish, as compared with its classic history'.[62] Dirty (life for the city's Jews in the ghetto, Hawthorne noticed disapprovingly, was 'close, unclean and multitudinous, resembling that of maggots when they overpopulate a decaying cheese'), Rome had few of the comforts and none of the modernity of his American home.[63] Under papal misrule, Hawthorne cautioned, present-day Romans were perversely superstitious, passionate and murderous. They 'speak truth so much as if they were telling a lie, that their auditor suspects himself in the wrong, whether he believes or disbelieves them; it being the one thing certain, that falsehood is seldom an intolerable burthen to the tenderest of Italian consciences'.[64] Romantic and enticing, to be admired, painted and photographed, but, for Hawthorne and many foreigners, in the 1860s and afterwards Rome lived on chiefly through its beautiful pasts. To be of present or future value, they contended, the city would have to be purged. Even the revolutionaries, they complained, were not really in tune with modernity. As the Russian liberal, Alexander Herzen, who had been resident in the city in 1848–9, put it some years later, Mazzini and the nationalists were 'children, but wicked children'.[65] To become adult, he implied, they must be re-educated in modernity; only then might they be inoculated against the decadence of their history.[66]

Recalling a journey to the city in 1864, Hawthorne's co-national, W.D. Howell, was even more dismissive. He found the Forum no better than a 'dirty cow-field, wandered over by evil-eyed buffaloes, and obscenely defiled by wild beasts of men'. Modern Rome, to his mind, was 'first and last, hideous . . . the least interesting town in Italy, and the architecture is hopelessly ugly – especially the architecture of the churches. The Papal city', he complained, 'contrives . . . to hide the Imperial city from you.'[67] Any Rome that mattered, Howell concluded arrogantly, 'really belongs to the Anglo-Saxon nations, and the Pope and the past seem to be carried out entirely for our diversion'.[68] Yet, he noted, a friendly sacristan who, he implied, clung to democratic aspirations, told him that 'they', by which he meant the Church and its supporting aristocracy and high clergy, 'have robbed us of everything, as if he and the Pantheon were of one blood, and he suffered personal hurt in its spoliation'.[69] No doubt, the USA, Britain and Germany were the best heirs of classical empire. However, Howells learned from this conversation, when their history was channelled into a new course, maybe Italians could yet aspire to join them, at least in a secondary role.

More nuanced in his assessment of the city and its heritage was the German Ferdinand Gregorovius, who was a resident from 1852 until the Italian conquest in 1870. In his diary he remarked on the events that occurred around him, even while he penned a multi-volume history of Rome through the Middle Ages. Like many another, Gregorovius portrayed his arrival in Rome in phrases that rendered the place portentous. He entered the city at 4.30 p.m. one autumn afternoon, only to hurry out to view the Campidoglio and the Forum, 'later the Colosseum, lit by the moon'. The city, he decided, was 'so overwhelmingly silent that there [a scholar] can feel, think and work in divine peace'.[70]

By 1854, conscious of parallels with Gibbon, Gregorovius had decided to write his history, even though he feared that 'Rome sometimes does not let itself be seen, but rather closes itself into its antiquity'. 'Rome', he reflected, 'is the demon with which I struggle. If I can be victorious over it, that is, if I succeed in dominating this powerful and universal being, and make it an object of observation, analysis and art, then, I, too, shall deserve a triumph'.[71] After all, he aimed to chart an ascent and not a fall, nothing less than the rise of modern freedom and civilisation.[72] The history that he wanted to hymn there was not restricted to the local in its meaning. 'Deeply stirred by the sight of Rome,' he explained, 'I resolve not only to depict the ruin of the city, but to follow it on its re-awakening to a new world-governing power'.[73] Indeed, perhaps there had never been a fall, since 'during the Middle Ages the reverence of the nations for the city was unbounded. . . . All the institutions of mankind had originally sprung from this single city'.[74] In curious parallel and competition with the Church, Gregorovius imagined a Rome that was universal or it was nothing.

Despite his personalisation of his relationship with the place and impelled by his joy at the approach of German unification and pleasure at the prospect of the extinction of papal power, in 1859–61 Gregorovius watched the process of Italian unification with approval – Cavour, Garibaldi and King Victor Emmanuel II were, he thought, real heroes (Mazzini, he ignored). Writing about the political battles and sufferings of the Middle Ages had a strange ring in a present, he mused, 'when a work is completed that the centuries had despaired of'. Three types, he claimed, regularly reappeared in Italy: Machiavelli, the *condottiere* and

Cesare Borgia.[75] Now they were again happily embodied in the three (rival) leaders of the Risorgimento.

To be sure, neither Garibaldi nor Cavour nor the King was genuinely Roman in background. Watching contemporary political events, Gregorovius observed in March 1861 that Rome was all but completely passive, sullenly awaiting its fate. Yet, he worried, was it destined to become just another national capital suitable for this Eternal City? Would an Italian Rome be too lightweight properly to represent its grandiose historical heritage? Although a Protestant and proud in the freedom he thought had been achieved through the Germanic Reformation, Gregorovius warned that Rome resounded with the Catholic spirit and with many Catholic pasts. 'The King of Italy here', he maintained, 'would turn into a figure like that of the prisoners represented on Trajan's Column.' Rendered Italian, Rome would 'lose everything, its republican air, its cosmopolitan breadth, its tragic stillness' and its commanding historical universality.[76]

For Gregorovius, a Rome whose history was to be nationalised would be transmogrified into a city that had been sundered from its most meaningful pasts, ones that were now being taken up by the Germans and other modernised peoples. As he predicted in October 1870, Italian Rome 'will lose its atmosphere of being a world republic, an air that I have breathed for eighteen years. It will descend a rung to be the capital of the Italians', a people who were natively weak and whose success on 20 September was owed to the exercise of German power in France. Gregorovius was glad, he remarked, at last to have finished his own historical reconstruction. In 1870 a medieval legacy was being destroyed just as was the classical one. 'The Middle Ages are being swept away as though by the *tramontana* [the wind from the mountains to the east], along with the whole historic spirit of the past. Rome has lost its enchantment.'[77] By 1874 he had made up his mind to go back to Germany and stay there. His own 'monument in the place', he believed, was to have 'created what did not exist and to bring to the surface eleven obscure centuries and so give the Romans their medieval history'. So familiar was his treasured past, he thought, as he walked down from the Campidoglio for the last time, that the 'monuments, the statues and the stones called me loudly by name'. But this old Rome was, he concluded, now 'fated to disappear and become a ghost like the world created by Prospero in Shakespeare's *The Tempest*. Roma vale! Haerat vox et singultus intercipiunt verba dictantis' (Farewell, Rome. My voice falters and weeping interrupts my words as I speak).[78] His Latin repeated tellingly, at least in his mind, the phrasing of St Jerome on hearing of the sack of Rome by Alaric and the Goths.

In his retreat from Rome, Gregorovius was eloquently making a case that had long underpinned a foreign presence in the city and would be taken up again by those from abroad who came there after Liberal conquest. At its simplest, for such visitors it was a Rome of the mind that mattered, and therefore one Rome or other of the past. The practical Rome of shopping and eating, of copulation and childbirth, as well as of rival and bickering liberal politicians envisaging or planning a future, could be left to the locals, even if, it was widely suspected, they would make a mess of things.

While events were leading to what foreigners feared was perhaps the latest sack of the city and certainly the Italian rewriting and so belittling of the meaning of Rome and its histories, Pius IX had tried with deepening desperation to summon and arm words to stave off the looming nationalisation of the Eternal City. The events of 1859–61 (more than 5,000 of his citizens then accepted exile in order to join the various Italian armies) he tried to combat through the exercise of his God-given authority.[79] In April 1860 he formally excommunicated King Victor Emmanuel II, justifying the act as demanded by the history of the temporal power granted by 'divine providence' to the Church as a substitute for the collapse of the Roman empire. When that interdiction did not check the making of Italy, Pius sought to prompt international diplomatic and military action to destroy the nation state.[80] Meanwhile, news of the sudden demise of Cavour in June 1861 was greeted uncharitably, with the Jesuit journal, *Civiltà cattolica*, always close to the pope, detecting signs of a 'heavenly vendetta'.[81]

Cavour, after all, a few months before his death, had pronounced that Rome was 'the only Italian city whose memories were not exclusively municipal'.[82] Given the need for a united national history, it was therefore required to be Italy's capital, being, Cavour contended in unaccustomedly florid phrases, 'the Eternal City which, for twenty-five centuries, has piled up glory of every kind'. 'Destiny', as expressed in 'the irresistible force of public opinion and the logical unfolding of history and civilisation', he stated in words taken as prophetic after his death when the language of nationalism at once anointed him a 'martyr', must take Rome out of the hands of the pope and put it at the head of Italian rule.[83] During the 1850s Cavour may well have shared the view of his Piedmontese aristocratic compatriots, D'Azeglio and Cesare Balbo, that it was time for Italy to surpass history, whether it be that of the Caesars or of the medieval republics. In this view, the real error of 1848 had been to be too obsessed with ghosts. However, once he became Italian Prime Minister, Cavour could not forbear to read historical lessons to his successors. Another for whom Rome, before the Risorgimento, had always been foreign territory, Cavour on his deathbed decreed that its present, future and past must become Italian.[84]

While seeking to block this ambition and awaiting godly vengeance on Italy, Pius chose the tenth anniversary of the proclamation of the dogma of the Immaculate Conception, 8 December 1864, to issue his Syllabus of Errors, a list of eighty faults in modern understanding, attached to his encyclical, *Quanta Cura*.[85] Summed up in a final clause which denied that 'the Roman Pontiff can and ought to reconcile himself to, and agree with, progress, liberalism, and civilization as lately introduced', the Syllabus constituted a root and branch attack on rationalism and science as understood since the

Enlightenment, and an assertion of the perpetuity of papal authority. It was an error, Pius declared, to think that 'the Church is not a true, and perfect, and entirely free society', that 'she does not enjoy peculiar and perpetual rights conferred on her by her Divine Founder', that 'the civil authority may interfere in matters relating to religion, morality and spiritual government', or that 'the Church ought to be separated from the State, and the State from the Church'. As far as the Risorgimento was concerned, he added, it was similarly a delusion to believe that 'the abolition of temporal power, of which the Apostolic See is possessed, would contribute in the greatest degree to the liberty and prosperity of the Church'.

Was not the crucial proof of the eternity of the Catholic mission the pope's continuing presence in, and possession of, Rome? As a clerical commentator argued in 1865, it remained 'the *city*, the *world*, the *compendium of the world*', a place staffed by heroic spirits. 'Every family has a hero, or rather a Pleiad of heroes. Every stone records a hero. Every tomb shuts in a hero.'[86] In rivalling it, such citadels of modernity, science and Protestantism as London were only replicating the role taken by Carthage in its battles with classical Rome, conflicts that ended not in victory but in total defeat. At least as bad were the Anglo-Saxon cousins of the English in the USA, who had just been engaged in vicious civil war that would 'shame the followers of Mohammed'.[87] Maybe, clericals urged, in spite of much evidence to the contrary, including the Garibaldinian raids blocked at Aspromonte in 1862 and at Mentana in 1867, God might still abidingly watch over the city of cities.[88] Maybe its Catholic history could defend it yet. As a French cleric put it emphatically: 'Our strongest argument against Rome capital of Italy is Rome capital of Catholicism'.[89]

Building on massive celebration of Catholic martyrs, killed in Japan in 1597 and in 1862, canonised before an ostentatiously international congregation, underlining the universality of the Church compared with little Italy, Pius called a special jubilee for 1866–7. It attracted to Rome a claimed tally of 500 bishops, 20,000 priests and 130,000 ordinary pilgrims.[90] So well were they received that some Italian nationalists despaired of the national loyalty of the Roman populace, once again seemingly blinded to Italy and its future by their credulity and love of festivals.[91] In the aftermath of these celebrations, the pope prepared the Church to hold a General Council of Bishops, the first since the sixteenth-century Council of Trent, fount of the Counter-Reformation. It was planned to open on 29 June 1867, said to be the eighteen hundredth anniversary of the deaths of St Peter and St Paul in the city, but was delayed by political events both of the Risorgimento and within the Church, where liberal Catholics were mounting resistance to the pope's ever more drastic assertion of his own authority and charisma. In the event, with a chronology that was becoming obsessive, Pius IX opened the council at St Peter's on 8 December 1869. The congregation numbered 80,000.[92]

Over the next months, four public sessions and eighty-nine assemblies of bishops debated the issues at hand, with Pius seeking to reaffirm a Catholicism that, with refurbished universalism and perpetuity, could rebut the errors, refute the disbelief and stem the changes of modernity. Ironically foreshadowing the rise of the celebrity and the accompanying populism that has so fretted democracy into our own era, Pius made the key question that of papal infallibility. Now not only would the Church be alone in comprehending Rome's passage through time, but the pope would be its only 'truthful' interpreter. Converting himself to 'History Speaking', 'I, I am tradition; I, I am the Church!' he maintained to one critic.[93] With this endorsement of infallibility, Rome was to be refreshed as a uniquely holy city, and the pope clothed in a cultic power greater than that possessed by his predecessors.[94] Throughout the 1860s the clerical line had drifted into being 'whoever is not with the Pope is against the Pope and whoever is against the Pope is against God'.[95] Overriding the doubts of quite a few bishops, Pius on 18 July 1870, as a summer thunderstorm broke over the city, drove through the final vote. Already the international atmosphere was electric. The Ems telegram, doctored by Prussian Prime Minister Otto von Bismarck, was published on 13 July and the armies of Napoleon III in France mobilised on the 14th. The formal French declaration of war on Prussia came on 19 July. The French garrison in Rome now trooped home to rapid defeat and the humiliating collapse of their imperial regime. With their departure, the Italian state readied 60,000 men to move towards its 'historic' capital.

On 19 September, with the military situation hopeless, Pius made one last attempt to deploy the power of historical mystery in the cause of the survival of the temporal power. Ignoring the fact that he was by now almost eighty and heavily overweight, the pope knelt to ascend the Scala santa outside his Lateran palace, a sacred stairway said originally to have been part of the house of Pontius Pilate and mysteriously translated to Rome by St Helena, mother of Constantine. Reaching the summit, Pius prayed loudly and in tears, before turning to give the Papal Guard and the few score foreign volunteers, who had offered to resist Italian aggression, his blessing.[96] Thereafter he retreated to make himself what would soon be termed 'the prisoner in the Vatican'. When, the next day, the Italian armies penetrated the Porta Pia and seized the last of papal territory, Rome seemed to have ended its long life as Catholicism's holy city. Certainly, through the next decades, the official account of the place was to be produced by anti-clerical liberals and not by Catholic priests. Rome and its histories were now to be nationalised. But that ambition, too, was destined in its turn to be curbed and checked by the multiple pasts that even the nation proved unable to remove or control in the city.

PIAZZA CAMPO DEI FIORI

Monument to
Giordano Bruno ●

PIAZZA CAMPO DEI FIORI

VIA DEI BALESTRARI

VIA DELLA CORDA

VICOLO DEI GIGLIO

VIA DEI BAULLARI

PIAZZA FARNESE

VICOLO DEI GALLO

FARNESE

PIAZZA FARNESE

PIAZZA FARNESE

PIAZZA FARNESE

FARNESE

PIAZZA FARNESE

Palazzo
Farnese ●

50 feet

20 m

0

0

N

6. Campo dei Fiori

———— ✳ ————

5

ITALIAN ROME: RATIONAL AND HUMANIST

An instructive place to ponder the historical order that Liberal Italy sought to impose on newly annexed Rome after 1870 and its fate over succeeding time is the Campo dei Fiori, located not far from the classical Campus Martius and the Tiber and, by that decade, becoming 'a centre of commerce among the working classes'.[1] Today the Campo is a more ritzy square located in a bustling shopping area between the Corso Vittorio Emanuele and the Palazzo Farnese. This latter is defined by the guidebooks as 'the most magnificent Renaissance palace in Rome'; perhaps appropriately, it houses the French Embassy.[2] On weekday mornings the Campo is devoted to a food and flower market, serving tourists and those Romans who live in this part of the old city. Amid the bustle, obscured in its message and purpose is a dark statue of a cowled figure, standing on a plinth at the centre of the square. When the market is closed, it is possible to approach and survey the site: a monument to the Dominican priest, Giordano Bruno (1548–17 February 1600), judged a heretic and sent to the stake by the Inquisition but, to many, a champion of rational enquiry and opponent of clerical obscurantism. The inscription reads: '9th June 1889, to Bruno, the century that he divined, here where the fire burned'. Bruno has his head bowed and his face shadowed. He is clutching a book by its cover, its contents obscured. Lunettes commemorate the lives of such critics of the Church in their times as John Wyclif, Jan Hus, Paolo Sarpi, Tommaso Campanella (these last two troubled by the Inquisition but not its martyrs) and four other lesser-known religious dissidents prominent during the Counter-Reformation.[3]

Once again, then, a history, is inscribed here, saying that Bruno was one hero among the many brave opponents of clerical obscurantism who, in sombre times, fought for science, fearlessly asserting the human right and ability to know. In this urban setting he is presented as another 'father of the

13. Inauguration of Giordano Bruno statue, 1889.

Risorgimento', like Garibaldi, a prophet of a liberal and anti-clerical nation possessed of a long and virtuous history. Further tablets affixed to the monument's sides record prominent moments in Bruno's life, including his preaching (at Oxford), his trial and the preparations for his public incineration. Small print explains further that the statue was erected by 'Roman students with the approval of the civilised nations'.[4]

For the inauguration of the monument in 1889, an event that foreshadowed the erection of the Garibaldi statue six years later, a crowd estimated at 30,000 (judged more like 6,000 by the hostile Jesuit organ, *Civiltà cattolica*) assembled, with moderate papers insisting that the majority were by no means violent radicals.[5] One thousand of the richer or more respectable proceeded to a public banquet that evening.[6] As far as the liberal mayor of Rome, Marchese Alessandro Guiccioli, was concerned, it was a good day. The square looked 'imposing', with 'only five or six of the better houses fronting it having their windows hermetically closed' out of loyalty to the clerical cause. Some 1,900 representatives of various anti-clerical groups assembled, with flags waving. One was the mayor of Nola, Bruno's birthplace in the hills east of Naples.

Having marched across Rome down the modern Via Nazionale, the liberal worthies had filed into the Campo, so cramming it that Guiccioli had trouble pushing his way through to the speakers' platform.[7] There, the ambitions of more extreme anti-clericals had been encapsulated in a speech delivered by republican philosopher and member of parliament, Giovanni Bovio, vehemently proclaiming: 'Today Rome inaugurates the religion of reason.'[8] Guiccioli was neither republican nor radical, but he dutifully presided over the unveiling of the monument to 'general applause and acclamation' since it was, he conceded, 'a noteworthy work of art'.[9]

All in all, the mayor noted in sober review, the affair had 'passed off with perfect tranquillity'. 'The truth is that the city as a whole remained indifferent and uneasy, given the fear of disorder. The greatest number of the participants actually came from outside. In Rome itself there are no more than five hundred convinced radicals, who are confronted by five hundred militant clericals.' His Prime Minister, Crispi, who, on that sunny June day, was away parleying with Imperial Germany, Italy's ally in the Triple Alliance, received the mayoral report with a shrug, remarking 'it is the merit of Providence'.[10] Yet a recent historian has concluded that Crispi had by no means opposed the public parading of anti-clericalism and the hailing of a monument to a hero rescued from past shame by those who most strenuously objected to a lingering papal presence in Italian Rome.[11] The Vatican, Crispi enjoyed complaining, did not always behave in a Christian manner, and so must accept that its once holy or clerical city was now national and Italian. In Crispi's not so hidden agenda, the Bruno statue, and the lay and rational history that it encapsulated, here traced back to the Reformation and before, proved that Italy, not the Church, owned all Rome, all its space and all its time. That Catholicism which had judged and executed Bruno was itself now implicitly tried, found guilty and had its conviction publicly displayed in the monument. Clericalism's antique vice, Bruno's statue preached, had no place in a modern, liberal and national Rome. Even the slightest whisper of Church gospel must hereafter be silenced by the nation.

Not surprisingly, the Vatican was affronted by the event, patently displeased at Liberal Italy's aggressive adoption of anti-clericalism. Already in June 1888, Pope Leo XIII, in his encyclical *Libertas Praestantissimum*, had declared that 'history' had showed the error of 'that widely-spread and powerful organization, who, usurping the name of liberty, style themselves Liberals'.[12] Now *Civiltà cattolica* joined in remonstrating against a national government 'that was the servant of the wicked Masonic sect' and whose commemoration of a heretic was 'sacrilege', 'scarring the face of God and religion'.[13] Leo XIII let it be known that he spent 9 June, Pentecost Sunday, prostrate in prayer and fasting before an image of St Peter.[14] As another conservative diarist, Giuseppe Manfroni, in charge of public security in the city, recalled, in the face of 'an affirmation of an extreme anti-clericalism that is very far from the ideas of the great majority and has been deliberately imposed on the citizenry', that day the Church had 'put itself ostentatiously in a state of siege'. 'By the personal order of Leo XIII, the gates [of the Vatican] were shut, the sentinels doubled, a battalion of Swiss Guards was called into service, none who worked there was allowed to leave, provisions were brought in.'[15] To counter the sin of the inauguration, the Vatican held a special expiatory mass at St Peter's on 29 June, inviting as many Italians and foreigners loyal to the Church as possible to attend. At a papal consistory the next day, Pope Leo XIII suggested that, should Italian policy at home and abroad become any more radical, he would remove the Church to another place, perhaps Malta, perhaps Salzburg, perhaps Spain.[16] By no means cowed, on 18 July Crispi informed his diplomatic representatives in Berlin, Vienna and London of the matter, suggesting for his own expansionist nationalist purposes that a papal flight was a likely signal for general conflagration.[17]

A war there would not be, if only because Crispi found no other European diplomat anxious to join his cause and he was not foolhardy enough to launch a conflict alone.[18] Crispi's intention to nationalise the Italian masses, if necessary through aggression against Republican France, thereby seizing history for the nation and it alone, was scuppered for the moment. During the next decade his hope in battle switched to Ethiopia. In March 1896 imperial intrusion there met its comeuppance in the disastrous defeat at Adua and in the rancorous demonstration thereafter that modern Italians were by no means united in willing a Third Roman Empire. As a young and patriotic historian in the making recalled sadly and using his own Roman explanatory frame, the 'mob, drunk with their own cowardice', then cheered for 'barbarians'.[19]

The absence from the historical record of a 'War for Bruno's ghost' makes sense since the name of the victim of the Inquisition carried, and carries, not just Italian but international connotations, a number of which are French. The statue in the Campo dei Fiori is not printed with just one history as Crispi desired. Although Roman 'students' were said to have floated the idea of the monument, in 1885 a cosmopolitan committee, boasting among its members such intellectual celebrities as French Republicans Victor Hugo and Ernest Renan, as well as Herbert Spencer, Henrik Ibsen and Ferdinand Gregorovius, worked to achieve a permanent commemoration of Bruno's sacrifice. Once the statue was inaugurated, its message retained broad currency. In 1898 a visit to the spot by the French writer Emile Zola caused enough interest for it to be recorded by the *New York Times*.[20]

As if to prove that Bruno was as much a symbol of cosmopolitanism as of nationalism, a few years later, William Thayer, an American historian of the Risorgimento, pronounced admiringly that 'Bruno was so far in advance of his age as to be [in scepticism] . . . level with our own'.[21] Thayer has had plenty of successors in this view, with the monk possessing a fruitful afterlife in culture, high and low. Giovanni Gentile, the later philosopher of Fascism and advocate of a strong state, edited the first full collection of his works in 1906–7. James Joyce mentioned him positively in *Portrait of the Artist* and expended quite a few words on his trial and execution in *Finnegans Wake*. Giuliano Montaldo made an adulatory film of his life in 1973, starring Gian Maria Volonté as Bruno. A Cuban singer paralleled Bruno's personal oblation with that of Martin Luther King, Salvador Allende, John Lennon and the victims of 9/11. The Dominican has been invoked by a Swedish metal band, had an interplanetary spaceship named after him, and been the protagonist of a modern opera. Bruno was used by the Polish dissident poet, Czeslaw Milosz, to evoke comparisons with the German liquidation of the Warsaw Ghetto, while a popular version of his life was fictionalised by the Australian Catholic, Morris West. A commercial radio station in Sydney, first owned by local theosophists, is still called 2GB in his honour. There is even a crater on the moon named after him.

Bruno's Roman history lives into many presents and yet kindles a struggle between clericals and anti-clericals. Late in the 1990s a body calling itself the World Pantheist Forum announced plans to hold a ceremony in the Campo dei Fiori on 17 February 2000, there to give the Catholic Church and its latest *Giubileo* a public drubbing. In a trial run in 1998 the pantheists welcomed a potential alliance with local anarchists whose graffiti on the plinth of the Bruno monument urging 'Morte ai preti' (Death to all priests) had been quickly painted out by the anti-graffiti squad of the Rome Comune (then in moderate leftist hands).[22] An organisation devoted to ending what its website calls the 'dark age of pharmaceutical medicine' is similarly anxious to exalt Bruno as a hero of 'science' and therefore its patron saint.[23] In the 1920s Pope Pius XI strove unsuccessfully to persuade the newly installed Fascist dictatorship to dismantle Bruno's statue and, perhaps in compensation, canonised the Dominican's main prosecutor, Robert Bellarmine, in 1930. However, eventually, John Paul II's Church did regret those processes of the Inquisition that led to Bruno's burning (his file in the Inquisition archive had been suppressed by a watchful Leo XIII in 1886, not being 're-discovered' until 1940).[24] But the damning of Bruno in Church courts has not yet been disavowed. According to a recent account, most ordinary Romans still view the statue of Bruno with affection, yet perhaps less for the clarity of the past that it might embody than for the difficulty in pinning it down as expressing a single historical message.[25] Certainly, into the twenty-first century, a battle over the interpretation of his victimhood continues.

Plainly, then, the monument in the Campo dei Fiori is a site of memory of remarkable geographical and chronological spread. It demonstrates again that the history of Rome retains over the centuries the power to move not just those who have lived and now live in the city but people from many places. Yet, above all, it is a prime manifestation of the way that, once Italian troops burst through the Porta Pia on 20 September 1870, the new Liberal nation sought to map and harness a history in its cause, and to disencumber this allegedly good and instructive new history from the sorry old one of the Church. When Italian politicians confronted the task of 'making their nation', it must be asked, which other Roman pasts best assisted them? And how did the Church and the many foreigners who possessed their own understanding of Rome respond to a national Italian assertion of primacy in crafting the city's history?

With their easy victory, the new rulers of Rome were sure that they were fortified with virtue; their commanding nation would purge the decadence and torpor from Roman lives and overcome what was bad in its history, all its history. As an editorial enthused on 23 September: now came the end of 'fifteen centuries of mourning, of misery and pain. . . . For Rome, it is only today that the Middle Ages are over.'[26] In the mind of the Italian military commander, Raffaele Cadorna, his army, in eliminating papal rule, was disposing of a 'complete anachronism'; its fall was 'a historic necessity'. National government, Cadorna predicted, would, by contrast, swiftly ensure the 'material regeneration' of a city where 'the testimony of past grandeur and sumptuous wealth made such a contrast with the lurid huts and utter wretchedness of a good part of the population'.[27] To begin work on this happy future, on 30 September he established a Commissione di architetti e ingegneri per l'ingrandimento e l'abbellimento di Roma (Commission of Architects and Engineers for the Expansion and Beautification of Rome).[28]

What was happening, then, was that the triumphant Liberals and the defeated Catholics now and for some time cleaved to 'two separate cultural and social universes', each dependent on a different way of comprehending the connections between past, present and future and each requiring its own networks of activity and identity.[29] As Pius IX was reported to have homilised in 1871: the Liberals 'are attempting to subvert Rome both materially and morally. . . . To their schools we must oppose our own schools, to their universities ours, to their clubs, organisations and congresses, rival clubs, organisations and congresses.'[30] Their gimcrack histories would be bested by age-old papal wisdom; their concocted 'modern' truths yield to perpetual Catholic truth. To show that battle was joined, on 1 November Pius formally excommunicated those who had seized his holy city, while *L'Osservatore romano* predicted that the new government would soon perish as once had fallen the false idols of Nebuchadnezzar.[31] More wide-ranging in his list of villains and with an all but eternal time frame, Pius IX paralleled King Victor Emmanuel II with Holofernes, Absalom, Pilate, Herod, Caiaphas, Goliath and Attila.[32]

If the Church was girded for battle with the liberal State through usable histories across the ages, some of the new rulers preferred peace. As Fabio

Gori, a deputy, reported gladly, in the aftermath of 20 September there had not been 'a single cry of damnation to the priests and the pope, and not the slightest disturbance of any male or female religious who passed through the streets of Rome'. There was no reason, he maintained, why the pope could not be fully independent within his Leonine walls, while, just in case, 'a garrison of royal troops stationed in Castel Sant'Angelo could defend the government against any reactionary plot'.[33] With the matter of Church–State relations easily resolved, the new rulers could rework the city productively, drawing out its happiest past and linking it with a lofty future. The King, Gori believed, should be emblematically housed in the restored 'upper storeys of the immense imperial palace' on the Palatine. Parliament could meet in the historic Palazzo Venezia or, if that palace's Austrian owners demurred, in what was left of the Augusteo (burial place of the Emperor Augustus).[34] These and other ruins, he emphasised, were a crucial part of the city since 'they illustrate our history and draw foreigners to admire them'. Their past must be woven into the Liberal nation's present and future. The city drains functioned effectively, Gori added with liberal practicality, since they were still those of classical times. Now, an enlightened and again rational administration could lift the curse of malaria and flooding, the latter best achieved by diverting the Tiber into a canal. They could clean the streets and rest the more secure because Rome's positioning 20 kilometres inland secured it from naval bombardment.[35] At peace with the Church, Liberal rulers would make Rome improving, modern and scientific as well as national, indeed, as a natural and prime corollary of nationalisation.

But was it going to be as easy to invent a liberal Rome as Gori imagined? A Tiber flood on 28–29 December 1870, that shut down the gasworks and reduced the city to darkness, stirred papal preaching about its symbolic proof that God had turned His face from a now unholy city. Italian offers to guarantee papal independence were, wrote *Civiltà cattolica*, sacrilege, a repetition of the policies pursued with wicked endurance by Nero, Domitian, Caracalla and Napoleon.[36] Moreover, when they tried to ignore Catholic anathemas, the Liberals were scarcely united in their interpretation of what was best for the city or the nation. Only a few months after Rome had been made Italian, the dying Mazzini, still a republican, wrote of his disgust at the 'materialists who misgovern us'. In the mind of the prophet of the nation, the new rulers were tawdrily unable to sustain a transcendental history, a civic religion, that, in its purity and spirituality, could match and surpass Catholicism. As Mazzini preached: 'We look on Rome as the sanctuary of the Nation, the Sacred City of Italy, the Historic Centre, where by providential mission came Italy's message to Men, the message that makes for unity and our *initiative* in the world. . . . To us, Rome did, and does belong to Italy, as Italy to Rome. Country and metropolis form, like human organism and brain, an indivisible unity'. The city's sublime 'message' should compel all to acknowledge Italian primacy over such competitors as France, England, Germany and the Slavic world. The 'Third Rome', Mazzini vowed in terms so fate-laden and vague that many would claim their inheritance, must astonish the world or be as nothing in the great drama of human history.[37]

The other popular hero of the Risorgimento, Garibaldi, its brave and incomparable warrior (if the official line was to be believed), was equally ready to draw counsel from Rome, although a finicky Mazzinian might have found his ideas disturbingly materialist. No doubt, for Garibaldi, as for many others of the incoming regime, Rome was 'as much a spiritual ideal, a private shrine, a public aspiration, as a real urban space, a city with a physical form'.[38] Back in 1849 the Hero had told his wife, Anita: 'One hour of our life in Rome is worth a century of life elsewhere.'[39] Still a fervent anti-clerical – in 1875 he predicted that, soon, flim-flam Catholic priests would 'disappear like the priests of Jupiter' – Garibaldi now became an advocate of a rational and scientific approach to urban problems.[40] He was one among many liberals for whom modernity and 'historic cleansing' went hand in hand. Ever since Napoleonic occupation, modernisers had urged the 'isolation' of those parts of the city that they valued – usually some ruin from classical times – and the purging of what were termed 'accretions', parts of the cityscape that had been built in historical periods regarded as less evocative and meaningful, no longer worth preservation or resurrection.

For Garibaldi, the salutary issue became the Tiber, the historic river that had flooded in 1870, with further inundations in 1873 and 1874 and onwards until 1900. In December 1878 floodwaters in the Via del Corso were so deep that a sailing race was held there and archaeologists rejoiced when the dispersing waters revealed a statue of Emperor Valentinian I (364–375), 'headless but otherwise in perfect condition'.[41] In the 1870s some commentators took to arguing that the river, flowing with a past that ran into the present, miraculously understood when great events were occurring in Rome. Had not it been in spate when Romulus and Remus were nourished by the she-wolf?[42] Whether or not he agreed with such pompous readings of history, Garibaldi – who from 1875 to 1877 held the parliamentary seat for Rome I – steeling himself for what might be his last act of heroism, advocated dealing once and for all with the recalcitrant river and channelling its purpose into modernity.

In January 1875 he visited the city for the first time since his flight in 1849, to be lionised as was now the custom and his not always entirely modest expectation. Victor Emmanuel II invited him to stay at the Quirinale. When Garibaldi refused royal hospitality, Crown Prince Umberto came to see him, saying that 'he wanted to know him up close' and adding humbly that the Hero 'had a great attraction for him'. The common people, for their part, were reported to be ecstatic at the Great Man's presence, with Roman women showering him with flowers on more than one occasion. Faced with such adulation,

Garibaldi tried to be austere: 'Be serious, Romans,' he told a crowd cheering beneath his hotel balcony, 'Be serious, serious, serious.'[43] Local workers, he advised sternly on another occasion, must be like their English brothers, 'wise, well behaved, strong.'[44]

The task at hand, however, was the wayward Tiber. The river, Garibaldi urged, needed discipline. It would be best to direct its waters around the city and away from its centre. A Tiber canal could be dug for 30 kilometres, thereby giving Rome a real port. The Aniene river, which flowed into the Tiber just outside the city, could be similarly regulated and, as a result, those who resided in the malarial Campagna could be restored to health. What flow remained in the *centro storico* (historic centre) could be usefully employed carrying away the city's waste to the boundless ocean. Lest sewer outlets every hundred metres become too noisome, the stream could be covered over and the surface paved into a wide road, suitable for parades and other grand and doubtless historic celebrations of the new nation. Garibaldi explained that, in planning such a major engineering project, he wanted his nation to conquer time. History was to be channelled along with the Tiber: 'Italy, recovering its capital after so many centuries, must make Rome worthy both of ancient and of modern civilisa-tion.'[45] The project was of such moral loftiness and physical size that it could reverse 'the deterioration of the fine Italian race, which was so marvellous but has deteriorated over time', vitiated by such papal degeneracy as 'kneeling, kissing hands, genuflection.'[46]

Garibaldi's touting of a new and didactic purpose for the Tiber was thwarted, however. The parsimonious government could not see its way to funding the transformation and, on 27 November 1875, the Ministry of Public Works rejected the entire canal scheme. Instead, from 1877 the building of an ugly concrete embankment went slowly ahead; it would not be complete until 1910. When it came to celebrating modern mastery over the Tiber, Romans had to make do with the erection of an iron bridge, the Ponte Palatino. It was constructed in 1886–91 to join the Palatine and Trastevere. Under Liberal rule, eight other new but more elegant crossings of the river were added. Three deferentially saluted the Savoyards – the Ponte Vittorio Emanuele (1911), the Ponte Umberto I (1885) and the Ponte Margherita (1886–91); and three those heroes of the times, Cavour (1891–6), Garibaldi (1888) and Mazzini (1904–8). One was generically named for the Risorgimento (1911), being supplemented by the Ponte Aventino (1914–19). A crossing that was not built was suggested in the 1880s to run from Piazza della Consolazione to the Via Bonella, thereby becoming a flyover for the Forum.[47] As for Rome's sewage, much continued to dribble into the Tiber, although the wandering cows and the flocks of goats brought in through the city gates each day to provide morning milk, familiar under papal rule, were gradu-ally excluded from the modernising city.[48] Rubbish collection, a new fangled idea in the last days of papal rule, now became a daily event.

What, then, of 'the people', so often invoked by the Mazzinians and yet, for almost all liberals, so troubling in their perceived 'backwardness' and their renewed reluctance to assume a heroic place in a national history? Could they be any better disciplined and channelled than the Tiber? Could they be cleansed of the sad accretions of their past and stand forward reclothed in good histories adapted to a modern national purpose? Did it matter that, in the decade after 1870, they seemed neither for nor against the new order, as a historian would admit a century later, 'giving no tangible sign of nostalgia, rather absent from high politics just as they had been before 1870'?[49]

After all, many Romans were still illiterate (in 1901, 22 per cent of them, while, in the 1890s, public letter-writers were an everyday sight on the city's streets).[50] Admittedly not devout, they remained superstitious, addicted to being salved by priestly charity in a fashion that liberals thought demeaning and irrational. Worse, they might be vulnerable to dangerous and novel hopes in social 'combination'. As early as 1872 liberals were alarmed by strikes by garbage collectors and the drivers of horse-drawn buses, men indicating that they might see themselves as belonging to a 'working class' and tempted to adopt a Marxist reading of history instead of a liberal one. Such protests, which allegedly 'paralysed the city', reflected the challenge offered to the elite by a workers' association, the Lega operaia d'arti e mestieri, that had just been founded.[51] Equally troubling to liberal 'decorum' were the more traditional habits of Roman men of combing their hair or urinating, shouting and swearing in public, and of adults and children wandering around Rome's streets with running sores and other bodily ills exposed to public view.[52] Such unwholesome popular traditions needed purging even more than did medieval or baroque accretions on classical remains.

What, after all, should be done with the unemployed, now a group to be counted, watched and, if need be, repressed? 'A modern people', one liberal wrote severely, is not to be formed by 'those plebs who, with thoughtless blackmail, made manifest their authority by putting their fingers up or down in the Circus or by hailing a new emperor, even when he was Claudius or Elagabalus.' No; the modern citizen, official or soldier, united in disciplined ranks to 'enjoy the benefits of civilisation', must be 'devoted to work and industry'. Italian Rome needed more than monuments and museums. Bankers and Manchester-style industrialists were required. Despite the temptations offered by memories of 'the grandeur of papal spectacles and by the shadows of the Pantheon and the Colosseum', some liberals demanded that industry forge Rome into becoming 'the capital of a great state and a leader of world civilisation'.[53]

Fostering progress might be a vexing task. In occupying Rome and seizing its histories, Liberal Italy had placed itself in a tantalising dilemma. Commentator after commentator, both local and foreign, were sure that owning Rome carried ramifications beyond those of ordinary people, space and time. Already in the

1860s Alexander Herzen had pondered the matter and its meaning for the *'future of the Latin peoples'.*[54] Once Rome was retaken, he questioned: 'What act will be announced to us from the height of the Capitol and the Quirinal? What will be proclaimed to the world from the Forum or from the balcony, where for ages the pope has pronounced his blessing "*urbi et orbi*"? To proclaim "independence" *sans phrase*. But there is nothing else', he lamented. In these circumstances, would not '*bourgeois* parliamentarism' soon reveal its spiritual limitations, its materialist failure to bear deep history? Would not such heroes as Garibaldi and Mazzini be exposed as of sham greatness? Would Italy really be able to come up to their ideals and lead its neighbours?[55] Ferdinand Gregorovius had been similarly flummoxed by the Risorgimento. 'Rome', he feared, had 'lost its enchantment', while, among the new rulers, he could discern 'only the courage to act violently. Nowhere can I see a grand moral ideal. Anyone can demolish', he warned, 'but a new edifice is not to be achieved without the moral force of the people'.[56] Every new structure that was being erected in the city, he commented sadly, either was or looked like a barracks.[57]

Although not sharing these foreigners' nostalgia for papal pomp and picturesque dirt and not endorsing Mazzini's soaring ideological ambition for the Third Rome, prominent Liberal leaders were susceptible to the view that it was impossible to occupy the Eternal City without expressing a timeless and global idea. Typical was the Piedmontese Quintino Sella, Minister of Finance, 1864–6 and 1869–72, a convinced advocate of the occupation of Rome, an act which, he reckoned in modern metaphor, could and must provide 'an electric shock' to the people.[58] Once government was installed there, Sella, in February 1871, argued for a double solution to the Roman problem. In terms of town planning, best, he thought, would be to design a new city, wholly constructed outside the Porta Pia.[59] It must be isolated from the old, which should be conserved for its 'ruin value', for the revelations positive and negative that echoed through its streets and buildings about the Catholic and imperial pasts, and so for its mellow history lessons. Old history could keep its place in the old part of the city; new history would need new surrounds.

Despite the seeming approval of novelty, essential in Sella's mind was that Rome should not be tempted along the path of industrialisation that was being pursued in Milan or Turin, was common in the cities of Western Europe and was then advocated by the city's Mazzinian mayor, Luigi Pianciani. The latter wanted Rome to be equipped with 'comfortable and healthy housing, wide, straight and secure streets that were brightly lit at night, efficient drains, well-stocked markets, and plenty of fresh, clean water'; only then would it be worthy of its monuments and past.[60] Italian Rome, Sella agreed, must indeed fulfil the dream of modernity. However, for it to be a model capital, it must not be menaced by a numerous proletariat or polluted morally and practically by the spread of factories. Workers, Sella maintained, would distract from the serious intellectual debate that must occur there. Kept free of popular lust, prejudice and superficiality, Rome would not falter from its destiny simultaneously to lead Italy and the world.[61]

Asked by the great German classicist, Theodor Mommsen: 'What do you intend to do at Rome? This question worries everyone: you cannot be in Rome without some world-ranging intent. What do you plan to do?',[62] Sella had an answer. 'We did not come to Rome just to set up a colony of office workers,' he explained. The new Italy must stand for 'science' and endorse the Enlightenment project of human perfectibility. It must work for 'truth' against 'ignorance', 'prejudice' and 'error'. It must do so not merely as a nation and within the nation but as part of a European and even global project.[63] The Third Rome must signify a pacific and universal liberal empire of Peace and Progress. It must transmit good to all peoples.

Alas for these grandiose ambitions, what might be termed this liberal utopianism, that so poorly fitted the reality of the city and of the nation. While Sella and his colleagues debated the place's meaning, Rome had indeed begun to change as it experienced a building boom that would last for two decades and would more than double its population by the turn of the century. Not particularly checked by town plans scrupulously adopted in 1873 and 1881, and ignoring demands that an eye be kept on historic preservation, an Italian Rome was being constructed by rapacious developers and an immigrant workforce drawn from Lazio and the other ex-papal and ex-Bourbon territories that lay not far beyond the Aurelian Walls. The history of boom-time Rome in its first two decades under Italian control was to be less elevated than Sella had hoped. In the bust of the 1890s, when the national banking system threatened to collapse from its base in Rome, optimistic talk about world leadership seemed well out of place.

Nonetheless, initially, there was plenty of open space to work with; only 203 of the 1,467 hectares framed by the Aurelian Walls were occupied by housing.[64] Despite Sella's dismissal of their spiritual merit, clerks poured into the city as the Italian administration organised itself. Bureaucrats rose from 14.1 per cent of the population in 1871 to 19.6 per cent in 1901.[65] To find the newcomers accommodation in the city, in 1871 it was reckoned that 40,180 rooms were urgently required when only 500 were available.[66] Quickly many Church lands were seized by the State, with the number of religious houses pared down by 134, even if an ample 164 remained in 1895.[67] Yet the sequestered buildings were insufficient to meet demand, and 53 of the 142 villas that had existed within the walls of papal Rome also fell to demolishers.[68] Soon modern apartment buildings were rising pell-mell in replacement, and elegant heritage took second place to modern utility.

Similarly expanding in number were soldiers. Conservative liberal Guiccioli confided to his diary in 1877 that the Army was all that mattered for the new

State. As the only genuinely national force, it must be perpetually primed against enemies, external and internal.[69] In 1889 the garrisons that surrounded the city were staffed with 12,649 men, up from 4,000 in 1871.[70] Rome was rapidly equipped with fifteen forts and three batteries, and its defences were thereafter regularly reinforced.[71] No longer reliant on the picturesque Papal Guard, Liberal Rome was militarily modernised to be like other European cities in the current age of blood and iron.

More congenial for the moment was the symbolism of the first major public edifice of Italian Rome, the Ministry of Finance, facing a newly straightened and renamed Via Venti Settembre (20 September Street, completed in 1877; it ran from the Porta Pia to the edge of the royal palace, the Quirinal), concrete proof that Liberal Italy had opted for capitalism. The Liberal government, unlike its papal predecessor, the extensive offices made plain, wished to tax the population in an ordered, reasoned, mathematically precise and effective manner. Not long after, in 1878, a new Post Office, further essential symbol of the efficiency of modern communications, opened in Piazza San Silvestro, while eucalyptus trees, that global export of colonial Australia, were usefully planted on Monte Mario as a counter to the malaria-bringing mosquito.

Other perhaps less healthy bastions of modern or ancient living were part of the urban scene. In 1883 forty-six brothels were counted, offering clients what sounds like an underestimation of 538 prostitutes.[72] At around the same time, the city gave its first hints of adopting the modern sporting life with the foundation in 1877 of a Rifle Club and an association for rowers on the Tiber. Soon the most popular sport of papal years disappeared: *pallone con il bracciale*, a combination of football and handball that drew crowds of 20,000 to a *sferisterio* or stadium near the present Piazza Quattro Fontane and was accompanied by much betting and some riot; it was judged too undisciplined to gain modern favour. Horse racing began at peripheral Capanelle, with a 'Derby' being contested from 1884. Ten years later, a velodrome opened outside the Porta Salaria for the rapidly expanding number of cyclists.[73] Nonetheless, many liberal gentlemen still agreed with the Marchese Guiccioli who had learned from his reading of history that sport always attracted 'brutes' like the Emperor Caligula.[74] It would take quite a while before sweat and leisure won a central place in respectable Roman life.

Despite some developments, when Liberal Italy began to make its way in the world its capital city, perhaps held back by too much history, was scarcely the dynamo that sparked a modern economy. The national stock market remained, and remains, in Milan. Italian factories in time hummed in Turin and other northern cities. Italian agriculture accepted a capitalist devotion to profit or loss in the Po valley, and Bologna claimed the right to speak for agrarian Italy. Modern trade habits were pioneered in the port of Genoa.

Intellectuals who mattered were more likely to assemble and publish in Florence than in Rome. For many years, the closest Rome had to a 'national' paper was, with considerable irony, the Vatican's acidulously anti-Italian *L'Osservatore romano*. In the first decades of its existence, Liberal Rome did not win hegemony in the making of the Italian nation, be it in industry or finance, culture or history.

By the 1880s, emblematic of the ambiguities about the function of the new in urban planning in Italian Rome was the broad Via Nazionale. This 'street of the nation' was gouged down from the Viminal Hill towards Piazza Venezia (itself not yet fully framed) and the heart of classical Rome in the Forum and Capitol. At the height of the Via Nazionale lay Piazza dell'Esedra, completed in 1888, with its Fountain of the Naiads, which still surprises today in the exuberant sensuality of its statuary, added in 1901 by sculptor Mario Rutelli. The street was, however, never given the more grandiose entry statement of a triple triumphal arch as initially imagined. One charitable American observer declared it an avenue 'really worthy of a great capital', but another American, the wife of a French diplomat, perceived instead 'an abomination'.[75] With its four- or five-storey apartment buildings and spreading shops and hotels, the

14. Voluptuous Naiad on the fountain in Piazza dell'Esedra marks the summit of the Via Nazionale. Sculptured by Mario Rutelli, more decorous lions were replaced in 1901 and rather clash with the nearby monument to the '500' fallen at Dogali in Ethiopia in 1887.

street was modern in its way, but scarcely able architecturally to emulate the flair of the Champs-Elysées or the best boulevards of *fin de siècle* Vienna or Berlin – or, indeed, the imagined glory of imperial Rome.

It was hard, after all, to distinguish it from other streets in its vicinity. Away to the south-east of the Via Nazionale, a whole suburb grew on the Esquiline, its central piazza being yet another place named for Victor Emmanuel. Generally the new streets of this part of Rome, with their dense ranks of apartment buildings, worshipfully recorded the heroes of Piedmontese royal history – Prince Eugenio, the Conte Verde, Carlo Felice, Carlo Alberto – or commemorated the politicians of the new state, themselves likely to be Piedmontese or immigrants to Rome from elsewhere in the north: Cavour, Rattazzi, Farini, Gioberti, Sella, Garibaldi, Bixio and, perhaps to the disgust of his ghost, D'Azeglio. The historic names that stood out in this new sector of the city underlined the fact that it had been seized and occupied by outsiders; the streetscapes evoked their history and not that of old Romans. In reaction to what they bewailed as Piedmontisation, clerical papers habitually derided the new rulers as '*buzzurri*', fat, alien and barbarous, unable to speak the pope's tongue or to comprehend the great history of Church and Eternal City. The lower classes, with their own linguistic assumptions, labelled the newcomers 'the Italians', with much the same implication.[76]

Yet, when it came to usable pasts, classical history was, once again, the easiest to adapt to a new, now national, purpose. Among the foremost undertakings of Liberal Rome was the labour of archaeology. Its chief interpreter, notably to the English-speaking world, was Rodolfo Lanciani, the son of an architect turned papal archaeologist. Lanciani was educated at the Collegio romano, once the Jesuit centre in the city, and, in 1867, he took an engineering degree at Rome University. He began employment on excavations outside Rome for the rich Torlonia family, before, in 1872, winning appointment as secretary to the Commissione archeologica comunale. A decade later, he added the chair of Roman Topology to his quiver.

From 1876 Lanciani, who had married an American and nourished many contacts in the English-speaking world, began to publish reports in the *Athenaeum* in London and they would continue until 1913. There, and in other voluminous writings, Lanciani acted as a reporter to home and the world about the achievement and the meaning of Roman archaeology in a city being made Italian. Although he grew more nationalist over time, his tone was always confident – here was a firm believer in the science and 'progress' that liberalism stood for and endorsed. His initial article in the *Athenaeum* characteristically praised the 'improvements' being achieved through work near the railway station: 'It may be said that not one but two Romes are being reconstructed at this moment – the modern, with its boulevards, squares and churches; the ancient, with its temples, thermae, aqueducts and theatres.'[77] The engineer in him loved to tally the massive movement of soil; in the summer of 1878 he was delighted that 80,000 cubic feet had been shifted over the previous three months.[78] Ten years later, he earnestly listed further statistics. Under Italian occupation, 82 miles of new streets had been built and paved, 1,158 acres were occupied by new quarters, 3,094 apartment blocks had been erected and they contained 95,263 rooms. During the same years, archaeologists had located 192 marble statues 'in a good state of preservation', 266 busts and heads, 36,679 gold, silver or bronze coins. From the fourteenth century to 1870, 3,925 inscriptions had been unearthed in the city. Since then, he boasted, he alone had collected more than a thousand.[79] The Colosseum had been cleaned, the Forum purged of refuse, the Pantheon isolated; in 1883 this last structure was stripped of the two *campanili* placed incongruously at its side during the pontificate of Urban VIII (1623–44). Progress on the archaeological front was dizzy, and Lanciani happily applied to his labours military metaphors when he defined the latest dig as 'the winter campaign in the neighbourhood of the Sacra Via'; the Forum, he added, looked like a battlefield so sweeping were the labours there.[80] All in all, he would often say, the first purpose of the new archaeology was to demonstrate how effectively modern

15. Façade of Termini station *c.*1890 allows Rome to board the locomotive of history.

Rome and modern Italy had been marshalled. The place was busy as never before:

> The embankment of the Tiber, the new railway station in the Trastevere, the military and civic hospitals, the barracks of three regiments, the military school, the palace of the National Bank, the Law Courts, the Ministry of War, the monument to Victor Emmanuel, the Via Nazionale from Piazza di Venezia to Ponte Sant'Angelo, the Via del Tritone carried as far as Piazza Colonna, the widening of the Corso, the new bridges on the Tiber, the twenty-one large fortresses, the new ramparts, or inner circle of defence, twenty-two miles long, the new drilling and parade grounds between the Tiber and the Via Angelica, the new system of drainage – all these works in course of construction require the excavation of many millions of cubic metres of ground, every one of which may provide a surprise for the archaeologist.

They also provided employment (and fame). Of course, he added, the 'work necessary for the transformation of Rome into a clean, healthy, comfortable town, requires some sacrifice'. Losses of the picturesque were inevitable. Yet too much aesthetic or archaeological nicety should be avoided and, anyway, 'our antique, medieval and Renaissance [predictably he ignored the baroque] monuments do not lose a particle of their interest if they are delivered from their shameful and dirty surroundings'.[81] The allure of the old city, 'so deeply mourned only by a handful of artists or pseudo-artists, was the direct produce of filth, and of a half-savage state of moral and material life'.[82] Neither Italians nor their foreign friends should repine for the death of that past and its idleness. It could readily be replaced by a new past, scientifically brought back to light and teaching modern lessons.

When he addressed foreigners, Lanciani could be ingratiating. 'The old Roman aristocracy', he wrote, 'was educated under the same principles as the English aristocracy is at the present time. Latin gentlemen of the republic and of the empire, as English gentlemen of nowadays, were not brought up in laziness and inactivity, but served their country with their intelligence and their strength, fighting gallantly in their youth against the foes of the commonwealth, and sharing the cares of government in their mature age'.[83] Equally, he could, on occasion, admit that the new Rome had quite a bit that was ugly and bogus about it. Yet his firm belief in science and patriotism told him that Rome simply must assume 'the look of a modern capital, with all its comforts and disadvantages'.[84]

Foreigners should not presume too far. It was good that many nations were opening or expanding institutions in Rome devoted to the exploration of its archaeological heritage. The Germans had arrived well before the invention of a German nation state, with the creation of the Istituto di corrispondenza archeologica in 1828 (later it would be called the German Archaeological Institute). Other nations trooped behind with the foundation of their own institutions in Rome, including the British School, which opened in 1901. Before that event, a young enthusiast like Thomas Ashby was welcomed as a colleague in work on the ruins of the Campagna.[85] Nonetheless, with the creation of an Italian nation state, the accustomed cosmopolitanism of archaeological labour in the city lost traction. As far as the 'profession' was concerned, Italians and only Italians must take leadership in the field. Their views on history must predominate. So, for example, the excavation in 1899 by Lanciani's younger colleague, Giacomo Boni, of the *Lapis niger*, the 'Black Stone', possibly marking the grave of Romulus in the Forum, was read as a victory of 'Latin tradition' over that German scholarship which, since Niebuhr early in the century, had been relegating Livy's stories about the city's origins to mere myth. It also allowed Boni to press for more coherent celebration of 21 April as the 'Birth of Rome'.[86] On that day, as early as 1882, the Via Sacra (Sacred Path) from the Colosseum across the Forum to the Capitol was thrown open to a genteel public who included King Umberto I and Queen Margherita.[87]

Archaeological advances were only one aspect of what liberals viewed as a reworking of history whereby 'the Italian spirit' could supplant the papal soul in Rome.[88] Yet doubts still surfaced. By the 1880s the Italian political and intellectual elite were divided in their appraisals of their nation's achievement in occupying the city. An official account might boast that Rome had become a hive of activity and that whereas in the sleepy papal city it took ten minutes to buy a cigar and two hours to eat a meal, now everyday life had become busily efficient. Under pontifical rule, it was added, the Romans had been people 'who had seen too much of the world to be able to marvel'; 'this eternal Rome had an effect like the sea, before which it simply seems stupid to worry about our annoyances, vanities and enviousness and where the heart simply has to widen into benignity and indulgence'. This Rome, it was argued with liberal propriety, had been 'for time what the ocean was for space'; there, mere flotsam on the whirligig of time, the eras had mingled without reason.[89] Now, harnessed into a sleekly modern history serving the Italian nation, the city could progress headlong and intrepid to a great future.

A more common reaction among the liberal elite, however, was to feel dwarfed by the histories of Rome and depressed or angry at the thought that the Italians were not mastering them. The metaphor of the moment was that Liberal Rome had become not the capital of a dominating empire but rather a corrupt 'Byzantium', degenerate despite its youth. As has already been noted, the thought that what Rome really taught and embodied was not power but decay, was, after all, an interpretation that had long been attached to the city. Thus the journalist Rocco De Zerbi phrased it in a speech delivered, fittingly, in Milan, in 1882: 'Now what Italy is missing is Rome! What they call Rome isn't Rome. It is Byzantium.' A real Rome, he prophesied, would only reacquire meaning when it could refresh and rally 'the tired youthfulness of the Italian spirit'.[90]

The most celebrated spokesman of a generation of intellectuals convinced that something had gone wrong with Italy since its political unification was the Bolognese poet, Giosuè Carducci. Once a Mazzinian, Carducci had argued for a return to the models coined by Cicero, Virgil and Horace. In the 1850s he urged that the classical empire offered a contemporary example; only by celebrating and mimicking it could the 'disgraceful stupid, drunken, base, small, [and] womanly' present be revived by a worthwhile history.[91] After 1870, however, these hopes seemed blighted and Carducci grew frustrated and irritable. He parodied Pius IX's ascent of the Scala santa with the claim that the Liberal government had done the same or worse in its appeasement of the Vatican after its troops had justly seized the city: 'on its knees with a rope around its neck, crossing its arms and shouting "Excuse me – I cannot help doing this – they have shoved me from behind!" '[92] Now Carducci's radicalism switched into a generic disgust with his present. 'Vulgarity', he lamented, had 'invaded art, thought, politics, life – from the Palace of Finance in Rome vulgarity dominates, the only god'.[93]

Thus uprooted from the contemporary and the past, Carducci began to think of himself as an aristocrat of the intellect, drifting right to applaud those who preferred an authoritarian solution to Italy's inability to stand tall as the heir of what mattered in Rome. In 1887, backed by Bovio, he was offered the chair of Dante Studies at the University of Rome but rejected the chance to employ the national capital as a forum for his strident nationalising of the medieval religious poet or to purvey his view that Dante was by definition a Ghibelline, hostile to all popes.[94] In 1895 Carducci again sought to decipher the messages left by the classical past, paralleling the contemporary enthusiasm for a cosmopolitan 'Third Rome' with the disgraceful fate of 'the Syrian Rome of Elagabalus'. Rome must not be suborned by 'Protestants, Lutherans, Calvinists and Anglicans', he warned. It must not sponsor 'a bourgeoisie of people who rent out rooms ... antiquarians, who sell everything – conscience, holiness, erudition, the fake relics of martyrs or of Scipio, and real women [*sic*]'. The city must rise above its false foreign lovers. Goethe, Chateaubriand, Niebuhr, Gregorovius and Mommsen – each was doubtless clever but each in his heart disdained contemporary Italians.[95] They must be ignored when they gave counsel about Rome. Where Sella and his generation – and, somewhere amid his phrasing, Mazzini, too – had deeply desired a national-liberal internationalism, Carducci was drifting towards xenophobia, wherein the pretensions of foreigners to partake in the history of Rome must be checked. In this new contest, anti-clericalism might no longer be the central matter. In the minds of Carducci and his fellow national liberals, the real issue was that Rome must possess only one history, an Italian one that was above all imperial. In its manufacture, the Church was doubtless still some sort of foe. But its threat was not nearly so immediate as that of liberal (or socialist) cosmopolitans, be they foreign or Italian.

A generation younger than Carducci, Alfredo Oriani was another Romagnole writer, eventually to earn fame as a Hegelian nationalist. Soon after 1870 Oriani travelled south by train to see and comprehend his country's capital. As he approached Rome, he grew pensive. The swampy country outside the city, the *agro romano*, devastated by malaria, seemed 'sad like the threshold of old age'. As he watched it pass, 'an inexpressible feeling of melancholy invaded my soul. I was penetrating the tomb of a civilisation that had delighted my adolescence. I was penetrating a solitude where silence was more eloquent than any voice and squalor was more masterful than any chance of flourishing.' Once 'the rulers of the world' had lived here, bejewelled with every conceivable treasure. Now all was altered except the sky that mocked the peasant as he harvested death from the cursed land. Only a sudden view of San Pietro offered Oriani some redemption.[96] Yet Catholicism could not provide the formula that a modern nation demanded. For Oriani, history taught that the solution lay in 'Africa' and the renewed imperial destiny that must be confronted there.

Here were ideas with a future. The fledgling national empire, however fated never to be more than a thing of rags and patches, began to be accorded significant monumental space in Rome. On 26 January 1887 an expeditionary force of 540 men, patrolling the border between the partially established Italian colony of Eritrea and Ethiopia, was attacked by indigenous forces. Four hundred and thirty Italians perished in what was called 'the Battle of Dogali'. The loss set

16. Huts in Campagna with 'anti-malarial' mosquito nets present a less than modern life for the poor, 1911.

in motion a wave of patriotism in political and intellectual circles, with the decision rapidly being made to name a square after the heroic '*Cinque cento*' (they
had been rounded up to 500 in doubtful historical parallel with the Spartans
who had died at Thermopylae, although some commentators preferred a
connection with the 300 Fabii fallen in 477 BCE).[97] Piazza dei cinquecento would
stand between the massive ruins of the Baths of Diocletian, the National Roman
Museum, opened at its side in 1889, and the modern railway station. At the
piazza's centre and confirming the parallel with imperial Rome would be erected
an Egyptian obelisk that had recently been discovered during excavation in the
Via Sant'Ignazio.[98] It was set on a piece of Bavarian granite and on its plinth the
names of the gallant dead at Dogali were recorded in gold lettering.[99]

Ruggero Bonghi, Professor of Latin and Ancient and Modern History,
journalist, parliamentary deputy, Minister of Education (1874–6) and first
president of the patriotic society named after Dante Alighieri, gave the key
historical interpretation. The shedding of blood in Africa and its commemoration in Rome demonstrated that Italy was a nation. Bonghi summoned the
dead to transmit their historic meaning: 'For the first time because of your
acts, the workers of the countryside [and] the workers in the city have felt
deep down in their hearts that the fatherland for which the soldier dies, for
whose future he sacrifices himself, is not the town of his birth or this or
that region of Italy . . . but it is Italy itself, the whole of Italy, which has had so
many glories in the past, and barring a failure on our part, will have as many
in the future.'[100] Even the Vatican, it was thought, embraced the Italian colonial
cause (hopeful that a new Italian empire, while seeking glory and gold, would
bring God to the natives).[101] Now and later, when first Crispi and then
Mussolini made Ethiopia, a territory where the legions of the Caesars never
trod, the prime target of expansion for the 'Third Italy', Rome and *romanità*
were repeatedly joined in clamorous if jumbled justification of a new
imperialism.

Yet, while Italian nationalism conscripted the Caesars to its cause, foreigners
were hardening in their opposing views of the inadequacy of contemporary
Italians, all the more when measured against what might be agreed was any
Roman past. Few European statesmen demurred when Bismarck joked that, in so
far as empire was concerned, Liberal Italy had a large appetite and very poor
teeth. As the nineteenth century ended, racial theoretics were everywhere
spreading in respectable discourse and were fusing with Social Darwinism in
persuading many that the world must be driven forward through a struggle of the
fittest. Few believed that modern Italy – alleged home since the mists of time of
the 'Mediterranean race', third and most deficient in Europe – was a natural victor
in such a contest.

Memory of classical times, if sometimes in the humble garb of tourist
commentary, was ironically reinforcing effortless foreign superiority at the

very moment that it was pushing Italians towards imperial adventure. As ever, Rome was the place where lessons could be most easily read. The works of Augustus Hare, republished in twenty-two editions over the decades leading to the First World War, are an example.[102] For Hare, Rome or, rather, Rome's past was glorious but its new Liberal owners could do little right. Typically sordid was the area around the Ministry of Finance:

> Here, since the change of government in 1870, have arisen many of the ugliest buildings of the new town; – wide, shadeless streets of featureless, ill-built, stuccoed houses, bearing foolish names connected with Piedmontese history, and a wretched square called the *Piazza dell'Independenza* [sic], in the construction of which much of interest and beauty was swept away, though its ill-built houses tumbled down before they were finished. Whilst some of the improvements in the old town are well executed, there is not a single point in the entirely modern Rome which calls for anything but contempt. Hastily run up, with the worst materials, and by the most unskilled workmen, its buildings seem destined to perish within the century.[103]

The Esquiline was, to Hare's mind, now covered by 'buildings of the most pitiful and mean kind'. The square in front of San Lorenzo had been similarly wrecked by the expansion of the Campo Verano, 'a hideous modern cemetery'.[104] Only the old retained its magic; its message and meaning were more salutary for stout foreigners than for feckless modern Italians.

Other commentators, even those lavish in expressing love of the place, agreed. As F. Marion Crawford, a long-term American resident, explained: 'a man can no more say a last farewell to Rome than he can take leave of eternity. The years move on, but she waits; the cities fall, but she stands; the old races of men lie dead in the tracks wherein mankind wanders always between two darknesses; yet Rome lives, and her changes are not from life to death, as ours are, but from one life to another.' Yet doubts lurked about the present day. 'Rome is one of the poorest cities in the civilised world,' Crawford conceded, 'and when she was trying to seem rich, the element of sham was enormous in everything.' The inhabitants of Trastevere, he feared, occupied the same lowly rank of civilisation held by the 'scalping' 'Indians' of his own country's West.[105]

In the eyes of many foreign observers, modern Italians, fickle and overtalkative, in their capital a thievish people dwarfed by the giant's robe of history, were failing the test of time and, it was automatically assumed by most who visited from north of the Alps, had yielded the imperial and governing torch, Roman greatness, to the British or Germans. As nationalist historian Heinrich von Treitschke put it, the classical Romans had 'impregnated the German races with their genius for State construction' but thereafter tragically 'lost the moral strength to enforce and uphold its own beliefs'.[106]

One pressing issue for European elites was how the masses, especially given their predilection for voting socialist, striking and forming themselves into menacing unions, could be blended into the weft of the modern state. In Italy as elsewhere, the socialist movement for the most part remained cool to Roman myths. The empire, after all, had been a slave-owning society and could scarcely be plumbed for socialist lessons suitable for the present or future. Marx had in the 1850s pointed to 'the horrors recorded of the latter times of the Roman empire' as having some potential parallel with current 'symptoms of decay' in Europe. However, he failed to follow up his insight with rigour.[107] It might be true that somewhere in the left's index of a useful past was saved a statement of Marx to Engels in 1861 that Spartacus, leader of the slave revolt of 73–70 BCE, was 'a great general, a noble character, and the authentic expression of the ancient proletariat'.[108] But Marx was testy about his Italian socialist contemporaries, writing them off as 'lawyers without clients, doctors without knowledge or patients, billiard-playing students, commercial travellers and various more or less unsavoury journalists of the gutter press'.[109] The Italian socialist movement did organise a political party for itself in 1892 and its Rome Chamber of Labour, founded that same year, became a serious player in the city's local elections. Its watchword gave qualms to Crispi and any who believed in a nationally united modern people: 'for us, Clericals and *liberals* are all the same'.[110] However, even if quite a few in the ruling elite were, by 1900, fearful of socialism's advance in Italy, the worst threat was confined to such working-class redoubts as Turin, to the peasant unionism of the Po valley or to dissident southern intellectuals, who were more likely to be found in Naples than in Rome. In 1900 only a few Romans as yet were converts to the Marxist charting of time.

Instead, in the capital for the moment at least, the most overt political battles and the major disputes over history were still those between the liberal nation and the Church, as the controversy over the monument to Giordano Bruno made evident. In 1881, for example, the transfer of the body of Pius IX, who had died three years earlier, to the basilica of San Lorenzo prompted street brawls late at night between partisans of the two causes. Into the 1890s the Church maintained its half-threat one day to desert impious modern Rome for some more sacred place where history still stood undisturbed. Leo XIII, for all his acknowledgement of modern social and economic life in his encyclical *Rerum Novarum* in 1891, continued to expect priests to address him as the *Papa Re* (Pope King).[111] In 1900 he moved to celebrate a Holy Year, despite being restricted by the forms of his 'imprisonment in the Vatican' (no religious processions were yet permitted in the city). He did so while complaining that Rome lay under 'enemy domination', but was still ready to predict the eventual restoration of temporal power.[112] Despite the fact that, once in office, he had quickly sold the last vestige of the papal navy, a paddle steamer named the *Immaculate Conception*,[113] the pope sonorously invoked the hope of a 'second Constantinian age', when the 'paganism' that had overwhelmed modern society would be checked and beaten and the course of true history resumed.[114] The *Giubileo* was hardly begun when *L'Osservatore romano* was inveighing against the temptation to immorality being offered in plush city shops; foreigners of any religion, it predicted unconvincingly, would be shocked by the 'sink of iniquity' evident there.[115]

In reaction, anti-clericals took pains to assemble in front of the statue to Bruno, both on 17 February and on 20 September 1900. Yet, in the decade since the monument's inauguration, times had changed. For those men of Liberal Italy who governed Rome, the practical and modern estimation of a revived *Anno Santo* was expressed in the establishment journal, *Nuova Antologia*. For them, to all intents and purposes, religion had now become a private matter. Church history could be divorced from that of the State; it might not need to be liquidated. In the rational present, Holy Year, rather than proving an intellectual or spiritual threat, could be treasured 'as an economic resource'. Apart from real pilgrims, it was noted, in 1900 many 'curious' would arrive in Italy's capital, 'attracted by the special reductions made available for rail travel and by the illusion of joining in a major spectacle'.[116] According to the diarist, Giuseppe Manfroni, liberal society, despite its rationality and its unabashed anti-clericalism, sought as many front-row tickets as possible to the public events in St Peter's; he was, he wrote wryly, in that regard 'literally besieged by all political, military, judicial and administrative authorities and by the two branches of parliament'.[117] Now, papal evocations of the Church's glory and longevity no longer fired an anxious frisson through the liberal elite lest the national capital was not really 'theirs'. For them, Catholic history, rather than offering a clarion call to battle, was withering into a pleasing opportunity for sellebration (that is, a marketed celebration). Now, rather than being feared and countered, it could simply be consumed.

Yet, if peace of a kind had, for the time, broken out on this front, other wars about the past smouldered or ignited. At various moments since 1870 liberal internationalist, rationalist-scientific, liberal nationalist, national imperialist, Savoyard, Catholic, republican, socialist and populist readings of a past, present and future for Rome had won followers in the new Italy, while foreigners still energetically drew their own messages from a real or imagined Rome. But, in the twentieth century, this span was to narrow. A radical libertarian like Bruno (if that is what he really was) did not point the way to the future. Liberal tolerance of multiple histories would prove shallow and short-term. The nation could not subscribe to the cosmopolitan. Rather, for a generation and more, Rome's present, past and future were read to mean empire, authority and, eventually, war and Fascism. In retrospect, of all the contending commentators who wrote about the new national capital, the Neapolitan novelist, Mathilde Serao, had seen the future most clearly, when, as early as 1884, she wrote in a novel entitled *Conquista di Roma* (The Conquest of Rome):

> Someone must come to disturb that serenity, to vanquish that indifference [that still flowed through the city]. Someone must conquer Rome, whether for ten years, for one year, for one month; but he must conquer it, must capture it, must avenge all the dead, all the fallen, all the feeble who have touched its walls without being able to overcome it. But, ah! such a one must have a heart of brass, an inflexible, rigid will; he must be young, healthy, robust, and bold, without ties and without weaknesses; he must apply himself profoundly, intensely to that one idea of victory.[118]

Four years later, a visit from the new young German Kaiser, William II, touched off similar boasts in the semi-official Liberal journal, *Nuova Antologia*. Italian Rome, the Kaiser was instructed, shone anew with its 'splendid memories and sublime traditions'; they led inexorably to 'new grandeur'. United Italy was not really creating a fresh Rome but merely allowing all the Romes and their magic and conquering destiny to shine through again.[119] Yet, as thoughts of empire revived and flourished, of the very many historical ghosts evidently alive in the Eternal City, bald Caesar would, over the next decades, prove the hardest to bury or contain.

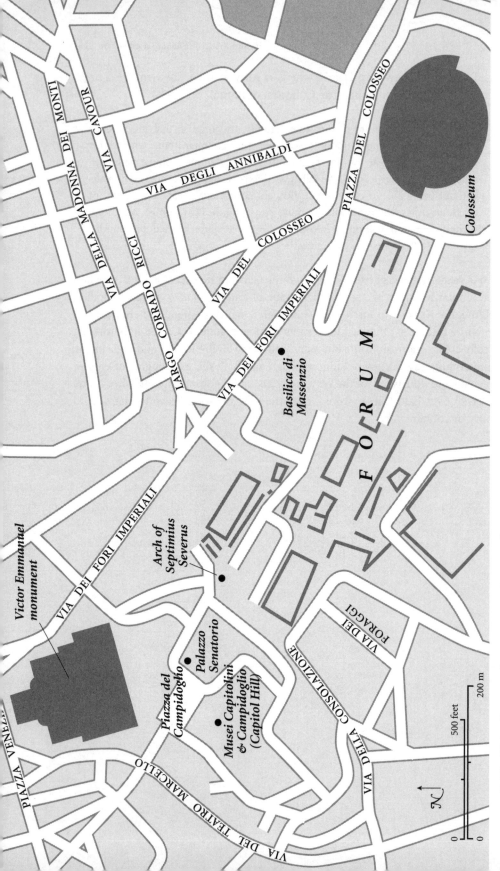

7. The Victor Emmanuel monument and surrounds

———— ✳ ————

6

ITALIAN ROME: NATIONAL AND IMPERIALIST

Of the city sites whose histories are explored in this book, the most obvious and unavoidable is the glaringly white, massively pillared and stepped, confrontingly imperial-looking Vittoriano. This commemoration of King Victor Emmanuel II (d. 1878) stands at the heart of Rome, brazenly outshining the half-hidden monuments to the *carbonari* of 1825, the Garibaldis, Cavour, Mazzini and Giordano Bruno. It proclaims loudly that a monarch matters more than any politician or intellectual. Its placement is as strident as its architecture. The Vittoriano faces Piazza Venezia, rendered notorious between the wars by the presence of the *palazzo* where, from September 1929 to July 1943, Mussolini had his office. It was from this *palazzo*'s balcony that he harangued the crowds and it was in those surrounds that dictator and followers bellowed their approval of 'Mussolini's Roman Empire'. Still more emblematically, the Victor Emmanuel monument is dug into the hillside of the Capitol, sacred place of Roman government, whether in classical times or during the Middle Ages and Renaissance. Here stands the statue of Marcus Aurelius (161–180 CE), sitting majestically on his horse. The Emperor, raising his hand in what Fascists could interpret as a 'Roman salute', seems perpetually to bless the monument to the first king of Italy. Everything about the Vittoriano's site and bulk shouts its desire to represent the 'Third' Rome, its intention to connect the monarch's story with a glorious and imperial past and so to pave the way to as grand and imperial a future.

The architecture and furnishing of the building confirm this purpose. Today few can fail to notice on its summit the twin burnished Winged Victories, charging northward in their chariots as if to repel a renewed 'barbarian' challenge, and the Tomb of the Unknown Soldier, each added after the First World War. The tomb was erected beside the Altare della Patria (Altar of the Nation), designed by Angelo Zanelli – a sculptor who was effortlessly to transfer from

17. Victor Emmanuel monument under a slow and tardy construction, *c*.1900.

Liberal to Fascist subjects – as an austere and 'Roman' structure.[1] Allegedly inspired by Virgil's *Eclogues*, one side of the Altar celebrates labour, mainly agricultural but with a segment on industry. The Altar's other face displays three women bringing crowns to Rome, the *labari* or legionary standards of the late empire, a chariot of victory, a hero and the sacred fire of the *patria*. An inscription reads PATRIAE UNITATI CIVIUM LIBERTATI (nation be united, citizens be free).

Elsewhere on the vast monument (135 metres wide and 70 high), the historical references grow more eclectic. The fame of such Italian cities as Amalfi, Ravenna and Urbino, despite being relatively fleeting, is united with the more lasting significance of Florence, Naples, Milan, Palermo and Venice. Sixteen colossal statues represent Italy's chief provinces. On the sweeping stairway at the front stands an equestrian statue of the dead king, itself 12 metres tall. A droll photograph from the time of its erection displayed workmen at the site communing with wine and bread from a table set up in the horse's belly. Within the whole edifice is located a Museum of the Risorgimento, erratic in its record of being open, but stoutly offering a patriotic account of modern Italian history, as well as rooms that house standards from one national military triumph or another, added on 24 May 1935, the twentieth anniversary of Italy's entry into the First World War.[2]

18. Workers socialise in the belly of the horse that King Victor Emmanuel II sits upon.

In much of its appearance, and particularly in its insertion into Rome and its histories, the monument might seem well to express Fascist aggression and hyperbole, a totalitarian dictatorship's drive to world power. Yet, although it was not fully complete until the interwar period, the Vittoriano was conceived and largely constructed in Liberal Italy. It was officially opened in June 1911 at a high moment of the *Cinquantennio* or fiftieth anniversary of national unification. It was indeed meant to make concrete the achievements of the Risorgimento and to bond the present and future of the Third Italy and the Third Rome to the history of their predecessors. It reflected a time when the Italian nation was drifting into its version of imperialism but when some of the more generous and cosmopolitan aims of early liberalism had not yet been renounced.

True, as always in Rome, whispers of heretical doubts about renewed dreams of empire were easy to hear. The London *Times* found it hard not to be patronising about the assertion that present-day Rome was now ready to live up to its ancient glory:

In the Victor Emmanuel Monument, which has been erected in Rome in this year of [national] Jubilee, the Romans seem to insist that their city belongs to the present as well as to the past. The position, the size, and the character of the monument have all been resented by foreigners, for whom Rome is the great city of the dead, and who wish living Romans to be mere caretakers

19. Inauguration of Victor Emmanuel monument, too early for the summer heat.

of what the past has left to them. They complain that the monument dwarfs everything near it and is an arrogant rival even to the Dome of St Peter's; and indeed it is true that in any wide view of the city the monument and the church are now the two chief landmarks. But the Romans themselves are not content that Rome should be a city for tourists and students. They regard it as their own city, which, in its triumph over time, has taken on a new life as the capital of United Italy. For them the present means more than the Imperial or Papal past; and they are determined that the past shall not tyrannize over them. The monument is a symbol of this determination; and we ought to admire the spirit of a people who, not being over-rich, are ready to make such huge material sacrifices for this expression of their pride in the present and their confidence in the future.

After all, the editorial added in terms that seemed borrowed from a head-master's speech day oration:

We have to remember that, if Rome in the fall of ancient civilization had remained spellbound by its past, it would never have been the Eternal City and unique among all the cities in the world because, through all the changes and catastrophes of history, it has, out of its primacy in the past, developed some new kind of primacy in the present, and expressed them all in the monuments of successive ages. . . . Foreigners . . . resent these pretensions of the modern Romans, and scoff at their attempts to express their present in art. No doubt the monument to Victor Emmanuel has many faults, but it also has this great merit, that it is alive, and in spite of some triviality and vulgarity of detail does express the spirit and pride of modern Rome. It proclaims to the world that Rome is once more a city of free citizens and mistress of her own destinies.[3]

Whether all Italians rejoiced at such a magisterial review must be doubted. However, there was relief that the monument was at last open. Plans to honour the dead king had been mooted in the Rome City Council in January 1878, only a few days after Victor Emmanuel's death and before he was buried in the mighty surrounds of the Pantheon, extolled by Augustus Hare as 'the most perfect pagan building in the city'.[4] Over the next years suggestions were made for a royal monument that could be lit by electricity in the most modern manner imaginable or that would tower above anything else in the city, a pillar combining the artistic appeal of the Leaning Tower of Pisa and Trajan's Column but much taller than either.[5] There was also talk of ousting the statue of Marcus Aurelius in favour of the 'Father of his Country', as Victor Emmanuel was regularly called. Confronted by such chatter and anxious that the modern should trump the ancient, Ruggero Bonghi reprimanded the Chamber of Deputies for being too fixated on past designs. Members must not become bogged down by 'the residues of ancient Rome, mistress of the world'. The new Rome, 'Italian Rome', Bonghi believed, had a 'different destiny. The times have changed,' he urged, and the monument must express that modernity.[6] The architect and *littérateur*, Camillo Boito, by contrast, preferred a monument that would be 'a kind of historical synthesis, a philosophy of history'.[7]

The debate between these and other commentators about the relative space to be granted to past, present and future in any monument to the King and the variety and level of nationalist celebration to be expressed there threatened to be endless. To resolve it, in 1880 an international competition was announced and, after assessing the 294 entries, its selection committee, with what seemed liberal internationalist propriety, gave the prize to a Frenchman, Henri-Paul Nénot. He had designed a gateway to the city at the top of the Via Nazionale and in front of the railway station, where a stately column was to be surmounted by a statue of the King with arm raised.[8]

But soon there were mutinous murmurs that his project was hackneyed, as might be expected from a personage who, although resident in Rome, was alien, no better than 'a pensioner of the French Academy' in the Villa Medici.[9] The journalist, Carlo Dossi vehemently denounced the whole exercise, deriding the 'holy madness' that, he could only conclude, had inspired many of the designs, thereby expressing if not analysing the ideological confusion of Italian liberalism as the nineteenth century drew to a close. Quite a number of contestants had opted most aggressively for anti-clericalism as the point of any monument, flaunting Liberal Italy's boasted modernising victory over antiquated religion. One concoction, centred at Castel Sant'Angelo (to be entered by a little train), featured Christ with his back symbolically turned to the Vatican. Another, less scientifically, portrayed the King in a kind of Assumption, lifted into the clouds and there mystically surpassing the Virgin as the protector of the people.[10]

Whatever the detail eventually to be made concrete on the monument, most agreed that, if memory of the King's spirit was posthumously to accelerate the nationalisation of the masses, it must be crafted by an Italian, all the more given the never eliminated fear that the Savoys were themselves a foreign Piedmontese dynasty. The offer to Nénot was revoked and a second contest held. This time the victory went to a man who more securely embodied Liberal Italy, Count Giuseppe Sacconi, born in 1854 near Ascoli in the Abruzzi, but later a student at Rome's Istituto delle belle arti.[11] On 30 December 1884 Sacconi formally took charge of the building. He rejected suggestions that the monument should feature a 'national style' that would mimic the Renaissance, opting instead for what was deemed 'a highly cultured re-elaboration of ancient Greek and Italic-Roman' architecture, a structure, it was explained, that would 'bring the past into the present and backdate what was current'.[12] Despite complaint from Rodolfo Lanciani, who, in 1883, called the location 'a national calamity' in what he deemed its modern clashing with the ancient messages being unearthed by archaeologists from classical times, the Vittoriano was to be situated in the area between the Palazzo Venezia and the Campidoglio.[13] Work, both of demolition and construction, commenced. Its intention was to merge the ancient and the modern; in its historical synthesis, the monument must teach the people that they were Italians and always had been.

In March 1885 King Umberto I turned the first sod, and by 1897 the altered Piazza Venezia was being hailed as 'the Italic Forum of modern Rome'.[14] However, progress was sluggish and the initial prize-winning plan was soon subject to amendment, notably when the eight statues of such 'national heroes' as Mazzini and Garibaldi were dropped; their presence, it was feared, might infringe the glory of the King. Costs skyrocketed; from an initial budget of 3 million lire, by the early 1890s Sacconi was talking about 21 million, and that figure was soon exceeded.[15] Amid the lengthy financial crisis of this vexed decade for the national economy, construction at the site faltered. Sacconi himself was finding his architect's task arduous, as well as being haunted for a while by the fear that his officer brother had been captured by the Ethiopians at Adua.[16] Moreover, Sacconi had not approved the appointment in 1889 of the young and radical-sounding Freemason, Enrico Chiaradia, to sculpt the statue to the King, and there were further complications when Chiaradia died suddenly in August 1901, with his labour incomplete.[17] By then, Sacconi was himself sickening from heart trouble, his medical condition not improved by his obsessive keeping of a dossier of attacks on the monument, reckoning that they spitefully exhibited 'an anti-national spirit'.[18] Sacconi died of a cerebral haemorrhage on 22 September 1905. Just before his death, he approved the idea of the addition of the Altare della patria; but when he went to his tomb his edifice was anything but finished, its purpose and meaning, its place in urban history, anything but clear.

Yet by now nothing could stop the Vittoriano and, as plans for the 1911 anniversary began to be unveiled, such rationalist liberals as recurrent Prime Minister Giovanni Giolitti and Ernesto Nathan, the radical mayor of the city, defended the project. In 1910 the 50-ton statue of the King was heaved to the site on a number of horse-drawn carts. The edifice, it was now declared, constituted a *Nuovo Capitolium fulgens* (a shiny new Capitol). The historian and journalist Guglielmo Ferrero reckoned it was the 'triumphant monument of a philosophy representing the new Italian state . . . not only in its past glories . . . but also in its future efforts, struggles and duties'.[19] Giolitti, in his speech at the opening ceremony on 4 June 1911, held at 8.30 a.m. lest foreign dignitaries be too discomforted by the city's torrid summer heat, was studiously moderate by comparison with such flights of rhetoric. He did agree that the Vittoriano recalled 'the glories and greatness of Rome' but he took pains to welcome the presence of delegates from the 'allied and friendly nations' (required terminology due to Italy's involvement in the Triple Alliance with Germany and Austria, and its contradictorily happy ties with Britain, Russia and France, members of the rival Triple Entente). His country's mission, now that it had passed its fiftieth anniversary, was, Giolitti affirmed, 'peace and civilisation'.[20] At least on such an occasion, mention of empire could be avoided and Italian liberalism could remain a virtuous ideology of progress and improvement.

Other voices were more discordant. The socialist daily *Avanti!*, still edited in Rome but about to be transferred to bustling capitalist and proletarian Milan, had its doubts about what it sardonically labelled the *monumentissimo*. Generally, it reported, the ceremony of 4 June had done nothing to suture the gap between rich and poor, between the theory and the practice of the Liberal government and between the imagined glory of Rome and the social reality of the rest of the country. The real union of Italians, it pronounced, was 'no more complete than the monument was'.[21] Talk about three thousand years of national history should not conceal the fact that Italians drew their most powerful and modern identities from class. *Civiltà cattolica*, pro-Catholic and friend neither of socialists nor liberals, stated that, rather than celebrating, Italy should join in 'a year of mourning' in 1911; in a better world, the loyalty of Italians would turn back to St Peter's and the Vatican, which 'can offer the security of unshakeable strength against all the assaults of Hell'.[22] The Jesuits' paper was even more appalled when, a couple of months later, 'the Jew' Nathan led a grand public commemoration of 20 September, thereby displaying again 'his stupid and childish ambition to parade as an anti-pope'.[23]

The various dissident intellectuals of the country, whether Nationalist or 'Futurist', were similarly little mollified by the Vittoriano's expression of nationalised history. One of their more fertile wordsmiths, Giovanni Papini, damned the monument as a *Vespasiano di lusso* (a de luxe public urinal; the Emperor Vespasian (69–79), these days best known as the sagacious chief in Lindsey Davis's detective stories, had allegedly first sponsored such useful devices). Expanding the rhetoric of the city's enemies, Papini proceeded to excoriate Rome more generally; the city, he wrote, was a 'whore', corrupting her customers with 'chronic archaeologism'.[24] To his mind, the cheap, fake classical, history of the nation's capital gave no useful guidance to modern Italy. Papini's Futurist friends went further, suggesting captiously during a street demonstration they had organised in 1910 that Rome's classical remains should be bulldozed, the debris raked up and buried in an impenetrable coffin somewhere in the heart of town.[25] Despite the contempt they expressed for history, from December 1913 the group opened a 'Permanent Futurist Gallery', allegedly prompted by the desire to reverse what Giuseppe Sprovieri regarded as the palpable inferiority of Italian art compared with that of other nations.[26] He and his colleagues did not remark that the boast of permanence hinted at how inconsistent the Futurists were in their bourgeois desire to skewer the bourgeoisie. Impermanent in fact, the gallery failed within a few months. Dashing Futurist events in the city, however, went on being staged, often scandalously designed to mock the backdrops of ancient ruins, and Giacomo Balla and Ferdinando Depero, eminent members of the movement, influential in the rise of Fascism and expressive of young Italians' discontent with liberalism, pursued their careers in Rome.

In 1911, then, the Victor Emmanuel monument shimmered in the sunshine. But its historic meaning was by no means settled and would remain in dispute for many years. Why, it should be asked, were there such divisions at a time of commemoration and celebration? What did they show about Rome after four decades of national government with its more or less emphatic desire to nationalise the masses through a patriotic reading of the passage of time? What did the wrangling over the monument and Rome signify about the history wars in Liberal Italy at a time when, in retrospect, it can be seen that the First World War was looming?

Despite all the emphasis on national history, Rome was still, after all, in quite a few senses a holy city, given the surviving presence of the Vatican and the retention of the Catholic version of past and future. In 1903 Leo XIII had been succeeded by Pius X, marketed as a 'peasant pope', although his father had been a village postman in the Veneto and later a bailiff. In calling himself 'Pius', the new pontiff was endorsing the inheritance of Pius IX, whether in regard to papal infallibility and the Syllabus of Errors or the determination that some version of the temporal power should be restored. The new pope's special concern became aggressively to check the spread of what, in Catholic circles, was anathematised as 'modernism'. Society, in Pius X's view, should be arranged hierarchically as God intended and as the Church itself was, or should be, governed; to ameliorate the fate of the suffering poor, those who assumed leadership roles could disburse charity where required (and earned). All modern politics, the new pontiff preached, especially anything that smacked of liberal, let alone socialist, democracy, should be eschewed. Any more critical, divided or national readings of history and of the possible path towards the future were heretical. As a sympathetic historian has explained, Pius 'forbade the ordinands to read newspapers or periodicals unless the bishop selected a few which he thought helpful to their studies. . . . He forbade any clergymen to use language which would cause in the poor an aversion for the upper classes for this is contrary to charity'.[27]

In sum, for Pius X, the Church's relationship with the past was much the same as it had been for Leo XII, eighty years earlier. Human sinfulness was always with us and must be contained by the Church, bearer of Christ's eternal message of warning and hope. Mystery must overbear rationality; the Enlightenment had tempted human beings into a sinful delusion that they could manage and master the world. To save men and women from the punishment that their blasphemy must incur, in 1907 Pius made the day of the alleged appearance of the Virgin Mary at Lourdes into a feast for all the faithful. The Mother of God in Her gentle universality could teach the people to reject contemporary heresies about nation and class. In the Rome serving Pius X, the Church remained far from compromise with modernity and clung as tenaciously as ever to its own abiding history.

In 1905 a survey in *L'Osservatore romano* claimed there were 442,394 Catholics residing in Rome, as against 7,121 Jews, 5,993 Protestants, 312 Orthodox, 38 believers in 'other religions' and 2,689 atheists.[28] The Protestants were split between locals and foreigners – the American Episcopalian church of 'St Paul's within the walls' (erected in 1879) stood out from the more prosaic buildings on the Via Nazionale and was embellished with romantic neo-Raphaelite mosaics by the English painter, Edward Burne-Jones. In 1883, in what to the Vatican seemed impious marking of the fourth centenary of Martin Luther, the Waldensians opened a church in what was eventually to be named the Via Quattro Novembre (4 November Street in honour of the national victory at Vittorio Veneto which successfully concluded Italy's First World War). In 1914 these Italian Protestants built a second and larger church (and one nearer the Vatican) in Piazza Cavour.[29]

But the most celebrated new religious structure in Liberal Rome was the imposing synagogue, completed in July 1904 and apparent proof of a humane liberal acceptance of difference. The building was, according to some, an artistic triumph, with its exterior attractively 'reminiscent' of 'Greek and Assyrian art', although a little 'out of tune with its Roman ambience'.[30] King Victor Emmanuel III, who had succeeded his assassinated father in 1900 and was a lifelong anti-clerical, soon visited the synagogue. He let it be known that he rejoiced in its size and resonant placement on the Lungotevere de' Cenci beside the river and near the classical relics. During his reign, he hoped, no grander religious edifices would rise in Rome.

The ancient ghetto, symbol of the centuries of papal tyranny and anti-Semitism, had been destroyed in 1883–4, the Jews having been liberated as soon as Italian forces had conquered the city. As if in proof of their ready devotion to the new nation and its historical course, thereafter Rome's Jews abandoned their own dialect, the so-called *giudeo romanesco*.[31] By contrast, Pius IX had been a traditionalist believer that Jews had betrayed Christ,[32] and the Jesuit paper *Civiltà cattolica* over the years did little to curb its hostile comprehension of the meaning and the exclusivity of Jewish history. In 1892, for example, it still wrote that Jews 'do not work, but profit from the work by others; they do not produce, but live and grow fat on the artistic and industrial products of the nations that give them shelter. The Jewish nation is a polyp that attracts and embraces all with its outsized tentacles.'[33]

Despite such prejudice, men and women who were by some definition Jewish were able to make their own histories as never before under Liberal administration. During the First World War, the national armed forces contained fifteen generals of Jewish background and three admirals. In March 1910 one person of Jewish extraction, Luigi Luzzatti, succeeded another, Sidney Sonnino, as Prime Minister, and all the time Nathan was mayor of Rome. By then, it seemed established, 'being a Jew ... [had become] a perfectly natural thing' in Rome.[34] Certainly Italy's Jews were very likely to be patriots, fully endorsing the Risorgimento settlement and the takeover of Rome from the pope. They were rarely seduced by rumours spreading from Vienna of the Zionist cause aiming to 'restore' a Jewish state as was appropriate for the 'oldest nation', but instead centred their identities in a nationalised Italian history.

Typical of this process of identification of Jewishness with Rome and Italy was Ernesto Nathan, a man who incarnated many of the key features and enduring ambiguities of Liberal Rome. Nathan had been born in London in October 1845 to a numerous family who, over the previous decades, had moved from the Germanic world via Paris to Britain. There they became the financial backers of Mazzini during his long exile. After his father died relatively young, Nathan and the rest of his siblings moved to Italy (his mother had been born at Pesaro), living at one time or another in Pisa, Florence, Milan and Genoa. Mazzini in old age resumed his contact with the Nathans, and died in the home of Ernesto's sister, Giannetta Nathan Rosselli. Thereafter the Nathan family acquired the royalty rights to the prophet's publications. They themselves financed a Mazzinian paper with the didactic title of *Il Dovere* (Duty).[35]

Ernesto, who never ceased to speak Italian with the London accent of his youth, only opted for citizenship of the country in 1887, the same year he joined the Freemasons. In 1895 he was elevated to the post of Grand Master, replacing Adriano Lemmi who had warmly prosecuted the running battle with the Church – Leo XIII devoted 118 separate texts to reviling Freemasonry – by stating blasphemously that the body acted as 'the way, the truth and the life' for its members.[36] For Nathan, the emphasis was more dignified. Freemasonry, he explained in 1901, was 'not a political organisation but rather a patriotic association . . . a humanist institution'.[37] As for his own base, 'Rome', he stated a little later, still echoing the cosmopolitan hopes of the 1870s, 'is no more a city. It is an idea and a world institution. Rome is no longer a slice of land; it is a spiritual frontier', the potential ideal proof of all that progress meant.[38]

By then, Nathan, who had completed his Grand Mastership in 1904, was active on the city's Communal Council. In May 1902 he founded the Unione democratica romana (Rome Democratic Union) to unite the liberal left yet remain open to contacts with the growing socialist movement. Five years later there was political triumph, helped by support from the daily, *Il Messaggero*, with a campaign pledging that the new mayor stood 'above parties'.[39] Thereafter, the Nathan team became busy in bringing what might be termed gas and water liberalism to Rome. The city budget rose spectacularly for education, utilities, public transport and housing; the neat two-storey houses now erected around San Saba, near the Porta San Paolo and the Protestant cemetery, may still be explored as an example of the human dimension of the town planning of the Nathan administration. One of the mayor's chief aides, the economist, Giovanni Montemartini, coined the phrase 'democratise consumption' as the winning slogan of the moment, endorsing the idea that city planning should accept the pre-eminence of 'science' and democracy.[40] Long-excluded workers and women, he counselled, should be pushed forward to play a proper part in city life.[41] In 1909 a plan termed the *Piano Sanjust* (after another of Nathan's collaborators, Edmondo Sanjust de Teleudamade), was ratified. It marked the greatest effort in the city's history so far to discipline its spread, in this aim earning the ire of the major local real estate interests, men with close ties to the Vatican and to Catholic banks.[42] The scheme did, however, win the backing of Lanciani and patriotic archaeologists by suggesting the 'isolation' and excavation of the Baths of Diocletian, the Mausoleum of Augustus, the Theatre of Marcellus and the Portico of Octavia, along with the creation of an 'archaeological park' across the Palatine and part of the Caelian and Aventine hills. Lanciani was also ready to applaud the idea that more generous welfare should be offered to the poorest citizens who, he lamented, were still 'seeking shelter, like the hermits of the Middle Ages, amongst the ruins' or in mouldering city stables, 'unfit for beasts of burden'.[43]

While the Liberals got to work with alacrity, those loyal to the clerical interest who had governed Rome before 1907 gave few signs of accommodation with the Nathan administration, with *Civiltà cattolica* deploring the presence of a city leader who, in their view, was neither Roman nor Italian but 'the son of Shem',[44] while the local paper, *Il Popolo romano*, guilelessly uniting its historical horrors, feared carnage from 'uncivilised Jacobins'.[45] The conflict boiled over after a speech that Nathan gave on 20 September 1910 at a fortieth anniversary ceremony of national rule held at the Porta Pia. In a published version, 'Papal Rome and Italian Rome', Nathan set out the modern choice of two approaches to past, present and future. The rational and patriotic one he represented, he explained, favoured 'free thought' and global contact with the fraternal nations, while the alternative, locked within the city walls, stood for the repression of the intellect. Typical was the declaration of papal infallibility. 'It was the reverse of the biblical revelation of the Son of God making himself man on earth. Rather it meant the son of a man making himself God on earth!' Churches in Rome, Nathan lamented, 'were superabundant'; schools by contrast could never be built quickly enough. Equally deluded was the superstitious habit of Roman women of relying on the Madonna in times of epidemic and not on medical science.[46] Here, it seemed, was a Roman who passed to the other side of the road whenever he walked near the statue commemorating the Immaculate Conception.

After an outraged Pius X issued an angry public reply, remonstrating against Nathan's 'blasphemous . . . effrontery in contesting the mission entrusted by Christ Our Lord to St Peter and his successors', Nathan countered sardonically by asking was not the pope, the anti-modernist Catholic warrior, implacably bent on banning any who sought 'a faith that makes peace between intellect and heart, tradition and evolution, knowledge and religion'. The fulminations of the Vatican, he stated defiantly, merely exposed the continuing battle between 'the

Rome of the past and the Rome of the present'.[47] All sensible citizens, he urged, must prefer modernity and science to the antique absurdities of Catholicism. Still a self-conscious heir of the more innocent hopes of the Risorgimento, Nathan preached a liberalism that was rational and humanist, sprung from Enlightenment optimism and not yet stirred by that exacerbating nationalism which, also in Italy, was learning how to hate its neighbours and drive forward to empire.

Who, then, were the Romans of Nathan's modernising city? After four decades of Italian rule or 'occupation', a fifth of the city's inhabitants were workers and almost as many were bureaucrats. Education percolated through to some. By 1911 there were estimated to be 45,000 pupils of one level or another domiciled in the city (Rome University took 2,800, 12 per cent of the small national tertiary total), while 8,000 religious were housed in the many Catholic institutions. Up to 10,000 foreigners resided in Rome, quite a few on a long-term basis. Until the First World War, the traditional area around Piazza di Spagna was their mecca. The English were likely to congregate at 'Mrs Babington's Tea Rooms', where they could console themselves with food and drink to their tastes, indulging in their own culinary history. Until the 1890s they could also cheer themselves by patronising an English Arts and Crafts shop which sold 'ladies' crafts'.[48]

Rome's own women typically looked after their families but could also find remuneration as domestic servants (there were 24,000 in 1911), prostitutes, lower-grade schoolteachers and in the occasional white collar post. Totalling 12,000 in 1911, people of independent means, ranging from traditional papal aristocrats to modern rentiers, bankers or other beneficiaries of Rome's expansion, stood at the top of a steeply hierarchical society.[49] Class and gender divisions yawned.

As if to prove the matter, the sociologist Domenico Orano, in the aftermath of Italy's fiftieth anniversary celebrations and in the reforming tone of the Nathan administration, published a survey that he had compiled over the previous five years surveying how working people lived in the poor suburb of Testaccio, whose tenements were rising south along the river from the Aventine. Men from this part of town worked either at the new modern municipal abattoir or Mattatoio, built between 1888 and 1891 (it now houses the Rome Museum of Contemporary Art) or at the power station on the Viale Ostiense (now the Museo Montemartini).[50] This edifice, with its promise of making electricity readily and cheaply available, was a special achievement of Nathan's rule as a result of which, in 1909, the Azienda Elettrica Municipale (Municipal Electric Company) was established; its 477 consumers in 1912 had risen to 21,093 by 1915.[51]

Orano had begun his account by noting that, in bourgeois eyes, Testaccio was a coven of criminals, threaded with streets where respectable people did not dare to tread, a place therefore with its own 'unspeakable' history. Such prejudice was mistaken, he counselled with liberal generosity, since 'the people, in spite of everything, are better than we believe'. Certainly, for many of the 9,262 men and women who lived in this part of Rome, conditions were harsh. Ten people could crowd into a one-room flat where, Orano reported, 'adultery, free love, the corruption of minors and epidemic disease find fertile terrain'. Dishevelled beds stood in kitchens, corridors and in such toilets as existed; Orano estimated that many of these last serviced thirty or more people and frequently lacked access to light or water. Abortion was common and infant mortality rates high; 44.9 per cent of children died before their fifth birthday while, in 1901, one-quarter of city-born infants were illegitimate. 'Food, mainly a single plate, was often eaten from the same pot wherein it was cooked,' Orano recorded. 'One fork and one spoon served the company.' For ordinary people, meat reached the menu once a week or less. As for drinks, father, mother and children gulped down a rough liquid from a single wine bottle, while the tavern (*osteria*) acted as 'a social safety-valve'. It was pointless to deplore the resulting drunkenness and squandered money.

The women, Orano complained, knew nothing of their own physiology; their ignorance should be blamed on the residual dominance of the Church. For Roman women, 'religion is the universal panacea and it wants nothing to do with clinics, infant schools or any of the marvellous discoveries of science'. The people of Testaccio were utterly cut off from Roman high culture. A product of past and present brutalisation, their histories were their own and official Roman history was not theirs. Fitting the pattern which ensures that rising cities are always places of immigration, where newcomers automatically add their histories to those of the autochthonous, more than half the inhabitants of Testaccio had not been born in Rome, originating either in Lazio or in the nearby provinces of the Abruzzi, Molise, Marche or Romagna. In these mean streets, Orano counted fourteen 'foreigners' from outside Italy.[52] Only the 'incredible fascination' of the infant cinema offered some relief to 'the worker deafened at his factory' or to 'the illiterate peasant'.[53] Perhaps with a hint that the project of nationalisation might nonetheless eventually penetrate Testaccio via the screen, the first narrative film made in Italian (1905) – and naturally focused on history – portrayed 'The taking of Rome: 20 September 1870'.[54]

On the other side of the city, the zone of San Lorenzo offered a life that was little different. There, in 1907, the reforming educationalist, Maria Montessori, complained that 'the streets are a constant theatre of crime, blood, riot and other foul spectacles, all scarcely to be believed by us', the respectable bourgeoisie. Often two families were housed in a single room, and the area looked as if it had just been devastated by a natural 'disaster'.[55] For the nationalist sociologists Alfredo Niceforo and Scipione Sighele, crime ruled thence almost as far as the Piazza Venezia and the police were cautiously absent. Locals spoke an impenetrable argot, while witches still told fortunes and promised other maleficence. Numerous beggars pursued their well-regarded and inherited vocation.[56] A brewery (it opened in 1902), a mill and a pasta-making enterprise (1905) offered some local employment, as did the nearby Verano cemetery and a garbage dump. A new church (Chiesa dell'Immacolata e San Giovanni) commenced services in 1909, while a restaurant on the corner of the Via Latini and the Via dei Savelli was known to be the haunt of anarchists. Socialist and republican groups had initiated an uncertain existence, but the socialists, although they were making a splash nationally, recorded just 1,260 party members in the city in 1914.[57] To the poor and unemployed of Testaccio and San Lorenzo, religion and politics of the formalised kind promised only a distant and wan utopia and so, ironically, did the city of Rome. People from such quarters lived the great part of their lives in their own streets and rarely mingled with the forbidding society that strutted inside the Aurelian Walls. There, the comfortable classes, whether 'Italians' or foreign tourists, were like aliens from another world. The poor, by contrast, muttered that they had been 'cursed' by nameless forces, pessimistically believing that they could not kick against the pricks.[58]

The traditional popular area of the city was Trastevere, across the river. Augustus Hare typically thought that its residents belonged to 'a stronger and more vigorous race' than did other Romans, and half believed that a residue from the classical bloodlines of the city still coursed through their veins. Hare's racial stereotyping convinced him that the *Trasteverini* committed more murders than did other Romans, thereby expressing their (charming) passion and (picturesque) fondness for wielding a knife, characteristics that were a predictable accompaniment of their (childish) good-heartedness in ordinary dealing.[59] What Hare ought to have been seeing instead was the politics of poverty in a place that was not yet modern but where time had not stood still. Modernity of some sort was actually reducing crime; muggings in the city fell from 349 in 1874 to 64 in 1901, murders from 244 (1893) to 91 (1901).[60] Nonetheless, in total, it was estimated in 1908 that 160,000 Romans lived in inadequate housing, while 80,000 were indigent and, certainly, the histories cherished by such ordinary Romans in all their ethnic and gender variety were not yet homogenised into merely that of a single Italian nation.[61]

Compared with the fate of the poor, the story of petty bureaucrats or of those serving the tourist industries is thinly documented. Yet social and gender difference could be discerned everywhere. Class appeared on the chins of men of the city since the petit bourgeois were accustomed to visit the barber every two or three days, workers only on Sundays, while the best-off kept servants to look after these and their other daily toilet needs. The patriotic,

Catholic (and partly Jewish) historian, A.C. Jemolo, who grew up in Umbertine Rome, remembers how food, too, divided the people. Ordinary men and women, he recalled, did not sit at table but ate from a bowl held between their knees, their humble fare consisting of bread or a *frittata* with some condiment or with fresh tomatoes. Petit bourgeois men at lunch, the main meal in a society that still observed siesta, ate two fried eggs (their wives and children one), augmented by some vegetable matter conserved in oil or a lettuce leaf. In winter, this dish would be followed by 'some poor quality little apples that would today dishonour the worst fruit vendor of the outer suburbs,' or a few chestnuts. At dinner there would be clear soup, a slice of boiled beef and a vegetable. On Sunday, *festa* would be marked with a plate of pasta (the habit of eating such 'southern' food had only entered the city after 1870), covered with 'a very thick tomato sauce that had a nauseous taste.' Such families, proud to be respectable, were assisted by a servant (earning 15 lire per month). Few homes of such people possessed a bath or aspired to have one. The Church, too, was not omnipresent, with priests being on the defensive in most public disputation and relying on their traditional charity to remain in touch with the people.[62]

Most Romans, in other words, as in the past remained happier to think of themselves as *poveri cristi* (poor Christs) than as adepts of an intellectualised or 'disciplinised' and so modern Catholicism. Equally, even quite a way up the social scale, they were typically disconnected from, and disconcerted by, the state-sponsored, national modernity applauded by their betters in their city during the various *Cinquantennio* events and giving worthy expression to what liberalism meant to reformers like Nathan and Giolitti, with their surviving faith in Italian and human progress.

In this regard, in 1911 the city, although it had to dispute with the arguably more appropriate Turin and Milan over which was the ideal venue for evocations of the Risorgimento, saw one event or initiative follow another. (By 1906, twenty-nine museums of the unification process had opened in Italy, all but seven in the north.)[63] During the year, Rome successively hailed the inauguration of new law courts, its first modern race track and zoo (January) – German-designed, it stood in the Borghese gardens, now a public park – the inception of a modern art gallery and an international photography exhibition (March) and a display on peasant life in the Campagna (May), the exordium of the Victor Emmanuel monument and of a new bridge named for the King (June), the holding of an international archaeological exhibition to be made permanent in the restructured ancient Baths of Diocletian (July) and a collection on Risorgimento history (20 September).[64] With a mixture of liberal nationalism and internationalism, the archaeological material collected to illuminate the history of the Roman empire made much of the complex of regions that fell (and prospered) under the control of the Caesars. It partially accepted thereby that the history of Roman Britain, for example, was as worthy of consideration as that of Rome itself. Similarly, the English architect, Edwin Lutyens, was encouraged to design the structure that still houses the British School at Rome, while the other European nations and Japan were politely asked to provide their own pavilions and artistic works for another large exhibition that assembled around the Valle Giulia.[65]

As a further sign of the intrusion of ideas from abroad and their still generous welcoming, Italian feminists met in Rome in June, dismaying the Vatican by their 'morbid' preoccupations with promoting modern education for women, although, a few months later, there was something of a cross-party alliance when the feminists and the Catholic press joined in deploring the elevation of a poor girl from Trastevere to be beauty 'Queen' of the festival.[66] Male desire meanwhile attracted the attention of the Liberal paper, *La Tribuna*. 'The imagination of the male is much more easily excited' than that of the female, it warned parents in words that provide evidence that liberalism was anything but libertarian in its approach to the history of childhood. The unmentionable threat, an editorial affirmed, could be avoided through the scrupulous surveillance of a boy 'in his games, in his friendships, in his corre- spondence'. Physical exercise, 'sport *all'inglese*', was the best remedy against the onset of dangerous sexual fantasies.[67] Yet, with the tolerance that still charac- terised liberalism, however ambiguously, exhibition space was even found for gay history (at least of an upper-class and foreign variety), with the photo- graphic display of the studies of nude boys by the Prussian baron, Wilhelm von Glöden, homosexual pioneer of the Taormina tourist industry.[68]

Equally expressive of what its friends thought was liberalism's span and its enemies its weakness was the decoration of the parliament building, Montecitorio. This palace had been designed by Bernini during the seventeenth century but, in the decade following 1900, was massively reworked, leaving only the façade unscathed. The meeting place of the deputies now offered many loyal historical invocations of Piedmont and the Savoy dynasty, while also depicting in ethical and historical amalgam the Virtues of Justice, Strength, Constancy, the Renaissance, Young Italy, the national tongue, Humanism, Art, Discoveries, the classical world, chivalry, ardour, the unknown, form and faith. There was space, too, for the she-wolf foster-mother of Romulus and Remus. As a contemporary explained the purpose of the whole, in the allegory of the painter, Giulio Aristide Sartorio, 'the history of Italy is soberly synthesised and symbolised at two great moments: the barbarian invasion which the free Italian Communes opposed with supreme heroism, and the heroism that revived when the Garibaldinian anthem resounded and the Heroes rose again. Those who fought for the Patria thus acquire a new vigour, and Destiny presses them on to the triumph of the tricolour flag, in whose shadow the House of Savoy raises the young to freedom.'[69] On the walls of Montecitorio, the pasts of classical Rome, the Middle Ages, Renaissance and the Risorgimento were promiscuously blended to teach a liberal national and a liberal internationalist lesson to the present and future.

It was true that rumours of a cholera outbreak in the summer of 1911 (its news was deliberately suppressed by Giolitti and was soon framed by Thomas Mann into his novella, *Death in Venice*) discouraged some from visiting Rome, with the Catholic press crowing that the number attending the celebrations had fallen below predictions and that, financially speaking, the *Cinquantennio* was proving a 'huge disaster'. Yet there were foreign dignitaries enough to blazon Liberal Italy's place in the comity of nations, and they included Crown Prince Wilhelm of Germany and ex-Chancellor Bernard von Bülow, a slew of Russian archdukes and General Miguel Primo de Rivera of Spain. The Duke of Connaught, an early visitor to the Photographic Exhibition, was feasted by the British ambassador James Rennell Rodd and his wife, with their guests including stylish Italian Queen Mother Margherita. Somewhat eclectically and hinting that English liberalism had its own ambiguities, the historic theme represented in the embassy garden was an artistic spectacle in the style of Watteau, amplified by a children's chorus, dressed in period style and presenting rococo, Hellenic and Spanish modes. Queen Margherita, it was reported, was so moved by the talent on display that she embraced the leaders of the chorus, who, beneath their costumes, in predictable touch, were Lady Rodd's own children.[70]

Yet the time for such pleasing manifestations of international amity and urbanity was running out in Rome. Empire was at the gates. Through the summer of 1911 a conflict rumbled on between Italy and Turkey over what might be an acceptable Italian presence in the *vilayets* of Tripolitania and Cyrenaica, regularly bracketed in Italian discourse as Libya, the name they had possessed under the Caesars. On 11 June 1911, only a week after the opening of the Victor Emmanuel monument, the Second Congress of Italians abroad assembled in the national capital, pledging to end the situation that saw Italian emigrant 'blood' dribble away in the Americas rather than being conserved for the nation in real colonies, a new Roman empire. Among the delegates was the young Achille Starace, born near Lecce, far to the south. By the 1930s Starace was to become the most ideologically driven secretary of the Partito Nazionale Fascista. Now his patriotism or xenophobia stirred and so did that of others.

For the moment, more influential than Starace was Enrico Corradini, the chief philosopher of new-generation Nationalists. In 1910 he had established the Associazione Nazionista Italiana (Italian Nationalist Association, ANI) in Florence and, in March 1911, began publishing a newspaper entitled *L'Idea Nazionale* (The National Idea). As he imagined a way to forge modern Italy into a genuinely great power, Corradini was no special fan of Rome. Japan, he argued, proffered the best current model of 'the cult of warrior morality' that could educate modern Italians.[71] Tales of social conflict from the Middle Ages or cosy memory of a Cincinnatus returning to his farm, let alone the florid constructions of the baroque, were, he warned, no longer pasts that could well instruct the nation.[72] Rather the prime lessons of classical Rome were austerity, rigour and empire, and they alone should be drummed into the new genera-tion by 'national education.'[73] When Italy did launch imperial war in Libya, Corradini expressed the hope that his countrymen might not discover too much wealth there since, he argued, the empire of what he called a 'proletarian nation' needed much more work and must avoid the soft distractions that were already enfeebling the richer states.[74]

The die of colonial aggression had been cast on 26 September. Giolitti's government drafted its ultimatum to Turkey just six days after the inaugura-tion of the Museum of the Risorgimento in Rome; it was presented in Constantinople on the 29th. No reply was sought or desired. Italian ships were at sail, heading south across the Mediterranean. Rome, as the language of the moment portrayed it, was 'regaining its empire'. Not far behind the troops and sometimes in front of them, Italian archaeologists mobilised to enhance the 'national work' of examining the 'Arch of Marcus Aurelius' at Tripoli and a number of other allegedly evocative sites.[75] Now, the lessons of history must teach that modern Italians could best be national by being simultaneously imperial. Now, and to this new purpose, Rome was 'alive again'.

Within the nation, however, the Libyan campaign was a contested war. The socialist movement, with Marxist virtue, loudly objected to what it condemned as cynical aggression. A popular song of the moment backed party leadership in invoking a permanent struggle between the 'plebs' and the aristocracy, a battle that was as central now as it had been to the Gracchi brothers in the second century BCE.[76] Among the noisy campaigners against the war was the young 'maximalist' socialist and aspirant dissident intellectual, Benito Mussolini, who at that stage of his life had no time for a 'Third' Rome or its history. In the news-paper that he edited at provincial Forlì with the laboured title of *La Lotta di Classe* (The Class Struggle), he lamented in September 1910, using phrases half adapted from the discontented patriot Carducci, that Rome was 'a parasitic city, full of landladies, shoe shine boys, prostitutes, priests and bureaucrats'. It lacked a healthy 'proletariat worthy of the name'. The place was 'not the centre of national life but rather the hot-bed of the infection of national political life'.[77] Its history marred the nation.

Yet the attitudes of many young Italians were changing and, when the Libyan escapade turned out to be the prelude to Italy's First World War, the political class soon downplayed the mixture of 'power and the pursuit of peace' that had nourished the city of Ernesto Nathan and had been cherished by Quintino Sella and his friends. In 1914–15 Nathan became an advocate of

Italian entry into the war and, after Italy joined the Triple Entente states against Germany and Austria, served, aged seventy, as a lieutenant on the bleak Carso above Trieste.[78] His radical administration had lost office in 1913, thereafter being bested in an election in June 1914 by a combination of clerics and Nationalists, bearers of histories that he had once disdained.

In the national poll held in 1913 after the signature of the so-called 'Gentiloni Pact' promised to bring Catholic voters in from the cold, one victor had been the Bologna journalist (later to be a leading Fascist), Luigi Federzoni. He was elected for Rome I after a close contest, first with the more moderate Liberal prince, Scipione Borghese, and, in the run-off, with a socialist. Federzoni became the chief spokesman in parliament for the Nationalist Association, preaching a xenophobic imperialism far removed from the optimistic assumptions about European fraternal advance about which Giolitti had expatiated not so long before at the opening of the Victor Emmanuel monument. When the Italian navy seized the eastern Mediterranean island of Rhodes (sometime 'friend and ally of the Roman people') during the war with Turkey, Federzoni expressed his joy at the 'regaining of an ancient family jewel'.[79] He deplored, meanwhile, the neglect of the Austro-Hungarian empire in allowing the 'monuments of Rome' to decay throughout Dalmatia.[80] The entire Mediterranean basin he deemed '*Mare Nostrum*', the term prefiguring his Fascism. The Third Italy and the Third Rome, he urged, must 'reclaim' the inheritance of the classical empire. History taught that, if you want peace, you must prepare for war, and readily launch it.

Federzoni's profile in parliament and the enhanced role of the ANI in Rome city politics helped to ensure that the campaign of the *intervento* (the period between the outbreak of the First World War in August 1914 and Italian entry ten months later) was, to a considerable degree, disputed on the streets of the city. Unsurprisingly the rival factions accoutred themselves with what they claimed were telling lessons from Rome's history. The interventionist cause was composed of many factions – local Republicans, through their paper, *Il Fascio romano*, were strenuously pro-French (the term *fascio* as yet spanned the political spectrum). The interventionists united to demand war and national grandeur, while damning the 'neutralist' Giolitti and those socialists who clung to the cause of the international worker.[81] There was even a Comitato nazionale femminile per l'intervento (National Women's Committee for Intervention) set up in the city.[82] By January 1915 the authorities had closed Rome University on the grounds that student patriotic excitability too easily got out of hand there. A month earlier, the Futurist Balla had aroused some on the campus by designing 'anti-neutralist clothes', suitable for pro-war demonstrations.[83] The patriotic devotion of the sort of middle-class youth assembled in Italian academies in 1914–15 and during the rise of Fascism from 1919 to 1922 demonstrates that a nationalisation of adolescence was proceeding apace (although not among the children of peasants and that part of the working class already politicised as socialist). Frequently, history was this relatively gilded youth's best and most potent subject.

Matters came to a head in what patriotic propaganda christened 'Radiant May' 1915, when the man of the moment was the hyperbolic poet, Gabriele D'Annunzio. Although in the past he had been promiscuous in his evocation of the Venetian, Florentine and even French empires along with the Roman one, D'Annunzio now focused his rhetoric on the classical shades of the Eternal City and their need to march Italy into the world war. They were mustered in his speech from the balcony of the Hotel Regina on 12 May, a week after he had adapted the Sermon on the Mount to the national cause at Quarto, near Genoa, the departure point of Garibaldi's Thousand in 1860. On arrival in Rome, D'Annunzio had been met at the station by a throng alleged by the patriotic press to be 100,000 strong.[84] The poet's high-flown words were widely echoed, with *Il Corriere della Sera* insisting that, in deciding for war, modern Italy had 'drawn its sword and spoken in the Roman manner'.[85] Even the archaeologist, Lanciani, argued that now was 'not the first attempt of the Huns and their allies to crush the Latin races and to annex the most beautiful and fertile country in Europe' and in 1916 he published a book with the title, *La difesa del confino veneto-istriano sotto l'impero romano* (The defence of the Venetian-Istrian border under the Roman empire), to prove the case.[86] Moreover, Lanciani was sure that Hannibal, great but murderous and barbarous enemy of Rome, had been first to dismiss treaties as a 'scrap of paper'. When, in October 1917, Italy suffered military humiliation at Caporetto and seemed to have been routed by the forces of the Central Powers, Lanciani added that Livy had experienced a premonition of the role social disunity played in producing defeat when he described 'Italian' divisions during the Second Punic War.[87]

A nationalist and later Fascist journalist, Paolo Orano, agreed in the journal, *Il Soldato*, that the assault on his country came at the hands of refurbished 'Teutons, Alemanni, Goths, Huns, Pannonians, Marcomanni and Vandals', evil and overweening 'barbarians'. They must, he wrote, be 'massacred' in the Roman manner, in this view cheerfully reviving that classical bloodthirstiness which had once repelled liberal nationalist D'Azeglio. The Germans were, as far as Orano was concerned, still the enemy of 'fourteen, twelve, ten, seven and four centuries past'; they were always 'the sacking races, the voracious tribes, the incendiary hordes, the bestial torrent, lusting for rape and mutilation'.[88] History did not change, he and his patriotic friends urged. Modern Italians and ancient Romans were fused by destiny. So, a few issues later, on New Year's Day 1918, a lead cartoon in *Il Soldato* portrayed a soldier wearing a toga and a laurel wreath, carrying in his right hand a set of fasces that stretched from ground to shoulder and in his left hand the tricolour, swirling into the other Allied flags. Italy joined its British, French and Russian allies in battle against Austria-Hungary on 24 May 1915. A declaration of war against Germany, however, was timidly delayed until 28 August 1916. Despite the politicians' caution, for many an intellectual and for almost all Italian historians, it was self-evident that every positive strand of the history of Rome must be woven into the cause of the eternal nation, blessed now as ever by the god of battles.

Foreign historians of Italy, if from Allied countries, agreed that centuries of the national past united in the conflict against the Germanic enemy. Typical was G.M. Trevelyan. With Italian entry into the war, Trevelyan arrived in Rome to help organise and then command a British Red Cross motorised ambulance unit. Once he was serving at the front he took care to carry with him 'a handkerchief which had belonged to Garibaldi', a holy relic of the heroic and virtuous history of the Risorgimento.[89] He had not, however, renounced his own nationalism. When he came to review his experiences, he was confident that, during Radiant May and afterwards, 'the touchstone of enthusiasm for the war has been the friendliness to England' of the Italian elite. Among such people, he added, notably impressive was the King, whom he described as 'quiet and shy, with an "English" manner that has oddly distinguished several of the makers of modern Italy. . . . Duty and democracy are his two watchwords.'[90]

For German commentators, Italy's war exposed not the virtues of Italian history but its vices. Italy's actions in 1914 and 1915 and then the Caporetto defeat confirmed the view that modern Italians were the racial inferiors of both present-day Germans and their own classical forebears. Even while Oswald Spengler urged that '*Rome*, with its rigorous realism – uninspired, barbaric, disciplined, practical, Protestant, *Prussian* – will always give us, working as we must with analogies, the key to understanding our future', he knew that any perceived progress that had spread from Western Europe (and a revived Rome) since the beginning of the Middle Ages was a delusion.[91] The sparky Italians of the Renaissance and after were, he argued, the bearers of nothing of value to the present and had no special bond with the citizens of contemporary Italy. They could not arrest the 'decline of the West'. The Risorgimento, he explained contemptuously, whether that of 1798 or 1859, was 'essentially no more than a change of political costume for a people long since become insignificant'.[92]

Italian propagandists of war might annex the city's mythistory, and foreigners from the rival sides might dispute its meaning. Yet Rome at war, during a conflict fought on Italy's Alpine borders far to the north, was, it soon became plain, a peripheral place from where to spark national victory. With every passing month of battle, the everyday reality of Rome contrasted more blatantly with the grandiose imperial history ascribed to it. When victory, however uneasy, came at Vittorio Veneto on 4 November 1918, Rome of the Romans was, if anything, less integrated into a country whose history was meant to have been better nationalised than it had been in 1915. Ironically, the actual history of Italy's war, and the social, political and cultural divisions that it had exposed, left Italians in 1919 more doubtfully united than they had been in 1915, and the constant evocation of Rome's mythistory could not disguise the fact.

One evident element in this regard was the Church, which the war had failed to reconcile with the Italian state and nation. On 20 August 1914 Pius X died, to be replaced two weeks later by Giacomo della Chiesa, the Cardinal Archbishop of Bologna, but long a member of the Vatican's diplomatic staff in Rome.[93] The new pope took the name of Benedict XV, thereby hinting that he might be open to a greater accommodation with the Italian state than had been his immediate predecessors. In 1919 there would indeed be some progress in regard to the Church's 'Roman Question', half-plans for reconciliation with the Italian state. However, Benedict's papacy had as its major dilemma coping with the international struggle where Catholics were fighting and killing each other. Benedict's early nostrums, blaming the battle on a spreading 'disrespect for authority' and the 'unchecked spirit of independence' stirred up by deplorable modern individualism, was transmuted in time to a more serious peace plan of 1 August 1917 and a cry that the war had become a 'useless slaughter'; to little avail, given that the Papacy had no battalions to impose its own version of peace.[94]

An unspoken assumption of the Catholic encounter with the war surfaces when asking what might have happened had the Central Powers won. Had, say, the defeat at Caporetto in October 1917 precipitated surrender, an Italian version of the Treaty of Brest-Litovsk would have entailed some restoration of the temporal power. While stubbornly clinging to that hope, the Vatican uneasily kept itself above or separate from the rival nationalist explanations of the past and present, championed so fervently by each of the combatant powers. Rome, the Church still believed as battle raged, might, through the mystery of a beneficent providence, again be the Holy City and yet reunite sinful humanity across a Catholic world.

Although no friends with the Vatican, the majority of Italian socialists similarly remained uncommitted to the war, pursuing their equivocal line of 'neither support nor sabotage'. Rome was not their stronghold, whether in myth or reality. Throughout the province of Lazio, party membership fell from 1,260 in 1914 to 681 in 1915 and to 572 in 1918, before reviving to 1,619 in 1919. By November 1918 it was reckoned that there were only 280 card-carrying socialists in the city and most were inactive.[95] Yet an ongoing detach-ment from the rhetoric of the nationalists and a cynical discountenancing of the value of the nation and its history to ordinary people was well expressed in a popular song:

> O Roma, Roma, città tanto cara,
>   Dove se magna, se beve e poco se paga.
> E si c'è quarche disoccupato che nun ha magnato
> c'è San Cosimato, c'è villa Borghese p'annà a diggerì,
>   Reggina Celi p'annacce a dormi . . . .
> E allora, cara gente, a Roma nostra nun ce manca gnente,
>   c'è la gran ricchezza e la gran povertà:
>   chi magna tanto e chi sta a sbadija.[96]

(O dear, dear, Rome, where you eat, drink and pay only a little. And if there are some unemployed, who haven't eaten anything, there's always the hospice at San Cosimato or the Borghese gardens where you can go and digest, or the Regina Coeli gaol where you can sleep. . . . And thus, dear people, at Rome you don't lack for anything. There is great wealth and great poverty, those who eat too much and those who yawn with hunger.)

Talk about the nation and its everlasting glory seemed misplaced, then, to quite a few Romans, even though the demands for functionaries in a state committed to 'total' war meant that the urban population rose from 593,000 in 1914 to 629,000 in 1919. That growth brought some gain to the city economy. However, the war was bad for the richer money-spinner, tourism, and a body to serve the cause of unemployed guides, interpreters and hotel staff had already emerged in the summer of 1915. Soon, it became plain, Italy's participation in global conflict in Rome meant hunger, disease and social conflict. Meat consumption fell by more than half during the war years. From January 1917 women led regular protests against the quality and quantity of bread supplies (now for quite a few families again, as before 1870, the major element in their diet), although those on fixed incomes as well as public servants may have been affected by wartime inflation more than the popular classes; by 1918 bureaucratic pay was half that of 1914.[97] Rationing, that proof of national democratic social unity in suffering and of commitment to fair and efficient modern organisation, had proceeded slowly and ineffectually in the city, with the Prefect doubting that it could be adopted by a population that was, in his mind, 'very needy, poorly educated and given to riot'.[98] Malaria revived in the *Agro romano*, and the number suffering from syphilis multiplied. From February 1918 the police stopped arresting prostitutes on the grounds that the gaols for women were full. In 1919, 4,000 in the city died in the world epidemic of Spanish flu (twice the death rate of Milan),[99] about the same total as those Romans who perished in the Italian armed forces during the war.

This tally suggested that an early modern history of medicine and hygiene remained as palpable in the city as was the scientific modern and national version. Beggars multiplied, with some commentators sure that those returned soldiers who exhibited their wounds on city streets were shameless and shameful fakes.[100]

Along with the social, urban cultural fissures gaped, and there were anonymous denunciations of shirkers or of such foreign residents as the Vatican's Swiss Guards, who might be conspiring 'spies' or saboteurs. With the continuing war, the interventionists of the left in the city readily swung over to the reactionary cause of the Nationalists, while their spokesmen orated about how the battle in the north was 'the greatest event' in '3,000 years of history' and required that enemies and allies acknowledge Italian imperium 'in the Alto Adige, Istria, Dalmatia, the Gulf of Cattaro, Albania, the Middle East' or 'any part of the world where Italian production and Italian labour find outlets'.[101] After Caporetto, with the country on the edge of defeat and/or revolution, paramilitary *Legioni rosse* (Red Legions; coloured so in homage to Garibaldi, not Marx) were secretly enrolled in Rome, their task being in a crisis to undertake 'the physical elimination of their opponents, socialists, Giolittians and even the Prime Minister himself, [Vittorio Emanuele] Orlando'.[102]

Doubts whether the war had been zealously enough embraced in the national capital were well expressed in the diary of Ferdinando Martini. This elegant Tuscan landowner embodied the strengths and weaknesses of national liberalism in the early twentieth century and embodied its drift towards authoritarianism and empire. Martini had long wanted Italy to 'go back' to Africa in the 'Roman manner'.[103] He had served as Governor of Eritrea, where he built Tuscan colonnades in the capital, Asmara, ruthlessly advocating the genocide of the locals and their replacement with Italian immigrants. Minister of Colonies in 1914, he had favoured Italy's entering the war and, after Caporetto, his diary is full of 'anguish' at the defeat, fear that Italy was about to be conquered and dishonoured, half-admiration for the violence contemplated by the *Legioni rosse* (whom he called the 'Red Society') and impatience with parliamentarism, which required that he listen to orations by Giolitti or the socialists, with their rival and unacceptable comprehension of Italian history and purpose.

On 29 December 1917 while he was travelling from Rome to his estates, Martini recorded meeting an artillery major who had come back from emigration to the USA to fight for Italy. This officer made remarks to him that expressed his own thoughts with yet another surfacing of what might be called the 'black legend' of Rome: 'He said he could not stomach the Capital, where the war had not been felt and everyone just went on doing what they had done before the war, only accepting personal sacrifice out of necessity and then making plain their reluctance. The theatres were full; the cinemas flooded with customers. Yet everywhere whingeing [could be heard]. It seems that the [Romans] did not have the slightest comprehension of the suffering of those who actually served at the front. The smallest privation or inconvenience caused irritation and brought protest. Whoever had lived in America reacted with profound disgust to this lack of discipline' growing everywhere in the corrupt, unwarlike and decadent, no longer imperial, city.[104]

Angelo Staderini, the main contemporary historian of Rome's war, has concluded that a society which was still fundamentally split between Catholics and liberals in 1914 had been transmuted by the end of the war to a place divided between those who accepted the values of the nation and those who did not.[105] Yet a binary division oversimplifies the complex and varied course of the many histories that, during the war and in its aftermath, continued to flow through Rome. To be sure, those who sought to be the war's heirs on the national political stage tried to keep its lessons simple. Orlando, hoping to be entrenched as 'the Prime Minister of Victory', typically proclaimed to the national parliament on 20 November 1918 that 'never as at this moment has Italy seemed a more worthy heir of Rome'. Similarly, when, on 4 November 1921, the nation, following the model of other ex-combatant powers, got around to burying its 'unknown soldier', the chosen site for national mourning and memory was the Victor Emmanuel monument,[106] with the *ignoto* being entombed next to the statue to *Dea Roma* (The Goddess Rome). Interment there was meant to signal a natural course from the Risorgimento to the post-war years, the King and the soldier both having upheld the constant national cause with Roman sobriety against invading (and barbarous) Germans.

However, by 1921, it was evident that the surviving liberals did not have a monopoly on the myth of the Italian war experience. Rather, in the cities and villages of Italy, social and cultural battle spread between socialists, Catholics and the new group of Fascists, this last recruiting many returned soldiers. Each of these rivals was anxious to understand the meaning of the war in its own fashion and each, but especially the Fascists, aimed to impose their version on the public and cancel that of their opponents. In the resulting mayhem, any hope that might have once driven D'Azeglio, Sella or Giolitti to tolerate historical debate and difference under the banner of a liberal nation was fading from view.

The city of Rome was not yet the most active front in this civil conflict about the nation's and the war's meaning. Yet, whatever the reality of the capital, its history had too much potential not to be claimed by the clashing factions. The meaning that could be drawn from Rome's past especially attracted the Fascist movement while it aimed to forge a total nation as the product of total war, and march forward, once the people were properly marshalled, to a new Roman empire. Soon, with what it called totalitarian purpose, the Fascist Duce, his title adapted from the Latin *Dux* (military chief), was demanding, with few of the beg-pardons of his liberal predecessors, that the history and spirit of Rome, its *romanità*, carry a single and Fascist meaning. The dictatorship was soon proclaiming its ambition to win a final and absolute, a total and totalitarian, victory in Rome's history wars. Now the historical truth was not so much whispered as barked to a people whose duty it was to 'believe, obey and fight'.

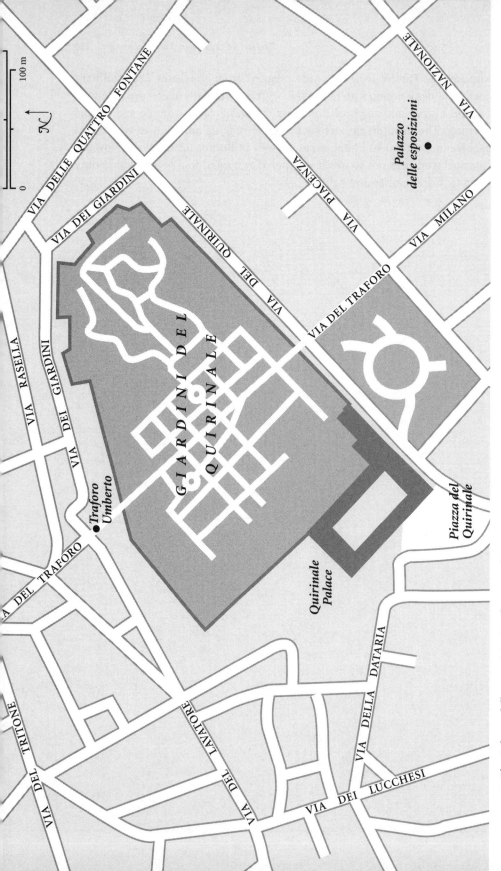

100 m

VIA DELLE QUATTRO FONTANE

VIA DEI GIARDINI

VIA NAZIONALE

Palazzo delle esposizioni

VIA PIACENZA

VIA MILANO

VIA DEL QUIRINALE

VIA DEL TRAFORO

VIA RASELLA

VIA DEI GIARDINI

G I A R D I N I   D E L
Q U I R I N A L E

Traforo Umberto

A DEL TRAFORO

Quirinale Palace

Piazza del Quirinale

VIA DELLA DATARIA

TRITONE

VIA DEL

LAVATORE

VIA DEL

VIA DELLA DATARIA

VIA DEI LUCCHESI

8. The Palazzo delle esposizioni and surrounds

* * * ✳ * * *

7

ROME, ITS HISTORIES AND FASCIST TOTALITARIANISM

Among the vast array of eras that are today expressed in Rome's architecture and urban planning, that of the Fascist dictatorship and its Duce, Benito Mussolini, is the most obvious. Tourist guides as yet rarely draw attention to it; however, to any with eyes to see, there it is, arguably the city's best enduring and most pervasive history, and certainly a major competitor with the papal line that Rome is a holy, eternal and universal city. In this and the next chapter, we shall visit many Fascist sites in order to discern what, under Mussolini's regime, may have been the Fascists' ambition in marshalling time and space and to explore what, after the expulsion of the dictatorship from the city in 1944, has become their present reality, necessarily adapted to the history of the Italian nation.

Because Fascist history is still so conspicuous in Rome, it is appropriate to start analysis at a city site where totalitarianism once was most aggressively hyped. The graceless structure of the Palazzo delle esposizioni is located down the Via Nazionale from the Baths of Diocletian towards the Forum and beside the church of San Vitale, dedicated in 416 CE and beautifully frescoed, but now sunk so far below road level as to be almost invisible. The *palazzo*, planned from 1876 and inaugurated in 1883 with the promise that it would enhance the image of the city as a capital of European weight, was the work of Pio Piacentini, founder of an architectural dynasty in the city. It is scarcely a glory of the Liberal era.[1] Rather it confirms the views of those commentators who disdained newly Italian Rome as ugly and pretentious, promiscuous and confused in its historical reference. The *palazzo*'s façade is crowded with pillars and bas-reliefs, vacuously invoking a scene from the Florentine Renaissance as well as depicting the rediscovery of the Laocoön near the Arch of Titus in Rome in 1506. The roof carries the statues of twelve worthies, culled mainly from 'Italian' history but including Rembrandt and the French mathematician,

20. Still not Fascistised Palazzo delle esposizioni in the 1920s.

Etienne de la Roche. At the apex stands a representation of Art sustained by Peace and Study. The main figure, whose head is crowned by black spines (meant to be the rays of Apollo), seems a louche precursor of the Statue of Liberty. The overall intent of such architectural ostentation, it has been argued, was 'to convey a tranquillising message: the centralising of art at Rome, made possible given the Palazzo delle esposizioni's construction, would not lead to local privilege but rather would embrace all artistic activity', whether in Italy or abroad. Despite what might be understood as the positive internationalism and cosmopolitan histories being woven into the building's fabric in the sanguine mode of early Liberal Italy, at least by comparison with what was to be Fascism's murderous xenophobia and imperialism, the souls of 'neither passers-by nor students', then or later, were quickened by the edifice.[2]

The *palazzo's* interior is no more compelling than its exterior. Piacentini decided that its initial purpose as a site for regular art exhibitions could best be achieved by avoiding exterior windows. The only natural illumination in its large rooms therefore comes through skylights. In recent years the communal administration has struggled to find appropriate and rewarding use for this building, necessary given its prominent position in central Rome. An expensive restructure in 1990, converting the *palazzo* into 'an interdisciplinary space for contemporary culture', capable of 'being in dialogue with the major European capitals', may not be convincing, even if it is now equipped with an upmarket restaurant, while a cinema and a library offer more intellectual sustenance.[3]

Like other buildings in the city, the Palazzo delle esposizioni has lived through time and carries a number of historical resonances. Yet the most significant event in its story occurred on 28 October 1932, tenth anniversary (*Decennale*) of the Fascist March on Rome, when the Mostra della Rivoluzione Fascista (Exhibition of the Fascist Revolution) opened there. Then, and for the next two years, while the Mostra remained in the *palazzo*, and with a less successful reopening from September 1937 across town at the Galleria Nazionale d'Arte Moderna, more than five million visitors viewed this display with greater or lesser awe and appreciation.[4] The Mostra was the pre-eminent place where the dictatorship's version of the history of Fascism was enacted and presented, a significance that was underscored by the dictator's decree in 1932 that every town and village in the country call one of its main streets the Via Roma.[5] All Italians were meant thereby to see every day that the nation's capital was the beating heart of their own identity and heritage, indeed the repository of their history.

Rome was to be the Holy City of the nation and pilgrimage to it was an obligation for all true Fascists. Once they reached the Mostra they found that it combined intransigent accounts of the recent past with what was portrayed as a fully happy present and destined future. The exhibition was intended to act as an engine of totalitarian control, with history harnessed to achieve an 'anthropological revolution' that would temper every man and woman of the nation into adamantine Italians and Fascists. Through its inscription of contemporary history, it would root a Fascist belief system deep in Italian hearts and minds. After all, its organisers stated bluntly, 'winners with their victory achieve the right to compose [the nation's] history', while adding sententiously that, in this regard, Livy and Tacitus had paved the way in writing forceful contemporary accounts when political passion remained alive. With residual international reference, they also maintained that the spirit of Beethoven, Carlyle and Michelet strengthened their resolve to make the story of the times dramatic and accessible.[6]

Although the Mostra was designed to sum up a past, its technique in approaching the task of chronicling it was stridently trend-setting, especially for the ordinary inhabitants of a city like Rome who remained in large part excluded from the Industrial and Commercial Revolution that had long made an impact further north. Throughout the exhibition there was much radical use of photomontage, as well as of a self-consciously Futurist dynamism in representation. The Mostra urged that Rome and Italy were now modernist or nothing. Crucial was the need to cover up the manifest failings of the Via Nazionale and the Palazzo delle esposizioni, sad testaments to the 'pomposity, clumsy grandiosity and tasteless richness' of the slackly Liberal past.[7] To hide its architectural and political sins, the *palazzo* was symbolically covered in a 'rationalist red mantle', and the building's old-fashioned statues and bas-reliefs were veiled.[8] In their place, four giant 25-metre metallic fasces stood as pillars beside the entrance, while massive capital letters announced that here was found the MOSTRA DELLA RIVOLUZIONE FASCISTA. Liberal history, it was proclaimed, was now lifeless; only Fascism could explain the world.

Inside the building, visitors were conducted through nineteen rooms arranged in a spiral.[9] The first five focused on how Italy intervened in, and fought, the First World War, with the third respectfully hailing the '*Re Soldato*' (soldier king – the diminutive Victor Emmanuel III). The next ten took history from the foundation of the *fasci*, the initial grouping of the men and women to be called Fascists, in Milan in spring 1919 to the March on Rome in autumn 1922. Having swung round the right and left sides of the building, the itinerary switched to the centre, and to grander sights. First was an 'honour room', designed by Mario Sironi,[10] where gigantic lettering shouted DUX, BELIEVE OBEY FIGHT and ORDER AUTHORITY JUSTICE, with the dates 1919 and 1922 for any who might have grown chronologically confused. Acting as a special focus, a tabernacle in a corner offered a reconstruction of Mussolini's office in Milan as the owner-editor of the newspaper, *Il Popolo d'Italia* (The People of Italy), with its Mazzinian-sounding purpose.

Next was the 'Gallery of the *fasci*', also designed by Sironi and lined with menacing dark statuary that seemed to merge fasces and the Roman salute. At the end stood an equestrian statue where rider and horse retained some classical connotations, aiming to inspire the place with 'Roman greatness'.[11] Third in the central series was a 'Mussolini room', designed by Leo Longanesi, another adaptable intellectual of the era, and commemorating the Duce's survival of six assassination attempts. This redemptive tale was supplemented by further relics of Mussolini's life. Beyond stood a final shrine or 'Hall of the Martyrs'. There, in a dim and reddish light, a visitor could discern the word '*presente*' (present and correct) inscribed one thousand times on a wall. At its centre rose a 7-metre-high illuminated metallic cross bearing the slogan 'For the immortal patria'. Then visitors had to turn on their heel again to traverse the rooms concentrating on the dictator and the movement, before going upstairs to a second and less flamboyant reconstruction of Fascist achievement in the years after 1922.[12]

The framers of the Mostra were emphatic about its 'revolutionary' purpose and the essentiality of its presentation of history. 'Pilgrims' (as the regime, sedulous in highlighting its religious and 'mystical' intent, called visitors) would find in their course through the exhibition spiritual uplift, an appeal to the emotions that entailed 'a delay or truce in the quotidian and humdrum efforts of the Regime'. The passage of time would be suspended and the visitor would enter in mystical fashion fully into Fascist history. To sustain this suspension of an individual's selfish daily preoccupations, the facts were rehearsed in a consciously theatrical and new manner, 'very modern and so audacious, without melancholy

PER LA PATRIA
IMMORTALE!

21. The Fascist 'Martyrs' Sacrarium', Mostra della Rivoluzione Fascista from 1932, promises dynamic cultural revolution.

echo of the decorative style of the past'.[13] The exhibition eschewed the old-fashioned and hortatory museum fare of 'the arid, neutral and irrelevant', preferring to excite 'fantasy' and 'imagination'. Its novel way of bringing the past to life was meant to conquer the souls of Italians and foreigners alike and, its organisers were sure, it would become the model in its field, earning Italy a 'primacy' there, as in so many other aspects of life (as Gioberti had once predicted).[14] The Mostra aimed to preach a gospel whereby 'the Fascist cult became the national cult, and both of these flowed into the cult of the Duce'.[15] At least for those devotees who came, saw and believed, it had made the Palazzo delle esposizioni into a 'temple', a Fascist St Peter's.[16]

Rome being Rome, the congregation who attended the Mostra della Rivoluzione Fascista was both Italian and foreign, a quirk of the totalitarian Fascist economy being its dependence on monies disbursed by tourists. Even if one (pro-Fascist) English visitor grumbled that the exterior of the exhibition was 'a small, futuristic sort of place, looking something like a cinema in an English country town', dismissing the drill of attendant party militia as ragged, and surmising that most of the visitors were allured by the 70 per cent discount offered in rail tickets to Rome, foreigners from many places did come to the Mostra's rooms to mark, learn and inwardly digest how the Fascists represented recent history.[17] Just what ordinary Italians absorbed from the lesson taught in the exhibition's rooms may be hard to decipher confidently, but the display certainly aroused intellectuals, whether those making their Fascist careers during the 1930s or those who, in more recent times, have been anxious to illuminate what was 'fascinating' about Fascism. The exhibition still prompts keen debate between those who believe the dictatorship achieved a cultural revolution and those more doubtful about the matter. Did totalitarianism make Rome thoroughly and infrangibly Fascist or did it not? At least while it was in office, did this dictatorship win Rome's history wars and impose a final solution on them?

To plumb these matters, it is worth asking how the city and its histories had been faring while Fascism solidified its rule. In this regard, it is at once evident that, however momentous Fascism's effect on Rome, the movement, its ideology and its leader did not directly draw their origins from Italy's capital. Any Roman spirit that might have whipped Fascism forward was based in historical myth, not present reality. In its first development, Fascism came from the north. Its paramilitary squads began their activity by 'cleansing' newly acquired Trieste on the north-eastern border with xenophobic attacks on Slovenes and Croats, and by 'occupying' the cities of the Po valley and Tuscany. There, the chief purpose of *squadrismo* was to reverse the social and economic advances achieved by socialist peasant unionists in the immediate aftermath of the war. Mussolini, by contrast, already an adroit politician, based himself in Milan, economic capital of the nation, where, armed with his newspaper, he honed his contacts with those for the moment greater and more powerful than he. While Fascist raiding spread ever more boldly across northern Italy, bureaucratic, unmilitary, Catholic and tourist Rome in 1919–20 lay tranquil in the south.

In Mussolini's mind and that of his followers, 'Rome' therefore was at first little more than a rhetorical device, doubtless to be summoned when need be, but usually in a negative sense. Rome was the unworthy and corrupt capital of the nation, home of mild and unwarlike clerks, men serving weak Liberal politicians, who combined to make the unlovely place 'vice-ridden' and 'artificial'.[18] Rome's other evident characteristic, its clericalism, was equally hidebound and unattractive to anyone hoping to thrust Italy towards the future.

Mussolini, in his socialist phase before 1914, had known that political action in Italy came from modernising Milan and not 'timeless' Rome and, when he converted into a Fascist, he did not initially change his views.

However, with the outbreak of the First World War and Mussolini's decision in October–November 1914 to favour 'interventionism', and with the resultant demand that war obtain primacy in Italian life and acquire justification in history, a mythical Rome – on most occasions a clichéd, mythical, Rome – surfaced in the Duce's prose. Borrowing his phraseology from the regular evocations of Rome by others in the variegated pro-war camp, Mussolini began endorsing historic messages allegedly left by classical Rome to its national Italian successors. When the Caporetto crisis seemed to threaten national dissolution, the Duce-in-the-making perceived that discipline, hierarchy and dictatorship (of the emergency variety typified by Cincinnatus rather than what was to become the long-lasting modern version) were helpful ideas that needed to be better harnessed in the cause of an Italy in crisis.[19] So was the 'birthday of Rome', 21 April, an anniversary read as assuming that the city and nation possessed 'three thousand years of history' all going in the same direction.[20] Classical *virtù* was what could be best invoked to defeat those misguided unpatriotic socialists who were flirting with importing Russian revolutionary ideas to Italy. 'Rome', Mussolini wrote combatively, 'is not a place confined to two centuries of life as Petrograd is.'[21] In February 1918 a booking to speak at the Augusteo, the sometime Mausoleum of Augustus still utilised as a public hall but soon to be accorded a pre-eminent place in the dictatorship's reworking of 'eternal Rome', encouraged him to rousing phrases. Now he preached that 'you do not deny the Patria. You conquer it!' 'Italy', he added, making the nation permanent and infallible, 'cannot die, because Italy is immortal.'[22]

Yet, despite such slashing oratory, the city and its history did not yet have him in thrall. A Fascist, Mussolini would for quite a while maintain, was too clear-eyed and 'practical' to parrot cheap ideological formulas and certainly did not wish to be enslaved by the past. Dynamism in the present (and future) was what mattered. So, when the war was about to end, Mussolini was sure that current events were greater than anything that had happened during the fall of the Roman empire or under Napoleon.[23] In reality, it was only in 1920–1, when Mussolini began to mould the Fascist movement into a party and the expansive range of his thoughts into an ideology, the prime purpose of both being to service his path to power, that Rome began to acquire a central place in his historical reference. Speaking at Trieste on 20 September 1920, for example, he had enough memory of the seizure of the Porta Pia to remark that 'a man had no claim to civilisation unless he knew Rome's history'. 'Rome', he added, 'is the name that has filled all history for twenty centuries'; its story was 'the most prodigious and marvellous of humankind'. With this city as its capital, Italy must resume a universal mission.[24] Fascism must end liberalism's weakness and confusion and win all Italians to unquestioning allegiance to the nation. So Mussolini, almost Mazzini reborn, began to enthuse about the 'religious concept of *italianità*', a gospel that would 'set the bases of Italian grandeur in the world'.[25] For this new or refreshed creed, Rome must be where the central truth, the meaning of history, reposed. 'It is fated that Rome will return to being the leading city of civilisation in the West'.[26]

The capital's other evident virtue, Mussolini maintained, was the same as had been perceived by Cavour: Rome, alone in the nation, through its antiquity soared above the municipal and parochial.[27] This natural supremacy was all the more significant given that the Fascist movement long remained prey to local bosses (called *ras* after Ethiopian chieftains). Put crudely, the Mussolini who determined to overawe the Fascist movement needed the myth of a Rome dominating Italy to justify and underpin his own power as Duce and dictator. History could be made to teach that Rome had always lorded it over Italy's numerous other beautiful and historically luminous cities and towns, just as Mussolini's grasp of thought and action meant that he must be without peer among his henchmen. As was emphasised at the Mostra della Rivoluzione Fascista, Mussolini's personal version of the past fused dictator and city as masters of time and empire, Italy and the world.[28]

Ideas still meshed uneasily with facts. In November 1921 delegates of the newly formed Fascist Party (Partito Nazionale Fascista), confronting with greater or lesser reluctance the process of 'disciplinisation' to their Duce's will, came south to a city that, Mussolini did not fail to tell them, pulsed with 'thirty centuries' of history. Predictably the Fascists met at the Augusteo. In the city streets, however, they were greeted with a mixture of apathy and suspicion, whether from the heights or depths of local society, with Mussolini restraining his hotheads with the sage (if sexist) advice: 'the Roman is by nature neither a Fascist nor an anti-Fascist. Rather he is a man who does not want to be bothered. When he is bothered, a man of the people and of the *popolino* is likely to become pugnacious. We should not provoke him but merely defend ourselves. If a Roman wears a red handkerchief, that's no reason to send in a punitive expedition'.[29]

Such prudence made sense since few Romans were yet loyal adepts of Fascism. The Rome branch of the movement had been founded in April 1919 in the offices of the genteel local irredentist Trento and Trieste Society, with a membership hard to distinguish from that of the reactionary and authoritarian Nationalists.[30] Thereafter it grew slowly and hesitantly, beset by schism over whether it should aim at respectability or revolution. From time to time, *squadristi* did provoke disturbances in the city, usually after the passion of the Roman membership had been fuelled by party members arriving from elsewhere. One affray broke out on 21 April 1921, when the Fascists, led by Achille Starace, emerging on to the national stage, tried to make the commemoration of the 'birth of Rome' their own.[31] They were fired by their Duce's comment from Milan that 'celebrating the Birth of Rome means celebrating our type of civilisation, it means exalting our history and our race, it means rooting ourselves firmly in our past the better to launch ourselves towards the future'. The Rome to be treasured, Mussolini explained further, was not really that of 'the glorious ruins'. 'I am not talking about famous stones but about live souls, not about a nostalgic contemplation of the past but a tough preparation for the future.' Fascists, he explained, were dreaming of the wisdom, strength, discipline and empire of Rome. But they were not looking back. Rather, 'it is necessary that the history of tomorrow which we are absolutely determined to create must not be a contradiction or parody of the past'. In their constructive labours, ancient Romans had challenged time. So must their Fascist heirs.[32] A year later, a fiercer riot erupted when a Roman *bersagliere* (infantry soldier), Enrico Toti, was buried with fanfare in the Campo Verano. Toti was represented both as a war hero and a Fascist 'martyr'; already such religious terminology had become automatic in the party lexicon.[33]

By the summer of 1922, Fascism had won some presence in the national capital. Yet, even if the moderate Rome paper, *Il Messaggero*, fulsomely compared Mussolini with Garibaldi, Cicero, St Paul and, for some reason, Plautus, Roman Fascists were scarcely as yet mustered into a powerful modern legion.[34] As Giuseppe Bottai, to be the most emblematic local leader under the regime, was a little ruefully to explain the events of October 1922, then 'we marched on Rome to bring Rome back to the city'.[35]

Bottai had been born in Rome in 1895 to a wine-shop keeper of Tuscan origin, who lived modestly beyond the railway station and was fond of spinning thrilling yarns about Mazzini to his son; his was a history that treasured republicanism and social change to the benefit of the poor in a manner that would scarcely prove Fascist.[36] Bottai volunteered to be a junior officer in the First World War, was wounded, and thereafter served cushily in front-line journalism. In the post-war years, he made his political debut in the city as a Futurist, disdainful of obsessions with the classical past. By 1920 Bottai had switched to the Fascist movement and, a year later, was appointed the Rome correspondent of *Il Popolo d'Italia*. He thereby became the most visible Fascist in the city, although one striving to look respectable while fluctuating in his commitment to the more radical or conservative factions of the movement. Once Mussolini was installed as dictator, Bottai held a series of important positions, being appointed *governatore* (non-elected mayor) of Rome (1935–6), as well as Minister of Education (1936–43), and in both offices acted as a major patron of the regime's intellectual life. In this regard he was vocal in his evocations of *romanità*, aimed at binding Roman histories to the cause, like the axe to the rods in the fasces, if only to bolster the image of Mussolini, a chief about whom Bottai was frequently to express an adolescent-style crush. Bottai's ambition to control the past was prefigured during the

'March on Rome' in 1922 when he advanced into the city at the head of a squad from a base at nearby Tivoli. On 30 October he led his men in a brutal raid on the poor streets around San Lorenzo. It culminated in the Fascist manner with the burning of the area's small socialist library as a symbol of Fascism's determination to wipe out any hostile Marxist reading of future or past.[37]

Despite this rampage, Fascism commenced its rule in Rome with a paradox never wholly to be resolved. The dictatorship's spokesmen grew ever more lofty in announcing that it was reactivating the Roman spirit and would rearrange the city to carry its message. Romans, Fascist propaganda now maintained with an unexplained switch in emphasis, were by definition possessed of a sense of eternity and a matching ability to synthesise the new and the old and thereby speed progress to the future.[38] Yet these and the other myths about the city were not easily reconciled with the ordinary lives and beliefs of Romans, whether those born in the city, the flood of Italian immigrants who were now attracted there or the foreign visitors (and residents), including those in the Vatican, who never ceased to experience or imagine their own Romes. When Fascism was in radical vein, its intention often seemed populist, designed to win over the 'people' and thoroughly convert them to its creed. However, talk of a participatory or 'democratic' Fascism jarred with the regime's prime repressive purpose. After ten years' rule, the assertion of the organisers of the Mostra della Rivoluzione Fascista that the regime's version of history made its consumers active, not passive, in their reckoning with the past, present and future, in practice never quite rang true.[39]

Certainly, in 1922, the city, with such economic and social progress as had been occurring arrested by the economic travail of the war, was anything but modernised. In the San Lorenzo area, for example, the locals, in quite a few senses still 'peasants in the city', kept pigs in their apartment rooms and clung to ancient *mentalités* in their attitude to savings, delayed gratification and the gender order.[40] Here, throughout the years of dictatorship, most, despite a minority defection to Fascism and a surviving reliance on Catholic charity, continued to root their identity and purpose in the family, first and last redoubt against a threatening world.[41] Established inhabitants viewed with suspicion the arrival of newcomers; by the 1930s many were labourers, attracted to Rome from the south by the city's building boom. These immigrants were labelled '*baresi*' (people from Bari), with the pejorative implication of men and women alien to the 'civilisation' of Rome. Another rumour was that the incoming settlers originated from the *paese di Starace* (Starace's home town was, actually Gallipoli in the province of Lecce, but the reference was generic). Starace was the party secretary in the 1930s who tried most flamboyantly to 'go towards the people' and give Fascism a populist veneer, but, at least in Rome's poorer urban quarters, his policy and personality did not cancel the traditional suspicion that his origins were 'barbarous' and ensured that he could not have history on his side.

There were plenty of social explanations as to why Romans clung to a familial understanding of the process of time rather than opting for a modern and ideologised one. In San Lorenzo, Testaccio and Trastevere, as well as in the new suburbs (*borgate*) on the city's periphery, quite a few citizens still lacked access to electricity and running water. TB and trachoma were among the endemic diseases. For the less well off, bathing remained a rare occurrence and babies were swaddled by their mothers.[42] In 1933 and 1935 typhus again struck the poor (in the latter spring, while Mussolini was noisily preparing to invade Ethiopia, there were 6,000 cases in the city, with 500 dead).[43] At least 25,000 Romans were homeless, with many eking out a living in what were ironically termed 'Ethiopian villages' or *baracche*, huts that, in the 1920s, spread across much of the area between the station and the Via Tiburtina, for example.[44] An estimated 6,500 of these hovels disfigured the city's periphery in 1930, with 6,000 still present in 1933, despite loud Fascist campaigns for their elimination.[45] Among the less well off, families of eight, nine or more children were common, again with some irony since Fascism, needing soldiers for the battles to come, had committed itself to 'win' the 'battle of the births' but did little to counter the decline in reproduction among the middle and upper classes, including most leading Fascists (except Mussolini).[46] For ordinary Romans, the first daily task remained to get by (*arrangiarsi*), as it always had been, and, to this end, there was much reliance on borrowing and barter. Employment remained precarious and Rome continued to lack any major industries, except tourism, Catholicism and bureaucracy, despite efforts by the Duce, especially in the 1930s, to foster an armaments factory on the city's outskirts.[47] At that time, the global Depression hit the city hard, with unemployment, according to official figures, rising from 1,473 in 1929 to 8,015 in 1931 and 38,358 in 1934.[48] After ten years of Fascist totalitarian pestering, the people of the suburbs had doubtfully surrendered their souls to Fascism and its understanding of the world.

Education was reserved for the wealthy, with fewer than 20 per cent of pupils proceeding past elementary school.[49] Contrary to Fascist rhetoric about national unity dominating all, class divisions still gaped in the city and did so graphically in its local administration. There, rather than sponsoring a revolution, most officials changed their shirts to a Fascist black and always remembered to salute their Duce but otherwise retained their social purpose and world view. Thus, on 2 March 1923, the City Council was abruptly dissolved. However, the existing mayor, Filippo Cremonesi, wealthy leader of a Conservative and Nationalist coalition and sometime head of Rome's Chamber of Commerce, was simply transposed into *Regio Commissario* (Royal Commissioner), the most obvious effect being a repressive one, ending any intrusion of democratic principles into his governance. This switch was made permanent on 28 October 1925, when the Comune was relabelled a *governatorato* (government), with Cremonesi as *governatore* (governor). He was seconded by nominated counsellors, baptised with equal novelty and pomposity 'rectors' (these *rettori* only lasted for a year) and *consultatori*, chosen in what would become the 'corporate' manner through their work qualifications rather than from spatially determined electorates. By November 1926 Cremonesi was driven to resign, amid rumours that he had yielded to pressure from Fascist (and Catholic) real estate merchants whose 'gold fever' had become too blatantly rapacious.[50] Once again, no radical change resulted. His successor until September 1928 was another nobleman (though of relatively recent coinage), Ludovico Spada Veralli Potenziani, characterised unflatteringly by his contemporaries as a 'gentleman' who was 'incompetent', 'indolent' and 'dozy'.[51] He was in turn replaced by Francesco Boncompagni Ludovisi, heir of an ancient aristocratic family with popes in their number, who lasted in office until he made way for Bottai in January 1935. The social pattern was restored at the end of 1936, when Bottai was succeeded by Pietro Colonna, son of the noble mayor of the city 1899–1904 and 1914–18 and, like the others, *persona gratissima* in the Vatican.

Fitting this process where, should the roar of propaganda about revolution be ignored, Roman Fascism remained more Roman than Fascist, and where pre-war social elites were little disturbed in their power, a report on party membership in the city conducted for the secretariat in October 1926 emphasised that most followers of the movement had opted for a comfortable life. Local officials, it was stated, had succeeded in 'purging from Fascist lists those elements who retained the mentality of a squadrism that liked to engage in hooligan acts'.[52] Four years later, the tone was little different. Now, party inspectors noted, 'Fascism in the Capital is much improved in behaviour and perfectly disciplined'. Order was the chief watchword. Thus arrayed, Fascist Rome was hard at work and in a newly dynamic manner: 'the whole city has been speeded up; everyone does everything now more in haste and so clerks have more time to take lunch'. That was just as well, it was added a little defensively. The 'foreign press has been greatly in favour of our reforms which have been described as <u>acts of courage</u> by the regime', the report ran, but Roman life was permanently 'under a kind of <u>examination</u> by thousands of individual foreigners who observe a lot and judge', and such recurrent inspection was all the greater reason for local party members to concentrate on discipline and order rather than enthusiasm.[53] A more guileless account in May 1932 alleged that the ancient urban tradition of *pasquinades*, lampoons about the fatuity and corruption of the great and powerful, had now at last died out, given 'the lack of any material that might foster irony'.[54]

Whether or not Pasquino had been finally silenced, there were plenty of reasons to doubt that Fascism was proving a radical engineer of human souls in Rome, shunting the populace on to new historic tracks, with the more honest officials admitting that, despite profound and pervasive popular admiration for Mussolini, beneath the surface of the city abuses lay unchecked, rusting the reputation of the Fascist party and its ideology.[55] For the moment, however, stubbornly surviving social divisions and the intellectual doubts that they prompted could be disguised by dramatic modernisation of Rome's cityscape; indeed in the late 1920s and 1930s it was bulldozed into a new shape. Fascism pledged to dominate the outward and visible in Rome, contenting Mussolini and his henchmen with the hope that they were thereby conquering the inward and spiritual. Perhaps a more solidly orthodox comprehension of the time, it was implied, could be achieved by the remoulding of space?

The compass of the urban plan, propaganda did not cease to recall, had been set by the Duce in two speeches in April 1924. Then, Mussolini had pronounced, while typically merging nation and empire, 'Rome is no more the capital of a little people of antiquarians. Look around and you will see that, already, the streets of this incomparable city are thronged with a traffic that is growing more intense from one day to the next. You will see . . . [building projects] driven by an ever expanding energy. The Rome of which we dream must not merely be the living and pulsating centre of a renewed Italian nation, but also the marvellous capital of the entire Latin world.'[56] To this end, urban cleansing was fundamental and must commence here and now. It must rigorously separate good history from bad. 'All of ancient Rome must be freed from what contaminates it.' Moreover, 'next to the ancient and the medieval, a monumental Rome of the twentieth century must rise', the Duce affirmed. 'Rome cannot, must not, be a modern city only in a banal sense. It must be a city worthy of its glory, and this glory must be incessantly renewed in order to transmit the legacy of the Fascist era to future generations.'[57] Even while he accepted honorary citizenship of the national capital that he had once disdained, the Duce was announcing his career as Rome's wielder of a pickaxe (*piccone*) and expert in demolition (*sventramento*).[58] Soon any who doubted Fascist pummelling of the urban fabric could expect to hear from the dictator that they were utterly absurd in wanting to save 'a pile of privies' (*un mucchio di latrine*).[59]

In first proof that the city had become modern, on 21 April 1925 (the birth of Rome was now proclaimed a national and Fascist holiday) a railway was opened from the city to Ostia, illuminating site of the classical port and of an enticing beach resort in construction. It was followed up with a motorway, opened on 28 October 1928. Work also began on 'isolating' the Forum of Augustus, with the demolition of a baroque monastery, and on a similar 'cleansing' of the area around the Tempio della Fortuna Virilis, near the Tiber. In 1925 the subsidiary classical museum in the Palazzo Caffarelli on the Capitoline was upgraded into the Museo Mussolini, allowing permanent exhibition of material about the ancient Roman empire collected during the *Cinquantennio* in 1911 and driving a visiting professor from Wellesley College to grow misty about how, under the dictatorship, 'while Rome is constantly planning for the future, it never loses consciousness of its past'.[60]

On 31 December 1925 Mussolini trumpeted a programme that would convert Rome into 'the great metropolis, the Capital of the [totalitarian] State'. 'Within five years,' he declared, 'Rome must appear a marvel to all the world's people: vast, ordered and powerful, as it was under the first empire of Augustus.'[61] Builders and town planners must now isolate the Augusteo and cleanse the accretions that, it was alleged in familiar phrases, demeaned the attractions and blunted the historical messages of the Campidoglio, the Pantheon, Piazza Colonna and the parliament building (in the case of these last three, the work was not pursued). On 21 April 1926 Mussolini swung his pick to mark the commencement of the destruction of what was deemed unworthy about the surrounds of the Theatre of Marcellus. In this act, he took pains to be photographed and have his image, then as on many further occasions, relayed to an admiring public.[62] Soon the demolition was making room for what was called the Via del Mare (the start of which now bears the less grandiose name of the Via del Teatro di Marcello), a road designed to lead the nation, practically and metaphorically, towards sea and empire. A plan was also launched for an underground railway or Metropolitana in the city (although its first track would not open until the 1950s).[63]

More elegant, if more ambiguous in regard to the scientific and rational modernity projected by Fascism, was what is now termed the Quartiere Coppedè, after its Tuscan architect Gino Coppedè, near Piazza Mincio in bourgeois Rome. Completed in 1926, these apartment buildings are worth viewing today as the supreme example of the Liberty style or Art Nouveau in the city, and, between the wars, were the luxurious home of such period notables as tenor Beniamino Gigli.[64] At the same time, the first new cheap mass housing for workers was erected around Piazza Verbano; over the years more would follow, with an increasing emphasis on narrow exits and entries, the better to allow surveillance by the regime's never numerous but always active secret police.

If, despite Fascist boasts, class difference in accommodation was not altogether overcome in the city, maybe healthy exercise could unite the people. Under construction on the northern outskirts of the city along the Tiber was a model sports complex called the Foro Mussolini (now the Foro italico). Its entry was marked by a tall marble obelisk, erected with applause and effort on 23 November 1929 (amid rumours of peculation at the height of the regime over payment for it). While the Foro's completion was awaited, the city's budget for school construction was raised from 5 to 50 million lire between 1922 and 1927.[65] Further examples of the Fascist version of welfare and modernity were the new Ospedale del Littorio (Lictors' Hospital, now San Camillo) and the Casa Madre dei Mutilati (Home for War Invalids), planned by Marcello Piacentini, son of the architect of the Palazzo delle esposizioni. This Casa was inaugurated on 4 November 1928, tenth anniversary of the victory in 1918 at Vittorio Veneto, celebrated under Fascism and under the succeeding Republic as

Armed Forces Day. A dreadfully ugly building, it still detracts from the nearby Castel Sant'Angelo.

But, with steadily increasing insistence, it was the regime's concentration on classical and imperial *romanità* that demanded changes to the city's historic centre. Modernity was all very well, but the dictatorship was convinced that it needed the blessing of the ancients to achieve real legitimacy. In 1927 excavations in the Largo Argentina unearthed four temples from the ancient Republican era that were quickly 'systematised' (at the cost of the demolition of a medieval church and more recent housing) and officially inaugurated, with the customary vibrant words about the 'three thousand year history' of the city, on 21 April 1929. Anniversaries were easy to find. On 28 October 1930 (eighth celebration of the March on Rome) the bimillenary of the birth of Virgil – first in a series including Horace and Augustus that would stud the coming decade – was given public memory with the establishment of a new Parco Virgiliano, opened for public use along the Via Nemorense. In 1931 the city plan of 1909, amended in 1926, was updated, with the chief emphasis on hammering the place into what was called the Fascist style, as well as a prediction that the future population should be two million. The document was, the regime boasted in characteristic words, a 'real plan of battle', even if, for the moment, it was explained primly, the struggle was to be a 'bloodless' one.[66] Nonetheless, the implications were clear. Under Mussolini's infallible governance, past and future were to be fused. The ancient was to come alive and light the modern way to ever greater Fascist power and ever more extensive empire.

The most revealing reconstruction in this regard was announced on 28 October 1931 and inaugurated twelve months later for the start of the *Decennale* as concrete proof of the dynamism of Fascism. To match the Via del Mare, another wide new street was to cut through old Rome. It would be called the Via dei Monti and symbolically carry Fascism through the hills and dales of the peninsula. But the area where demolition proceeded most aggressively ran from the Victor Emmanuel monument and the Duce's new office in the vast and ornate Sala del Mappamondo (Room of the Globe of the World) of the Palazzo Venezia to the Colosseum. Soon it was grandiloquently named the Via dell'Impero (Empire Street; after Fascism it would be redesignated the Via dei fori imperiali – Street of the Imperial Fora). To be sure, the idea of such an avenue went back to the Liberal era and even to French administration under Napoleon. Now, however, previous sketches became concrete at the cost of a number of churches, palaces and apartment buildings, containing an estimated 6,000 bedrooms, and the expulsion of those who dwelled in them to rapidly rising tenements on the city's periphery or wherever else they could find substitute housing.[67]

The Via dell'Impero scarcely matched the Champs-Elysées in Paris, relic of the grandiose Caesarian ambitions of Napoleon the Little (Napoleon III), but

22. Mussolini visits the Via dell'Impero with a pick-axe utmost in his mind, 1931.

it was an impressive venue for military parades and was, during the decade after 1932, regularly used for flamboyant Fascist ceremony. As instructive ornament, on 21 April 1934 four maps were set into the Basilica di Massenzio, tracing the expansion of ancient Roman power from tiny first settlement by the Tiber to the Mediterranean world. On 28 October 1936 after the conquest of Ethiopia, a fifth map, this time of the Fascist empire, was added. The message rang out that the Duce was a modern Caesar whose legions had vast fields yet to conquer. Meanwhile, many Italians for whom Rome was still a far-off place came to know this part of the city through film; a cliometrician has estimated that, during the 1930s, the Victor Emmanuel monument and its surrounds acted as a backdrop to *Cinegiornale* (the newsreel playing in every cinema throughout Italy) on 249 occasions.[68]

Yet, as contemporaries began to notice, the Fascist construction of wide streets through the heart of the ancient city was having unplanned effects. The conquests of Fascist armies were to prove fleeting. Motorised traffic, however, was to master Rome. In 1925 a propagandist had hailed the rigour of Fascist government in imposing on 1 March the rule of driving on the right in the city (until then Rome, Milan, Genoa and Turin had all weakly been permitted to retain driving on the left despite the fact that the nation had opted for the right in 1912 in its first Highway Code). The journalist joked that, 'with Fascism, it is no longer possible to talk about the left'.[69] Yet the car was not necessarily funny in Italian cities and soon 30,000 vehicles were choking the capital.[70] In

1934 a Scottish fan of Fascism commented disconsolately in prose that sought to imitate Futurist militancy and dash: 'Noise. Klaxons. ROME. Traffic that rushes at you, roaring as it rushes. Motor-cycles with exhausts full open. Bicycles like malign mosquitoes darting for your flesh. Eternal Rome. Infernal din.'[71] As a more recent commentator noted, the dictatorship, in its failure to foresee this coming history, was creating not so much a modern Rome as 'a *modernist* city which defied rationalism', a place whose historic centre was not so much accorded Fascist meaning as converted into 'an uninhabited space, filled by ruins and surrounded by fast-moving traffic'.[72] Maybe in seeking to pin down the city's history into a Fascist meaning and no other, the regime was actually frittering away much of Rome's memory and atmosphere?

Such debates lay in the future. For the present, Fascist control over Rome seemed secure and purposeful. True, to the north there was a shadow on the horizon with the rise of Adolf Hitler, leading what might or might not be a fellow Fascist movement, but soon advancing with a dynamism that the Italian dictatorship had not matched to set Europe aflame. Was the answer for Mussolini to drive his people on to greater deeds and make more drastic the reworking of Rome? As if in reaction to German pressure, the dictator's rhetoric shifted from the line that his ideology was for domestic consumption only to asserting that Fascism was 'universal', the winning 'idea of the twentieth century'. If universality was now what the dictatorship aimed at, where better than Rome and its history to find physical and spiritual expression of that quality? As a local Latinist put it in early 1932 in *Capitolium*, propaganda organ of the *Governatorato*: 'Rome, which has had, and must always have, a global function', could, given its history, never be 'a limited phenomenon of a limited nation'.[73] 'Onward Fascist legionaries' was the ringing motto for the 1930s and Rome was meant to be an ever more important historical base for their imperial actions.

One surviving emblem of this ever more militant Fascism is the menacingly authoritarian Tempio di Cristo Re, the temple of Christ the King, opened in 1934 in the Viale Mazzini (presumably to the disgust of the ghost of the anti-clerical prophet of the nation). It had been designed by Marcello Piacentini ten years earlier as a 'temple of peace', patriotically recalling the First World War. Its construction lagged, however, to be resumed in 1932, with the soldierly now overwhelming the pacific. Mussolini singled it out for praise as expressing Fascist style and purpose; its vividly modernist interior carries quite a few themes from the display at the Mostra della Rivoluzione Fascista. Its crassest feature in the 1930s was Arturo Martini's sculpture on the arch of the portal of Christ donating his sacred heart to the faithful, while giving a 'Roman' (or Fascist) salute. As threatening is another large Christ worked into mosaics on the apse by Achille Funi. The Christian Saviour is here represented as a sturdy son of God being offered regalia by two angels. If rather clumsily, he looms forward ready to trample down any un-Fascist sinners in the congregation.

Here, more than anywhere else in the city, it seems, even Catholic history had been annexed to the dictatorship.

In a book published just after his death in 1960, Piacentini, who, during the post-war years had shrugged off his reputation as 'Mussolini's Speer' to resume a major role in Rome's architecture and town planning, rearranged any reading of the church's message to convert it to 'a redoubt of human, family and social values'.[74] It was in the shadow of the building's campanile, Piacentini contended, that, after 1944, 'the hopes of the Patria' were 'reborn in difficult times'.[75] As will be seen further below, such tendentious claims would commonly feature in Rome's effort to disguise its Fascist past in the post-war era. But they can also prompt the query whether the dictatorship's home base was as secure as its propaganda and its increasingly commanding place in Roman streetscapes seemed to proclaim.

Had the Church really surrendered its history and its vision of the future to totalitarian Fascism? What, after the signature of the Lateran Pacts promised amity and accommodation, had happened to the long-standing history war between a nationalist, now Fascist and imperialist Italian reading of Rome and the enduring and universalist Catholic one? According to some historians, who take the regime's rhetoric at face value, Fascism, despite its deal with Pope Pius XI, was fully and aggressively determined on an avant-garde project designed to imbue the masses with a 'collective historic imaginary'. Adapting to its cause deeply embedded 'Latin Catholic rhetorical codes', it aimed to create its own novel 'immanent conception of history' and replace the Catholic religion with its own.[76] However, the success of this project, if it in fact existed, may be doubted. While the Vatican stood, neither numinousness nor liturgy was a Fascist monopoly on the streets of Rome. For most of the time, through the years of dictatorship, the popes and Mussolini cohabited with reasonable cheer. Yet Catholicism had not surrendered its mastery of history in the *longue durée*. Even if it might appear that Fascism was becoming the triumphant political doctrine of the twentieth century, the Vatican's version of Christianity ran inevitably on through all time.

The double meanings that can therefore be detected in Church–State relations can be explored by examining further the story of that 'Christ the King' given presence in Rome in Piacentini's 'temple'. There, analysis will show that a Catholic empire marched onwards as proudly as did a Fascist one. On 11 December 1925 when his first Holy Year was drawing to its close, Pius XI had issued an encyclical, *Quas Primas*, instituting the feast of *Christus Rex* as a particularly significant liturgical celebration, a sacred moment when the faithful would rally globally to repel any advances by the dread forces of secularism and anti-clericalism, committed to error and crime. Images of this version of Christ, the Church now took pains to recall from its vast compendium of useful pasts, had been utilised in the Vendée, homeland of the counter-revolution, to combat the de-christianising aims of the French Revolution. The sway of 'Christ the King' was not confined to Italy. His commanding message was to stir and rally anti-Republican forces in Spain after 1931. By the time that country had descended into civil war, the name would be further borrowed by the Belgian Fascist movement – the Rexists – led by Léon Degrelle.[77] In Catholic intent, *Christus Rex* stood for the counter-revolution, militant and triumphant, Fascist if need be but too abiding to be merely that.

In his encyclical underlining that the regal 'power' of Christ was manifest in legislative, judicial and executive arenas where it guaranteed 'a just liberty, order and tranquillity, peace and concord', Pius XI set the date of the feast marking this aspect of the Saviour's relationship with an ideally more obedient humankind as the last Sunday in October.[78] It was a choice full of unspoken meaning. This date meant that, in Italy, the counter-revolutionary and integralist as well as universal role attributed to Christ the King could directly coincide with the anniversary of the March on Rome (28 October) and always implicitly conditioned it, while similarly abutting and qualifying Vittorio Veneto Day (4 November), the patriotic commemoration of Italy's victory in the First World War. Through the 1930s the annual celebration of the festival of *Christus Rex* denied any acceptance by the Church that a lay Italy of Mussolini (or of the Savoys) had taken the destiny of Rome and its people out of its hands. As if in proof that a purpose had been served, once Fascism was defeated and the Savoy monarchy expelled, Pope John XXIII, in 1960 striving manfully to loosen the Church's ties with counter-revolution, downgraded the significance of the feast. His successor, Paul VI, cut any chronological connection with Fascism by moving the commemoration a month forward to the first Sunday in Advent. With these post-Fascist adaptations, the festival of *Christus Rex* dwindled into its present condition as one among a multiplicity of Church holy days. Its history has not been liquidated and is likely to be treasured by the more reactionary in the Catholic flock. However, for the present, it is not as useful as it was between the wars.

The story of *Christus Rex* in Fascist Rome is a specific one. More ample in the conscripting of history by the Church in open or implicit rivalry with the Italian nation and the Fascist dictatorship were the two *Anni Santi* or jubilees presided over by Pius XI. As Achille Ratti, he had been elected pontiff in February 1922 from a previous position as Cardinal-Archbishop of Milan, where he had been able to scrutinise the strengths and weaknesses of Fascism. Moving south to Rome while retaining his Lombard entourage, Pius XI in 1924 announced through a Bull with the bold and assertive title, *Infinita Dei*, that, during the following year, the Church would hold another *Giubileo*.[79] Mussolini, he was implying, may have made himself an 'all-powerful dictator'. Soon he might aim to be totalitarian and indeed infallible, at least according to the regime slogan that 'Mussolini is always right' (*Mussolini ha sempre ragione*). Yet, in the Church's view, he did not cease to be a feeble and imperfect man when measured against the infinity of God and the divinely endorsed and so 'real' infallibility of successive pontiffs. As if to prove the matter, Pius moved more actively than had any pope since the French Revolution to make his Holy Year memorable and salutary.

There is plenty of evidence that he did so with success, thereby highlighting that the Church was the bearer of the most significant and durable history of Rome, while he himself donned a charisma that could outshine (and outlast) any dictator. One testimony is that of the English travel writer, E.V. Lucas, who attended the closing ceremony of the Porta Santa (Holy Door) at St Peter's on Christmas Eve 1925. However sceptical an Englishman, he perceived transcendence there:

> all strangers in Rome, when the opportunity arises of seeing a great festival of the Church, should seize it; for there is nothing like it anywhere else. On this occasion, the most precious relics are exhibited ... but it is the procession, heralded by the papal march played on the silver trumpets, that one remembers most vividly. The members of the Pope's bodyguard of gentlemen, moving about the church in their capacity as ushers, are medieval enough, in their ruffs and capes and knee-breeches, with dazzling sword-hilts; but clothes are mere accessories, whereas faces are facts, and the true Middle Ages arrive with the procession itself and the countenances of the princes, prelates, priests and monks of the Church. For these faces do not change. ... Some of the clerics are in purple, some in black, some in cowls; one or two are bearded; some austerely robed in white, with cabbalistic design. Many are incredibly old; almost none look happy, care-free; many are lined and marked with anxiety. And then the cardinals, in their dazzling white ... and then, carried high above all the rest, by servitors in red, and accompanied by two bearers of lofty feather fans, the Holy Father himself seated in his chair [the *sedia gestatoria* or portable throne], with a great yellow mitre on his venerable head, and softly waving his hand from right to left in blessing.[80]

Such a rite was, thought Lucas, an expression of timelessness. It made manifest the real and abiding Rome.

Similarly, for the American Catholic journalist, Anne O'Hare McCormick, the ceremonies of this year mystically transformed the chief figure involved. When the pope was borne 'in his uplifted golden chair [after being summoned by a silver trumpet], those ineffable waving fans of white peacock feathers somehow hedged him in and brushed him aside, so that the man inside the Pope did not matter at all. He was lost in something impersonal, perpetual, obliterating. It was the Papacy that one saw moving in the hush, swallowing up good Popes, bad Popes, indifferent Popes, and surviving them all.'[81] For many onlookers, the Church could, through its self-consciously 'ancient' ceremonial (or its ceaseless ingenuity in inventing tradition), express an aura and a mystery which modern regimes, preaching the gospel of political religions, whether nationalist or Fascist, could seek to emulate but scarcely equal. The durability, even the eternity, of the Papacy overbore the most grandiose claims of Musssolini's personality cult.

Certainly the Church, in its own explanation of *Anno Santo*, took for granted that it stood above contemporary trumpery and human concerns, and did so from a Rome that it staunchly believed still belonged to the Church and God. The Jubilee offered a more vivid sign than usual of the Deity's conquest of time. The semi-official introduction to the current *Anno Santo* was emphatic that its purpose went back to Mosaic law when 'the chosen people do penance once every fifty years in order that the sins they had committed might be forgiven'.[82] While the faithful awaited expiation, the *sedia gestatoria* could prove that, in Church events, the pope was lifted above the human ruck halfway to heaven, just as the Host was raised above the altar at the most solemn moment in a mass.

If permanence was an insistent Church claim in any Holy Year, universality was another. Throughout 1925 *Civiltà cattolica* reported on the succession of activities in Rome, interpreting them often with some reflex comment on the 'totalitarian' dictatorship that was in those same months tightening its control over Italy. Italians, one writer feared, were too given to political disputation. But they could apprehend from the Jubilee that religion united them, given its basis, not in human discord and error (or in short-term history), but in 'immutable truths and eternal principles'.[83] In Rome itself, another author underlined, visiting pilgrims from home and abroad learned how classical and early Christian ruins and relics expressed a providential triumph. In 'overcoming every modern tumult of passion or self-interest', it was announced, the Church 'dominates, invigorates and conquers the people who come together here from every known part of the world'.[84]

Before this grandiose global mission, Italian events might seem frail and fleeting. The Fascist predilection for violence, it was still cautioned, made it hard for loyal Catholics to accept the regime's recipe that being Italian and being Fascist were now the same.[85] As if further to display and challenge the parochialism of Mussolini's dictatorship and to exhibit its own span, the Church that year appointed Monsignor Roche of India as its first 'coloured' bishop from the extra-European world. At the same time, Pius XI eagerly encouraged the updating of the missionary exhibition at the Museo missionario-etnologico in the Vatican complex, a site that exhibited a global range that might be thought to overwhelm Italy's petty international ambitions.[86] Typically imposing legitimacy on present actions by reference to deep historical roots, papal commentary explained that Catholic 'imperial' interest was not new but had been normal since 'the time of St Paul the apostle'. The museum was not the only place to tell such a story. Already in February 1922 the church of Santa Susanna, dating back to the third century but frequently altered, was nominated as reflecting the enhanced Catholic American presence in the city and potential lay American power in the world.[87] In 1925 even regime journals celebrated a monument to a black man in Santa Maria Maggiore, testimony to an embassy from the Congo to the Vatican in 1608.[88] Fascist Rome, in other words, might be national, it might quest for empire and win a (meagre) place in the sun. But Catholic Rome, the real Rome, was universal, as it always had been; the *Urbs* was the capital of the *Orbis*.[89] The sun never set on the Church's empire and God had charged it to rule the world for ever and ever.

To be sure, Catholic commentators conceded, maybe Fascism, despite its deplorable worship of the State, had something to be said for it in the short term compared with the scandalous evils of liberalism, socialism and communism.[90] The events of this Holy Year had proceeded with calm and comfort, and the illumination of St Peter's and its square at Easter, allegedly for the first time since 1825, signalled the growing practical accommodation between Church and State in Italy.[91] Moreover, Catholic pilgrims flocked in, 600,000 of them.[92] The receipts, much richer than those of 1900, were reckoned to be almost 3,600 million lire, covering 61 per cent of the annual national debt.[93] Whatever might be their dissonances throughout history, Church and State had plenty of practical reasons for the newly friendly contacts that were to culminate in the Lateran Pacts.

Yet, however heralded in Italy and the wider world, this plan for the Vatican to rub along comfortably with the dictatorship did not mean that the Church was renouncing its claims to primacy in Rome. The most telling demonstration of the fact came in Pius XI's second Holy Year, held between Easter 1933 and Easter 1934. Allegedly commemorating the two-thousandth anniversary of the death and resurrection of Christ (indeed a long and deep history), this *Giubileo* was summoned in the immediate aftermath of the *Decennale* and while the Mostra della Rivoluzione Fascista still drew Fascist pilgrims to Rome. Since 1929 no longer a 'prisoner in the Vatican', Pius XI could now sally forth into the streets of Rome for the first time since the Risorgimento. With this happy prospect, Catholic 'pilgrims' thronged the city, quite a few taking in both the Fascist and the Church sights. Catholic ceremonials, however, usually outweighed Fascist ones, both in attendance and in solemnity or glitz. Hundreds of thousands assembled in and outside St Peter's for Easter mass, or at the other three great basilicas, as the calendar of feasts moved in stately progression to San Giovanni in Laterano, Santa Maria Maggiore and San Paolo fuori le mura. On each occasion, by implication, the power of Catholic history trumped that of the regime.

Typical was the Ascension Day celebration, 25 May 1933, at the Lateran. It followed hard on a Fascist parade of 24 May, eighteenth anniversary of Italy's entry into the First World War, applauded by 40,000 in the Via dell'Impero, where Mussolini spoke in militant mode to fresh conscripts in the armed forces. Yet, the Vatican festival was evidently grander in its appeal. Now holy

23. Pius XI in Piazza San Pietro, exhibiting his charisma and infallibility, Holy Year, 1933–4.

relics that had been locked away since the trauma of the Risorgimento were evocatively displayed; on the afternoon of 25 May a solemn procession, winding around the streets between the Lateran and the Colosseum, carried the *Acheiropoieton*, a portrait of Christ allegedly painted by St Luke that was conserved at the Scala santa, for public cynosure and worship.[94] Fascist monuments could demand observation; as he journeyed beyond St Peter's, Pius XI raised the blind on his car window so he, too, could inspect the triumph of Mussolinian town planning (and of the Fascist parading of history) on the Via dell'Impero. But the press also reported that, at the pontiff's exit from the Vatican, a throng of a thousand fell to its knees and any individuals or groups who spotted the passage of the papal car through Rome did the same. At the Lateran the crowd was 'massive', both inside and outside the basilica, at least 200,000 strong according to Vatican estimates.[95] During the rite, onlookers' emotions were stimulated by music, the varied colour of the gowns worn by the religious authorities and by the sight and aura of the *sedia gestatoria*, which had been brought there.[96] Fascism might be hard at work inventing tradition, but the Church effortlessly incarnated it, just as its every act made plain its universality with a span that vastly exceeded Fascist plots in Ethiopia. So, at a papal mass a few days after the events at San Giovanni, three Chinese were given Episcopal rank, when Pius was 'wrapped in a huge silver mantle interwoven with gold'.[97] Could the spartan or dowdy black shirt of Fascism or imperial rule in dusty Mogadishu really compete?

As ever, the Church could rely on a congregation that was not merely Italian. Distinguished international visitors flocked in to renew their dedication to Catholic Rome. Prominent were Austrian strongman Engelbert Dollfuss, his Hungarian equivalent Gyula Gömbös and Alfonso XIII, former king of a Spain being battered in Catholic eyes by its anti-clerical or demonic Republic. Hermann Göring and Franz von Papen, Nazi rivals, were appropriate German arrivals because papal officials were engaged in negotiating a concordat with the new regime in Berlin (it was initialled on 8 July). Many of those who came to Rome made some obeisance to Mussolini, but they did not forget to stoop to Pius XI and his Church. Whatever else was occurring in 1933–4 it was not the simple triumph of applied Fascist totalitarianism.[98]

After all, Catholicism had so many histories that it could summon, as Church activity made plain in a competition with the dictatorship that may have remained latent but did not diminish in its firmness of purpose. As was the custom in a *Giubileo*, the pope approved a number of beatifications and sanctifications, the most celebrated of which was that of Bernadette Soubirous (1844–79), the 'innocent peasant girl' of Lourdes. She was elevated into the company of the saints on 8 December 1933, in a five-hour ceremony that included a *Te Deum* and a pontifical mass, a sermon in Latin where Pius XI drew an apposite comparison between Bernadette and the Immaculate Conception, as well as a public blessing of the crowd. To attend this event, eager pilgrims slept overnight in cold and heavy rain. They filled St Peter's.[99]

But the best was to be saved for last. During the closing ceremonies of *Anno Santo*, the person to be elevated was Don Giovanni Bosco, the Piedmontese missionary priest and founder of the Salesian order. Tugging national Italian history free from the sins of Cavour, Garibaldi and Mazzini, Bosco, labelled by a recent historian a 'reactionary clerical' and hard-line defender of Temporal Power, was represented as a Catholic agent of Italian unification and so of a clerical Risorgimento.[100] Helpfully, his early missions to North and South America also made him a 'friend of emigrants', one with an imaginably imperial air.[101] In Church eyes, Bosco's life proved that there was nothing original in the nationalist and Fascist path through time; anything positive in this track was obviously Catholic.

On 1 April, 300,000 flocked into St Peter's Square to be present at the walling up of the Holy Door and, before that, at the mass that made Don Bosco a saint (and so, by definition, someone who, through his virtue and piety, had conquered time). A statue to him was being prepared in the Basilica; it was finished in 1936 and can be found, now darkened by the years, on a raised plinth above a commemoration of Pope Pius IX on St Peter's central aisle. Don Bosco is caressing a boy of the people and an 'Indian' girl. For Easter 1934 the worshippers included Crown Prince Umberto but not the Duce and, at least officially, none of his leading henchmen. In *Il Messaggero*, the excited press account of what was to happen did not fail to balance itself with a salutary article by Bottai on 'The power of Mussolini'.[102] Nonetheless, it was hard not to be impressed by what the papers elsewhere called the 'incomparable magnificence' of the show at St Peter's. As a weekly portrayed it: 'The Jubilee closed therefore on the Day of the Resurrection with a solemnity of apotheosis that has probably never been seen before in the many centuries of Christian civilisation.'[103]

The celebration of Don Bosco was not quite finished, however. The dictatorship could scarcely accept its implicit rout by Church power and sought to give its own imprint to the saint's asserted fame. So, on 2 April, the Campidoglio, another luminously meaningful Roman site, saw the Fascist State add its blessings for the new saint to those of the Church. Helped by the presence of five cardinals and many other religious, as well as by such regime notables as ex-Nationalist Federzoni, and 'Admiral of Victory' in 1918, Paolo Thaon di Revel, but most exalted by the appearance of Mussolini himself, another ceremony took place in the apt surrounds of the 'Julius Caesar room' of the local Roman government. Cesare De Vecchi di Val Cismon, a *quadrumvir* and murderous Turin squadrist in Fascism's salad days but now the ostentatiously Catholic ambassador to the Vatican, recalled how Don Bosco was 'an Italian Saint and the most Italian of saints'. Bosco, De Vecchi urged, expressed that 'Italian perfection which became for him *romanità*' and which led him and his Salesians to govern 'an empire as wide as the world'.[104] The rivalry in interpretation was stark. For the Church, Bosco's piety gave proof that, through Risorgimento and after, Italy's past, present and future belonged to it. For the dictatorship, Bosco was a proto-Fascist whose religion was more Roman than Catholic.

Egilberto Martire, the regime's staunchest clerical and a Fascist who in a few short years would fall out with the dictator, tried to blend the history of Don Bosco and of Holy Year in phrases that were meant to be solemn.[105] The new saint, he wrote, understood that 'Italy will be and the Church will be; one and the other, both will be, reconciled as they are in a new synthesis and in the new glory of Rome'.[106] He presumably convinced himself. Yet, despite the sunny atmosphere in Rome that Easter and the chatter about loving accord between Church and dictatorial State, there had been, and would continue to be, plenty of evidence that no full synthesis had occurred between Catholicism and Fascism or between their reading of past and future. In Rome, as the political storms of the later 1930s rumbled closer, disputes about history had not been silenced for ever.

9. Villa Torlonia

———— ✳ ————

8

THE ROME OF MUSSOLINI AND HIS
HISTORY WARS

In one of his more expansive broodings late in his life, Mussolini contemplated converting the position of Duce into a fixed-term one, perhaps of seven years, perhaps of five.[1] Had this idea been pursued, it might be imagined that Mussolini could have retired to his home region of the Romagna in 1932 or 1936. Either choice might have granted him a less dismal historical reputation than he possessed after his death in 1945 and after the rout of his nation, regime and ideology in the Italian sector of the Second World War. To be sure, a Duce, retired like Cincinnatus to his estates in the 1930s, would have had to explain away the violence through which he obtained office, the tyranny that he used to impose a totalitarian state and the murderous policies that his regime implemented in Libya and Ethiopia. Those seeking his historical redemption would also have had to assess his assault on the urban fabric of Rome, which, as has been seen, by the *Decennale* in 1932, had erased a number of fine urban legacies in the interests of imposing a totalitarian reading of history on the city.

Yet, it is also true that the second decade of the dictatorship was, in many ways, more radical than the first, and this broadcasting of Fascist fundamentalism can still be traced in Rome, where urban 'cleansing', building and rebuilding proceeded apace. In the political world now came the alliance with Nazi Germany and the adoption of racial legislation in the empire and at home, culminating in the Salò Republic and its damning in November 1943 of Rome's ancient and patriotic Jewish community as enemies of the nation and 'race' in the Italian chapter of the Holocaust. Towering over all was the personality cult of the Duce, elevated by regime propaganda into an infallible and omniscient God. Real Fascists were now meant to believe without doubt or hesitation that he held the whole world in his hands and had instituted a regime that would last for ever. With the passage of the years, the totalitarian urge of the dictatorship hardened, at least rhetorically. The regime was, it seemed, utterly determined to inscribe the dictator into 'his' city.

As if in proof of his mastery, rumour suggested that Mussolini was contemplating his own eventual burial place next to the mausoleum of the Emperor Augustus, whose bimillenary in 1937 was the spur to another of the dictatorship's loud campaigns to make every site of memory in Rome its own. There new buildings were added to the old, and in the resultant Piazza Augusto Imperatore, their Fascist message can still be read. In practice, however, the Duce was not to achieve empyrean posthumous glory. Instead, his corpse would suffer a bathetic fate, from its violation by the Milan populace and American doctors in 1945, its kidnapping by nostalgic fans in 1946, to its burial in the family tomb at Predappio, a not particularly memorable town in the province of Forlì in 1957. Rather than saluting the dictator's body, Rome expelled it. Yet the historical figure of Mussolini was never entirely silenced in Republican Italy, where, especially in the country's capital, neo-Fascism quickly acquired and retains a major political, economic and cultural role. Soon the Duce's complete works were reverently assembled in thirty-six volumes by La Fenice publishing house, whose name implied that the Duce's words, read properly, would one day allow the Fascist phoenix to fly again. Into the twenty-first century, the man Mussolini remains an object both of scholarly debate and popular memory. His personal history counts much more than does that of the ideology of Fascism or of the practice of its regime.

In Rome, a first approach to exploring this lingering of the dictator, the remembering and forgetting of Benito Mussolini, can be taken at the Villa Torlonia, 500 metres to the east of the Aurelian Wall and the Porta Pia where, in 1870, Italian control over Rome began. This villa is a place that has, in the twenty-first century, become one of the most popular museums, and most multifaceted memory sites, in contemporary Rome.

Here, from November 1929 to July 1943, lived the Mussolini family, the Duce and his wife, Rachele, their three rackety sons, Vittorio, Bruno (each in time to depart with a new wife) and Romano, and younger daughter Anna Maria, from 1936 cruelly afflicted by polio. The eldest child, Edda, was married from home to Galeazzo Ciano in April 1930 in a well-attended ceremony that began at the plain local church, San Giuseppe a Via Nomentana, opened in 1904–5 in the Liberal era. This young man about town was the son of the *ras* of Livorno. Nepotism ensured him a brilliant youthful career; he became Minister of Foreign Affairs (1936–43). After helping to dislodge his father-in-law in July 1943, Ciano was shot in January 1944 at the behest of the Germans and extreme Fascists, with the cowardly Duce, ignoring his daughter's impassioned appeals for mercy, too sad and frightened at his own fate to intervene to save him. The family life of the Mussolinis in Rome, in

24. Villa Torlonia, seeming stately and historic.

sum, was not a tale of eternal sunshine. The complications in their story add to those lurking from further back in the past in their surviving place of residence.

Despite its 'historic' looks, the Villa is a nineteenth-century structure, begun by Giuseppe Valadier in 1806 for Prince Giovanni Torlonia and finished for his son, Alessandro. The Villa's gardens are embellished with a 'Moorish' tower and two fake Egyptian obelisks, manufactured in Lombardy and illustrated with a nineteenth-century version of hieroglyphics. Writing before the onset of Fascism, the acerbic Augustus Hare counselled tourists not to stray in the villa's direction. The whole place, he wrote, was 'ridiculous', stupidly 'sprinkled with mock ruins'.[2] As he doubtless snobbishly knew, the Torlonia family was not an ancient noble one, with consuls or popes in their bloodline. Rather, Giovanni's father, Marino, in the eighteenth century had migrated to the city via the Kingdom of Naples-Sicily, adapting his name of Tourlonias to something that looked more Italian. Along the way he converted from Judaism and made a fortune as the chief papal banker. With this business success came honours, titles and estates. In 1809 Giovanni Torlonia, who had been elevated to Duke of Bracciano in 1794, was formally inducted into the Roman patriciate.

With succeeding generations, the family expanded its wealth and influence, marrying on occasion into the Spanish royal family, while Giovanni's great-great-great-great niece is the Hollywood star, Brooke Shields. The Torlonias took their place in the Risorgimento and Liberal Italy, if scarcely as people who speeded the progress of modern Rome or identified especially with its nation-alised history. In 1887 one of the Torlonia princes, thought too close to the Church, was sacked by Crispi in the lead-up to the inauguration of the statue of Giordano Bruno. As some reward, however belated, in 1958 the Torlonias assumed the responsibility of being 'Princely Assistants to the Papal Throne', an office held since 1735 by the ancient Orsini stock (the first owners of the frowning castle at Bracciano, not far north of Rome). From 15 November 1929 the Torlonia family, armed with its own special heritage, one that scarcely throbbed with Fascist purpose, generously or cannily lent their villa to the Mussolinis at a peppercorn rent.[3]

As tenants the Mussolinis, whose world view could sometimes seem as global as it was Roman, added a modernised annexe – the Limonaia – where films could be viewed; particular favourites of the dictator were those starring Laurel and Hardy, Mack Sennett and other American comedians. The Duce cagily ordered the digging of a couple of bomb shelters under the residence, sanctuaries that were meagrely supplied to ordinary Romans by the Fascist regime during the Second World War. The first refuge, initially entered from the garden but later from beneath the floor of the ballroom, was strengthened with reinforced cement and was devoted to repelling a gas attack, a significant choice given the regime's use of chemical weapons in its imperial wars (crimes stubbornly denied after 1945 by official Italy).[4] The hideout was 'equipped with showers and washbasins to eliminate any residue of gas on the skin'.[5] During the world conflict, the Duce became aware that air attacks were now of a different order from those experienced in the First World War and he ordered a new bunker stiffened with four extra metres of concrete protection against blast. On 25 July 1943, however, work was not yet complete.

During their stay, the Mussolinis did not prompt further archaeological labour on the extensive and richly ornamented Jewish catacombs, dating from the second or third century CE, which lie beneath the villa and its garden and spread for 9 kilometres. Indeed the eagerly installed bunkers did some damage to them. The tunnels were first identified in 1919 and mapped during the next years, providing ironical reminder of the Torlonia family's origins. In the interwar years the Torlonias earned international fame of a different kind by being portrayed as viciously greedy landlords of the peasants of the area to the east of Rome around the Fucino in the novel *Fontamara*, written by communist Ignazio Silone and translated into English in 1934. With its scary realism about the suffering of ordinary peasants at the hands of a grasping alliance of traditional landowners and unreliably modern Fascists, the book achieved global success and has been frequently reprinted.[6]

Once Rome was liberated in 1944, the villa became an Allied military head-quarters, whose lusty soldiers earned the ire of local restorers who damn the 'disgraceful misuse' of the place in those times.[7] Once the estate was returned to the Torlonia family, it failed to regain its lustre, passing into communal hands in 1977. A year later under leftist urban administration, the extensive grounds were opened to the public as a park. Thereafter, perhaps fearful of Fascist nostalgia, local politicians allowed the main villa to rot. It did. Only in 1993 did restoration begin.

At a formal ceremony in 2000, marking the completion of one stage of this reconstruction, the path leading from the Via Nomentana to the main villa was named the Viale Renzo De Felice in honour of Mussolini's certainly most pertinacious and perhaps most forgiving biographer.[8] Given De Felice's labour, and that of his followers, to remove what they viewed as too much negative ideological baggage from accounts of Mussolini's life, the designation may act as an appropriate entry statement for the restored villa and its role as a site of historical representation and memory in contemporary Rome. Further work on the park after 2000 saw the name of the Viale Luigi Calabresi (*Medaglia d'oro di vita civile*: Gold Medal for public service) accorded to one of the avenues that cross the estate. It was a slightly surprising choice by the Roman

25. Viale Renzo De Felice, Villa Torlonia, makes contemporary history historic.

City Council, then under the sometime communist youth leader, Walter Veltroni. Calabresi was the policeman murdered at his base in Milan in May 1972 by leftist terrorists, committed to writing their own new history into the city and nation, at the beginning of what are termed '*gli anni di piombo*' (years of lead). Calabresi was a target of attack because he had been in charge when, in December 1969, the anarchist Giuseppe Pinelli fell to his death from an upper-storey window at police headquarters, an event scathingly dramatised by Nobel Prize-winning writer Dario Fo, as *Accidental death of an anarchist*. Calabresi had been born in Rome in November 1937, but what message his ghost might relate to those of the Mussolini family must remain a mystery, seeming rather to give proof that history in Rome has a permanent potential to be syncretic.

If present-day crusaders against 'terrorism' feel an impulse to remember Calabresi, the prime heritage intention behind the restoration of the villa is aimed at forgetting. Despite or because of the fact that its halls and gardens echo with the history of Fascist racism, violence and war, the upper storey of the main building – where formerly lay the bedrooms of the Mussolini boys – houses a display of depoliticised painterly images of interwar Rome, with the dating carefully running from 1918 to 1946, thereby avoiding exact coincidence with Fascism. On the ground floor, in the ornately candelabra-ed ballroom, where Vittorio Mussolini used to play billiards, there is a display of classical archaeological material excavated from around the Via Nomentana in the eighteenth century. The Limonaia has been converted into a 'play-centre' for local children, and bankers are allowed to dine for a suitable fee in the bomb shelters, otherwise closed to the inquisitive public.

This medley of heritage and entertainment has made the Villa Torlonia into the most visited of Rome's new museums. The guidebook spends a few pages on the Mussolinis' time there, with some detailing of the bomb shelters, but is studiously apolitical in its main account, guilelessly relating how Rachele Mussolini planted a garden, 'encouraging Italian families to deal with the shortages occasioned by the outbreak of the Second World War, cultivating vegetables and raising livestock to allow themselves to become self-sufficient.'[9] There is no explanation of the curious nineteenth-century frescoing on the first floor where were located the (separate) bedrooms of Benito and Rachele. There, the racial messages are mixed, in what, in the 1930s, might have seemed a troubling fashion, since a Cleopatra appears in the 'Egyptian room', surrounded by more fake hieroglyphics, as a white woman with shining black hair. However, the 'Queen of Sheba' is portrayed as a half-naked black woman, looking rather grumpy at her fate.

Nowhere today is there any serious suggestion that the site could be ideal for a Museum of Fascism that would allow critical examination of what the dictatorship did to the city, Italy and the world, or more scrupulous

26. Francesco Podesti's Queen of Sheba (*c.*1838) from the interior of Villa Torlonia evokes Ethiopian conquest but has odd racial ambiguities, positioned as it was outside the Mussolini family bedrooms.

historical consideration of the larger ramifications of the Second World War. After protest at the ignoring of the Jewish catacombs there, it was agreed in 2004 that a Museum of the Holocaust could become a worthwhile addition to the villa's grounds. At the time of writing, it has still not opened, however, and, to complaints from Jewish sources that Rome is now the only European capital without such a memorial, there is suggestion that it may be ready in 2012.

In this as in other aspects of recollection of the dictatorship, the current presentation of Villa Torlonia scarcely expresses history well. Yet, as was noticed at the start of the last chapter, memory of Fascism eddies throughout the city of Rome and cannot really be reduced to being merely decorous. Certainly, the decade following the *Decennale* in 1932 and the supernumerary *Anno Santo* in 1933–4 saw a quickening in the dictatorship's physical reconstruction of old Rome and in the development of new areas of the city. One example lay along the road that connected Piazza Ungheria and the Via Flaminia, pompously named the Via dei martiri fascisti (Street of the Fascist Martyrs, after the war to be changed to the Via Buozzi, in memory of a trade unionist, murdered by Nazi-Fascists in 1944). The surrounding quarter of the Parioli – home to a Campo DUX, designed to house visiting Fascist scouts – was developing into a bourgeois redoubt. Less showy were the various *borgate*, peripheral suburbs that sprang up at Primavalle or Pietralata on the city's outskirts, mixing immigrant families with those local poor whom Fascist building projects had dislodged from the centre. The financing of new housing in Rome remained a complex process, if generally involving collaboration between private entrepreneurs and the State, amid recurrent rumours that massive peculation occurred at the interstices. In 1933, for example, more than 70 per cent of the new apartments were priced beyond the budget of any in the 'popular classes'.[10]

Similarly, while the 1931 city plan envisaged 896 hectares devoted to parks and gardens, in practice they were curtailed to 400.[11] More generally, despite the propaganda about Rome's glory, the government never funded the *Governatorato* to an acceptable level. Typical was the fact that the city administration was given no special monies for the much-hyped visit of German Führer Adolf Hitler in May 1938 – at a cost to Rome of 70 million lire – and the urban deficit continued to balloon.[12] One result of the Führer's trip, to be reversed after 1944, was the renaming of the short street running from Porta San Paolo to the Ostiene station, the Viale Adolf Hitler. The abutting square became Piazzale Adolf Hitler and was garnished with a statue of the Nazi leader as a token of Axis comradeship. After liberation, a different history was necessarily inscribed there, with the Viale Hitler turning into the Viale delle Cave Ardeatine (Avenue of the Ardeatine Caves, a place on the city's outskirts where, as will be seen below, a Nazi massacre was committed in 1944) and the *piazzale* now commemorated the Resistance under the title Piazzale dei Partigiani.[13]

Another major Fascist building initiative was the construction of a new home for Rome University beyond the railway station. Here Marcello Piacentini led a group of often squabbling architects from 1932. The site was inaugurated with patriotic fanfare on 31 October 1935, a few weeks after Fascist Italy, contravening the League of Nations, invaded Ethiopia. The modernist university buildings certainly then and perhaps later intimated to faculty historians the need to approve the Fascist version of the past. In 1933 four new post offices of greater or lesser architectural elegance were opened in the Via Marmorata, Piazza Bologna, Via Taranto and Piazza Mazzini, each at the heart of an area where the population was rapidly growing. New museums were instituted to recount in the official manner the history of crime (1931), of the *bersaglieri* (1932) and of the *carabinieri* (1937).[14]

Yet, even when Bottai held office as *governatore* in 1935–6, demolition was given preference over construction, and the city was characterised by 'a chaotic expansion of housing, through the erection of new *borgate*, with their more or less ramshackle rooms. There, however, the key matter was social and geographical isolation.' Metaphorically imprisoned in their peripheries, the ordinary people were excluded more actively than in the past from participation in the history being made and represented in the historic centre of Rome. 'Any plans for bureaucratic reform or the provision of acceptable infrastructure were left on the table' and the popular classes perforce sought, as they always had, to make do through their families and useful friends. Whereas the Duce was alert to what could be read into the grand monuments, old or new, he remained impervious to suggestions that the dictatorship should actively improve the lot of the Roman poor.[15] The regime gloated over its resurrection of *romanità* in every Italian soul, but its everyday practice remained repressive, not engaging; ostentatious 'oceanic' parades and the excitation they encouraged and demanded were the exception and not the rule in ordinary people's lives.

As the decade wore on, Mussolini's own image developed a more syncretic historical reference than it had possessed in the early years of the dictatorship, while it simultaneously hardened into more 'granitic' form, almost as though the Duce was turning into a living statue, ironically more Byzantine than Roman. Blacksmith hammering his people into modern Fascist power,[16] invincible *Condottiere*, legionary or Caesar, Greater than Napoleon, Prophet, Hero, Colossus, Sun God,[17] each likeness and past comparison, no matter how grand, had to be acknowledged as falling short of the dictator's sublimity.[18] His power and infallibility were such that, by definition, he governed time. So Giovanni Viganoni, author of *Mussolini and the Caesars* published in 1933, maintained that he had been stimulated to write his book when, on attending a reception for the dictator, he had spontaneously greeted him: '*Ave, Caesar Imperator*' (Hail, Imperial Caesar), just as he would have done in classical Rome. Moreover, when he turned to his historical research, Viganoni quickly realised that the Duce was greater than Julius and Augustus Caesar, each of whom had also 'marched on Rome'. Mussolini outdid all their successors as well, being a fiercer soldier than Trajan, a more subtle philosopher than Marcus Aurelius and a better organiser than Diocletian. When it came to the late empire, Mussolini effortlessly 'surpassed the virtues of Constantine, the power of Theodosius and the wisdom of Justinian.'[19] Maybe Viganoni's parallels were too drably human. Another Fascist ideologue placed the Duce in a celestial trinity composed of 'Homer, the divine in Art, Jesus, the divine in Life and Mussolini, the divine in Action.'[20]

Or was even that status insufficiently elevated? In his conquest of time, could it be that Mussolini was immortal? Certainly, it was stated by one propagandist, He [the use of capital letters for every reference to the DUCE had become mandatory) was ineluctably destined to dominate the twentieth century and every succeeding and preceding age, being 'an infallible anticipator'.[21]

In fact, somewhere beneath the spin and pretension, the ageing dictator was growing more cynical about the human condition and more curmudgeonly at his failure genuinely to refashion Italians to his will. Yet he was still ready to argue that he had overcome history in his fusing of the glory of the past with a dynamic modernity. In 1937 he boasted to Anglo-Saxon interviewers that he had taylored himself into a machine man. 'I am never tired,' he told them. 'I have turned my body into a motor, which is under constant review and control and which therefore runs with absolute regularity.'[22] His public image, once multiple and displaying him smiling and mobile, now narrowed. In photo, portrait and statuary, the Duce stood apart, perpetually in uniform, grave and unmoving, sculpted into something fixed and unchanging, infallible and eternal, the Master of history, space and time.

Mussolini, who in reality liked to work in a battered blue suit, needed reading glasses, did not always remember to shave and had opted for a bare head after his hair turned prematurely white, was now constantly represented as a soldier or airman, commander of land, sea and sky, ever victorious. Any reference to battle no matter how modern its waging, as ever, stimulated classical parallels. It is therefore no surprise to find that, in his ringing speech from the balcony of the Palazzo Venezia on 9 May 1936, a few days after Italian troops had entered Addis Ababa and won the war against Ethiopia, Mussolini donned the mantle of the Caesars to blazon the 'return' of empire to 'the fatal hills of Rome'. To be sure, after they had cheered Mussolini, the crowd, with motives that mixed nationalism and Fascism, went off to salute King Victor Emmanuel III, who had just accepted the title of emperor from the hands of the Duce.[23] Calling a perhaps more reliable dead emperor to his side, Mussolini ascended the Campidoglio carrying a laurel wreath armed with fasces to proclaim, as Augustus had advised in his memoirs was his practice, victory and the outbreak of peace. As one commentator put it, the African conquest marked a destiny that tied the classical empire through the '*verbo*' (gospel) of Mussolini to 'the history of the future'.[24]

Italians were not the only people to enjoy Fascist razzmatazz. Foreigners, too, found it hard to resist the belief that something 'Roman' had happened in the Italian rise to empire and that Mussolini was its unchallenged chief. For a guileless English journalist, Rome had never 'forgotten that, in its days of glory, it deified those leaders who conquered an empire. Now Rome did what it did in the past. While the Duce stood on his balcony, he was given a triumph and made into a God.'[25] Matters, however, were not always read so positively. Two of the most bitter journalistic attacks on Mussolini condemned him as a cruel 'Caesar' leading Italy's brutal assault on Ethiopia[26] or dismissed him as a 'sawdust Caesar', avowing sardonically that 'History and monuments will recall Benito Mussolini as a Caesar – not a Julius but perhaps a Caesar Borgia or perhaps a Kaiser Wilhelm. If not a Napoleon Bonaparte, then at least a Louis Napoleon.'[27]

Such deprecation is worth noting because a considerable number of historians continue to see Fascist Rome as personally 'made' by Benito Mussolini.[28] Yet was the city being structured in the interwar period really a novel creation of the Duce? Was it the product of 'one man alone', as Churchill would put it in a propaganda bid to divide Mussolini from the Italian people during the Second

World War?[29] To what extent was the city imprinted with Mussolini's version of history (and that of his party and regime)? Or, somewhere beneath the bluster and the pyrotechnics, did a continuity survive with the Liberal era and with the nationalist but not reliably Fascist historical imaginings of those who had, since the Risorgimento, wanted Italy and its capital city to be modernised and Italianised, yet simultaneously to express in its architecture and people three thousand years of history? The verbiage of the 1930s is heavy with the dictator's personality cult. But what happens if the florid words are held in abeyance for a moment? Maybe then it will be concluded that, in Rome as elsewhere under his rule, Mussolini required less that Italians 'work towards' him; rather more the dictator worked to make concrete the durable dreams and delusions of the more imperially minded of the national ruling elites.

Certainly, throughout the 1930s, the 'cleansing' from Rome of undesirable histories inexorably proceeded. It was now that the Corso del Rinascimento, at the usual cost to the previously existing urban fabric, was driven through the Campus Martius, the oldest part of the city, running beside the Senate building, the Palazzo Madama, and very near the magnificent Piazza Navona. The avenue was inaugurated on 21 April 1938 and has proved a bottleneck for traffic ever since. Work was also commenced in 1936 (under the ubiquitous Piacentini) to 'open' Piazza San Pietro to the public and to traffic, at whatever damage to Bernini's brilliant design (although the change had been mooted by the French before 1814). A street to be called the Via della Conciliazione, in honour of the reconciliation achieved between Church and State in the Lateran Pacts, replaced the previous homes, alleys, squares and a total of five churches there and in the adjacent heavily populated *Borgo*, 'cleansed' from 1937.[30] The regime boasted that it had shifted 600,000 cubic metres of material in the process. The demolishers were cheered that October by a personal visit from Pope Pius XI, who, in this instance no enemy of Fascist work, took pains to congratulate Piacentini and the other urban planners on their design.[31] The Via della Conciliazione was not completed until 1950 and remains a controversial part of the Roman streetscape, with one contemporary urban planner advocating its complete destruction and the rebuilding of all that had been razed in its path.[32] Along the Tiber, a bridge named in honour of the Duke of Aosta, the most military of the Savoys, and illustrated with telling scenes from his campaigns, was begun in 1937 and opened in 1942. It led to the Foro Mussolini, which was continuing to expand its sporting facilities (and, to contemporary approval, had acquired a large car park), and to a new modern palace, called the Farnesina, designed by Enrico Del Debbio to become the new headquarters of the Fascist party.[33]

All over the city, building continued. However, the architectural purpose of the regime and the attitude towards history that underpinned it were most vividly expressed in two zones, the Augusteo and its surrounding Piazza Augusto Imperatore, and the expansive new suburb of Esposizione Universale di Roma (EUR, Rome Universal Exhibition). This latter scheme to build an entirely Fascist quarter south-west along the Tiber and a Via del Mare that would push well beyond the Aurelian Walls from old Rome was initiated by Bottai in June 1935. Its ordered streetscape and numerous major Fascist edifices can still be viewed by visitors, although they will need to ignore the clutter of post-war buildings that have filled in the area and ironically house unmilitary bureaucrats.

EUR was given formal approval in October 1936 for the first anniversary of the attack on Ethiopia. Its then chief administrator, Vittorio Cini, promised that it would express 'the definitive [architectural] style of our epoch: that of the Twentieth Year of the Fascist Era', being both good to look at and 'rational'. Above all, Cini asserted, there 'the sense of Rome, eternal and universal, will prevail'. The regime was determined that the model that EUR provided would 'last for fifty or a hundred years' without ageing or tiring.[34] As if in proof of its durability, in October 1937 its foundation stone was laid in a ceremony where Mussolini glorified in Latin 'the [spiritual] mustering of the nations' to be achieved there.[35] Once Quintino Sella had hoped that a liberal humanist Rome could rise outside the Aurelian Walls, safe from the corrupting legacies of Pope and Caesar. Now Fascism proclaimed that its (universal) history was to be made concrete at EUR, even if, in reality, the zone was not ready for 1941, as initially promised, nor for 1942 and the *Ventennale* (twentieth

27. Esposizione Universale di Roma (EUR) and the adaptable new model city, 1953.

anniversary of the March on Rome). Hampered by the war and by the costliness of its buildings, EUR, like the Via della Conciliazione, was left to post-Fascist governments to complete and there inscribe a historic meaning that was not merely Fascist.

The major but less extensive work on the Augusteo, by contrast, was completed in 1937 for the Emperor's touted bimillenary and made the occasion for a grandiose Mostra Augustea della romanità (MAR). This new exhibition, held in the again refurbished Palazzo delle esposizioni (with heavy imperialism rather than dynamic modernity as its motif), was meant to express the expansionist ambitions of the regime with the same force with which, only five years ago, the Mostra della Rivoluzione Fascista had advertised the regime's totalitarian control over past and present within Italy. The MAR's slogan urged, 'Italians, make sure that the glories of the past are surpassed by the glories of the future'.[36] Archaeologists, led by Giulio Quirino Giglioli, had been excavating the site of Augustus's mausoleum since 1926 (utilising plans first sketched in 1909). During their work, they had identified further substantial remains of the Ara Pacis, an altar consecrated there on 4 July 13 BCE, and formally dedicated by the Emperor Augustus four years later when he proclaimed perpetual peace, having returned to Rome from victorious campaigns in Spain and Gaul.

With the site's historical sacrality thereby enhanced, in 1936 the building long ago erected over the ancient mausoleum was closed and demolished. In 1937–8 fragments of the Ara Pacis were hastily blended with reproductions of material, excavated earlier and owned by museums that included the Vatican, the Uffizi and the Louvre, to 'recreate' it as a holy site of empire (one by then as evidently bent on war as peace). The reconstituted altar was placed at an elevated spot near the Tiber and roofed over by leading urban designer Antonio Muñoz (Director of Antiquities and Fine Arts in the city, 1928–43), while inevitably stamped with modern fasces. In uncovering the Ara Pacis, the archaeologists had located the burial places of many of the Julio-Claudian imperial family and even of Vespasian, with Giglioli talking unconvincingly of parallels between the younger princes and Fascist boy scouts, as well as proclaiming the supremacy achieved by Italian archaeology over the perfidious French, who, he lamented, were engaged in 'a work ever more ruthless and obscene (the word is no exaggeration) to denigrate Rome and *romanità*'.[37]

When not digging, Giglioli took time off to urge his country's imperishable historical connections with Malta and Corsica, touted objects of Fascist irredentism.[38] On 23 September 1937 he gave the formal speech dedicating the Augustan exhibition to the Duce and in doing so he appositely tied together classical Rome, Risorgimento and Fascism. He, like others of Mussolini's subjects, Giglioli stated, had been impelled to action 'not only by Your sayings but also through the spontaneous and inevitable merging of so many of Your actions with those of the greatest Romans of two thousand and more years ago'. Julius and Augustus Caesar, he explained, had taken over a Rome 'already bold and powerful but a prey to destructive factionalism'. The Caesars had 'gone to the people and there divined the new dictatorial order' that would last so long.[39] For this classicist, Mussolini's presence in the city had resurrected the glory and the purpose of the Caesars, and Giglioli was committed to 'working towards' both them and the classical emperors. History was alive and would remain so, at least for him. On 24 July 1943, the day when Mussolini learned at the meeting of the Fascist Grand Council that he had lost his henchmen's confidence, Giglioli wrote effusively to his Duce, asking to enter active military service at the age of fifty-seven and so making an ironical claim to be the 'last Mussolinian'. His impulse, he explained, was a combination of 'Fascist faith' and 'all that I have done to illustrate and exalt the work of civilisation of eternal Rome'.[40]

Meanwhile plans continued to frame the mausoleum with Fascist buildings in the still extant Piazza Augusto Imperatore. Signalled in October 1934 by the arrival of Mussolini wielding a pick, the area was rigorously cleansed of what were deemed unsightly old houses (the baroque church of the Santa Annunziata had been demolished in the 1920s). These edifices were replaced with sterile office buildings, most notably the headquarters of the para-state insurance office, and were to be made meaningful, it was hoped, by Fascist mosaics and inscriptions hailing the virtues of work and peace. Simultaneous demolition to make the Via di Ripetta and Lungotevere more friendly to motor cars ensured that, for many years under the Republic, the mausoleum's lack-lustre first purpose would be to act as 'a monumental traffic directing device'.[41]

Over recent years the worst of the flow has been diverted. However, the history of the Ara Pacis remains alive. In 2006 Muñoz's weighty structure was refashioned at the hands of the American rationalist architect, Richard Meier, who added rooms to the site that could allow reflection on the purpose of the altar.[42] Conservatives reacted badly to Meier's work, which is starkly white in a way that seems ironically to replicate the Victor Emmanuel monument. In 2008 the new *sindaco*, Alemanno, promised to demolish what Meier had done and was backed by Berlusconian Minister of Culture Sandro Bondi (author of poetry in honour of his boss), who loudly expressed his disdain for 'modern art' as a whole. Perhaps prompted by such attitudes and while action to change the monument stalled, in June 2009 rightist demonstrators splashed the struc-ture with patriotic red, white and green paint. They also installed a porcelain toilet and some packs of toilet paper next to Meier's structure to indicate a neo-Fascist view of his 'insult' to so sacred a site.[43] Whether such protesters will get their way and the ghosts of Augustus and his family will again be troubled by the sounds of demolition remains to be seen.

Yet, as one Fascist commentator perhaps incautiously remarked, in 1922 Mussolini had admitted that he had never visited a museum.[44] When, therefore, he listened to Giglioli's words (morally preparing for his departure on the next day for a state tour of Nazi Germany), was he hearing himself and knowing that Rome was being remade in his image? Or, despite the extravagant grovelling to the dictator necessary on such occasions, was the applauding crowd having its wishes made concrete? Already it has been seen that neither the Church nor the people of the suburbs were true believers who meekly drew their identities from the official Fascist version of Rome. Is the same true of the respectable classes, very likely to be Italian nationalists of some kind but not always fundamentalist Fascists?

A good way to answer this question is to examine those architects who were key assistants of Mussolini in the Fascist reshaping of Rome. One illuminating figure was Gustavo Giovannoni (1873–1947), whose career therefore spanned Italian rule in the city from national occupation to the fall of Fascism. In the pages of the Liberal establishment journal, *Nuova Antologia*, in 1913 Giovannoni had promulgated a credo about town planning in urban settings where pasts circulated. It combined nationalism with a softer liberal internationalism appropriate to the 'Giolittian age' but already being torn by the new imperialism and soon to crumble under the dictatorship. A debate, Giovannoni wrote, was growing between 'Life' and 'History', the past and the future, and on its results depended the look of the historic centres of all major European cities and the quality of services available to their inhabitants. It was important, Giovannoni argued, to deny the extremist conclusions of the paladins of each side. An expanding Rome, for example, should open itself to the 'garden city' concepts being sponsored in contemporary Britain and Germany. Communications were of key significance, all the more because local urban planners since 1870 had ignored this crucial modern issue almost completely. Ruins needed to be cherished but roads had to be built. Regrettably and humiliatingly, under Liberal rule, Giovannoni grumbled, a 'genuinely elevated approach to modern Rome' had been avoided. Now 'science' and 'art' must blend fruitfully to achieve a 'healthy and balanced renewal of the historic centre'. Then, and only then, could an Italian Rome revive its boast of being eternal, that is of continuing value to the nation.[45]

Over the next years, Giovannoni remained prominent in his profession as he campaigned for its elevation to full professional status. In October 1919 he was made head of the Scuola superiore di architettura di Roma, the leading tertiary training school for architects, with his chief assistant being Enrico Del Debbio, the later 'radical' Fascist and, from 1927, designer of the Foro Mussolini, as well as technical expert on the adaptation of the Palazzo delle esposizioni for the Mostra della Rivoluzione Fascista. A rival of Marcello Piacentini, Giovannoni was accepted as the national expert on the restoration of monuments and the advocate of the view that continuity with the past of Vitruvius, Vignola and Palladio should not be sundered in the implementation of a 'national style'.[46] In 1923 Alberto Calza Bini, a man of parts – architect, Fascist deputy and prominent in the lively debates and conflicts of the Fascist party in Rome (belying totalitarian boasts about total discipline and order) – was made national secretary of the Sindacato fascista degli architetti (Fascist League of Architects), and was thereafter courted by both Piacentini and Giovannoni.

With the passage of the years, Giovannoni occupied a key place on the conservative edge of Fascist urban planning, trying, for example, to ban his pupils from reading Le Corbusier and highly critical of the modernist urges that had surfaced among the younger generation serving the regime.[47] In 1931 he developed his thoughts in a book entitled *Vecchie città ed edilizia nuova* (Old cities and new building), which, by implication, cast doubt on too much enthusiasm for the *piccone* and urban cleansing. For twenty-seven centuries, Rome, he remarked, had expressed 'an admirable continuity and had responded to the three great revivals of human civilisation in a wonderful and unparalleled fashion'.[48] The city's historical weight made Giovannoni no unalloyed fan of modernity. Urban planners should not be seduced by the false allure of the soulless skyscrapers of New York. Artisans and art must hold their place, while, he emphasised, 'the wish to transform the old central zone into a place full of movement and business in the way of a modern city is an immense, definitive and irrecoverable error'.[49] When he came to give examples of planning failure, he cautiously focused on the mistakes of the Liberal era, ending his work with an apt citation of the 'masculine voice' of the dictator, seconding Mussolini's demand that Rome be loyal both to its past and to its future.[50] Yet Giovannoni was not agreeing to dutiful silence in any dispute over Rome's look and meaning. As he explained circumspectly but unbowed in 1939, Fascist Italy was 'like an army led by a great captain, but still spread out in its units. Where the activity directed by the Duce reaches, there can be found creative will and victory. Where it is absent, there can be blockages that lead to conflicts and a failure to achieve.'[51]

His recognition, however polite, that the Duce did not control everything was, however, pushing him still further from the internationalism of the Liberal years. For Giovannoni, town planning was a crucial matter since buildings bore history, or did so at Rome, more reliably and durably than could any partisan book.[52] The implications of his understanding of the relationship of the city with its past led him, on the imposition of racial laws, to harness them to his theme. The continuity that he had long treasured in the cityscape could now be ascribed 'to the great permanent element' in the population, 'which is that of race'. Throughout history, Giovannoni contended, national architecture had 'reacted to the numerous invasions and infiltrations by always restoring its purity, just as water does in a rushing stream after the passage of a storm'. Rome's buildings were the perfect example of how, 'with intense activity, sometimes slow, sometimes swift', architecture 're-absorbed those foreign influences that had been able to corrupt or dominate it and thus returns to being more Italian than ever'.[53] With this line, the conservative Giovannoni had been driven by his comprehension of history and its value to join with the regime's most radical elements, linking himself, by implication, with the Nazis (although he continued to write derogatorily about 'Nordic' impulses in architecture, town planning and history).

What, then, of Giovannoni's more successful rival, Marcello Piacentini? What were his ideas about the representation of history in Rome and how did they relate to chatter about Fascist cultural revolution? Like Giovannoni, Piacentini had made his name before the onset of the dictatorship and was another who was as influenced by a nationalist (and Catholic) understanding of history and heritage as an exclusively Fascist one. In 1915 he accompanied Ernesto Nathan on a trip to the USA that combined war propaganda and instruction in the virtues of transatlantic rationalism (as well as proving that the architect had excellent ties with Freemasonry, ones which, despite Fascist condemnation of that organisation, Piacentini never renounced).[54] Back home, in 1916 Piacentini sketched the best way to preserve Rome's beauty and simultaneously advance its modernity. For the present, he feared, the place was 'picturesque and not grand' and so failed in any comparison with New York. Yet, as Italy's capital, Rome had a glorious future; its population could expand to two million, a figure that Piacentini imagined well before Mussolini did.[55]

Reworking the ideas of Quintino Sella, Piacentini suggested that the best way for Rome to be both modern and yet hold its 'ruin value' was to concentrate new building outside the historic centre. 'Old Rome' could be the 'Citadel and Acropolis' of the city, thereby acting as 'the precious Tribune from where the treasures and traditions of past epochs will be religiously preserved'. This area could 'sumptuously entertain astonished and admiring foreigners', as well as 'high-quality artists and the best antiquarians, all those, and there are a lot of them, who live from and for the ancient'.[56] Trams should be removed and any electricity lines should be hidden underground. Ordinary people should be encouraged to translocate elsewhere, since 'the classical areas must be isolated and tranquil so as to allow concentration on the past, meditation and ecstasy'. The dividing line should run from Piazza del Popolo to Castel Sant'Angelo and St Peter's, along the base of the Janiculum to Trastevere. It should cross the Tiber at the Via Marmorata and, from there, proceed to Santa Maria Maggiore and so back to Piazza del Popolo.[57] Outside should rise the modern quarters, 'palpitating with life and movement: tramways, railways, airlines, shops sparkling with light, industries, villas and gardens' and equipped with wide roads with ample access, while popular housing could spread in such areas as the Tiburtino (beyond San Lorenzo), Trastevere and the Trionfale (behind the Vatican). In Piacentini's dreaming, Rome's ancient soul and its modern one might fuse spiritually but they would remain separate spatially.

Although Piacentini counselled that monuments kept their historical meaning best if left in their 'ancient surroundings' and doubted the virtue of 'isolating' them too starkly, he did agree that some demolition was necessary.[58] Certainly, once Fascism took over, Piacentini moved adroitly into his position as the regime's most favoured architect and town planner. If he did not take out PNF membership until 1932, he carefully honed his ties with such Fascist notables as Bottai, Costanzo Ciano and Calza Bini, and with Mussolini himself, nudging the Duce to express the view that 'architecture is the greatest of the arts' (even if, on a different occasion, the Duce gave this palm to modern cinema).[59] In 1929 Piacentini was made a member of the Fascist Academy and contracts poured in, with the architect talking confidently about having developed a 'Fascist style', although without ending dispute about its meaning.

His rivals, old and young in the profession, remained split into bickering factions, with each sedulously seeking Mussolini's backing. Their warring was helped by the inscrutability or confusion of the dictator's 'real' thoughts, since, contrary to his official myth, the Duce could change his mind about architecture as about other things. In 1934 the dictator was said to lean towards the enthusiasts of modernism but in 1936 he decreed 'the architecture of the empire must not be modern'.[60] In the nature of the Fascist elite, Piacentini also became the focus of malicious rumour, pointedly collected and preserved by the Duce's private secretariat, implying that he was guilty of peculation, plagiarism and sexual exploitation.[61]

Within the architectural profession, the battle grew fiercest over the rich pickings and public importance of EUR, where, in 1937, Piacentini again emerged victorious, although without fully silencing his critics. A danger here was the young Giulio Carlo Argan (later, from 1976–9, communist-supported mayor of the city). By the outbreak of the war Argan had won the ear of Bottai, telling him in 1942 that two decades of Fascist rule had shamefully failed to create 'an architectural school, properly speaking'. The plans for EUR, Argan advised, embodied 'the gravest defeat imaginable' of the 'culture of the Revolution'.[62] Piacentini, meanwhile, had foreseen the collapse of Mussolini's dictatorship. His dissidence had become so notorious that, in September 1943, he was arrested by the invading Nazis and released only when the papal Undersecretary of State, Giovanni Battista Montini (from 1963 to his death in 1978 Pope Paul VI), charitably intervened in his favour.

The sometime friend of the Freemasons had, under the regime, nourished his ties with the Church and they were again useful in 1945 in helping Piacentini discount his Fascist career and resume his university place and his position as a leading architect. Always, he told the purge commission modestly, he had been 'a mere technocrat', a man who had never won a contract 'through personal interference or pressure of any kind'.[63] In Piacentini's argument, the city, its expansion and greatness became the explanation or the cover of his flirtation with Mussolini but simultaneously cleansed his personal history of Fascist corruption.

The key elements in his defence were brought together in 1952 when Piacentini published an account of changes in Rome since 1870, reiterating his view that 'the popular masses' read the history of the place through its monuments and buildings rather than through books.[64] The city, he maintained, 'is an organism, which has its own life, bound to the life of man'. In 1918, he recalled, the peace, scoured by strikes, disorder and a 'civil war', had 'deluded' those who wanted Rome to be once more its grand self. Fascism, 'accepted by the great majority of Italians', was first aimed solely at 'the restoration of the authority of the state'.[65] Thereafter the regime's urban planners, drawing their inspiration from 'an organic and noble synthesis of archaeological and papal' constructions, as well as from celebrated modern cities outside Italy, indeed remade Rome.[66] All, in other words, had been for the best in the best of all possible worlds, and post-Fascist Rome bore no negative connotations from its decades under dictatorship. The Eternal City was too great for that. It soared above the brief Fascist parenthesis. Its architectural message was national, Italian, Catholic and popular but never 'really' Fascist.

Just as his booklet of 1916 was something of a manual for the rearranging of Rome to be implemented under Mussolini, so the post-war work was a blueprint for the way conservative Rome sought, after Mussolini's fall, to remember and forget its experience of totalitarianism (Italian-style). Piacentini, like Giovannoni and his other colleagues and rivals in their adaptable careers, offer evidence that, for all the talk about Mussolini's genius and power, those with influence in his regime had by no means lost the ability to think (or manipulate), and to frame personal and urban histories that were not identical with those of the dictator and his ideology.

If architects drew benefits from the regime and cast their work in what they called Fascist style, Italy's historians were at least as assiduous in their public seconding of the dictatorship (in their self-interest). The regime offered them employment and fame and, in return, the great majority of the nation's historians found past justification for present actions and policies, while not necessarily converting themselves into credulous Fascists.[67] Mussolini's repeated evocations of *romanità* especially raised the profile of classicists. Ettore Pais, once the pupil of Mommsen, from 1920 a Senator and a historian with ample international contacts and reputation, was ready in the 1920s to laud the regime's demographic plans, while paralleling the present destinies of 'young Italy' and those of early Republican Rome.[68] Academician Roberto Paribeni was sure that Rome was eternal and universal and that the values established in classical times remained the basis of civilisation.[69] In 1939 he expatiated on the glory and justice of the first Roman empire, heralding Fascism's revived exaltation of *romanità* in Ethiopia and elsewhere (while finding time to defend Gallienus: arguably a Roman emperor possessed of 'lively ingenuity, a lover of culture and art', but regrettably overwhelmed by the intractable issues confronting him).[70] Paribeni also declared publicly that Jews had been a deleterious and disturbing element in imperial Rome.[71]

Foreign classicists did not demur. The French student of the Roman everyday (and supporter of Action Française), Jerome Carcopino, during the *Decennale* orated in Rome about the sublime virtue of European imperialism, a modern duty inspired by ancient Roman example.[72] A younger colleague stipulated a few years later, perhaps archly, that 'the history of Augustus and of the origins of the Empire was not for the French a foreign story, but rather a page of our national history'.[73] Further to the north, racist assumptions about the decline of Rome were common, with the Swede, Martin Nilsson, ascribing the fall of the empire to 'the equalisation of races and the mixture of blood among all the different peoples of the Empire' and to the concession of too much welfare to workers, who were thereby reduced to 'loafers'.[74]

English-speaking visitors to Rome and researchers there (some 5,000 foreigners were recorded as living in the city in 1931, with 889 Americans and 794 Germans leading the tally) often shared the enthusiasm for a reconstructed Roman empire.[75] Americans were easily persuaded that history was repeating itself in Rome. 'Two thousand years later, a young intellectual . . . and, like Octavian, a leader of men and lover of his country', one visitor stated effusively, 'was called by destiny as that other Italian had been so long before him.' Had not Augustus relegated his critics to islands as the Fascist regime did so effectively in the policy of *confino*? he added.[76] Rome, another classicist remarked with wider reference, 'symbolizes the fusing of the centuries'. The city was proof that history did not die, 'a kind of evidence of things not seen, but of things real and potent nonetheless'.[77] Eugenia Strong of the British School in Rome was deeply impressed by the Augustan bimillenary and ready to accept parallels between the Emperor and Mussolini. She did take pains to emphasise that Augustus had not been a warrior but a 'pacificer', adding with more sinister implication that he had 'searched by every means to revive the Latin element, purging from it every foreign contamination'.[78] Hints of criticism may be detected in young Ronald Syme's *The Roman Revolution* (1939). Yet even he ended with what might seem a fanfare, certainly of Augustus and perhaps of Mussolini: 'Dux had become Princeps and had converted a party into a government. For power he had sacrificed everything; he had achieved the height of all mortal ambition and in his ambition he had saved and regenerated the Roman People.'[79]

By the time Syme wrote, the Italian regime had instituted racial legislation and a notable immediate casualty was Arnaldo Momigliano, the most brilliant of Italy's young classicists and a Jew. In 1938 he fled to the UK and thereafter made a distinguished career at Oxford and London universities. In such exile he was freed, as he had not been in Italy, to give an anti-Fascist reading of *romanità*, in a review of Syme's book arguing that 'every revolution has its small group of leading or favoured men; but very few revolutions are explained by their chiefs. The study of the leaders is necessary but by itself is not enough.' Momigliano also charged that Syme had been too pessimistic in implying that the 'security of life and property is more important than political liberty'. The best message of the Roman empire, he now stressed, was 'that despotism imposes moral degradation upon men'.[80] What, then, it must be asked more generally, were racism and war by 1938–40 doing to the histories that eddied through Rome and to the lurking disputes about them?

Within the regime, the leading explicator of the meaning of the city remained Giuseppe Bottai, should the truth be told more Roman a Fascist even than the Duce. As Minister of Education he was suitably employed to give a modern gloss to the bimillenary of Augustus. 'In regard to the Italy of Augustus and the Italy of Mussolini, we have exhibited two great Chiefs who confront problems that are equal or similar and certainly can be assimilated in character, with each in response providing solutions appropriate to their time.'[81] Learning about the history of Rome, he contended, had a mystical effect in that it 'transforms the past into the future and again ensures the triumph of Rome at a time when its imperial mission had seemed over. You do not really teach Rome,' he explained with a false profundity that was his signature approach to matters of the intellect, 'you continue it, you develop it, as an idea and as a thing which is present in itself. Our Rome', he concluded, 'cannot be that of Augustus, or that of Gregory the Great. . . . It must be both [virtuous pasts and present] together and thereby mutually Italian and Fascist.'[82]

By 1940 Bottai, in his way the most racist of the Fascist chiefs, if studiously endeavouring to keep Fascism's 'spiritual' racism separate from the more mechanical and 'scientific' German variety, was urging that 'the spirit of Rome is no longer the exclusive patrimony of the city of Rome but belongs to all *romanità*, of which, however, Rome remains the centre and symbol'. What Rome had most to offer was living history. 'The monuments of pagan, Christian, medieval and Renaissance Rome [he did not mention the baroque] are not mere works of art but, over and above everything else, they are alive, present and at work.'[83] They expressed not so much the survival of uncontaminated Roman blood as that of an eternal Roman spirit.

Maybe an impulse for Bottai's lucubrations came from secret police reports about Rome, where the population were said to be ready to accept punitive measures against their Jewish fellow citizens but were hostile to suggestions that Italy was sliding into being the lieutenant or mimic of Nazi Germany.[84] Once Italy entered the war on the side of the seemingly victorious Germans on 10 June

1940, spies did not always bring comfort to the Fascist leadership, with one report on 14 June claiming that an isolated and light Allied bombing of the capital had produced 'panic' and 'grumbles everywhere', with the general impression being given of a lack among ordinary Romans of 'any spirit of sacrifice'.[85] To be sure, the seriousness of such attitudes was immediately denied and, the next day, a rival survey maintained that the population were united in a 'granitic block' with the rest of the nation.[86] Yet what was evident was that, despite a generation of Fascist propaganda and action, and despite the cherishing of the city by the regime, its massive building campaigns and its recurrently didactic use of history, Romans remained at least as detached from this conflict as they had been from the First World War. Once again, other Italians quickly joined complaints about the softness of the war for Romans, with an extreme example occurring in 1943, after the severe American bombing of Rome on 19 July. 'Among vast masses from every social sphere', ran an account from Milan about the reception there of news of the event, reigned a 'monstrous sentiment of satisfaction', and the same attitude was replicated in every northern centre. It was, the spy ran on with easy metaphor, as though a 'Neronian perversion had invaded the souls of a great majority of our fellow citizens'.[87]

Doubtless such comments were proof that, amid the disasters of Fascist war, 'the idea of the nation had long since dissolved'.[88] Yet something greater was being expressed; the massive efforts that the dictatorship had directed at mobilising history whether in books or in the streets of Rome and in marshalling it behind the boasted 'ideology of the twentieth century' were proving hollow. Analysts of Rome's experience of combat have shown how badly Fascist government performed in the city. For all the prattle in the 1930s about a war economy, rationing did not work, anti-aircraft shelters were far fewer than officially stated: Governatore Borghese blithely announced that Rome would never be bombed. There had been no preparation to transport people to a refuge in an emergency or to provide supplies of electricity and water in time of need.[89] Already in the spring of 1943 Romans were hungry, a black market was flourishing, child mortality spiralled up and those below the poverty line multiplied.[90] Any initiatives planned by the urban administration were halted by the limitless financial drain triggered by the building of EUR, in 50 per cent deficit when Fascism fell.[91] In the absence of public transport and petrol supplies, the *Governatorato* desperately suggested that walking was good for its citizens.[92]

One unkind historian has stated that the Fascist economic version of total war was 'risible' and the regime marked itself off from liberal democratic Britain, Nazi Germany and the communist Soviet Union by being utterly unable to increase production under war conditions.[93] Such practical matters were of major significance in explaining the botching of Fascist battles. But the Italian regime had one other evident weakness compared with its ally and enemies: despite its decades of braggadocio about harnessing Rome's pasts to the present and future, Fascism, now engaged in international struggle as it had always predicted would be its fate and purpose, proved feeble in summoning history to its side. In Britain's 'people's war', Laurence Olivier could resurrect the ghosts of Henry V (and Shakespeare) to foster national unity and resistance. In the Soviet Union, the spirits of Ivan the Terrible and Marshal Suvurov were made to stand shoulder to shoulder with Stalin. Among the Nazis, racism and nationalism commingled, perhaps assisted by the cloudiness of prehistory in bolstering an Aryan cause, to work for the creation of One Great Germany. In Japan, the Imperial Rescript and 'three thousand years' of dynastic history rallied the nation.

But what valued past could give historical weight to the Italian and Fascist war effort? During the First World War, there had been talk of Roman conquest but the more convincing theme had been that Italy was fighting 'the fourth war of the Risorgimento', achieving its natural borders and defending itself against those 'barbarous' *tedeschi* who had been the enemy certainly in 1859–61 and perhaps through all time. But in the second war Italy had reversed its alliances and was fighting on the side of the Germans, who, by now, were the fierce proponents of those pseudo-scientific racial theories that had consigned Italians to the lowest European rank. Fascism had, in manifold ways, been a regime that cemented itself in peacetime power as the bearer of the heroic history of Italy's First World War. But past triumphs over Germanic forces could scarcely be emphasised after 1940. Bottai was left to preach unconvincingly that 'Germanism' and *romanità* had always been in alliance, with each planted deep in the Italian soul, and efforts by young party intellectuals to talk about 'the last war of the Risorgimento' won little public response.[94]

If this version of history might not persuade everybody, how could the *romanità* which had launched a thousand monographs in praise of Augustus and the rest before 1939 best stiffen Italian arms? Certainly Mussolini picked up references to the possibility that Britain might be the new Carthage, talking knowingly about Italy's 'Fourth Punic War'.[95] But the phrase did not catch on, even if this ancient history may have retained a popular base of a kind since a memoirist from the San Lorenzo quarter recalled that boyhood games there were fought out between 'Romans' and 'Carthaginians'.[96] A youth growing up to be a communist remembered instead that, by early 1944, his friends were split between fans of Sulla (the aristocrat) and Marius (the commoner), rivals in their time under the Republic but now updated as contemporary class symbols, despite Fascism's pledge of complete national unity and the cancellation of any Marxist memory or history.[97]

Had familiarity with the classics bred not contempt but, worse for Fascist purpose, a lack of precise meaning or, that apparent oxymoron, a profound superficiality? To be sure, as early as the 1920s, some Italians endorsed the idea that the ancient Romans were 'more purely [Aryan] than any other people'.[98] But was that true of contemporary Italians? After all, a search for 'Aryans' could have negative as well as positive implications, as was demonstrated in one of Hitler's nightly verbal rambles when he remarked that there was 'only one Roman living amongst the Italians', Benito Mussolini.[99] And, once the Italian war effort proved ineffective, the Duce himself was given to bluster about how unworthy the people were of him, and how un-Roman they were showing themselves to be.[100] As he told Ciano as early as March 1942: 'This war is not for the Italian people. The Italian people are not mature or consistent enough for so grave and decisive a test. This war is for the Germans and the Japanese, not for us.'[101]

In any case, just what was the story of race in classical Rome? It was easy for Fascist propagandists to urge that Julius Caesar was best interpreted as 'the first Black Shirt in the story of the Nation', but had not ancient Rome pursued a policy of assimilation of those whom it conquered? The Duce himself had praised this line in proclaiming the 'restored' Roman empire in May 1936.[102] What were the racial implications? Perhaps the 'lessons of Rome' (like those of Catholicism) pushed members of Mussolini's entourage who enjoyed intellectual speculation to dream up an idiosyncratic Italian racism nourished by the spirit and the will, and a counter of the Nazi version, sprung from blood and (pseudo-)science. In Rome, Governatore Colonna had purged Jews from the city administration well before Italy entered the conflict.[103] Yet here, too, world war rapidly brought discomfort. The fine print of Fascist racial theoretics could scarcely assert itself against the passion and fanaticism of Nazi anti-Semitism (and Nazi anti-Bolshevism), all the more when, in battle, the Fascist empire in East Africa melted as though it had been built of snow in the tropics. In Libya there was greater resistance, but only when Erwin Rommel led Nazi troops in command of their Italian allies, viewed by enemies and friends less as iron-hard legionaries than as ragged auxiliaries.

Could the answer be that Mussolini's Italy, like the Caesars, was fighting for 'civilisation' against 'barbarism'? In that regard, communism might offer the best target. After all, Fascism had been invented to overthrow the Italian followers of Marx. Regime histories had always emphasised that Fascism amounted to a 'third way' between past and future that would avoid the excessive materialism and the cruel body count of Bolshevism as well as the spiritual malaise of capitalism. It was simple to label the Soviets as 'barbarians', and, in contesting communism, Fascist forces might well find allies in the wealthier, more conservative and Catholic sectors of national society.[104] And, in the summer of 1941, the Italians, although not informed beforehand of Hitler's war plans, joined their Nazi allies in the assault on the USSR in Operation Barbarossa (avoiding the fact that the red-bearded Emperor Frederick I had warred viciously in Italy and defeated a 'Roman' army, before being forced by malaria to retreat to his German territories). However, the military results of the invasion of the USSR for the Italians were unhappy and humiliating and it was not long before Mussolini was trying to press the Führer into a compromise peace with Stalin.

The Duce did so because he had decided that Italy's 'real' enemy was the 'plutocratic' Anglo-Saxon world, whose armies in 1943 strode inexorably through Libya to invade Sicily on 10 July. But here, too, history worked badly for the Fascist cause. Whereas the Germans could plausibly argue that, in Danzig and as far as the Volga, they were bringing Germans home to the Reich, the vast majority of Italians scattered throughout the world lived as immigrants in the USA or in its South American subordinates. There lay Italy's massive 'informal empire', one that not even the most deluded Fascist could claim had once seen the Roman eagle and might willingly hear history's demand to 'return' to rule by that city.

On every front, then, for Mussolini's dictatorship, identifying a Roman history that illuminated and steeled the virtue of the present was impossible. Fascism in battle was not comforted by a usable past. Rather, in the dictatorship's version of modern 'total' war, the diversity of histories that had always characterised Rome proved particularly hard to manage. Well before he fell on 25 July 1943 and was killed on 28 April 1945, Mussolini had lost control of the past, simultaneously surrendering his, his regime's and his ideology's present and future. Despite the noisy talk about the Birth of Rome, Julius Caesar, Augustus and the rest, despite the thwacking of the city into Fascist shape and the lasting creation of monuments to the dictatorship, the regime's attempt to take over the history of Rome had failed. While peace had survived, Fascist propaganda, undergirded by ceaseless urban activity in Rome, had hidden what in reality were surviving differences in the Catholic, popular and bourgeois nationalist readings of Rome's meaning from contemporary society. War exposed these fissures, casting stark light on the inadequacies of Fascist totalitarianism. In its total defeat, it must now be asked, had Fascism blotted the nation's contact with its capital's past, in the process offering the Church the chance to turn the clock of historical understanding back before 1870, and reassert that it, and not Italy, was the most authentic bearer of Roman history?

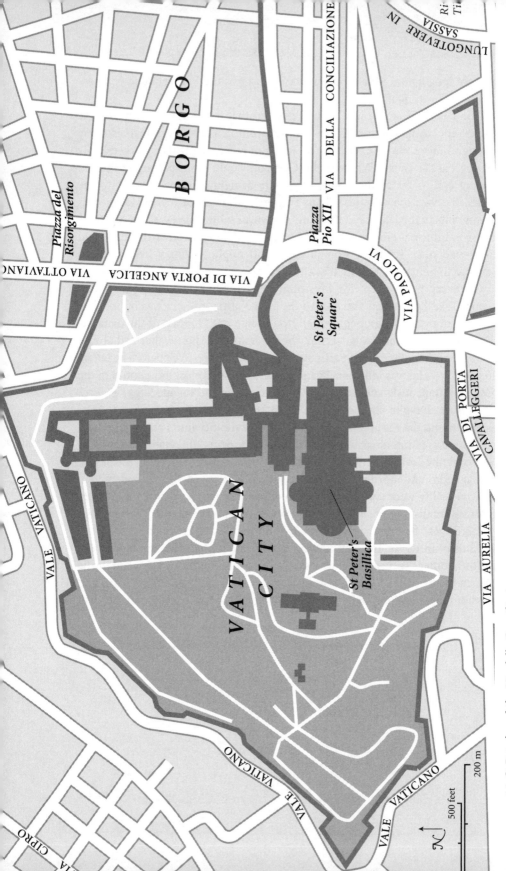

10. St Peter's and the Via della Conciliazione

———— ✳ ————

9

A SECOND RESTORATION? THE CATHOLIC
AND IMPERIAL ROME OF PIUS XII

The fall of one 'Great Man', who had been exposed in the war as by no means 'always right', inevitably burnished the image of his rival, the infallible pope, divinely inspired holder of the office whose power had always been said by the Church to run from one age to the next across the succeeding centuries. Even while Mussolini was still the warrior Duce, an event underlined the victory of the long-term histories marshalled by the Vatican over the short-term ones propagandised by the dictatorship. On 19 July 1943, with virtually no opposition, 662 American planes rained down 4,000 bombs on Rome, striking the airport at Ciampino to the south and the railway yards to the east near the Stazione Tiburtina. The raid inflicted considerable collateral damage on the urban fabric in those parts of the city and their surrounds, killing more than 1,500 Romans.[1]

Rome was scarcely the only European city to be bombed in the course of the Second World War and neither this attack nor a repeat on 13 August was anything like as severe as those that befell such German cities as Hamburg and Dresden, nor, indeed, other major Italian centres from Naples to Milan.[2] Yet, the bombing of Rome signalled the withering away of Fascism and the shattering of its totalitarian pretensions to offer a full and unchallenged explanation of life and history to the city. Not the dictator (who, on 19 July, was in the north at Feltre trying to get a word in edgeways in an ineffectual talk with Hitler), not the Fascist party secretary, not the King, but rather Pope Pius XII, at this time of emergency, assumed the task of salving public agony, calming public fears and incarnating Rome's past, present and future among the people. At 5.20 p.m. that hot summer afternoon, Pius stood alone and without police escort outside the shattered remains of San Lorenzo, the ancient basilica where Pius IX lay buried, to be greeted with 'popular delirium'.[3] The pontiff and Bishop of Rome stayed for three hours, more pallid than usual as he contemplated the ruins, genuflecting on the rubble and 'praying for the victims in this city and all who were afflicted by aerial attack'. He ended by intoning the *De Profundis*.[4]

Since 1967 a statue of Pius XII, funded by the rightist Rome daily paper, *Il Tempo*, has recorded this papal visit of succour. More memorable is a photo of the event, showing the pope, arms stretched and eyes raised to heaven, surrounded by an anxious and worshipping crowd (in recent times, sceptics have argued that the image was actually snapped after a second raid on 13 August). Whatever the case, on 19 July it does seem that Pius summoned God as witness and salvation to his suffering people, while his Undersecretary of State, G.B. Montini, charitably distributed banknotes to those afflicted.[5] When, a little later, the King tried to make an appearance in the quarter, he was ignored or insulted, even though his aides also handed cash to the populace. When Mussolini came back to Rome on the 20th, he was forced to inspect the damage at the dead of night and without fanfare, an infallible and eternal Duce no more to his people; instead, as he admitted, 'the most hated man in Italy'. As the Second World War brutally infringed their history, Romans remembered that they had

28. Statue of Pius XII outside Basilica di San Lorenzo offering austere salvation.

once belonged to a holy city and looked to the Pope as their refuge in time of troubles. Neither the nation nor the dictator could match his historic appeal.

Pius XII had become pope in March 1939 and his rule would last till October 1958, taking in not just the war, but the foundation of the new Republic in 1946, the Cold War elections in 1948 that would elevate a Catholic party, the Christian Democrats (DC), to national and urban government for a generation, the next scheduled Holy Year in 1950 and many other significant events. The momentous nature of his times ensures that it is easy to locate sites of this pope's memory in Rome.

The most obvious is inside the great basilica of St Peter's, the public heart of the universal Church. If visitors enter and turn to the right, their eyes are naturally drawn to the *Pietà* by Michelangelo, exquisite expression of human suffering and love. Sadly, since a hammer attack by Laszlo Toth, a deluded Hungarian-Australian tourist, on Pentecost 1972, this luminous statue must be viewed through a shatter-resistant acrylic glass shield. Proceeding down the right aisle of the massive basilica, pilgrims can identify more ordinary statues commemorating the two popes of the interwar era, Pius XI and Pius XII. The representation of the latter is by the long-lived Sicilian sculptor, Francesco Messina (1900–95), and was completed in 1963.[6] Messina was another of those Italians cheerfully able to serve Fascist dictatorship and post-war Christian Democracy, becoming director of the Brera gallery in Milan in 1936 and recovering his job in 1947 after charitable investigation of his Fascist connections. In between, Messina had been a paladin of the *Novecento* school, winner of the Venice Biennale prize in his field in 1942 (a potentially taxing year politically but one when competition may have been limited).

The image that Messina crafted of the pontiff is a severe one. Thin-lipped and wearing almost rimless glasses, Pius looks ascetic and a little reproachful, although, it must be admitted, few of the crowds that throng the church glance at him as they hurry by, seeking the more obvious glories of the place. The long, elegant fingers of the pope's right hand are raised in blessing, while Pius himself looks away and down to the right. He is frowning but seemingly less in anger than perplexity. Perhaps the problem is the placement of his statue, since his eyes may be fixed on two nearby naked putti, together holding a lunette of St Damasus, pope between 366 and 384 CE during a restorative phase for the Church after the unsuccessful efforts of Emperor Julian the Apostate to reverse its growing power. The alternative is that Pius has been left eternally to stare at the adjacent monument to Queen Christina of Sweden (1626–89). Although she sought sanctuary in Counter-Reformation Rome and renounced the Protestantism of her birth, Christina was a historical figure of a nuance that might not fully appeal to the rigour of Pius XII (all the more since she is now an 'icon' of European feminist lesbians).

A hint of ghostly discomfort in the statue's positioning is all the more ironical since, until his death in 1958, Pius gloried in the imperial Catholic majesty
of St Peter's, presiding over many gorgeous ceremonies there, uplifted on the
sedia gestatoria, cooled by waving peacock fans, hailed by the silver trumpet
and proud to be the *ancien régime*-style monarch of a Church that would last
until the end of time. Yet it is outside St Peter's that the ghost of the Pope can
find greater pleasure. There the Via della Conciliazione has plaques at either
end that record in Latin its completion during the Jubilee of 1950. At the
opening to the street (in front of the Roma Aeterna souvenir shop) stands an
area described on maps as Piazza Pio XII: Defensor Civitatis, although it
lacks the lineaments of a real square. An explanatory marble panel, its imprint
faded by time and the sun, clarifies (in Italian): 'June 1944–June 1960. On
31 May 1950 the City Council of Rome, cognisant of the work completed by
His Holiness Pope Pius XII during the world conflict for the salvation of
the city of Rome and determined to pass on the memory of the solemn and
spontaneous expressions of filial gratitude made to him by the whole Roman
people, acclaiming him the Defender of the City community, has unanimously
decided to rename this square to Pius XII on the day of 4 June 1950'.[7]

The panel in Piazza Pio XII adds that the pope had sent the Comune the
following reply: 'the tribute which the City Council has paid us with its unanimous resolution in giving our name to the reconstructed square abutting
Bernini's great forum is for us a fresh bond with the Eternal City and with its
Christian and civil fortunes; grateful for this noble testimony that recalls the
pain and happy salvation [of wartime] that we have shared, we pray God may
bestow for ever upon our beloved people of Rome the peace of which apostolic
blessing may be the hope and the promise.'

At least in the piazza named after him, those who revere this pope, who, in
2000, was elevated to 'venerable' on the high road to sainthood and who is said to
have in Pope Benedict XVI a weighty backer of his imminent canonisation, can
believe that there is only one way to read his story. Back in 1883 Leo XIII had
urged that, to counteract the malign effects of the national and liberal manipulation of the past, the Church needed 'true history, better history, impartial history.
We need to show the Italian people what they owe to the popes of past centuries.'[8]
Could it be that, during his pontificate and especially in the Holy Year celebrated
under his aegis, Pius XII had cleansed Rome of its errors since 1870, restored the
Catholic reading of present, past and future and re-sanctified the holy city?

Perhaps. Yet, in Piazza Pio XII, a jarring is not far away. Even in the shadow
of St Peter's, disputes over the reading of the past surface. Further down the Via
della Conciliazione, at its junction with the Via S. Pio X, stands an insurance
building, erected in 'ANNO MCMXLI' or, more faintly, it can still be seen, 'ANNO XVIII
[of the Fascist Revolution]'. Above is the emblem in bas-relief of the she-wolf
and the babies, Romulus and Remus, and a space where the shadow of the fasces

29. Plaque marking Piazza Pio XII abutting Piazza San Pietro, untroubled by the Holocaust.

that were once affixed there lingers. Here, then, is a hint of less agreeable histories of the era of Pius XII than the decorous ones recalled by officialdom. The outline of the fasces raises the question whether this pope's friendly dealings with Mussolini's dictatorship mean that Pius XII was, to all but fundamentalist Catholics, a flawed defender of the community of Rome and the world beyond – 'Mussolini's pope'? After all, until the Second World War was lost, his personal political preference for sinful human beings was Fascism.

Worse is that other soubriquet charging him with being 'Hitler's pope', the anti-Semitic head of a religious institution which, in the twenty-first century, has still made no proper moral reckoning with its racist sins.[9] For the Zionist polemicist, Daniel Goldhagen, the whole Church is dragged down by a 'past that will not fade away', and the most deplorable artificer of this malign history

30. Rome's Great Synagogue *c.*1930, when Jewish history was still welcomed by Fascism.

was Pius XII. According to Goldhagen, the pope's 'repeated approval during the Nazi period of the publication of vicious antisemitic polemics in the Jesuit journal *Civiltà cattolica*, and his failure during the time of maximum danger for the Jews to countermand the deep-rooted antisemitism of the Church leave no doubt that he was an antisemite'.[10] As a more charitable but still critical commentator has phrased it, did not this pope stay culpably silent while the Holocaust was perpetrated in Mussolini's Rome, where Jews were set to work as slaves, 'under his very windows'?[11] Whatever the appreciative words carved into permanence at Piazza Pio XII, this pope remains a focus of debate, a spirit circled by contested histories and rival memories.

One adjective that can be attached without excessive controversy to Pope Pius XII is that he was 'the Roman pope'. Perhaps he will prove the last such. Certainly, of all the recent holders of the pallium, Pius XII was the one who most evidently sprang from the city and most straightforwardly embodied its manifold histories and their jostling ambiguities. This pope of Rome was indeed a bearer of Roman histories.

His roots in the city were, at their most basic, familial. Among his predecessors, Leo XIII (1878–1903) and Innocent XIII (1721–4) came from noble stock, owning estates in the hills surrounding the city. But, before Pius XII, the last pontiff actually to have been born in Rome was Clement X (1670–6), and much had changed in the city and in the comprehensions of its pasts and purpose since then. Eugenio Maria Pacelli began his life on 2 March 1876 in a place that had fallen under Italian rule only six years earlier. His family were aristocratic, not by blood but of the service kind, rising through their skill in administration. His grandfather, Marcantonio, had been the most useful papal man of business for much of the nineteenth century, while also being nominated a member of the Censorship Council, formed on Pius IX's return to Rome in 1850 in order to arraign those guilty of what the Church damned as crimes under the Mazzinian Republic. Marcantonio Pacelli was soon promoted to be Secretary of the Interior (1852–70). He was also the person most directly involved in the launching of the papal daily paper, *L'Osservatore romano*, in 1861, just as an Italian nation was coming into being. Opposing the perverse triumph of liberalism, this organ aimed to read the present, past and future as it was said the Church had always done.

The Pacellis, then, were a family awakening to a Catholic version of modernity, to a degree ready to accommodate themselves to the rise of the nation of Italy but never identical with it. Their hedging was evident in the careers of the family's most distinguished members in law and banking. The pope's brother, Francesco, was the key legal negotiator on the Vatican side of the Lateran Pacts, where he worked closely with Mussolini but did not forget the Church's political, social and financial interest. A cousin, Ernesto Pacelli, in 1880 had helped found the Banco di Roma, over which he presided until 1916. This bank was always seen as 'Catholic', although it eagerly involved itself in zones of Italian national and imperial interest, pressing for government action in Libya, for example, before and during the invasion of 1911.[12] Despite his family's fame, Eugenio Pacelli remembered growing up with modest wealth and he was educated first at a public school, the E.Q. Visconti *liceo*, before attending the Catholic Gregorian university after opting for the priesthood at eighteen.[13] He did so formed by a family that stood at the summit of Catholic participation in modern Rome and, even under Liberal governance, was determined to pursue a Catholic track through contemporary history.

As a priest, Pius rose rapidly, becoming Cardinal Secretary of State in February 1930, promoted from his previous post as papal nuncio in Germany (stationed in Munich in 1919, he learned during that city's brief communist revolution, and never forgot, that good order and religion were threatened by the evil of 'Judaeo-Bolshevism'). Back in Rome, he flourished as a Church diplomat, sponsoring the Concordat with Nazi Germany in 1933. He also showed a comprehension of Rome's purpose in the life of the Church, rejoicing in April 1931 at the opening of a new Pontificio Collegio Urbano di Propaganda Fide (City Pontifical College for the Propagation of the Faith) on the Janiculum. He studiously turned his back on Garibaldi's statue there as he informed trainee priests that, when they climbed that hill, they must think about 'the ascension of the mind and the heart toward heaven'. The College, he added, was about spiritual and not military battles; it drew on the 'universality of the nations' and the 'universality of the Church', blending all people 'in the same faith, hope and love'.[14]

In a later sermon, Pius enthused over the Fascist cleansing of the chief classical ruins in the city, while drawing the lesson that the Church bore the inheritance of all that was 'healthy and vital in Graeco-Roman culture'. Despite the imprint of Mussolini's pickaxe, Rome, Cardinal Pacelli maintained, was 'indestructible', given that it had brought 'before the world in uninterrupted apostolic succession . . . unstained by error, the diadem of the blood . . . of its Divine Conqueror'. In the churchman's mind, the spiritual and metaphysical surpassed the practical and everyday aspect of the city. With its best focus on the early Christian period, Rome's archaeology was, he concluded, 'the archaeology of life'.[15] Catholic Action, the Church's youth organisation, a body always likely to annoy those Fascists aspiring to totalitarianism, was, he added a few months later, 'renewing the empire of the Caesars, but in a more extensive, more intimate, and more divine manner, one that would last until the end of time'.[16]

Perhaps his devotion to universality faded a little during the Ethiopian war when, in December 1935, reflecting on the twelfth centenary of the death of the Venerable Bede, he chose to underline that 'the real cradle of English Christianity lies in Rome. Hence came the light that guided those peoples from the shadows of error to the freedom of being the sons of God'.[17] There was an intimation here that Cardinal Pacelli was not fully persuaded by the justice of the League of Nations' British-led condemnation of Italian aggression in Ethiopia and was ready to bless a Catholic imperialism that could win back schismatic Coptic Ethiopians to the True Church (and its beneficent history) in alliance with Fascist arms.

But of his preaching in these years of preparation for the Papacy, the most celebrated moment occurred on 26 November 1936, some months after Pacelli had returned from a visit to the USA that may have taught him that American capitalism was the greatest lay contemporary power (and suggested to the Church financial authorities that they should shift their European investments to the US Federal Reserve).[18] The theme that Cardinal Pacelli now addressed was 'Rome, in order that you may know Christ is Roman' ('*Roma onde Cristo è Romano*'). 'The most sacred destiny of Rome', Pacelli contended, 'lies hidden in the faith of Christ, faith that is victorious over any form of paganism, be it ancient or modern'. The real centre of the city was the Vatican, where the pope held in his hands 'the destiny of Rome'. No other place could match Rome in a significance that, at its most profound, was 'not of this world'. 'Jerusalem and its people are no longer the city and the people of God', Pacelli intoned. 'Rome is the new Zion, and every people who live the Roman faith is Roman'.[19]

Just what target Pacelli had in mind in these phrases remains unclear, although the Church was suspicious of the drift of Mussolini's dictatorship into Axis with Hitler, and when, in May 1938, the Führer came on an official visit, the Vatican rebuffed any suggestion that he should be allowed to inspect work on the Via della Conciliazione. They let it be known that Pius XI viewed the swastika as a twisted and malign cross that should not be confused with the true Christian one and its eternal message.[20] Certainly, once Pius XII had been elevated to the Papacy on 2 March 1939, he continued frequently to blend Church history with that of Rome, repeatedly implying that Catholic universality was older, better and more permanent than anything that might result from 'universal Fascism'. As his Christmas message of 1941 explained, the *Urbs* was the 'lighthouse of civilisation', radiating a glory that the whole world perforce acknowledged, 'a city more for Christ than for the Caesars, a city that is eternal and timeless'.[21] Its beneficent imperial destiny, he implied, soared beyond the fate of whichever new world order would in the short term be imposed by the victorious side among the presently warring nations and the geegaws of their empires and ideologies. And he himself embodied this timelessness that soared beyond politics and did so with a grandeur that dwarfed Mussolini and other possible competitors. So, in the summer of 1942, a film entitled *Pastor Angelicus* recounted the pope's life and continuing work, tirelessly occupying every day and night. Thereafter papal propaganda regularly revived this theme that Pius was indeed an 'angelic pastor'.

So the war passed. When liberation came on 4 June 1944, the pope's initial reaction was to look beyond little Italy again to emphasise the universality of Rome. The history of the great city surpassed that of the gimcrack nation. Even while Allied troops were still approaching the city, on 2 June Pius preached that 'any who raise their hands against Rome are, in the eyes of the civilised world and of the eternal judgement of God, guilty of matricide'. After the Americans arrived, he added that, although he mourned the fate of all bombed cities, 'Rome is <u>unique</u>: unique for the grandeur of its history and for its preponderant role in the evolution of universal civilisation: unique for its supernatural mission which places it beyond the flux of time and above any national distinctions.'[22] In the mind of Pius XII and many in the Church, whatever the ups and downs of the Italian nation or the rise and fall of Great Powers in the mundane world, Rome's prime and transcendental indentity had always been as the Holy City.

Its place was all the more significant and its message must be all the more heeded since the welcome defeat of at least the Nazi side of the Axis did not bring perpetual peace. The death of Hitler and Mussolini ended the Second World War but, well before their demise, Pius was anxious to approve the global Cold War, now to be fought to a bitter end against Stalin and communism. A prime site of battle was Italy where the national communist party, the PCI, was threatening to carve out its own road to power and legitimising its rise by claiming that, through the black years of dictatorship, it had been foremost in resisting Fascism. It did not take long for Pius XII to assume a leading role in seeking to roll back this interpretation of recent history and to reveal his worry that the Christian Democrat party, led by Prime Minister Alcide De Gasperi, might not be tough enough for present needs. Did its commitment to democracy render it too soft for the current situation? Maybe, as a propagandist near the pope put it in 1946 in the pages of *Civiltà cattolica*, 'the time had come for reconciliation between fascists and all anti-communist anti-fascists'.[23]

Until the DC triumphed in the 'Cold War' elections of 18 April 1948 and even after, Pius XII remained alert to any threatened advance of communism in Italy. In his Easter message on 28 March that year, he warned that the nation's history was confronting a 'turning point', and demanded that the faithful rigorously eschew 'pusillanimity, appeasement or irresolution' in opposing and destroying the political left.[24] The victorious Catholic slogan for the poll – 'At the urn, God sees you but Stalin does not' – carried the usual implication of the eternal superiority of Catholic spirituality over Marxist historical materialism. So, too, did Pius XII's fervent backing of regular and disciplined 'Pilgrimages in the spirit of Mary' (*Peregrinatio Mariae*) in Rome, Italy and the world.[25]

In his steely determination to keep his people wherever they were to be found outside the Iron Curtain safe from Marxist contamination, Pius XII regularly summoned the providential power, the salutary history, that he had always known to reside in Rome. In December 1945 he had already re-emphasised that the place was 'The Eternal City, Caput Mundi'. In 1948 he rejoiced when friendly journalists argued that 'Italy means Rome, and Rome is the synthesis of a civilisation the opposite of that of Muscovite barbarism'.[26] As proof of the revival of clericalism, Christian Democrat city mayor Salvatore Rebecchini, who led a junta dependent on votes from such far right forces as the monarchists, the neo-Fascists and the 'know-nothing' Uomo Qualunque (Everyman) party, that year applauded the special consecration of the city to the Sacred Heart of Jesus. This devotion had been especially dear to Popes Leo XIII and Pius XI and was destined to be affirmed again by Pius XII in 1956 and by Benedict XVI in 2006, with its promise that, through appropriate prayer, God would be able to touch the most hardened of hearts of any who allowed the illumination of Rome to pour over their souls.[27]

In 1948, however, the electoral defeat of the Popular Front coalition of communists and socialists might still have proved temporary even though Italy was encouraged to join NATO in early 1949, cheered by a papal Christmas message that 'a people which is menaced or is victim of an unjust aggression, if it wishes to act in a Christian fashion, cannot remain in passive indifference'.[28] Pius did not fear to suggest that, in a crisis, God would stand firm on the West's side should the Cold War turn hot.

This ambition to impose a second Restoration on the erring people needed one further grand historical event to exalt the sacrality of Rome and the permanence of its lessons – a Holy Year. So the coming *Anno Santo* was formally announced by the pope in the same week that Italy joined NATO.[29] After all, as the pope put it in June 1949 when he had excommunicated Italian communists and their collaborators (thereby cutting them off from the Church and its history): Rome was 'the city where you search for God, know God, love God, serve God. Rome must be the place where every one and every thing cooperates to carry out the purposes of God.'[30] Not Nazi, no longer Mussolinian and certainly not Marxist, it was and ever would be the Catholic light to the world. At the coming Jubilee, all could worship its eternal glory. Then, one history, and only one history, would shine out to the farthest reaches of the globe from Holy Rome.

Happily, as Pius preached on the radio in March 1949, things were looking up, the war was over and the 'moral plagues' that had afflicted the early post-war years were checked. Yet, during the coming celebrations, the Catholics of Rome must give the best example to those who would arrive from everywhere as pilgrims to the city in Holy Year. Romans must be disciplined, in stringently discountenancing non-Catholic newspapers, for example.[31] Catholic women must refuse the seduction of 'luxury' and must devote themselves to children and family, educating the young to 'obedience and respect for authority'. Had not 'simplicity of life and parsimony, throughout time, been the special virtue of the Italian people?' Pius asked in phrases that Mussolini had been accustomed similarly to murmur when the war started to go badly.[32] Foreigners, too, should listen in obedient silence and awe to the pope in Rome. A delegation of American congressmen were welcomed to a city that, they – cold warriors from a New World – were instructed, was possessed of a 'long, long memory', whether of pagan 'heroism and cruelty' or, better, of its 'purification and ennoblement by Christian civilisation and culture'.[33]

It is no surprise therefore to find that the pope's Christmas message for 1949, coinciding with the opening of the Porta Santa, was grandly addressed to 'beloved sons and daughters of the universe'. As the pope explained, the Church in Rome was 'the perennial source of truth, salvation and good'; it stood above and beyond the nations and the competing ideologies.[34] The Church and its Rome were certainly not communist. But, it was time to indicate, they were not naively capitalist, either. As a Jesuit observed in *Civiltà cattolica*, the Church led human resistance to materialism and false science, that 'hybrid mixture of materialist agnosticism, evanescent humanism and an ingenuous faith in badly defined progress and mistaken evolution'. 'Science, philosophy, progress, revolution, socialism, communism, and all such myths', the priest homilised, 'are now discredited and exhausted as oracles, they have nothing whatever to tell us'; their history was past, the falsity of its reading exposed.[35] Liberal democracy, another added, had been 'born under the sign of religious agnosticism', had always tended to persecute the true faith and was very likely to degenerate into 'the militant atheism of rigid Marxists'. Catholic doctrine must not flinch from opposing the 'pseudo laws and freedom' that, ever since the French Revolution, had wantonly led men astray.[36] Whatever the temporary political doctrines that so excited and so pointlessly agitated humankind, the Church was a rock that resisted cheap talk about modernisation. Human nostrums 'pass, and the Church stays', it was asserted.[37]

As for Italy, a third Jesuit maintained, the most important matter was to stick closely to the provisions of the Lateran treaties, that wise deal between pope and dictator. 'Since the so-called "liberation" (better defined in the diktat of the peace treaty), the Italian people have endured a series of dreadful humiliations which, together with the material destruction, the general impoverishment of the economy, and the admission into the political arena of alien elements or those come back from long and not always involuntary exile, uncompre-hending of the national spirit', should have illustrated to Italians the meretri-ciousness of human answers. Since it seized Rome in 1870, the nation had proved no solution to the people's ills and sinfulness; it could not satisfy their longing for truth. The real message of war and calamity was in future to obey the pope, giving faith less to the fleeting nation than to the eternal empire of the Church, so much greater than that of Caesars, old or new.[38] 'The sun of this Rome', it was declared in words not dissimilar from those that had once hailed the Duce as a contemporary Apollo, glistered, 'with its rays that are so alive and so penetrating that no part of the world can hide from its light and colour'.[39] Holy Year, it was proclaimed with a further echo of Fascist phraseology, had amounted to a 'Marian muster' (*adunata mariana*) of unparalleled appeal and success.[40] Pilgrims had flocked to Rome to know that Christ was Roman.

The city shone with papal power, or so Church spokesmen maintained. Appropriately received by the pope at his New Year's blessing was the mayor, Rebecchini, who was congratulated on the way his rightist coalition communal council was enhancing the 'good and decorum' of Rome, while helping 'the less well off' and any in need of (Catholic) social action.[41] In the following weeks, Holy Year was punctuated with the customary round of papal visits to the ancient basilicas and by various other religious events, including the publica-tion on 12 August of the encyclical, *Humanae Generis*, something of a repeat of the Syllabus of Errors in its denunciation of evolution, existentialism and historicism.[42]

Among the more notable ceremonies of the year was the canonisation on 24 June of Maria Goretti; coincidentally the day before, in the larger world, the West moved to resist 'communist aggression' in Korea. Goretti was a poor peasant girl, murdered in 1902 in Lazio province when defending her honour against an attempted rape by Alessandro Serenelli. The rapist repented in prison and eventually emerged from it to become a Capuchin lay brother. He and Maria's elderly mother, Assunta, attended the holy ceremony in St Peter's with more than 300,000 worshippers, where Maria was lauded as a virgin saint, 'a humble child of the people' as the pope expressed it, and the 'St Agnes of the twentieth century', a model to erring womankind, untouched by the vulgar sin of feminism.[43] Her elevation, and that of a number of other new saints that year, were proper, *Capitolium* explained, since all expressed in some fashion a holy *romanità*.[44] Whether or not this was the quality that mattered, since 1950 Maria Goretti has retained a considerable presence in the religious imagining of Rome and its periphery, rivalling in the urban popular mind Italy's most celebrated post-war saint, Padre Pio of the Gargano peninsula on the Adriatic coast, as specially blessed.[45] At least in Catholic eyes, Santa Maria Goretti embodies all that is best in women's history.

The other major religious moment of the year, presaged in Assunta Goretti's name, was the pope's dogmatic and infallible definition on 1 November 1950 of the bodily Assumption of the Virgin in his Apostolic Constitution, *Munificentissimus Deus*. As Marina Warner has explained, in this document Pius XII was again underscoring the Church's transcendence and its ability to master time. 'Belief in the Assumption', she comments, 'extends an idea fundamental to the virgin birth: that time itself belongs to the material world and is alien from the spiritual, from the supernatural. Death, like birth, belongs to time; freedom from death, like freedom from sex, overcomes it.'[46] As far as Catholic rhetoric was concerned, it might be concluded that the Virgin's path was curiously paralleled by Rome, a place that was eternal and 'perpetually young', as Rebecchini put it in a speech of 21 April: since its foundation Rome had been ensured against decay and unconfined in its universality through the will of God in its providential destiny to be the Holy City.[47]

Yet, it might need somewhere to be admitted, pope and Church were protesting too much in their sermonising about a fully restored holy city. Had they really achieved total control over understanding of Rome's histories? After all, the *Giubileo* brought many foreigners back to the city for the first time since the war. A delegation from distant Australia turned up in June led by the sometime admirer of Mussolini, Archbishop James Duhig of Brisbane, while to show its superiority over human law, the Vatican had negotiated a deal with the Italian government that relieved 'pilgrims' from needing passports to enter Italy so long as they were equipped with a Catholic guarantee.[48]

So much was triumph. But the fame of the *Anno Santo* gave less worshipful foreign visitors the opportunity to resume their efforts to frame a historical meaning in the city, often more cynical in its interpretation than was the line pushed by Catholic officialdom. To be sure, the comprehensions of Rome that were now expressed were rarely new, instead reviving familiar disgust with the hypocrisy and self-interest of priests and people, and the natural and even eternal sinfulness and corruption of Rome. The place, an opinionated Englishman remarked in words that seemed to bear the echoes of Augustus Hare, had been further consigned through Fascism and war to 'the tradition of indifference and the tradition of the parasite. . . . Consuming much, producing little except departmental memoranda and papal bulls, modern Rome', he stated, 'stands as a hostage to a by no means certain fortune.' Damaged by the poverty of Liberal and Fascist architectural trends, the city had 'lost the attractions of its papal period without acquiring the principal advantages of a great European capital'.[49] It scarcely mattered any more. Another English visitor was struck by the way that Rome lacked anything Italian: 'It is the age-long internationalism of Rome, first under the Empire, then under the Popes, and now under the reign of the tourist, that causes Rome to be less Italian than any other Italian city.' Mind you, it was not clear that he regretted this difference. The new apartment buildings that were spreading like an ink stain beyond the walls, he grumbled, were quarters so wretched that 'no one would go [there] unless driven by whips'.[50] In his mind, they were very likely too 'Italian'.

Eleanor Clark, an American sojourner, was more charitable. Rome, she agreed, sometimes seemed no more than a place of 'roaring motors and other dreadful noises, ... whose churches are junk shops of idolatrous bric-à-brac, ... a place of no grandeur whatever of any kind you expected, ravaged by fascist vulgarities'. Yet, she hoped, despite the grossness carried over from the defeated immediate past, a tourist, with a bit of thought, could realise that Rome's history was not single but multiple. With all its faults, this city, Clark contended, still could be found at the heart of 'everybody's memory, as it was a hundred or a thousand years ago'.[51] During a *Giubileo*, all roads led there. 'Three million', Clark noted, was the official tally of pilgrims. But they seemed 'twenty million'.[52]

Foreigners might applaud or complain according to their insight or prejudice, but more reliably pious in their commentary were a number of ex-Fascists who now detected that Catholicism, patriotism and opportunism allowed them to promote Rome's history (and themselves) in a revised key. Egilberto Martire, once the fan of Don Bosco, now enthused over a Colosseum blessed with the holy signs of Catholicism. The restoration in 1927 (by the Fascists) of the cross there, he wrote, had been 'the wish of everyone'.[53] Martire had re-emerged in Rome in 1947 when he presided over a 'Morality Congress', urging more zealous campaigns against pornography and greater press censorship; among those to applaud him was the leading Fascist historian, Gioacchino Volpe.[54] Then and thereafter, Martire was alert to every chance to exalt Pius XII as the defender of community and civilisation, his chief; whom, in his secret heart, he may have again called his Duce.[55]

Giuseppe Prezzolini, once the youthful Mussolini's intellectual sponsor, was, during the dictatorship, accorded gilded rustication running the Casa d'Italia at Columbia University in New York, there adapting the Fascist story for audiences in the USA. After the war, he accepted a commission to write a guide for American visitors to the Jubilee, advising them what to think of Rome and multiplying his clichés as he strove to impress upon his readers a history he thought they wanted to hear. From the birth of Rome, he knew, the city had commanded a special but easily comprehended past, and so he began by remarking that, 'like the citizens of the United States, they [the Romans] were brilliant in organisation'. Indeed, he added ingratiatingly, 'Americans have much in common with the ancient Romans: like them, Americans have received more than given in the arts and philosophy; but like them also, Americans dominate their contemporaries in the social and practical sciences, in the tolerance of races and religions, in their political thinking, in their love of sports, and in the conscious effort of their government to appeal to and satisfy large average sections of the population'.[56]

Warming in his praise, Rome, he continued, 'is a kind of connective tissue among living cells of knowledge, of beauty, of history'. Liberated from 'the Germans', the city shimmered with an architectural glory that extended from the Caesars through the Renaissance, Baroque and Umbertine periods, while, he maintained, 'the architecture of Mussolini's period was more successful than his foreign policy'.[57] Perhaps there was a downside: visitors to the city would sniff the 'smell of time', odours that combined rotting cabbage, incense and candle wax. Romans might lack the seriousness of the transatlantic world: 'Work is not looked upon as a blessing of God in Rome. The crowds have intelligent eyes and like to see and be seen. They are quick to comment and, although at times impertinent, they are fundamentally good-natured. The traditional use of the stiletto has disappeared. Indeed, its use was seldom inspired by avarice or premeditation, but,' he added maximising his triteness, 'resulted from motives of love and politics.'[58] Yet, Prezzolini concluded, the city lived on and mattered. In the Cold War it might be the first and best ally of the USA or even its spiritual leader: 'in the present menace generated by the threat of Slavic Communism, Rome has sounded the warning cry of danger. The Marxists realise that their principal obstacle is the Rome of the Church and they have levelled their most vicious attacks against it. This is the point of view from which we must look at Rome: as the heart of our common world and one of the most inspiring works of our civilization.'[59] In Prezzolini's prose, here was a Rome manufactured anew, with its Fascism papered over to allow its eternal pre-eminence in defending civilisation again to emerge.

Similarly, Guglielmo Ceroni, who not long before had been star-struck by the Fascist modernisation of Rome, returned to the pages of *Il Messaggero* at Easter 1950 to urge the pre-eminence of Rome as the national capital over any rival cities (if only for its traditional objection to localism, he added with unconscious irony).[60] Rome, Ceroni wrote, sloughing off the centrality of the Axis in Fascist policy, had objected to German occupation with its every sinew and in an *Anno Santo* must represent the nation by being 'the most admired and admirable city in Italy'.[61] Even while the bombs were falling, Ceroni had clung to his 'illustrious memories'. In the absence of military shelter, he had been protected by the history that was 'the universal patrimony' of 'this immortal city', natural home of 'saints, poets and geniuses'.[62] Here was another

Roman sometime Fascist for whom the forgetting or obscuring of the recent history of dictatorship was mandatory, and readily achieved by a brazen return to the history of other allegedly glorious events in the 'three thousand years' since Romulus and Remus had founded the city.

Although past believers in, or fellow travellers with, Fascism were now alert to the chance fruitfully to rework their histories, ever since 1944 anti-Fascists had also been crafting their accounts of the city, its role in defeating the dictatorship and its future as the national capital of a democratic Republic. If mostly polite in their dealings with the Church, their understanding of the recent past was not the same as that cherished by Pius XII. One group whose history was their own were Rome's Jews; in 1945 some 30,000 remained in Italy, of whom 12,000 resided in the national capital.[63] There, no doubt, they were little cheered by the pope's intimation in 1948–9 that he disliked the creation of the State of Israel, preferring that Jerusalem and the 'Holy Places' be placed under international guarantee and protectorate.[64] However, in 1948, as if to show that their community had forgotten little and clung to its special memory, a ceremony was held in the Forum to mark the foundation of the modern Jewish nation state. Led by their rabbi, the city's surviving Jews marched under the Arch of Titus in what was thought to be the opposite direction from that imposed on the defeated Jews of classical times, brought prisoner to the city after the Roman destruction of the Temple.[65] Their track proclaimed that the creation of Israel could now cancel centuries of persecution, as well as providing a future sanctuary from the terrible history of the Holocaust, as it was not yet automatically called.

Outright Zionists, Italian Jews might not necessarily be. It has already been noted that Jews were fans of the Risorgimento, joining with a will in the modernising and laicising project of Liberal Italy and in national Italian participation in the First World War. For the great majority, their Jewishness was a religion or a culture but not a national identity. Indeed, Rome's Jews were such patriotic Italians that they greeted the installation of the Fascist dictatorship with broad, if not full-scale, approval (a number of leading intellectual anti-Fascists were Jewish by culture). In return for mainstream Jewish backing of the nation, the regime's organs were often friendly to Jews. *Capitolium* in 1932, for example, rejoiced at the idea that Rome was 'the central city of all the Jews in Europe' and celebrated the alleged fact that some in the community had stayed so close-knit that they had transmitted 'the pure blood of their Semitic stock to their descendants'.[66]

To be sure Italian Jewish Fascism had aspects that, in retrospect, seem perverse. Ettore Ovazza, from a Turin family dedicated to 'fatherland, faith and family', was committed to an Italian nationalism that bitterly opposed Zionism, arguing that 'the history of Israel is strictly bound to the history of Rome'.[67] Ignoring the centuries of papal persecution, Ovazza focused instead on the endurance of Rome's Jews. In his opinion (ironically agreeing with

Pius XII), the national Italian capital was the beneficent *caput mundi*, by contrast with desert Palestine eternally swept by 'wars and fratricidal struggle'. *Romanità* was Ovazza's ideal and, he urged, it should gird all of 'the Jewish religion who are citizens of Rome'. Anti-Semitism was, by definition, a stupid heresy, of appeal only to 'barbarians'. Germans, he wrote in 1935, were behaving badly, but Jews would win in the 'great drama of history' so long as they were honoured to belong to Rome, 'the just and magnanimous *Patria* of all gods'.[68]

Such readings of history were soon to prove deluded when the Fascist regime moved into its anti-Semitic phase, having first experimented with anti-black racist legislation in its empire. Under Salò, legal persecution led to forcible collection, transport to the camps in the east, and death. Of Italian cities, Rome suffered the largest toll of deportees, more than 1,700. After the initial manhunt in October 1943, up to a thousand more were deported between February and April 1944, mainly after denunciation by their city neighbours, with 'minimal German involvement' (apart from an offer of blood money of 5,000 lire per individual caught). Those who gave information to the Nazis were of all social classes and all ages; some were Jews.[69] Nonetheless, from September 1943, a greater number of Jews than those expelled were given sanctuary in the city, the majority helped by charitable priests acting independently of direct orders from the hierarchy.

With the defeat of the dictatorship, Rome's Jews were again citizens of a nation, if one where most emerging contemporary histories excused or denied the dictatorship's racial persecutions and murders, blaming them on the Germans (or on Mussolini's craven mimicking of his Nazi masters). As though in proof of this insouciance, the Badoglio government, after 25 July 1943, moved slowly to amend racist legislation, while the *Enciclopedia cattolica* (Catholic encyclopedia) of 1948 repeated the truism, common in the country (and on more than one occasion mouthed by Mussolini), that 'in modern Italy, anti-Semitism has never existed'.[70] Liberal historian and philosopher Benedetto Croce, advocating the line that Fascism had been an unnatural 'parenthesis' in the positive course of Italian history since unification, was no friend of what soon would be called multiculturalism, demanding instead the full and absolute assimilation of the Jewish and, by implication, any other minority, into the nation.[71] Even in the 1950s, Rome City Council had still not got around to removing Fascist-inspired racial categories from its forms.

Gradually, however, the persecution of the Jews was more openly discussed and deplored in Rome. At the end of the 1950s community leadership gave backing to historian Renzo De Felice, who in 1961 published a lengthy account of Italian Jews under the regime, a book that launched his career as a student of Fascism. De Felice's conclusions were comforting: 'There is no doubt in fact that Mussolini's decision to introduce even in Italy state anti-Semitism was essentially determined by his conviction that, to make the Italian-German alliance firm and strong, it was necessary to eliminate any strident contrast in policy between the two regimes.' The vicious anti-Semitism of the *Repubblica Sociale* was similarly ascribed to German pressure.[72] The persecution of the Jews, it could still for the present be agreed, was not a native part of the history of Fascism, the Italian nation, Rome or Catholicism.

While anti-Semitism and the Jewish response to it were being given a place, perhaps too cosy a place, in urban memory, what was the fate in Rome of anti-Fascist history as a whole? After all, the Resistance, whatever its achievement and popular base (and Pius XII habitually labelled partisans as 'communists' with pejorative intent),[73] was largely confined to northern Italy and blossomed most in 1944–5, when it was clear to almost everyone that the Nazi–Fascist cause was lost. Although armed resisters did operate in central Italy after September 1943 and, within the capital, there were many instances of quieter anti-Nazi-Fascist actions involving intelligence collection and the hiding of those subject to persecution, Rome was neither the wellspring nor the ideal of the Resistance.[74] Furthermore, it was hard not to notice that, to the heroes of anti-Fascism, Rome was of little worth. Typical were the views of communist philosopher, historian and political activist Antonio Gramsci, who died following release from a cruel Fascist gaol in 1937, but thereafter his ghost was often summoned by PCI chief Palmiro Togliatti to act as a caring and national Marxist guide through history. The Sardinian Gramsci had grown to manhood in the Liberal era convinced of the corruption and irrelevance of the national capital: 'Rome, as a city,' he stated in 1920, 'has no function in Italian social life. It represents nothing.'[75]

Such contempt was ignored when, in 1944, Gramsci had a street named after him in the historic centre; previously it had been the Via dei Legionari (Street of the Legionaries). Perhaps such rebranding could plant anti-Fascist history into the Roman people's minds? Certainly, other anti-Fascist 'martyrs' were rewarded with similar sites of memory in the city, there being little concern over what had been their precise opinions on Rome and its place in the nation. The major socialist victim of Fascist brutality, Giacomo Matteotti, murdered in Rome in June 1924, now had the Ponte del Littorio (Lictor's bridge) changed to the Ponte Matteotti, while the name of the liberal Piero Gobetti, also killed by Fascists, blotted out the title of the erstwhile Viale Libro e Moschetto (once it had evoked the dictatorship's slogan, 'Book and rifle make a perfect Fascist').[76] Perhaps for the most humane hero of the anti-Fascist cause, the Turin-born Primo Levi, a Jewish survivor of Auschwitz, the historical detail posed a dilemma. From the 1960s globally if belatedly acknowledged as the most subtle teller of the terrible story of the Judaeocide, Levi, although he had taken a brief holiday in wartime Rome, had few practical or emotional connections with a city which, in his understanding, was malignly in thrall to Mussolini and Pius XII. His honesty and anti-Fascism had to wait until the new millennium for a site of memory in the city, with the opening of a high school (*liceo scientifico*) named after him in the socially and culturally troubled outlying suburbs.[77]

Yet the public inscription of a few place names scarcely amounted to thoroughgoing historical amendment. Nor did academic history elevate Rome to a capital of Resistance. True, in 1965, Enzo Piscitelli wrote an account of the wartime opposition in Rome from what might be deemed the official anti-Fascist stance, asserting that, 'during the months of passion' from 25 July 1943 to 4 June 1944, 'the Roman people . . . united spontaneously through the ups and downs of events in resistance against German domination. The Germans worked with Italian Fascists and were fought in a struggle that was at the same time local and national, animated by the same flame that burned in the hearts of partisans in every European country afflicted by German hegemony.' The Social Republic, Piscitelli continued, 'at no stage found backing in Rome. Its summons, proclamations and threats were wrapped in silence and immobility, both veiling irony. . . . The Romans, constitutionally alien to any form of fanaticism, simply did not believe in the RSI.'[78]

When it came to specific events in the city, Piscitelli did report that, under Badoglio, a manifesto critical of all the parties, including the PCI, had appeared on buildings urging immediate peace and signed 'Cola di Rienzo'.[79] Such evocations of past Roman republics had been foreshadowed on 26 July 1943 with spontaneous graffiti urging '*Viva Garibaldi!*'[80] In the people's minds, it seemed, some remembered shades could resurface to celebrate a dictator's fall. But, Piscitelli admitted, at a serious level 'the pope remained the only person who could express legal and traditional authority. The citizenry invoked his protection and, as in the High Middle Ages, the Bishop of Rome again defended his city from the overweening power of the new barbarians and from the dreadful effects of famine.'[81] After 4 June 1944 and liberation, Piscitelli believed that 'Rome finally rediscovered its function as guide and symbol of the life of all Italians' but did so primarily through the Vatican. On 9 June, Piscitelli concluded, at an open-air mass in Piazza San Pietro, 'all classes' 'rendered homage to the pope, thanking him for his achievement in leaving Rome relatively undamaged' by the war.[82] Even for this avowedly anti-Fascist historian, Pius XII and the settlement reached in the Lateran Pacts held the keys of national and urban revival and the overcoming of what was retrograde in the Fascist past.

If history-writing about Rome was scarcely radical in its appraisal of the city's path through and out of Fascism, how did other frames of memory, whether official or public, treat the violence and terror of 1943–4 under Nazi occupation (and its ally, the Social Republic)? While battle continued north of Rome, a myth of the war experience in the city was being developed. A graphic example was Roberto Rossellini's 'neo-realist' film, *Roma: città aperta* (Rome: Open City), first screened in September 1945, exhibited at the reconstituted Cannes festival a year later and a triumphant international success that still elicits breathless comments about how it 'permanently changed the landscape of film history'.[83] Certainly Rossellini offered a historical reconstruction of Rome's fate from September 1943 to June 1944 that eschewed profound confrontation with the Fascist years. The villains of the piece were members of the Nazi Gestapo, and, in an othering device acceptable at the time, homosexual as well. Italians, by contrast, even (Fascist) city policemen, were portrayed as heroes or good folk, rich in family values and all that is summed up in the concept *italiani, brava gente* (Italians, nice people). The major protagonists were a (self-sacrificing) communist and a priest (with a social conscience), happy to resist Nazi evil together, indeed implicitly merging when the communist took the pseudonym 'Giovanni Episcopo' (Bishop John). Rossellini portrayed the future as resting with winsome children of the people, mainly boys, who were led by 'Romoletto' (little Romulus). After the torture and death of the two anti-Fascist martyrs, the film ends with these lads marching together down the Via Trionfale, the ancient path for victorious returning warriors, restored under Fascism. They are heading towards St Peter's dome, silhouetted in the sky. Their 'March on Rome', it might be concluded, led to Pius XII, the Vatican, a Holy Year to come and true happiness.[84]

To be fair, such populist escapism was a common approach through which many combatant societies tried to blot out their journey to the abyss of the Second World War and start anew without too many thoughts of punishment or vengeance against the local perpetrators of the time of troubles. But, over the following decades, neither Italians nor Romans were quick to question what was becoming the established snug recollection of anti-Fascism and confront the trauma of what had been believed and done by the Fascist generation.[85] Inevitably enough, Rome, Italy's capital, became the epitome of this process, as the major national memorial to wartime suffering in a state whose complex real history had been as the premier ally and boasted ideological partner of Nazi Germany. The telling site was at the Ardeatine caves, just south of the then inhabited part of the city and not far from the Via Appia, the basilica of San Sebastiano and the catacombs of Santa Domitilla, a young woman martyred in the reign of Domitian (81–96). With an easy implied resonance between that era and the present, she was revered as one of the first Christian victims of religious persecution in ancient Rome.

At the Fosse Ardeatine a Nazi massacre had been committed, in its horror bearing comparison with those to be commemorated at Oradour in France and at Lidice in the Czech Republic and the unnumbered others too often forgotten or obscured in all the Russias. The killings had been prompted by an act of resistance on the Via Rasella. There, on 23 March 1944, twenty-fifth anniversary of the foundation of the Fascist movement in Milan, a squad of Nazi German reserve soldiers (many volunteers from what had, until 1943, been the Italian province of Bolzano) was ambushed by the communist Resistance. Thirty-three died in the attack. In retribution, the Nazi and Fascist authorities in Rome seized 335 Italians from prison or from those unlucky enough to be at home on the Via Rasella or other city streets. The next day, the victims were driven to the Ardeatine caves, where all were shot in the nape of the neck in groups of five, and then, whether dead or alive, thrust brutally into a mass grave. German military engineers then blew up the site. No informa- tion was passed to the victims' families, and the details of the executions were only discovered after 4 June and the city's liberation.

Once Rome had been freed by the Allied armies, there was a rush to commemorate this appalling deed and to claim its meaning for the anti-Fascist cause, somehow defined. The provisional national government at its first sitting after the liberation of Rome decided that a monument to the Nazi killing was necessary, justifying this choice by claiming that it acted at 'popular request'.[86] The first post-Fascist issue of *Capitolium* in autumn 1944 reported that 'pious pilgrimage' to the caves had already begun, despite the problem that 'the [Nazi-German] descendants of Attila' had still not been expelled from the nation (while adding that the best comfort to the people was now 'the religion of our fathers' as expressed by Pius XII).[87] Over the next year, with the help of the American military, the Ardeatine caves were opened and explored, with the names of 322 of the 335 victims identified by February 1945. In March 1947 it was officially agreed that the place be defined as 'a site of memory'. A monument, however, was not inaugurated until 24 March 1949, amid continuing dispute over whether there should be commemoration only of the specific victims or whether the monument should be nationalised to include those butchered by the Nazis in other parts of the country and notably at Marzabotto, a village in the hinterland of staunchly, or worryingly, communist Bologna.[88]

Despite politically inspired bickering, heightened by the emotion aroused during the 1948 elections and their aftermath, especially when on 14 July (a resonant date) a disturbed Sicilian anti-communist tried to assassinate Togliatti while he was standing outside the Chamber of Deputies in Rome, some agree- ment was possible. As a plaque still records, the Christian Democrat Umberto Tupini (holder of the relatively minor post of Minister of Public Works) in 1949 proclaimed the establishment of 'a national mausoleum for all those fallen in the struggle for liberation to give freedom and independence to the *patria*'. A further inscription recorded the story of the event, urging on all respectful recollection of 'the holocaust of our fathers'. So, too, on 25 April that year, representatives from the leftist ANPI and the Catholic Associazione volontari della libertà (Association of Volunteers for Freedom) joined to deposit floral wreaths at the entry to the cave in a ceremony that was to become annual and later to involve visiting foreign heads of state.[89] In March 1950 a statue evoking the three ages and classes of man was added to the site, with an article in *Capitolium* explaining that there symbolically were united 'all political faiths, be they socialist, commu- nist, republican, democrat, monarchist or liberal. All endured death, and in their

31. Statue of three ages and classes of man at the Ardeatine caves (Fosse Ardeatine), opened in 1950, adding a cosy memory to the austere memorial of the Nazi massacre there. The sculptor was Francesco Coccia (1902–82).

death were equal before God and man. At the final moment, all felt themselves brothers.'[90] There was as yet no specific recall of the Jewish victims.

During these first post-war years, 25 April was becoming established as '*il giorno della Resistenza*' (Resistance Day), beating off suggestions that the end of the war might be marked on 28 April (Mussolini's death) or 29 April (the formal surrender of German armies). A major advantage of 25 April was that it could imply that Italy had liberated itself, as well as deny that the enemy was anyone other than the (Nazi) Germans. This interpretation was ratified by the wide variety of men (there were no women) killed at the caves, ranging across class barriers from postmen to lawyers, and including communists and Catholics (one was a priest), seventy-two Jews and eleven non-Italians.[91] The fact that the massacre had occurred in Rome, the nation's capital, gave the memorial a natural primacy over other sites in the country where there had been similar slaughter. Its management is still patriotically kept under the aegis of the Ministry of

Defence. In sum, the Ardeatine site, its Roman history nationalised, has become the central memorial place for Italy's Second World War, one that entails scant analysis of the roles of Mussolini, Fascism and the nation as perpetrators in those terrible times. Here is expressed at its least questioning the 'myth of the resistance', an interpretation of Fascism and war that, in recent times, has been frequently denounced by the revitalised right, given courage in its convictions by successful entrepreneur and three times Prime Minister Silvio Berlusconi.

Yet no established line on the meaning of the massacre had been without challenge and in this, as in other instances, history wars smouldered. From the beginning, Christian Democrats and others asked whether the communists had been culpable in provoking the Germans with their 'terrorist' bombing in the Via Rasella. Had they deliberately brought down suffering on innocent civilians when the Germans reacted viciously but predictably? One of the minor events of Holy Year in 1950 was a failed prosecution of such leftist Resistance chiefs as communist Giorgio Amendola (greatest memoirist of his movement) and socialist Sandro Pertini (to be President of the Republic 1978–85) for risking civilian deaths in their approval of attack on German troops.[92] As the Cold War froze minds into rival blocs, objection to the evil of Nazism for some blended helpfully with opposition to 'totalitarian' communism. In 1959 Christian Democrat Prime Minister Antonio Segni (later President of the Republic, 1962–4) compared the victims of the Ardeatine massacre with 'those fallen for freedom in East Germany, Poland and Hungary'.[93] Soon the chief neo-Fascist party commentator on history, Giorgio Pisanò, went public with a conspiracy theory that what the communists had 'really' been attempting in the Via Rasella was the death of some non-communist partisans.[94]

When the Cold War seemed to be ending in the 1960s, the battle over the past took a new twist with the rise of the Holocaust as the chief moral yardstick of the Second World War prompting greater emphasis on Jewish victims and on the context of Nazi (but not Italian Fascist) racism. From the 1990s spokespersons of Rome Jewry have regularly defined the Ardeatine massacre as 'a Holocaust crime'.[95] They thereby obscure the anti-Fascist matrix of the event and ignore the debates about it, as well as the fact that Jews were a numerical minority of those murdered. By 2000 the fading of anti-Fascism as a credible ideological stance and a new moderate consensus that Italy between 1943 and 1945 was scoured by a civil war where neither side gleamed with historical virtue, renewed doubts about the anti-Fascist interpretation of the Ardeatine caves, with some commentators again seeing communist ruthlessness at the heart of the story. Could the passivity with which Romans waited through the spring of 1944 for their liberation by the invading Americans, it was now asked, have been proof of a popular moral rejection of the carnage in the Via Rasella and, therefore by implication, of any urban-based political violence?[96]

The official monumentalisation of historical tragedy is one thing, its popular memory another. Despite a generation of Fascist propaganda about militant *romanità*, and despite the gradual adoption for decades after 1945 of official anti-Fascism, with its claim of spontaneous and durable dissent from Mussolini's dictatorship, through the 1950s the meaning of history for the poor of the city and its outer quarters remained in great part its own, featuring a simple and cynical amalgamation of material hope and likely deprivation. Doubtless, especially on grand occasions like a Holy Year, the people could seem to follow Church teaching. But in the popular mind, high politics remained as imponderable and far off from their ordinary lives and meanings as they had in the nineteenth century. Rather, it was widely assumed, perpetrators and evil arrived in due time from a great world beyond normal ken. As oral historian Alessandro Portelli was to report, the American bombings of the city in July and August 1943 in retrospect were ascribed by popular memory to 'Germans' or 'Fascists'. They were believed to have irrupted into an almost arcadian experience of the war years in the Roman suburbs. Such recollection was unstained by any admission of Romans' guilt as perpetrators of Fascist crimes.[97] Instead, such memories, Portelli suggests, were likely to deplore the 'butchery' that battered Rome late in the war and to be accompanied by evocations of God and the Madonna as the permanent refuge and salvation of afflicted humankind.[98] In sum, for quite a few of the city's workers and petits bourgeoisie, whether male or female, history was still understood as familial, timeless (and, on occasion, cruel), governed not so much by orthodox Catholicism as by popular religiosity.[99]

True, as the 1950s began to pass, news spread that Italy was experiencing an 'economic miracle' that, in two decades, was to end the nation's 'backwardness' and raise it briefly to be the fifth industrial and financial power in the world behind the USA, Japan, Germany and France. Once again, however, a crucial national process did not begin or achieve its greatest dynamism in Rome. The miracle was occurring in the north, in Milan, Genoa, Turin, Bologna and other such places. One result was mass internal migration. Now Southerners flocked into the cities of those regions. It sometimes seemed as if their contact with Rome was confined to the brief change of engines undertaken by their train at the Stazione Termini.

Nonetheless, Rome did matter. Its history wars continued to have ramifications beyond the city's gates. Its economy may have depended more on bureaucracy, tourism and real estate deals than on genuinely productive business, but the city's population soon resumed the rapid rise that had commenced under the dictatorship. Even in the Rome over which Pius XII presided, modernity was in the air as never before. No doubt, in urban ceremonial and the evocation of Rome's history, the Church continued to preach the city's abiding holiness and set its universality well above any role that it might serve as Italy's capital. With the proclamation of a 'Marian Year' in 1954 on the centenary of Pius IX's elevation of the Immaculate Conception (this evocation of the Virgin Mary was repeated by John Paul II in 1987), Pius, armed as ever with religious anniversaries, pressed ahead with his hopes for the global 'reconquest' of erring souls and the restoration of Catholic empire.[100]

Yet somewhere in the fine print of the present, troubles were mounting for Pius XII's Roman imperial version of Catholicism. In 1951 a prefectural report suggested that, in the ranks of the DC, let alone among social groups influenced by Marxism, the Pope's 'intolerable absolutism' was causing distress.[101] Again irritated as he had been in 1946–8 by the moderation of Christian Democrat national governments, the pope was dallying with forces further to the right, including neo-Fascists, in the hope of a new 'crusade', a 'mobilisation' of good Catholics, commanded by a Roman Church that was 'the master of civilization, the seed-bed of social and moral renewal'.[102] The appropriate historical reference, Pius XII remarked, was Pope Leo VI's effort to stop Attila the Hun from sacking Rome.[103] However, the project of rightist alliance failed, and Pius began to seem not so much the universal pope, hailed so fulsomely in 1944, as the head of one among many Christian Democrat factions.[104] Yet, despite the sense of gathering failure and even irrelevance, and despite the accompanying globalisation of his Church, ironically manifest in the increasing ethnic diversity of the College of Cardinals, Pius went to his death in October 1958 still dreaming of a conquering imperial Rome whose sacred history could garrison it against the materialism of modernity.

It was therefore appropriate for the occasion that a writer in *Capitolium*, organ of a City Council that, since the war, had never forgotten to bow to the Vatican, should in an obituary draw attention to the special affiliation between Pius XII and Rome. Papa Pacelli, it was recalled, had perceived that 'Rome is the centre of civilisation, ordained by God in this eternal mission from the remotest times'. It could not be forgotten that, when a cardinal, he had urged that '*Roma onde Cristo è romano*', arguing that 'the Providence which governs the world' exempted the city from 'the rise and fall of influence that other places and countries experienced'.[105] For this loyal obituarist, Pius XII had never ceased to command a Roman empire.

However, even the most superficial glance at Rome in 1958 suggested that the pope's efforts to reassert total control over the passage of history, channel its multiple whispers into a single message and simultaneously proclaim that Eternal Rome had not changed and would not change in its profound meaning had failed. As his successor, John XXIII, soon admitted, the Church was in turmoil in Italy and elsewhere. In national politics, if not yet in Rome's urban administration, the idea was developing that, rather than the Vatican's preferred solution of DC coalition with monarchists and neo-Fascists, Christian Democracy should 'open to the left', embracing the socialists and hinting that the anti-Fascist alliance that had briefly bloomed in 1943–5 might be capable of resurrection.

Rome's Council remained under the control of rightists, hostile to this prospect. But they were increasingly at a loss when it came to confronting the social crisis precipitated by the city's huge and chaotic growth since 1944, with talk about the city's resultant 'Southernisation' and 'corruption'. From 1951 to 1971 38 per cent of dwellings erected in Rome disregarded any building norms and legal forms.[106] The city plan seemed to mean nothing to speculators with good contacts. In Italy at large, the economic miracle was bringing new riches to some Italians (and detaching them further from the moral simplicities of Church teaching). Soon Federico Fellini would set his satirical film about the emptiness of this new wealth, *La dolce vita* (1960), on the Via Veneto in Rome, a venue more redolent of fashion and celebrity than industrialisation. Rather than dealing analytically with a modernising 'miracle', the film gave fresh play to old assumptions about the natural vice and excess of the nation's capital. But, away from the gilded youth of cinema, the number of Romans who were suffering and deprived, excluded from whatever was happening in the historic centre, began to demand attention. In 1952 150,000 of them were registered as scrabbling for a life below the poverty line.[107] By then, 425,000 Romans lived within the Aurelian Walls, but more than a million outside them.[108]

In 1954 Aldo Natoli, PCI secretary in the city, launched a searing attack on Christian Democrat corruption and misrule in a book entitled *Il sacco di Roma*, finding his own historical parallel in bracketing current events with the devastating sack of Rome in 1527. The forces of change and of good, he maintained, must seize and renew the city's meaning. The DC's version of a national capital, Natoli lamented, was, with its focus solely on the historic centre, 'totally detached from historical reality. A political but above all religious capital, a bureaucratic and administrative centre, a place of sojourn for the wealthy and tourists, most coming from abroad, a city formed almost exclusively, or anyway essentially, by basilicas and monuments, princely palaces and ministries'. By contrast, the Rome of the people had won 'a primacy in Italy in the number of the homeless and of those forced to live in caves, grottoes and huts'. As a visiting American had noticed, families who had lost their houses in the bombing in 1943 still made do in 'cardboard shacks' and caves on the periphery.[109] This sad situation was the result of a historical process that went back to 1870 and, despite the ostentatious parades and ceremonies of the Church, had been reinforced by 'a city administration totally at the service of private interests'. Rome could only become modern, Natoli urged, if the people of the periphery had their sufferings addressed, and their history recognised, recorded and admired.[110] The Rome of the people, he implied, must at last overthrow the Rome of pontiffs and cardinals, entrepreneurs and real estate men, the rich in their unholy alliance.

Andrea Riccardi, a fine Catholic historian, has concluded that the death of Pius XII marked the end of an imperial history in Rome, the final fall of the myth of *romanità*, the successful burial of bald Caesar. Now and hereafter,

Riccardi explained, 'the collapse of the last universal idea present in Rome revealed the city to be more provincial and more real' than it had been perceived since the Risorgimento.[111] Hereafter, he implied, it should make do, as others cities did, with little histories and with being the capital of what, now, was not even the least of the Great Powers. Yet Riccardi exaggerated. No doubt, a current driving Rome into being just another modern European metropolis did sweep the place and would not be diverted. However, in its streets, older history was not easy to escape. To be sure, under John XXIII, the Church curbed its evocation of a Catholic Roman empire, humbly seeking reform that could help it to accommodate 'democracy' or, at least, achieve better contact with the global masses in processes that would culminate in the Second Vatican Council (opened in October 1962). However, others in the great world had not surrendered their hope of drawing global significance and profit from Rome. In August 1960 the city would be the site of the 'XVII Modern Olympiad'. That grandiose event would utilise what had once been Mussolinian stadiums for its athletic contests but try to do so with national or international liberal capitalist and not Fascist purpose. Roman histories would once again need to be flexible and capable of change.

As the date for the Games approached, the tensions implicit in this adaptation surfaced in Italian politics. That summer, a government led by Christian Democrat Fernando Tambroni followed the recipe long favoured by Pius XII, by seeking a parliamentary majority dependent on neo-Fascist votes. If Tambroni planned to bring Fascists and their history in from the cold, his move failed when confronted by massive popular demonstrations, notably in Genoa on 30 June, vociferously condemning plans to hold the national congress of the neo-Fascist MSI (Movimento Sociale Italiano, Italian Social Movement) there. In Rome, too, there was a large protest, organised beside the Piramide (and the erstwhile Viale Adolf Hitler) and the memorial plaque to the 'first resisters', who had died there on 8–9 September 1943.[112] On 22 July Tambroni was forced to resign, to be replaced, for the Olympics, by what is called a *governo balneare* (beach holiday government), led by another DC factional chief, Amintore Fanfani. Even if one recalcitrant cardinal defended Tambroni's effort to put down the protesters in Genoa as 'worthy of gaining him entry to the seventh circle of Dante's version of paradise, along with King David, Trajan, Ezekial, Constantine and William the Good', for the majority of Italians it now seemed agreed that anti-Fascist history underpinned the Republic.[113] Meanwhile, sometimes in parallel, sometimes not, throughout 1959–61 the Italian nation was commemorating its centenary. Officially approved historians were busily preaching a positive reading of the Risorgimento, now to be understood as the birth of a liberal and democratic nation. While athletes and fans from around the world assembled in the city, plenty of rival histories still swirled around Rome.

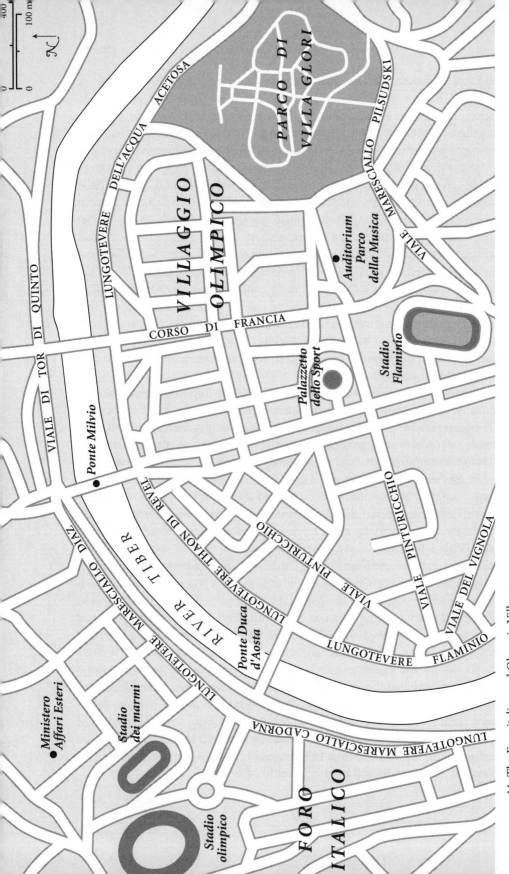

11. The Foro italico and Olympic Village.

※

10

OLYMPIC ROME: SPORT, BLOOD
AND HISTORIES

It is not difficult to find vivid traces of the XVII Olympiad held in Rome between 25 August and 11 September 1960, or to see that cladding the Games in historical legitimacy was a complex matter. An area of the Tiber plain running down from the more elevated Parioli district is still called the Villaggio olimpico and possesses some of the athletes' housing (most of it privatised in 1985), erected in 1958–9. At the entry to this village, competitors were unsurprisingly expected to salute a copy of the Capitoline statue of the she-wolf and the babies; Rome was inseparable from 'three thousand years of history'. Satisfying the needs of the visiting athletes in 1960 had come at a cost to thousands of urban poor who were expelled from the quarter. After the war, they had taken sanctuary there in huts and other precarious and illegal structures.[1] The Rome paper, *Il Messaggero*, had paved the way for this uprooting, lamenting in the self-righteous and hackneyed phrases of the respectable classes that the city centre was assailed by a 'disgraceful "Casbah" '; 'around civilised Rome, composed of people who work and live honourably, is a barbarous Rome, a ring of criminality and social anarchy that is fearsome in nature'.[2] Middle-class fears of theft and disorder from their poorer fellow citizens had, it seemed, not been assuaged by the opening in 1951, beyond the then eastern edge of the city, of the modern prison at Rebibbia, planned by the dictatorship in 1937 to blunt the threat of crime.

No doubt, in Christian Democrat Rome and Italy, Catholicism stood guard over bodies and souls. A small prefabricated church (made more concrete in 1987) was opened for pious Olympians and consecrated to San Valentino, the ancient past not being forgotten since the catacombs named for this saint could be visited not far away. Moreover, as the date of 1960 approached, it was emphasised that Pius XII had rejoiced in the assignation of the Games to Rome, bruited in 1951 and confirmed in 1955, and had even been their spiritual progenitor. Superficially at least, the slim figure of Pius XII had not seemed cut out for modern sports. His idea of exercise was a few morning stretches, communing with his pet canary and a longer but solitary, post-siesta, afternoon walk in the Vatican garden. His contemplative urge was so powerful that he grew furious if another human being then came into view.[3] His wartime had been sufficiently abstemious for him to weigh just 57 kilos in 1945.[4] Nonetheless, he had often enough preached in favour of the spread of the modern sporting life so long as it bore Catholic values. The cyclist Gino Bartali, a loyal member of Catholic Action, was personally blessed by the pope and made into a standard-bearer of Catholic virtue. In September 1955 Pius XII, endorsing Catholic Action's Centro Sportivo Italiano, homilised on the gains to youths achieved through a healthy mind in a healthy body and the accompanying commitment to playing the game.[5]

In his authoritarian manner, Pius was at pains to patrol the meaning of Rome's Olympics. He insisted that the holding of the global meeting of amateur athletics in a holy city should avoid the 'so-called "marketing" and the celebrity focus ("*divismo*")' to which, he feared, the 'high ideals, sense of fairness and health of athletes, and the good name of the nation' were 'sacrificed' in commercialised modern sport. Neither untrammelled capitalism nor ardent nationalism, he charged, should guide the XVII Olympiad. Rather, in the pope's Catholic view, Rome was the appropriate venue for the Games, less because it was the capital of national and liberal democratic Italy and more because of its long history as the fount of the global Church. Reaching the city, he counselled, the crowds, 'to their spiritual gain', could take in 'the many holy and beautiful things in the centre of Christianity'. In that sacred place, they would have the chance to 'breathe the air of universality' that marked 'Christian Rome'. They could see and digest its eternal history.[6] In his Catholic enthusiasm, Pius XII was not alone. The settings in the city were perfect, the Jesuits announced. With the Games, 'sports fans from the whole world would, willingly or unwillingly, come into contact with the real meaning of Rome', and so with its religious and Christian reality. St Thomas Aquinas, as well as the Bible, they added, had made plain the divine sanction of sport, especially if the contamination of lucre was kept out of it.[7]

The Church may have devoted itself to framing the Olympics in such suitable terms, even if some aspects of sport remained troubling to religious officials: in 1960 those training for the priesthood were forbidden to attend such unclothed events as swimming and diving if they involved females, and they were also instructed to avoid boxing and wrestling contests.[8] However, Rome's historical background could scarcely be confined to Catholicism. Indeed, across the river from the Olympic village, most track and field and swimming events were fought out in one arena or another of the Foro italico. This venue well expressed the contradictory messages that might be drawn from the holding of the Games in Rome. During the sporting contest, some still recalled the site's earlier name as the Foro Mussolini and remembered that it had been built under the dictatorship to express the Fascist version of the sporting life.

Pious in their own manner, the Italian organisers of the Games took pains to state that the Olympics were bringing great joy to the city, all the more because they fitted neatly into its historical processes. 'To the Rome of the Latin spirit and of the Papacy, to the Rome of the Renaissance will be added sportive Rome,' it was announced.[9] Yet, as ever, some of the past was here being remembered and some forgotten; the innocent-seeming list contains absences that are as worth noting as what is said. There was, for example and as usual, no mention of the 'unheroic' and 'un-national' baroque, despite its massive presence in city architecture. But, above all, there was no hint of memory of Fascist precedents and influences. At least formally speaking, Rome's Olympiad was to be purged of any overt connection with the nation's troubled recent past and with the war that Mussolini had fought as the prime partner of Adolf Hitler.

Despite such obfuscation, it did not take much effort to detect the ghost of the Duce at the Foro italico. For one thing, the place's entry statement was, as it still is, a tall and commanding marble obelisk with MUSSOLINI DUX inscribed on it. In 1944–5 there had been talk of its demolition, but the US military authorities intervened to save it, thus signalling their tolerance or approval of the survival of Fascist architectural history in Rome. This choice was not replicated in Nazi Berlin liberated by the Red Army (after vicious street battles).[10] Fascism may have committed crimes, the implication was, but it could scarcely be compared with the visceral evil of Nazism.

In 1960 the obelisk was not alone in the complex in evoking the dictatorship's past. The view to the north was framed by the aggressive male statuary of the Stadio dei marmi, even if prominent Fascist genitalia (and the history of the Fascist ideal of masculinity) in Pius XII's Rome had been veiled by cautious fig leaves. Eleanor Clark, the American visitor to Holy Year in 1950, had already been appalled by what she saw at the stadium. The loathsome athletes, she lamented, 'their muscles anatomically impossible, foreheads low, jaws out Duce-fashion, genitals in line with the virility policy whether behind tights or jockstraps or (until Holy Year) bare, gaze either belligerent or loftily dedicated, beneath collie-dog brows, hands the size of fur-muffs and tending to hang to the knees'.[11] Nor, a more politically attuned spectator might note, did worry end with aesthetics. The 'sixty provinces' represented in the sixty statues of sportsmen still unabashedly included Fiume and Pola, lost after bitter war to Yugoslavia, and here by implication the object of revisionist hope.

Slightly further away from the Tiber was the main stadium for athletic competition in the Olympics, remodelled in 1953 to take 100,000 spectators. Called the Stadio olimpico, today it is used for the home games of Rome's two major football teams, A.S. Roma (thought to be supported by 'real Romans') and Lazio (the majority of whose fans traditionally are southern immigrants). Nearer

32. Stadio dei marmi with Farnesina in the background recalls athletic support to the Fascist Party.

to the Tiber was the swimming complex (Stadio del nuoto), with its walls and other surfaces covered with Fascist art, didactically updating classical images to reflect the purpose of the regime. A further part of the complex was the headquarters of CONI, the Italian Olympic Association, housed in what had once been the offices of the Fascist Academy for Physical Education. Painted in the dictatorship's version of what was deemed the 'national' Siena red, the building's architecture replicated that of *Case del fascio* or party headquarters, erected under the dictatorship in cities and towns throughout the peninsula.

Most graphically, there was the avenue that led from the Mussolini obelisk to the Stadio dei cipressi, the Stadium of the Cypresses, as the Olympic Stadium had been called in the 1930s. This space is marked with two lines of thirteen marble blocks, each with a boasted Fascist victory inscribed on it. In between, the ground is paved with pebbles, fashioned into mock-classical mosaic images. They studiously exemplify Fascist *romanità*, while recording such regime slogans as 'Molti nemici, molto onore' (Many enemies, much honour), 'A Noi' (The world belongs to us) or 'Duce Duce Duce' (the title is repeated 264 times). In May 1938 Benito Mussolini and Adolf Hitler had tramped across this area together when they came to watch a militant and militarist display by Fascist youth in the stadium. What, for 1960, was to be done with the glaring nature of this Fascist history and what might be thought to be its lingering reflection?

Predictably enough, the first and fundamental official line on the matter was to ignore the Fascist past, however blatant. As a guidebook retailed for the Games by the Banca Nazionale del Lavoro put it, with studied amnesia in regard to the origins of the Stadio dei marmi, the statuary there represented no more than a 'vigorous classicism', composing 'a crown of severely white tall marble statues, erected on cylindrical plinths'.[12] Rome, the guide explained further in words that must have been endorsed by the bank's Christian Democrat masters, was 'eternal and classical'. It was a city that everywhere 'radiated that civilisation that possesses, in the Gospel, the clearest invitation to human brotherhood for all men and all peoples'.[13] As for the Vatican, the guide added politely, it was 'the smallest, greatest, strongest, most beneficent and silent state, and the one nearest to God'.[14] After the Games were over, Salvatore Rebecchini, no longer Rome's mayor but still a city father, similarly pushed a history that eliminated Fascism, or any of the ills of the dictatorship, from Rome's story. The period between the wars, he wrote sonorously, 'was characterised above all by a far-sighted development of public works and a major growth in the population'. Only in 1943–4 were there troubles because of German occupation. Yet, then, 'the hungry were fed and the persecuted found generous sanctuary through the effort of a great Roman Pope, Pius XII, whom the people would acclaim as "*Defensor Civitatis*" '.[15]

An eternal Catholicism might be of use in covering much. However, during the build-up to the Games, there had been open criticism from leftist politicians about the Fascist residues in the Foro italico and its surrounds, with the complaint that so visible a past had a bad effect on the present. It was, the Chamber of Deputies were told, inappropriate to have words inscribed there 'with an apologetic memory of a past which the Italian people and the world's democratic consciousness have condemned'.[16] True, in their present outrage, the PCI had forgotten that, in September 1948, they had held a party festival there, under portraits of Marx, Engels, Lenin and Stalin, designed to celebrate their party's 'deep popular roots' with no suggestion of being put off by the Fascist residue of this part of Rome.[17] However, in 1960, Christian Democrat spokesmen tried to stifle attack by arguing that the inscriptions at the Foro italico 'do not authorise anyone to think that democratic Italy approves or praises the principles enunciated there. On the contrary they are of use in recording the risks that men run when they decide too rashly to make a record in marble or bronze of events before they have been properly put into context by history'. Rather than fostering nostalgia, it was stated, they acted as 'a condemnation of Fascist presumption'.[18]

The debate grew more lively in 1960, with the new Fanfani government on the eve of the Olympics bowing to pressure to cancel the more offensive slogans, while maintaining that the 'tragic rhetoric' of the dictatorship could not really be buried 'by splashing on a bit of cement'.[19] Perhaps such caution and procrastination amounted to the best way to deal with such divisive signs from the past, because the announcement that something would be removed

provoked on 10 August a neo-Fascist demonstration at this site and a threatened bombing at EUR. The rightist slogan of the moment was 'You cannot
cancel history with a paint-brush or a chisel'.[20] Among those arrested while
protesting at the Foro italico was the racist ex-servant of the Salò Republic,
Giorgio Almirante, long-term party chief of the neo-Fascist Italian Social
Movement (MSI), which had one of its key power bases in Rome.[21]

Faced with political and ideological warring about recent history that threatened embarrassingly to spill over international visitors to the Games, the city
administration decided to preserve the mosaics and blot out only two of
the inscriptions, one that recorded the Fascist oath of allegiance and another that
remembered with xenophobic overtones the sanctions applied against Italy by
'52 nations' during the Ethiopian war of 1935–6. However, it was now that the
passage of time was given a different ending from that intended by the dictatorship, since three of the seven vacant pieces in the alleyway of memory were
inscribed with the dates 25 July 1943 (recording 'the fall of Fascism'), 2 June 1946
(the referendum approving the Republic) and 1 January 1948 (the inauguration
of the new constitution). By adding these facts, it was emphasised that the path of
history led not to universal and eternal Fascist empire as the designers of the Foro
italico had intended, but to its replacement by a democratic (and Christian)
Republic. As a minister explained not altogether convincingly: 'only the ideological writings will be cancelled. The historic ones will remain.'[22] They still do.

Yet, Rome being Rome, the Foro italico and its environs, neither in 1960
nor today, bore or bear a Fascist past and only that. Any reflection on the
surrounds of the sports complex illustrates the survival there of more than one
history, as well as giving further examples of attempts that have been made to
deny memory or adapt it for what has been viewed by one faction or another
as more wholesome remembrance.

Immediately opposite the Mussolini obelisk is the Ponte Duca d'Aosta,
opened in 1939 and adorned with heroic scenes from the Fascist version of
Italy's First World War. Emanuele Filiberto, second Duke of Aosta (d.1931), had
served as a general at that time and been known for his alleged competence and
admitted brutality. His wartime career left him with a reputation as the most
militant and militarist member of the royal family, potentially a pro-Fascist
replacement for Victor Emmanuel III, should the little king have refused to
install Mussolini as Prime Minister in 1922.[23] The recording in this part of
Rome of his life, its implied salute to the Savoy monarchy and its survival in the
Republic, meant that his sins had been forgiven or obscured through a generic
patriotism that still cheered national victory in the Great War.

Rather different in its resonance, the much older Milvian bridge stands a little
further up the river. It was erected by a Republican censor in 109 BCE, remodelled
by Pope Nicholas V (1447–55), a great patron of the Renaissance in the city, and
further worked on by Pius VII and Valadier in 1805, who added a triumphal arch.

This structure was blown up on Garibaldi's orders either to block the invading French or with anti-clerical malice in 1849 but was soon restored by Pius IX. The most emblematic history that the bridge bore was, however, that of the Emperor Constantine who, on 28 October 312 CE, fought a crucial battle here against his rival Maxentius, each man being the son of a previous emperor. Constantine, rewardingly adopting the symbol of the Christian God, won. His routed foe, whose 'Roman' spirit on occasion has been invoked in modern times (he did name his son, murdered by Constantine after his victory, Romulus), was ignominiously drowned in the Tiber.[24] From 313 the Edict of Milan offered religious toleration to the empire, in practice entailing the triumph of Christianity in Europe, although Constantine was not baptised until just before his death in 337. Following his victory on the Milvian bridge, Constantine had plainly become a 'great man', to be remembered on due occasions with advantages especially by the Catholic Church but not only by them. A rival message from the spirit of the Emperor, for example, resurfaced in the twentieth century, when that modern Caesar, Mussolini, 'marched on Rome' on 28 October, a full 1,610 years after Constantine, and also reached a deal with the Church while, it was boasted, he was organising a revived Roman empire. For those alert to its histories, on the Milvian bridge the purposes and achievements of classical *romanità*, Christianity, Catholicism, Garibaldi's Risorgimento and Fascism met and jangled.

Had Mussolini's dictatorship lasted and his party headquarters been ensconced in the building prepared for them behind the Foro italico, the so-called Farnesina, the parallel between Duce and Caesar might have been still more glaring. But, with the holding of the Games, this structure, only completed in 1956, had become the new home of the national Ministry of Foreign Affairs. Its location had been accorded greater propriety in post-1944 street renaming that obscured the Farnesina's Fascist origins by recording the careers of a number of patriotic liberals — Paolo Boselli (ineffectual wartime Prime Minister, 1916–17, but long president of the nationalist Dante Alighieri Society), Antonino di San Giuliano (expansionist Foreign Minister in 1914), Leopoldo Franchetti (an advocate of imperial advance, here blandly described as 'supporter of Italian colonisation in Libya and Eritrea, 1847–1917'), Armando Diaz ('Marshal of Victory' in 1918, and, in 1922, Minister of War in the initial Fascist coalition) and Salvatore Contarini (canny 'diplomatist', dropped by Mussolini in 1926). Also commemorated were the patriotic (and Jewish) diplomatic historian, Mario Toscano, and Giuseppe Volpi, man of many parts and, arguably through their variety, not a reliable Fascist, if the holder of a quiver of offices under the dictatorship. Officially, then, the streets that gave access to the Ministry of Foreign Affairs admiringly recalled liberal heroes. More critical observers might notice the ambiguous connections with dictatorship in most of these men's careers.

Behind the Farnesina on the height of Monte Mario which rises above the Tiber, a more recent history found representation and duly aroused controversy.

There, the Rome Hilton hotel had won planning approval from accommodating Christian Democrat councillors in the early 1950s and, with brutalist modernism of steel and glass, expressed not Fascist national architectural principles but those of modern global capitalism, even if the building remained unfinished for the Olympics. Its construction had been bitterly contested by the left as ugly, inappropriate for historic Rome, destructive of a public park, too crass a reminder of American power and, it was implied, a case study of DC 'corruption'.[25] Carlo Levi, author in his time of the classic anti-Fascist text, *Christ stopped at Eboli*, denouncing the cruelty or irrelevance of Fascism to the peasantry, damned the hotel as a 'colonial' excrescence in the city, by implication worse in the values that it expressed than those made concrete at the Foro italico.[26]

Back across the Tiber, in the area of the Villaggio olimpico, another ghost from Liberal times is recorded in the streetscape, enlarged in 2002 by the opening of Renzo Piano's highly modernist Parco della musica, the city's first new music auditorium for many years. It stands, perhaps a little ironically, on the Viale Pierre de Coubertin. The French baron, De Coubertin, is renowned as the founder and prophet of the modern Olympics movement, although his relationship with Rome possessed more than one facet. Predictably, at the end of the nineteenth century, a powerful factor in justifying the institution of the modern Olympic cycle every four years was inspiration from classical times and therefore from Rome. In his initial propaganda, De Coubertin had been emphatic that the purpose of the Games was to 'restore' the competitive values and social discipline of Athens and Rome (before, in his mind, decay set in under the later empire and early Christianity).[27] Personally he was proud to be descended from the Frédys (Fredi) family, a 'Roman' bloodline which, he avowed, ran back to the classical Senate.[28] The Fredis' legitimacy and virtue would be sycophantically recalled in 1960 by Rebecchini, who took the occasion to underline how De Coubertin, through his family sense, embodied 'the universality of Rome and its perennial moral teaching'.[29]

Yet, maybe in his appeals to history there had been a certain volatility in De Coubertin's search for meaning that would help to explain why Rome had to wait until the XVII Olympiad to take its turn in managing the Games. In 1896 De Coubertin had been glad that the first modern meeting was held in Athens, commenting that this small and scarcely wealthy or developed town was a better choice than Rome (where the irritatingly Francophobe Crispi at the start of that year was still Prime Minister). Displaying what might be read as Italophobia, De Coubertin complained that the city was too mired in the past and too slack in its present for a modern sporting venture. 'To play tennis before the Colosseum or to ride a bicycle under the Arch of Titus would indeed cause a disagreeable impression,' he then remarked.[30] 'The Roman monuments are dated; they belong to a definite age. The Parthenon has none; it belongs to all times; no manifestations of popular life can disfigure it.'[31] Yet, perhaps prompted by the rapprochement in Franco-Italian relations that burgeoned after Crispi's fall, De Coubertin soon changed his mind in this dismissal of Roman history. Appalled, after Paris hosted the second Olympics, when the next Games (1904) were relegated to St Louis in the 'unhistoric' New World, De Coubertin campaigned vigorously for Rome to be the fourth venue.

The Olympics, he urged, easily switching his identification of value in the past, could and should be 'an international tribute to Ancient Rome'.[32] Only in that city, De Coubertin maintained, 'after its excursion to utilitarian America, would Olympism be able to don the sumptuous toga, woven with skill and much thought, in which I had wanted to clothe it from the beginning'. So he imagined wrestling matches contested in the Baths of Caracalla and a marathon run across the Forum and along the Via Appia. The Villa Borghese he thought 'a natural stadium of perfect beauty that was, in fact, ideally suited to athletic sports'. The Vatican, he was pleased to report, was ready to end the 'sort of interdict laid on physical education in many clerical circles'.[33] In May 1905 the news came that the Games had been formally assigned to Rome, and King Victor Emmanuel III promised a special grant of 50,000 lire to facilitate them.[34] Preparations commenced for competition in track and field events, rugby, soccer, lawn tennis, cricket, polo, shooting, fencing, boxing, wrestling, swimming, rowing, equestrianism, cycling, sailing, motor racing, ballooning, archery, walking, mountaineering, hunting and fishing. There were even plans for prizes to be awarded for painting, sculpture, music, architecture and literature, so long as the works in this field were 'directly inspired by the sporting idea'. The two weeks around Easter were thought likely to be the best time climatically (summer was still ruled out by malaria).[35]

However, the cause was not won; Liberal Rome was not to gain an Olympic history. In the pages of the establishment journal, *Nuova Antologia*, Angelo Mosso, Professor of Physiology at Turin University and charmingly known as 'the philosopher of the national gymnastics movement', doubted if Rome and Italy were ready, when present-day Italians, he lamented, had the shortest legs in Europe.[36] They 'ran and jumped much less than did other peoples', he fussed, and, until that deficiency was overcome, holding the Olympics in the national capital made little sense. It may have been right that 'ancient Italians', he wrote, backdating national history with the usual aplomb, were the 'strongest men' to attend the classical Games but, since the fall of the Roman empire, Mosso noted bitterly, no one had bothered to build a single gymnasium in the city. Modern Romans were just not primed to resume athletic responsibility.[37] Furthermore, spokesmen for Milan, Turin and Florence, where at least some sport was practised, openly resented the choice of what they thought of as 'lazy', backward, Rome and, to De Coubertin's dismay, suggested that the Games could be shared around the country. Prime Minister Giolitti, circumspect as ever with national finances and himself a stolid belle époque bourgeois hard to imagine in rapid movement or being a keen sports fan, was also doubtful. In early 1906 he intimated to the Olympic authorities that Italy preferred to forgo its promise to host the next Games, which were hastily reassigned to wealthier and more sportive London.[38]

The Fascist dictatorship put greater emphasis on athletic achievement than had its Liberal predecessor, with Mussolini being photographed swimming, performing equestrian jumps, playing tennis, skiing, fencing and enjoying a kick around with his sons. Football now imposed itself on the Italian imagination as the major sport, although its fame, like so much else that was modern in Italy, trickled slowly from north to south; Rome had to wait for the troubles of wartime when the city's AS Roma won the *scudetto* or premiership in 1941–2, the first team below Bologna on the map to do so. Under the dictatorship, Italy did participate eagerly in the Olympics, with party propaganda highlighting the national sporting achievement in its fifth placing at Amsterdam in 1928, second at Los Angeles in 1932 and third in the Nazi Berlin Games of 1936. Fascism's enthusiasm for sport (and the political preference of many sports administrators for Fascism) meant that Mussolini's Rome was high on the list of potential venues for the Olympics. The elderly but still influential De Coubertin thought that the Eternal City should win the palm in 1940. However, pressure built against Eurocentrism and those Games were assigned to Japan, with Fascist officials agreeing to wait until 1944. In practice, however, war intervened and Italy (1960) and Japan (1964) were forced to delay their Olympics until after the fall of their imperial regimes.

If the sporting arena situated along the Tiber to the city's north hosted the Games in a setting with many encircling histories, among which Fascism uneasily predominated, the same was true of the other major venue, EUR, to the south-west of Rome's historic centre. After all, the Esposizione Universale di Roma had been planned to be the apotheosis of Fascist town planning. Indeed, after the dictatorship fell, it was asked with some insistence whether the quarter would survive without its sponsor. The Christian Democrat Prime Minister (1946–53) Alcide De Gasperi nourished public doubts and may have been pleased when an early plan, launched in 1948 to re-label the place a 'Progress city' that would enliven Holy Year, failed to find financial backing.

Yet, inevitably, work soon resumed on EUR, especially after, in January 1951, De Gasperi nominated Virginio Testa as Extraordinary Commissioner of the project (he had been the *Governatorato*'s chief agent in the matter, 1935–43).[39] With some effrontery, Testa now argued that the site was not so much the architectural epitome of militant Fascism as the Roman version of a 'garden suburb'; it did use open spaces as settings for some of its key buildings. In that regard, Testa expanded his case to declare that EUR must occupy an essential role in planning for the coming Olympics. It would be proof then of democratic Italy's 'international spirit'. Now Testa maintained that it had not been placed where it was near the mouth of the Tiber to laud Fascist imperial

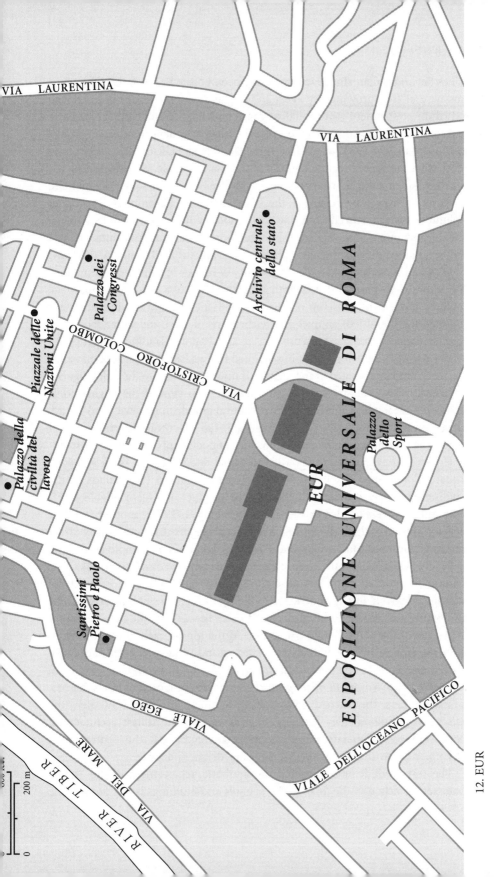

VIA LAURENTINA

VIA LAURENTINA

Archivio centrale
dello stato

ESPOSIZIONE UNIVERSALE DI ROMA

EUR

Palazzo dei
Congressi

Piazzale delle
Nazioni Unite

VIA CRISTOFORO COLOMBO

Palazzo della
civiltà del
lavoro

Palazzo
dello
Sport

Santissimi
Pietro e Paolo

VIALE EGEO

VIA DEL MARE

RIVER TIBER

VIALE DELL'OCEANO PACIFICO

200 m

0

12. EUR

sallies beyond Italian shores (as once had been boasted), but rather because it was 'natural' for a growing city to expand in that direction. Best he decided with a thrift in government that capitalists must applaud, it could easily be made to pay for itself.[40] So, *Linea B* of the much-delayed underground, inaugurated in the city in July 1953, opened its three stations at EUR in 1955. Already in 1950, what the Fascist regime had called the Via Imperiale, almost meeting the Via del Mare to unite highways of imperial dreams across the seas, reached EUR. However, it was now renamed the Via Cristoforo Colombo (Christopher Columbus Street), adroitly saluting early modern Italian primacy in nautical science and imperial voyaging and contemporary Italy's revised international status, no longer friend and ally of Hitler but loyal(ish) NATO aide of the USA.

EUR had been designed to be a repository of history in a more direct manner. Along its strictly parallel streets, with their evocation of a legion's encampment, could be located the Museum of Roman Civilisation, full of exhibits originally collected for the fiftieth anniversary celebrations of 1911 and expanded under Fascism. Nearby stood a Museum of Art and Popular Traditions, again with origins dating back before 1914, but adapted by Fascism to preach a nationalist message. Similarly situated in the quarter, if now dustily so, are the Luigi Pigorini Prehistoric and Ethnographic Museum and the Museum of the High Middle Ages, each ideally highlighting national cultural grandeur, longevity and span.[41] In yet another pompously pillared building, full of echoing corridors, EUR houses the state archives, the chief repository of documents on national history.

However, the quarter's deservedly most celebrated structure is the so-called 'Square Colosseum', the Palazzo della civiltà del lavoro (the Palace of the Civilisation achieved through Labour). The product of a team of able architects and engineers headed by Pier Luigi Nervi (1891–1979), another architect cleverly able to wriggle free from his Fascist origins, the luminously white building combines modernism and Fascist *romanità* in a splendid reworking of the classical Colosseum. Its construction was largely complete in 1943. The *palazzo* is adorned with twenty-eight statues representing most fields of human endeavour. On its outside, the building has six rows of nine arches. The numbering was meant to be meaningful since the six and the nine represent the letters of the name Benito Mussolini. At the top on each of the four sides is an inscription hailing Italians in a catch-phrase that was both nationalist and Fascist as '*Un popolo di poeti, di artisti, di eroi, di santi, di pensatori, di scienziati, di navigatori, di trasmigratori*' (A people composed of poets, heroes, saints, thinkers, the learned, sailors and migrants). In every way, then, the *palazzo* is simultaneously pleasing to look at and the fullest architectural expression of the dictatorship's intention to make EUR the centre of an 'Olympics of Civilisation', with Fascism as its driving purpose.

The rest of EUR fails to match the aesthetic achievement of the Square Colosseum, although the form of the squares and buildings is not unpleasing,

33. Square Colosseum, or 6 × 9 arches representing the letters of Benito Mussolini's name.

with the recurrent whiteness giving a luminosity to the modernist structures in a way rarely achieved by the drab brickwork often utilised in Fascist building in the city's historic centre. There are excesses; the church of San Pietro e Paolo is squat and heavy, aesthetically likely to repel the faithful rather than attract them, despite its alleged replication of Michelangelo's design for St Peter's. San Pietro e Paolo might therefore have been a suitable repository for the body of the Duce, as was rumoured to be its purpose late in the regime (somewhat confusingly, given earlier talk about the Augusteo). However, although planned in 1935, the church was not finished until 1955, too late for Mussolini. Somewhat similar is the story of the Palazzo dei Congressi, planned in 1938 but completed in 1954, a building whose hall was utilised in the Olympics for fencing matches, disputed beneath frescoes with classical Roman themes, which, like those on the walls of the swimming pool in the Foro italico, now looked pretty in their pastel colours but had once been charged with Mussolinian *romanità*.

As far as the Olympics were concerned, the major new construction in EUR was the Palazzo dello Sport, designed by the familiar team of Nervi and Marcello Piacentini, as a second major stadium after the Stadio Olimpico and seating 15,000. Made of pre-stressed concrete (Nervi's speciality), it has not weathered well, and the same complaint can be made of a velodrome which stands adjacent. Aesthetically the worst damage done at EUR was, however, the erection of the new ministries built of steel and glass that were being placed athwart the Fascist structures (the Ministries of Health, Finance, Foreign Trade and the Merchant Marine opened in this part of Rome between 1956 and 1967). Their admixture of bureaucracy and capitalism has left the quarter today the most soulless part of the city, empty of life and ironically deprived of a sense of history.

Perhaps this process began in 1960, when, with the justification of the Olympics, what had been intended as a quintessentially Fascist site, an urban expression of *romanità*, was pushed through to completion, with the trumpeted claim that the place's Fascist past had been purged by the disappearance of the dictatorship or because that regime's history was only a slight addition to the many, longer, more serious, durable and 'truthful' histories of Rome. So, in 1960, the Banca Nazionale del Lavoro's introduction to the Olympic venues there blandly explained that the whole zone was 'particularly original in its shape and buildings'.[42] In such prose, Fascism had indeed been blotted out of Roman memory and EUR was being readied for its future meaninglessness, all the more since the 'modernity' that it may have expressed in 1960 could scarcely be expected to last for ever.

Naturally enough, the Olympics, with their puffing of the modern religion of sport, encouraged much further sprucing of the city and its urban fabric, just as papal Holy Years had always done. A new airport was opened at Fiumicino, near Ostia, eventually to be honoured with the name of Leonardo da Vinci, a Tuscan who took up residence in France but was now nationalised and Romanised as a pioneer of flying. A new lighting system was introduced for the key classical remains and more elegant *piazze*.[43] As it prepared to welcome its latest wave of visitors, Olympic Rome tried hard to be modern as well as 'eternal'.

There were also attempts to paint Rome as national, unsurprisingly so at first sight given the coincidence of 1960 with the centenary of Italian unification. A trial of the Risorgimento past in the city had already been attempted in 1948–9, although, on that occasion, praise of the nation was hampered by the political disunity that had been so manifest in the revolution of 1848–9. During this centenary, not all lay commentators agreed when Catholic spokesmen urged that Pius IX was a proto-democrat and even Gregory XVI a reformer at heart.[44] Not all Catholics were pleased when leftist historians argued that a deep social disunity afflicted the Papal States in the period.[45] In 1949 Mazzini did get his statue above the Circo Massimo, the classical arena having been 'cleansed' during the Fascist years. But a single national narrative about the Roman Republic did not impose itself. The easiest escape hatch from dispute over past vice or virtue was, then as it often is, to slide into romantic populism. Rebecchini stated with cheerful vagueness that after 1848–9 there could be no doubt that Rome had made itself again 'the natural head of Italy'.[46] Another contributor to a special issue of *Capitolium* added that, at that time, 'the Roman people' had become 'the Italian people'.[47]

Yet, once this anniversary was past, struggle over the meaning and nature of national unification did not cease. Catholic uneasiness about the lessons of the Risorgimento for contemporary Rome was not allayed. In 1961 the mayor Urbano Cioccetti, who had held office since 1958, refused, for fear of offending the Vatican, to host a celebration that would mark the anniversary of Cavour's ringing oration designating 'Rome and only Rome' as the new nation's capital.[48] In his own speechifying, Cioccetti took care to underline the happy 'reconciliation between Church and State' in the Lateran Pacts, in his mind the most memorable event in a century of national and urban history. Cioccetti's political posture was a delicate balancing act since his majority on the City Council depended on MSI support, a formula that, after the fall of Tambroni, had been rejected nationally. Cioccetti was also a papal chamberlain as well as serving on the board of the Istituto centrale finanziario, which was heavily engaged in the burst of massive (and often illegal) housing construction in the city through the 1950s.[49] He and his City Council in other words still reflected the urban politics approved by Pius XII.

Oddly, therefore, despite the patriotic uplift of the Olympics, in their most recent manifestations in Sydney and Beijing so blatant an opportunity for the retailing of nationalised usable pasts, the centenary of the nation in 1959–61 was not lavishly celebrated in Rome. Nationalism remained muted even when Italian sportsmen and women came a creditable third overall with 36 medals, behind only the superpowers, the USSR (103) and USA (71). After all, in regard to the Risorgimento, the dating was awry; Rome had only joined Italy in 1870. Despite that recurrent adjective 'eternal', Rome was the belated capital of the country, and had never been able to achieve the economic or cultural dominance effortlessly assumed by London in Britain or Paris in France. Even Fascist rodomontade had not persuaded Italians that they should cherish their capital more than their home town nor had the dictatorship made them believe that Romans worked hard and with modern efficiency to their collective benefit. Confronted with these profound silences and contradictions in the national reading of Rome, during this anniversary forgetting had as much to be said for it as remembrance. As a result, the extensive visual and historical exhibition assembled to celebrate the Risorgimento at home and abroad opened in Turin, not in the nation's capital, and the introduction to the catalogue written by sponsoring Prime Minister in 1959–60, the Sardinian, Antonio Segni (he was Tambroni's predecessor), avoided much mention of Rome.[50]

Debates about the Risorgimento, and Rome's historic place in it, were contested internationally, with Sicilian historian Rosario Romeo defending the virtue and advantage of national unification against the American economic historian, Alexander Gerschenkron, and the English liberal, Denis Mack Smith, whose history of Italy, published in 1959, pursued a critical line; its theme was not the triumph of the united nation but its sad degradation into Fascist dictatorship.[51] Although both Gerschenkron and Mack Smith were scarcely Marxists, Romeo saw himself as warring against a mistaken and politically pernicious deprecation of the nation. Its worst feature in his eyes was that it bolstered the thesis of Antonio Gramsci, and so of the PCI, that the whole story of national unification had been a *rivoluzione mancata*, a political but not social revolution, with gains only for the elites and not for the people.[52] When in March 1961 President Giovanni Gronchi sent a formal message to parliament to acknowledge the centenary, he implicitly rebuked leftist criticisms by warning against history that had been read 'ideologically', with its necessary 'detachment' damaged by present 'political interests'. In the way of officials pronouncing on national history, he duly advanced a tendentious conservative line about such matters as the relationship, friendly or otherwise, between Garibaldi and Cavour. Ignoring the convincing evidence of popular disconnection from the Risorgimento (notably in Rome), Gronchi took as read that the Italian people, to a man and a woman, wanted their nation.[53] Nonetheless, despite presidential efforts at patriotic uplift, a debate about the past of national unification continued in Italy but whichever way the events of 1859–61 were examined, Rome was not at their heart.[54]

The result was that at the Olympics nationalist rhetoric was held on a careful leash. The Church, the classical empire and the ambiguity of the numerous Fascist residues all restrained patriotic excess. Not for nothing did the Roman Christian Democrat, Giulio Andreotti, who combined the posts of Minister of Defence and chair of the Games' organising committee, hail visitors at the opening ceremony on the Campidoglio, not in Italian but in Latin, and in his praise elsewhere of the event remind his audience that it had been hallowed by Pius XII rather than by some national hero.[55] The Olympics, Andreotti pronounced, were 'entirely removed from being national. Rather they are fundamentally and totally international and apolitical'.[56] Their purpose was to foster 'brotherhood across races and nations', an aim that Andreotti thought could readily fuse the spirit of the ancient and the highly modern city.[57] For this canny politician of all seasons, the city's history or histories and not the nation's were what mattered then in Rome.

Unlikely to be mentioned too publicly but fundamental nonetheless was the hope that the Olympics, even more than the last *Anno Santo*, could be fruitful for the national and urban economy. Umberto Tupini, still a leading figure in the DC, commented that the year after the *Giubileo* of 1950 had seen an upward leap in tourist numbers and the same expectation could nourish the Games. There might be gains on a number of fronts, he predicted, since the host country would 'draw advantage not merely from the economic point of view but above all in regard to national prestige and in the consideration with which we are held by other peoples'.[58] To assist this process, it was even urged that the daily siesta be abandoned for the duration of the athletic contest since it worsened the traffic problem in the city's streets and annoyed visiting shoppers. In reaction to the news, an emigrant Italian paper in the US credulously reported, 'business will go on all day and sandwiches will be eaten at local cafes or in the office itself'.[59] However, city restaurants did draw the line at a total reworking of their culinary history, ignoring the suggestion from one helpful foreigner that they should take the occasion to 'serve spaghetti in the shape of the five Olympic rings . . . [since] spaghetti would . . . [be] very suitable for this purpose'.[60]

A syncretic spirit did nonetheless surface in other features of the activities planned for visitors. Inevitably, the prime exhibition organised to coincide with the Games focused on 'Sport in Ancient Rome'.[61] A.M. Colini, in Fascist times the expert on the history of the *fascio littoriale* (the Fascist party's use of the symbol),[62] was again to the fore, now portraying how the city had been equipped for sporting contest under the Caesars.[63] However, the classical past was not all that was evoked, nor was Rome defined narrowly as a site of saleable pasts. Tourists, it was thought, liked festivals and so replicas of the *Palio dei Balestrieri* (Contest of the Archers) from Gubbio and similar 'historic' sporting competitions which, with greater or lesser invention of tradition, were fought out at Foligno, Ascoli and Pisa, were translated to Rome.[64] The special Florentine version of football, claimed by patriots as the origin of modern *calcio*, was also brought to the capital, a match between 108 players being staged at Piazza di Siena in the Borghese Gardens on 28 August.[65] In passing, there was even an admission that, through the Renaissance and after, Rome had not been the capital of sporting endeavour in the peninsula, again allowing to surface many Italians' recurrent suspicions that the city was not the 'real' fount of anything that brought them gain or pleasure.[66] No doubt, the imported 'heritage' entertainments were designed to express the nation, although their communal origins meant that they simultaneously laid bare the variety of Italian pasts, a diversity that had always made for 'divided memory'.

Further hints of historic irony could be found in the Games themselves. As had become the norm (allegedly replicating what had happened in the ancient Olympics), the final event on the programme was the marathon (for men; there was as yet no female contest). As is generally true of such occasions, the race's course mapped what the organisers wanted to be viewed as the host city's best, most luminous and approved history. Athletes heard the starter's gun on the Campidoglio. They then ran past the city's classical remains, the Forum, the Circo Massimo and Baths of Caracalla, before continuing down the Via Cristoforo Colombo to EUR. There they turned back along the Via Appia, past the Catacombs of San Callisto and the church of Quo Vadis, to re-enter the city through the Porta San Sebastiano. The finishing tape of the marathon was stretched under the Arch of Constantine. On the evening of 10 September 1960 the victor on this track through ancient, national, Fascist and Catholic *romanità* was the Ethiopian Abebe Bikila, son of a soldier who had fought the Italians in 1935 and now striding across the stones of Roman empires barefoot. Going and coming, he had passed the Axum stele, the Fascist seizure of which had been meant symbolically to entail the transportation, and the subjection, of independent Ethiopian history to Rome. The triumphant marathon athlete had run a route fuller of Rome's histories than the Games' Italian organisers wanted or knew, all the more since 'moderate' opinion in Rome had stubbornly gone on remembering the Fascist conquest of Ethiopia as a glorious national triumph.[67] In sum, during the XVII Olympiad, as on so many other occasions, Rome proved a site of multiple and contested memories and histories rather than an easily manipulated official memory and an authoritatively commanded national (or Catholic) history. The city remained swept by many voices.

Moreover, once the shouting and the tumult died, the dilemmas of post-war Rome and of its reckoning with its pasts had not been overcome by the city's staging of the Games. For the communists, a moment of sporting excitation did not mute their challenge to the rich and powerful. Rather, as party spokesman Alfredo Reichlin put it in reflection on the closing ceremony of 11 September, all that had happened beneath the glitz and despite the positive internationalism that the Games featured (with the long list of Soviet medals and the failure of various CIA initiatives to persuade communist athletes to defect), was 'the aggravation of the historic conflict between the "two Italies" and the "two Romes", between the exploited and the exploiters, between luxury and poverty, between the privileged and those who are always sacrificed'. As the athletes departed, he charged, they left behind two contrasting cities called Rome; one was 'the city of monuments, stadia, ultra-modern housing. The other was filled with *borgate*, squalor and the absence of civilisation'.[68] Christian Democrat rule left workers and their families, the majority of Romans, 'in a state of complete abandonment'.[69] Now their cause, with or without the Games, a comrade had remarked, must be championed by the party in a city that was 'the centre of a grand democratic and revolutionary movement that, thanks to the anti-Fascist struggle [under the dictatorship], had planted indestructible roots in the city'.[70]

Yet was it so? With every passing year, the population expanded and the new Romans crowded into spreading apartment buildings covering what had once been the Campagna. No doubt these immigrants, like their predecessors under

Fascism or after 1870, were deprived of most of the luxuries of life, including the art and grandeur, the splendid or strident histories, of the city within the Aurelian Walls.[71] But were they really united by anti-Fascist memory and a resultant determination to bring the Marxist project to fruition in the city, as PCI chiefs claimed? Were they true believers in a materialist reading of Rome? One who cast doubt on this idea was the homosexual novelist and film director, Pier Paolo Pasolini (born in Bologna in 1922 and murdered at Ostia in November 1975). Pasolini moved to Rome in 1950 and began to portray life in the poor outlying suburbs or *borgate*, notably in his films *Accattone* (1961) and *Mamma Roma* (1962). The latter featured Anna Magnani, once the vivacious and anti-Fascist woman of the people in *Roma: città aperta* but now a more equivocal figure. The Rome of the periphery that Pasolini painted in these and later works was a place of crime, exploitation and alienation, recalcitrant to political nostrums, excised from recognisable public history, be it of Church, nation, city or opposition. In other words, Pasolini repeated a familiar image of a 'popular' Rome that was detached from all official pasts, presents and futures and found its identity through the locality, family or gang, united by violence, suffering and endurance. His final film, *Salò or the 120 days of Sodom* (1975), is all but unwatchable in its desperate anger, now framed less in Rome than in his deeply pessimistic depiction of the universal human condition.

If unlikely to applaud Pasolini, one institution increasingly fearful that a majority of Romans were alienated from their city and any of its accepted courses through time was the Catholic Church. Its parishes in the city had expanded from 64 in 1930 to 116 in 1944 and 225 in 1964, reaching 299 in 1980.[72] But, during the 1950s, attendance at mass fell and there was other evidence that the Church was failing to reach the people as it once had; religious marriage, for example, declined from the 1960s; soon more than 30 per cent of weddings would be purely civil, while many couples avoided any formal ceremony of union.[73]

The Papacy's initial solution was the summoning of the Second Vatican Council between 1962 and 1965, a meeting which seemed on the surface to show, as official statements put it, that 'Rome, the centre of Catholicism is acquiring a newly dynamic character' (more than half the delegates attending the opening ceremony came from outside Europe, a situation that did give new relevance to the Church's claim to be world-spanning from its base in Rome).[74] Once again, well-worn words were spoken about the way 'the whole human family looked to Rome', the universal and Eternal City, even if Pope John XXIII, like his successor from June 1963, Paul VI, and unlike Pius XII, came from northern Italy.[75] The *Papa buono* (good pope), warm and natural, it was claimed, and so a vivid contrast with his predecessor, was represented as bringing a breath of fresh air to Catholicism in the city. He did take his role as Bishop of Rome seriously, and he was mourned as such in *Capitolium* on his death.[76] His admirers cherished the fact that, during his relatively brief pontificate, he had made 152 visits to various parishes in his diocese, being especially active in the city's periphery. There, he talked optimistically about seeing a 'flowering of life', while clerical commentators maintained that, through his urban journeys, he had at last given full meaning to the fact that he was no longer a 'prisoner in the Vatican'.[77]

Yet did this pontificate really change the course of Catholic history in Rome by making it local as well as global, social as well as political? After all, John was very much a conventional figure. When preparing for the priesthood, he had studied at Rome, while Leo XIII was pope. The messages that he then drew from the city were the usual Catholic ones about a 'holy city', illuminated by 'the tombs of so many famous martyrs and so many reverent priests'. The Roman history that mattered for him was that of the early Church. Liberal and national Rome, by contrast, was of trifling concern. Returning to the city in late 1923, alert not so much to the new Fascist government as to the approaching *Giubileo*, set for 1925, the young priest remarked that 'the ruins of the city of the Caesars speak to the eyes, they arouse memories, they sustain admiration. But they leave the heart cold. That was not true of the great basilicas of Catholic Rome', where the 'voice of love' could be eternally heard, rallying 'the people around the cathedral of truth'.[78]

Given these evident limitations in modern imagination, it is not surprising to find that, rather than forging a new bond with the masses, the pontificates of John XXIII and Paul VI in many ways signalled a retreat from Roman authority and power in the Church. Perhaps, instead, there really was a novel concentration on the world at large, an attitude that, as a corollary, brought a lessening in the traditional Catholic recourse to the historical power and meaning of Rome. John XXIII's major encyclicals, *Mater et Magister* (1961) and *Pacem in Terris* (1963), aimed to speak to the world with new urgency, while the Vatican Council was also pledged to shatter what an American observer called the Church's 'medieval cocoon', even if he then added tartly that the result was to advance Catholicism in its attitude and practice from the thirteenth to the seventeenth century.[79] Both John XXIII and Paul VI were reluctant reformers but they did endorse the first principle of the council that, in the complex modern world, the Church needed to avoid 'rigid uniformity' and become more flexible in its administrative practices and message.[80] They also tried hard to be more 'ecumenical', catholic rather than Roman Catholic, with John XXIII already in 1960 informing a visiting Jewish delegation: 'I am Joseph, your brother'.[81] The council went on to proclaim that Jews, Muslims and followers of the other great world religions were 'close to God' and shared a 'rich historical patrimony with Christianity'.[82] A slogan of the moment (borrowed from St John Chrysostom c.347–407) became 'Whoever stays in Rome, knows that his limbs are in India'. True to this enhanced sense of global range, Paul VI, in 1964, just after his accession, instituted what would soon become a recurrent feature of the modern Papacy by travelling abroad, to Israel and India. Rather than expecting the world to come to Rome as Pius XII had done, now popes took Rome to the world. Meanwhile, a defensiveness about anti-Semitism gnawed at the city's spirit, as was evidenced in 1966 when the Prefect banned the performance of Rolf Hochhuth's play, *The Representative*, with its thesis that Pius XII had failed in the war to intervene to save the city's Jews.[83] In official circles, open attack on the Papacy was still automatically regarded as intolerable blasphemy.

It was true that Paul VI, when he was only Cardinal Montini, had opted for somewhat oblique phrasing in urging that 'Rome would be reflected in the Vatican Council and the Council in Rome'. The city, he contended picking up a more familiar Church theme, was 'not afraid of time, of human dynamism, of progress, decadence and of its own possible destruction. It is a Rome that remains itself. Eternal Rome.' The council, he added, was bringing 'the world to Rome as though to its home'.[84] Yet, over the next years, it was the Church's struggle to accept or adapt to the massive social changes that were becoming evident throughout the world that was its most obvious characteristic, and reference to Rome could have little more than ritual significance in this process.

In his commentary on the city, Paul VI had also recommended that the Vatican Council stand for 'the affirmation of liberty and democracy in our country'.[85] However considered or clever the phrasing, given that the words could be read on the right as no more than Vatican endorsement of the Christian Democrat party, Paul was here announcing a shift in the Church's attitude to national Italian politics. The fiasco of Tambroni's flirtation with neo-Fascism had pushed the leaders of the DC into favouring the so-called 'Opening to the Left', accepting coalition with the socialists, if not the communists. This drift away from the right became the ruling formula of Italian coalition government for the next decade and a half. Paul VI, it was remembered, was the son of a member of parliament from the Partito Popolare (Popular party), who, in the 1920s, had rejected cohabitation with the Fascists. He, too, it seemed, had pledged his Church to endorse the myth of anti-Fascism.

In Rome's urban politics, this pattern was slower to emerge, and the accustomed post-war alliance of Catholics and the right long survived. The new city plan of 1962 may have set some limits to the rapacity of building contractors, but Rome continued to be a city where the gap between rich and poor was not bridged. The signing of the 'Gubbio Charter' in September 1960, which pledged to safeguard and revivify 'historic centres', did curb further Fascist-style demolition, blocking developers' schemes for the construction of skyscrapers on the American model within the Aurelian Walls.[86] However, it simultaneously reinforced the separation of Romans into those who, in company with the ever-growing tourist throngs, lived with the city's older histories, and those who dwelled in the spreading suburbs beyond the city gates and were ignored in most discussions of Rome's meaning. It was all very well for one enthusiast of this variety of city planning to announce in 1976 that every city worth the name had 'a soul', by which he meant a special history bolstered by a particular present mode of production.[87] But, in Rome, access was not guaranteed to all. The gap was not new, but now those who lived outside the walls and so outside the city's official meaning were vastly more numerous than they had been in 1900.

By the 1970s there was much talk in national politics about what PCI party secretary Enrico Berlinguer labelled a 'historic compromise'. The Italian government's inability to check social ills, fairly manage a modern welfare state and cope with the economic crisis brought on by the first 'oil shock' was being laid bare by the rise of leftist and rightist terrorism. Was the solution to extend 'Opening to the Left' as far as the communists? Such an arrangement, allegedly repeating what had once occurred during the Resistance in 1943–5, would create a national coalition of all men and women of good will, excluding only the neo-Fascists. Culturally, therefore, what was being advocated was a historiographical compromise, whereby the key history of recent times was acknowledged as an anti-Fascist one; the dictatorship had been overthrown and Nazism beaten when, already, (many) Catholics and (all) Marxists had worked fruitfully and courageously together, as they should now do again. Their heirs should agree that this story of opposition to Fascist tyranny was the most significant aspect of the past, and the one with the clearest and best lessons for the present, both in the nation and in Rome. The intention was for the ruling history of the city to renounce its imperial pretensions in favour of social ones; Rome was at last to embody equality (by some definition), as well as an ampler liberty than in the past.

In 1969 Clelio Darida, from the left of the Christian Democrat party, became the city mayor and in the following years he initiated some contacts with the Marxists.[88] However, the sense of urban malaise did not lessen and, in 1974, even Pope Paul VI appeared to blame the Christian Democrats for 'the evils of Rome' where 70,000 to 80,000 people still lived in ramshackle huts.[89] Were the communists on the edge of power? Yet in June 1976 national elections saw what had, in the preceding weeks, seemed a likely communist *sorpasso* (overtaking) of the Christian Democrat vote narrowly frustrated. No national government with Marxist ministers would yet assemble in Rome.

Nation and city were not necessarily identical, however. The left won the poll for the urban administration, with the PCI surpassing the DC by 35.8 to 33.9 per cent. However, the result of this victory for the Rome council was not the 'grand coalition' sketched by Berlinguer but a leftist administration under the elderly art historian, Giulio Carlo Argan, now an 'independent of the left', as the catchphrase went, sponsored by the PCI (despite in the 1930s and early 1940s having been a client of the Fascist, Bottai). Skirting such historical difficulty, Argan preferred to depict himself as the heir of Ernesto Nathan and so the bearer of a non-ideological radicalism, committed to improving the lives of 'ordinary Romans' in a way that conservative and Church-approved councils had signally failed to achieve.[90]

Very much an intellectual, Argan was emphatic about his cultural purpose. He was, he explained, determined to follow the recipe of Antonio Gramsci, philosophical hero of the 1970s PCI, in seeking to institute in Rome a counter-hegemony that could amend the misrule of the Christian Democrats and oust the mistaken ideas that had underpinned it. The new mayor was therefore bent on finding a new and better history for his city. As he explained his own past, a little tendentiously, 'our anti-Fascism was ignited by a resentment above all inspired by Fascist lack of taste, by its cultural crudity'.[91] Present-day Rome, Argan feared, scoured by the crass capitalism of his predecessors (politely he forbore to mention clerical obscurantism), was a city with a 'dismal cultural level'; it was a place 'that had changed without a plan of development'.[92] Although Rome could not be Rome without being imagined, since the war, he complained, 'the Italian bourgeoisie had no project of growth except one based on exploitation'; this greed meant that, by now, the city resembled Teheran or Cairo more than it did London, Paris or Berlin. Even its natural internationalism was corrupted into 'messy cosmopolitanism'. It must find a more rewarding history and renounce that which merely fuelled the profits of building entrepreneurs. Only by that revisionist mechanism could Rome overcome its 'identity crisis'.[93]

Despite the careful treatment of the Vatican, no doubt especially because Paul VI was no reactionary, there were hints of anti-clericalism in the debates of the new City Council, when Argan, speaking in the pope's presence, repeated the communist admonition of the 1950s that DC corruption had amounted to 'the third sack of Rome'.[94] In 1975 Paul VI had just watched over a less than exhilarating *Anno Santo*, one that he had announced ingenuously would advance the cause of 'social justice, fraternity and peace' and, more generally, would be 'radically new' in 'confirming the spirit' of Vatican II, thus opening 'a new phase of theological, spiritual and pastoral growth'.[95] Effective novelty was hard to see, however. Rather, the practical result of Paul VI's partial renunciation of history had further confirmed that the Church was not the power that it had been, whether in Rome or Italy; in the referendum on divorce in 1972, Rome voted 67 per cent against the official Catholic line (and, in 1981, 72.4 per cent supported abortion).[96] There was therefore some desperation in the visibly tired pope's public approval of the switch to the left in communal politics, with his unconvincing suggestion that Argan's expressed ambition to find a 'symbiosis of sacred and profane life' had long been one of Rome's best features.[97]

By the mid-1970s, the talk in city and nation was of 'the crisis of the Italian crisis', as it was named. In dramatic phrasing, the CIA reported to the guileless new American ambassador, Richard Gardner, that 'society is unravelling'; Italy, US spies feared, might no longer be trusted to fight the good fight in the endless Cold War.[98] The leading Christian Democrat, Aldo Moro, a politician close to Pope Paul and many times Prime Minister, Gardner has remembered, was 'not easily comprehensible to Americans. Although extremely erudite and with a penetrating intelligence, he sometimes spoke in incredibly ambiguous constructions.'[99] What Gardner, a political scientist by training, was not understanding was that, at this time, Italy and Rome had entered a major crisis in their search for national and urban meaning. For the moment, the truisms of neither Catholic nor Italian nationalist history could be relied on to pave an agreed path from past to present to future. Similarly under challenge were the rival interpretations of capitalism and of the anti-Fascist orthodoxy most closely associated with the PCI. As the leftist architect and town planner Leonardo Benevolo was acute enough to see in 1977: 'Rome after all is not the Eternal City, but rather the philosophical opposite of that mediocre literary myth. It is the city where major historic values, tragically and ironically, meet with the little threads of chance.' The way out, he contended, was for rigorous modernising action framed by a more enlightened social conscience and a clearer-eyed comprehension that 'past history becomes an eternal condition that can be accepted, refused or modified, according to the means and strength available.'[100]

But the moment was not that of a democrat like Benevolo, with his subtle reading of historical debate. Rather, left terrorists were about to carry their bloody challenge to the heart of the nation's capital, which had not been the epicentre of their movement until then. On 16 March 1978 the Roman faction of a group calling themselves the 'Red Brigades' (*Brigate Rosse*) kidnapped Moro as he was driving to work from his family house and local parish church, not far beyond the Foro italico. For the next fifty-four days Moro was locked up in what the terrorists called a 'people's prison' in the Rome suburbs, while the forces of the Italian state and of their NATO allies proved embarrassingly incompetent in rescuing him. On the morning of 9 May Moro was cruelly murdered by his captors, who then drove into central Rome, leaving the corpse in the boot of a Renault 4 car parked in the Via Caetani. Many commentators have noted that this street stood 'halfway' between the headquarters of the PCI in the Via delle Botteghe Oscure (widened under Fascism) and of the DC, opposite the Jesuit Church of Gesù (dripping with gold from the Indies and newer wealth, quite a bit ostentatiously provided by the Torlonia family). A more accurate measurement will show that the communist offices were nearer, and the car had been parked right outside the Palazzo Caetani,[101] home of Rome's Centre for Italian-American Studies and the Biblioteca di storia moderna e contemporanea, richest research library in the city for history of the times during and since the Risorgimento. If, throughout the two decades following the ending of the Olympic Games, Rome had seemed to be growing into just another urban centre in a globalising world where both history and memory were slipping into being no more than tourist infotainment and patriotic sellebration, now the Red Brigades were brutally proclaiming that their way of reading the past and future offered the best and sole lessons for their times. The meaning of Rome was being challenged with yet another interpretation of the historical process.

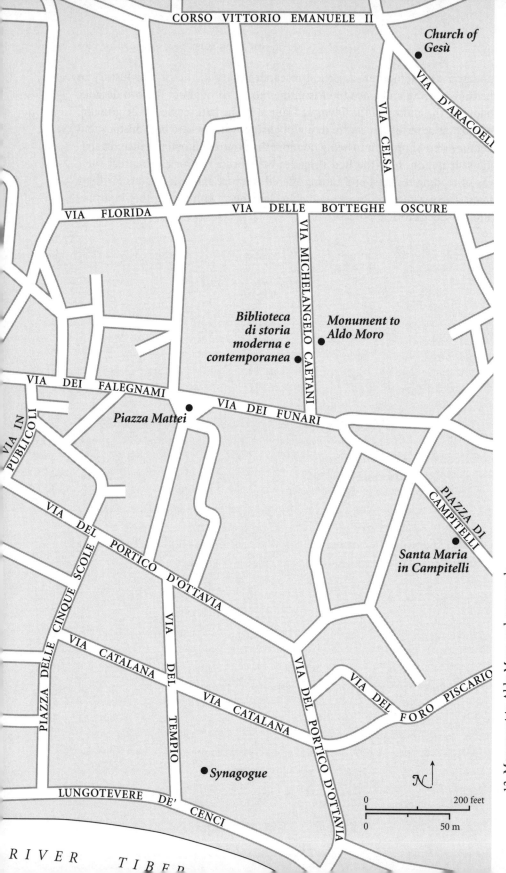

13. Monument to Aldo Moro and surrounds

11

✳

ETERNITY GLOBALISED

It did not take long for Aldo Moro to be deemed worthy of a site of memory in the city. Today any who wish to reflect on Moro's career, or the political travails and cultural wars that assaulted Italy and Rome during the 1970s, can find a bronze bas-relief portrait of him on the wall opposite the portal of the Palazzo Caetani and its libraries. The Christian Democrat whose life was so pitilessly and mindlessly ended by the Red Brigades' left terrorists is there accorded tousled hair and a more youthful look than was actually his in 1978; he had been born near Taranto in 1916 and grown to manhood under the Fascist dictatorship. A plaque tells of his 'barbarous kidnapping' and execution, while highlighting his 'lucid intelligence', his 'exquisite sense of moral rectitude', his 'faith' in 'liberty' and 'democracy', an ideological mixture that could solace 'the various emerging needs of an Italian society experiencing rapid transformation'. 'His sacrifice', the inscription concludes, 'coldly decided on with inhuman ferocity by those who uselessly attempted to prevent the achievement of a courageous and far-sighted programme, designed to benefit the whole Italian people, will stay as an admonition and instruction to all citizens. It will inspire a renewed effort for national unity in the cause of justice, peace and social progress.'[1]

In this ceremonious historical summary of Moro's life, two omissions might be noted. One is of any specific mention of the swirling rumours at the time of his kidnapping that Moro was flirting with communist entry into national coalition government through the 'historic compromise'. The other absence is Rome itself. Not the city, but the nation, onlookers are instructed, was the focus of Moro's career, actual and posthumous. Although today few pilgrims penetrate the Via Caetani and the narrow street is usually half blocked by parked cars and the other impedimenta of contemporary urban life, this site of memory goes further than that of the Ardeatine Caves memorial in stressing that sacrifice in the city above all serves and sanctifies the nation.

34. Aldo Moro's trashed body in the boot of a Renault 4 car parked outside the Biblioteca di storia moderna e contemporanea, 9 May 1978.

Ironically, Moro's murderers, the left terrorists grouped in the Red Brigades (BR), when they identified their historical justifications and explained their willingness to kill, also drew scant inspiration from Rome and its pasts. They did take history seriously; when it was discovered in October 1978, their hideout in the Via Montenevoso in suburban Milan contained a full archive of their activities, kept with scrupulous accuracy from the movement's beginning.[2] Their commitment to 'revolution', this record stated, had been fuelled by their interpretation of recent history but conceived with global span. As Marxists of some kind, they aimed to free the 'workers of the world', drawing their immediate models from the 'direct action' of Latin American urban guerrillas, 'Third World' peasant communists and Palestinian freedom fighters. As Renato Curcio, the founder of the movement, put it magniloquently in 1974, he and his comrades fought against 'the enemies of humanity and of intelligence. Those who have built and are building their wretched fortunes on the material and intellectual misery of the people'.[3] When the left terrorists grew more specific, their foe, they stated, was 'the imperialist state of the multinationals', world-ranging in its rule but, above all, sponsored by the USA. Had not Giangiacomo Feltrinelli, the wealthy publisher who was a pioneer of the armed opposition in Italy, in 1968 coined the apt watchword: 'in Italy as in

Vietnam'?[4] Thereafter, left terrorists sought to overthrow American power with the same intrepid doughtiness that armed the followers of Ho Chi Minh on what they perceived as a worldwide front.

When the BR and their fellow travellers on the far left switched their attention to Italy's national past, present and future, it was the 'Resistance' that they viewed as their historic mainspring, taking every word of the 'myth of anti-Fascism', still regularly hailed by official Italy as explaining the Republic's birth and purpose, as literally true. Even though the so-called 'Battle of Valle Giulia' had been fought dramatically on the streets of Rome on 1 March 1968, with 232 arrests and hundreds of students and police injured, and so signalled the years of contestation to come, the myths of Rome were not central to the BR's ideology, except in the familiar charge that the national capital was the epicentre of corruption.[5] When, in January 1973, the BR, whose membership lagged in the city, launched a fresh attempt to insert themselves into local 'resistance', they rallied against a neo-Fascist, MSI, party congress being held in the shadow of the dictatorship's architecture at EUR, with the catch-cry: 'War on the Fascism of Almirante and Andreotti [the latter then being Christian Democrat Prime Minister]. Armed struggle for communism.'[6] A year later, shortly before her death at the hands of the police, Margherita Cagol, Curcio's partner, besought her parents' understanding of her clandestine life and use of the gun by predicting that 'History will show that I am right, as it did with the Resistance in '45. . . . The police state is maintained by force of arms and anyone who wants to fight it must fight it on these terms.'[7] In the minds of the BR, in Rome real time had not advanced since 1943–4, and they were still engaged in pluckily opposing Nazi-Fascism as they thought partisans had then done.

With this profound belief that they were re-enacting a history which had first resulted in tragic farce but now could be amended to triumph, it is no surprise that, during the Moro kidnapping, Mario Moretti, hard man of the movement and in charge of the 'action' in Rome, for the occasion took the 'fighting name' of 'Maurizio'. It was the same as that used under Mussolini's dictatorship by Ferruccio Parri, leader of the radical democratic Partito d'Azione and fleeting Prime Minister of the failed anti-Fascist government of 1945. Moretti, born in 1946, had been trained as a Catholic (like Curcio and Cagol) and so did not have the direct family experience of the communist Resistance that was common among the BR.[8] Whatever their personal histories, by the mid-1970s the terrorists were sure that the lessons of historic anti-Fascism, in the hands of such compromisers as Moro and Berlinguer, had become fudged and enfeebled. They would have found it typical of the misuse of memory of Italians' struggle against ruthless dictatorship that, during the Moro kidnapping, the chubby and patriotic journalist-historian, Giovanni Spadolini, soon to be Prime Minister despite belonging to the tiny Republican party, automatically reached for an anti-Fascist vocabulary as he lamented that the BR were 'the direct heirs of Nazi barbarism'. 'Every season, in Italy,' he moralised, 'produces its own *squadrismo*.'[9]

The Red Brigadists angrily disagreed, outraged when they saw time-servers shamelessly exploiting the 'real' history of opposition to Mussolini. The actual partisans of 1943–5, they urged, had aimed at 'revolution', not a moderate Republic. They intended the complete liquidation of 'Fascism', both as a theory and as a practice. This joint target was all the more necessary because Mussolini's movement had been a coalition of murderous and racist hoodlums, deluded intellectuals hoping to impose an evil ideology, and the rich and powerful, cynically rapacious and repressive as ever. For left terrorists, communist leader Palmiro Togliatti's definition of Fascism at a party school in Moscow in 1935 as 'the open terrorist dictatorship of the most reactionary, most chauvinistic, most imperialist elements of finance capital' retained an exact truth.[10] The liberal capitalism (and Catholicism) of the post-war Republic, jockeyed into power in 1946–8 at the behest of the Americans, the BR believed, had camouflaged continuing Fascist rule in Italy with an appealing gloss. A generation later, their virtuous aim was to unmask the livid beast beneath for all the world to see its ravening wickedness. In the conceptual base of the Red Brigades, Rome only mattered in the sense that its habitual corruption and its unbridged distance from 'real' Italy made it a cosy sanctuary for the vicious and shameless agents of the Fascist Multinational State.

Like Cassius, the terrorists mistook everything. The pitilessness of their killing of the hapless Moro ensured that, after May 1978, they swiftly lost the considerable political credibility that they had, until then, earned in Italy. Even their own membership now found it hard to believe their historical line. As if in proof, *pentiti*, comrades who repented of their past views and activities, began to surrender themselves to the authorities. By 1985 the resultant internal fragmentation of the movement and more purposeful police work brought fifty-three Red Brigadists to trial in a special high security courtroom in Rome. The legal event possessed complex historical resonance since it was held in the buildings of the Fascist Foro italico, within a kilometre of where Moro had been seized. Thirty-two of those arraigned were sentenced to life imprisonment.[11]

Although the terrorists had regarded the PCI as supine and 'reformist', another enemy to be drubbed through a more candid and accurate interpretation of the historical process, the BR in their fall terminated the advance of Italy's communist movement in national politics. The terrorist version of 'anti-Fascism', ruthlessly used as an excuse for present murder, overwhelmed Berlinguer's claim that the Resistance had been virtuously led by a national communism with a human face. Simultaneously, the terrorists ensured the eclipse of the vaguer and more general contemporary interpretation of opposition to dictatorship, that 'myth of the Resistance' which had guided much Italian politics during the 1960s and 1970s.[12] In the new decade, support would instead rise for 'anti-anti-Fascism' as the best way to comprehend the recent past. From the moment that Moro's body was so callously deposited in the Via Caetani, the path was open to a general crisis of the left that would be deepened by the global victory of monetarist economics and the accompanying collapse of the Soviet empire in Eastern Europe and all the Russias. The consequences were heralded by the American sociologist, Francis Fukuyama, as 'the end of history'; in Italy and the wider world, they seemed to entail a dead end of Marxist and other left-leaning metanarratives of how societies progress through time.[13]

In Rome, however, these emendations of historical meaning ironically trickled down into the city just as it acquired a council further to the left than at any time since the fall of Nathan in 1913, with the result that the new right was muted in its presence for some years. In 1976 the victorious group of communists and fellow travellers had campaigned on the platform that their administration would bring the best of participatory democratic anti-Fascism to Rome, until then yoked into backwardness by traditionalist clericalism. Simultaneously, through their social understanding and their practical efficiency, they would save the place from the ravages of unchecked capitalism. As the mayor Argan pronounced, Romans faced a choice between the beauty and meaningfulness of its monuments and the devastation wrought by cars, winning applause from 200 Italian and international academics for planning to ban private vehicles from the historic centre.[14] No longer, the ruling left promised, would the Colosseum be reduced to a vehicular roundabout. As if to make the triumph of anti-Fascism concrete, plans were announced to reverse what the Fascists had done in the 1930s to the city's central archaeological zone, with the blocking of all or part of the Via dei fori imperiali and even its re-excavation to bring back to light so far as was possible what Mussolini's pickaxe had destroyed or buried. As a start, on 1 February 1981 the council instituted car-free Sundays for the central zone and, in the next month, cancelled a 'historic' ceremony, begun under Pius XII in 1955, of blessing the city's cars in the square next to the Colosseum.[15] Such initiatives, it was proclaimed, meant that a people's history was now at long last to win proper respect in urban life. In particular, it was announced, the left would pursue a radically diverse approach to archaeology and classical history, 'where the "ancient" is no longer comprehended as a "monument" nor viewed therefore as the bearer of illustrious histories but rather absorbed as a part of history potentially comparable with other historical moments – the Middle Ages, the Renaissance and the Baroque – that the city has never used properly'.[16] 'Great Men', with the Caesars in the van, must be pried loose from their domination of the city's public memory. Now, anti-Fascism, an interpretation of the past which had framed the Italian version of a people's war, would bring to the national capital the most humane and meaningful aspects of a people's peace.

But how, precisely, might the city's histories best be dressed for a popular cause? It was all very well for Argan's successor, the communist official, Luigi Petroselli, to urge in 1981, 'we do not want the historic centre of Rome to be a museum or a place of privileged luxurious residence and Levantine marketing' (*sic*; the adjective almost suggested that a residue of anti-Semitism lurked somewhere in the bones of Roman Marxism). 'The historic centre of Rome must live, and its life must push the whole city towards new values of civic association,' Petroselli added. 'It must be telling proof of a new administrative culture in the metropolis that opens wide the human dimension, and thereby reaffirms in modern terms the positive character of the city as it confronts the present.'[17] But what might these high-sounding words mean in practice? Just how were ordinary Romans to be integrated into Rome as they had never been before and how was the great history of the city to be successfully blended with the little histories of ordinary inhabitants?

The easiest way out of this dilemma for a political left, to which certainly neither Lenin nor even Gramsci could any longer provide a convincing guide to human organisation, was a populist recourse to appearance rather than rude effort to change reality. So, whereas once Nathan had worked hard to spread the advantages of science and modernity, bringing cheap gas supplies and clean running water into ordinary people's lives, now the council focused on culture. The people of the periphery were to be lured back into the historic centre by the regular staging of free public events. Renato Nicolini, in charge of this part of the council's activities and still worried by a recrudescence of terrorism among possibly alienated or giddy youth, took special pains with *Estati romane* (Roman summers). On these occasions, the social discontent that might bubble to the surface during the long, hot, months from June to September was to be diverted by a light, bright, array of festivals. To be sure, the entertainments were not quite Hollywood. But neither were they driven by the high culture that Marx, Lenin and Gramsci had envisaged as elevating the people to real freedom (even if, eventually, in 2003, the gardens of the Villa Borghese mysteriously acquired a replica of Shakespeare's Globe). In 1977 the Roman summer began with outdoor cinema in the Forum's Basilica of Maxentius and 'circus in the piazza' in the Via Giulia and Piazza Farnese. This repertoire was soon widened to take in public dances and rock concerts, and some effort was made to spread the partying to more peripheral sites at Cinecittà and Forte Prenestino.[18] Similarly, the vast square outside the Lateran was now more frequently utilised for entertainment than for the political demonstrations which, during the previous decade, had been common there.

By his own optimistic account in 1990, Nicolini was 'the angel, who, with an ephemeral beating of his wings, announced the arrival of a new Rome. New in a sense that would be very similar to the old in regard to beauty and the place of urban architecture in defining it.' His aim, he intimated, had not been aggressively to imprint a humanist hegemony, with the resultant forced silencing of the 'enemies of progress' in the manner that austere and ambitious communists had advocated before 1978. A leftist administration's task, he explained, was to bring all Romans up to the standard of life and leisure achieved in such global centres as Paris and New York, sparklingly modern 'cities of service industries'.[19] Everything, whether the sketched archaeological park running from the Via Appia to the Campidoglio or improved schools, hospitals and public transport, should work to that end, rendering Rome a 'post-industrial' world-class city that had simultaneously at last become a real national capital for Italy. Perhaps Gioberti's pre-Risorgimento dream of primacy could now come true. Central Rome, Nicolini maintained, could be taken out of the hands of those who wanted to freeze the historic zone into an unchanging past and instead prove that there, too, 'expansion' was possible and desirable.[20] As his leading collaborator, Carlo Aymonino, would express it more grandly, the hope of the future was 'to make Rome a capital diverse from all the others', where 'salvation . . . could lie in its very promiscuity, especially when planned'; a city not so much anti-Fascist as modern, democratic and multicultural, and perpetually in festive mood.[21]

For all the fanfare, however, whether under the aegis of the left juntas that ruled until 1985, or of their moderate successors until 1993, or, from then till 2001, of the returned centre-left embodied by Francesco Rutelli, head of the Margherita or Daisy party and the grandson of the adaptable sculptor of the Naiads in Piazza Esedra and of Anita Garibaldi, and despite the place sharing the global rise in prosperity of these decades, Rome remained a city frequently thought to be in crisis. Typical was the jeremiad of celebrated sociologist, Franco Ferrarotti, who complained in 1991 that Rome had still not risen to be the mother of the nation. It was rather its 'stepmother', a metropolis not in positive 'development' but merely in meaningless and wayward 'expansion'. Rome, Ferrarotti charged, was for ever doomed to be an agglomeration where *'the idea of a real city was lacking'*.[22] The starkest issue, the sociologist and others feared, was that Romans were themselves changing and the city was confronting another turning point, interpretations of which might differ in an alarming manner as they had in the 1970s. Once again the course of history was not running smooth. Whereas Italy had long been thought a country of emigration, now people from societies as diverse as Ghana, Ethiopia, Somalia, the Philippines, Iran, Poland and Romania were washing up in Rome, bringing 'with them needs, habits, behaviour, cultural models and values', and so new histories, all radically 'different from ours'.[23]

No doubt, it might be admitted, since 1870 immigration had not been a novel experience in Rome. Newcomers had flocked in under the Fascist dictatorship, and ever greater numbers arrived during the 1950s and 1960s. After all, such international and internal migration had long attracted the solicitude of the Church, with Pope Paul VI updating the Catholic line on such matters in his *Motu proprio, La cura pastorale dei migranti* (The Pastoral Care of Migrants). It asserted generously that all migrants had the right to preserve in a new society 'their way of thinking, their language, culture and religion', in other words their specific histories, with the Vatican humanely blessing what came to be called multiculturalism as the ideal for every modern society.[24]

Until the 1980s, however, many Italians parroted an accustomed discourse about being an emigrant country. Romans found it all the easier to endorse rhetoric about victimhood and persecution in that regard, the lament that Italophobia lurked in most host societies, since their city, unlike places further south, had only rarely driven its own people out into the paths of the world.[25] Now, suddenly, everything changed. Italy became a country of immigration and Rome was the epicentre of the process. By 1995 it was estimated that 20 per cent of legal foreign immigrants to Italy had taken up residence there, supplemented by perhaps twice as many illegals. By the turn of the millennium, ninety countries contributed to Rome's school population.[26] In the most recent survey, more than 200,000 foreigners are estimated to live in the city and its spreading suburbs, with 173,000 of them originating from beyond Europe. Officially, the five leading sources are the Philippines, Romania, Egypt, Bangladesh and China.[27] Given this situation, with the new millennium, it was, or should have been, clear that Rome had become multicultural in the modern sense of the term, a city with its 'foreign' histories exponentially on the rise. Admitting such multiplication and accepting that these pasts should join the city mix was, however, to prove a taxing and vexing matter.

One facile solution was to revive the assumption, familiar from other occasions reported in this book, of a 'barbarous' periphery that was excluded from the 'civilisation' of the city's centre and its long and glorious past. There, as one leftist historian put it in phrases that seem drawn from an ancient vocabulary about the history-less condition of barbarians outside the city gate, 'cultural syncretism' was the rule; there, 'no history exists, just the real or virtual present'.[28] With such unthinking phrases near the surface, Rome was not at the forefront in accepting the rules of the multicultural game of modern 'identity politics' or of endorsing the view that every 'community' must be able to express its own culture and history.

Yet, where political opportunity offered, some minorities grasped fuller cultural representation than in the past. Leading the way was a group with many claims to being one of the oldest in the city, the Jews, although in a process that owed as much to the global remembering and forgetting of the Second World War as it did to Rome's specific past. In July 2000 the Italian parliament, then with a centre-left majority, approved setting aside an annual *Giorno della Memoria*, Memory Day, to be marked, as in a number of other countries, on 27 January each year. It was the anniversary of the day in early

1945 when the Red Army had liberated Auschwitz and exposed its horror. The Italian parliament also passed legislation penalising Holocaust denial, while more generally condemning the fostering of prejudice about 'racial superiority'.

Even if such officially instituted recollection did not necessarily ensure a critical review of anti-Semitism in Rome over the centuries, these developments did signal that urban Jews had at last won an official place as contributors to urban history for what was proudly claimed to be 'twenty-one centuries'.[29] The surviving prejudices that had lingered through the 1950s were now written out of memory. Thus the centenary in 2004 of the great synagogue beside the Tiber, once approved by King Victor Emmanuel III as the best religious building erected in his reign, was recorded in an effusive history written by Luca Fiorentino and given an endorsing preface by Walter Veltroni, then the leftist mayor of the city. Fiorentino told a Whiggish tale in the manner that emigrant communities call 'filio-pietism', relishing the statement by Chief Rabbi Riccardo de Segni that, 'in Jewish Rome, every stone in the different layers, and every site' expressed the 'complex and articulated' history of the Jews. The unpleasantness of the Second World War was not forgotten but evil, in that sad time, came from outside – 'the massive deportation by the German Nazis [on 16 October 1943] opened up the black hole of the Holocaust'.[30] Fiorentino made no mention of the more difficult and divisive matter of Italian Fascist responsibility for the wartime persecutions nor did he examine Romans' part in the implementation of the racial legislation successively enacted after 1938. There was no space either for Fascist and Italian murder of Arabs, blacks and Slavs. Rather, Fiorentino explained carefully, the dictatorship's anti-Semitism had sprung from 'servile obedience' to Italy's Axis ally. In any case, the persecution had the advantage of forcing Rome's Jews to think more clearly than in the recent past about the special quarter of the city from which they were, in 1943–4, dispersed and so about their 'national' identity.[31] All in all, Fiorentino concluded, cheerfully fixing contemporary community politics into the *longue durée*, 'for more than two thousand years' the Jews had been 'considered more Roman than the Romans'.[32]

Another symbol of the acceptance of greater difference, at least in regard to those sectors of the urban population with the power to be taken seriously (a strength that was more international than Roman), was the opening of a grand mosque on 21 June 1995. If, unlike the synagogue, it was set outside the Aurelian Walls, it was also granted a prime site near the Tiber. It rose just beyond the Parco di Villa Gloria, land that had been converted in the 1920s into a patriotic memorial of the heroism of the 'martyred' brothers Cairoli in the Garibaldian attack on papal Rome in 1867 and of soldiers in the First World War. The suggestion that an Islamic centre be erected there was mooted in the 1960s, with finance being guaranteed after a visit to Rome by King Faisal of Saudi Arabia in 1973. Two years later the City Council set aside 30,000 square metres of land for the building and an attached cultural institute. An architecture contest was won by a team of two internationally celebrated Italians, Paolo Portoghesi and Vittorio Gigliotti, and Sami Mousawi, an Iraqi working in the UK. A splendid structure, able to house 2,500 worshippers, was eventually completed. The architects, with a palpable anxiety to get their history 'correct', explained that the mosque, 'although inspired by Islamic tradition, is not a mere synthesis of historical elements, nor is it eclectic or an imitation; it is a work of modern architecture, born from the universality and "modernity" of a long-standing tradition'.[33] In their minds, it fused the best of past and present, attaching a happy history and a hopeful future to the Muslims of Rome, people whose culture was now well rooted in the city and destined to burgeon along with the rest.

Admittedly, less splendid structures of Muslim worship, half hidden deeper in Rome's poorer and more peripheral suburbs, frequently confronted, and confront, harsher problems. The Bengalis, who were beginning to compose a major segment of the population of the Esquiline, for example, failed in August 2007 to get police permission to build their own religious centre, although the changing habits in that quarter of the city were already manifest in a Buddhist temple, a synagogue, a Jain prayer centre and a Chinese Evangelical church, which over the years supplemented the seven established Catholic places of worship there.

Despite the troubles that still afflict Muslim Romans, bottom of the heap among the city's communities were, and are, the gypsies, who certainly could not expect to have their long history in the city joyously celebrated in a museum or cultural centre. In most minds, gypsies remained utterly 'barbarous', a people by definition lacking an acceptable heritage or future.[34] Mussolini's dictatorship, as early as 1926, had urged their expulsion from the city, given their alleged fondness for 'crime, begging and vagabondage'. Thereafter Fascists talked about the need to 'purge' from the nation the 'caravans of gypsies' believed to be intruding into it. In 1940 a contributor to the journal *La difesa della razza* (Racial defence) wrote admiringly of the German solution to the gypsy problem, notably in regard to preventing miscegenation. During the war a number of gypsies were interned, although the regime stopped short of Nazi-style murder of that part of its population.[35] After 1945 Rome's gypsies re-emerged into city life, always present at those sites that attracted tourists, but mostly they operated outside the urban administration, and were excluded from its welfare and schooling and steadfastly denied any part in approved history. Since the end of communism, they have been replenished with migrants from various Eastern European countries; following persecutions, gypsies have been frequent refugees (if ones seldom granted respect or solace whether from international organisations or ordinary Romans).

As Roman urban administrations tried with some uneasiness to find a satisfactory modern approach to being a multicultural city in a globalised world, Rome's most ancient organisation, the Vatican, was reviving its claims to incarnate all that mattered there. Back in the 1970s, the fate of the Church had seemed bleak with Pope Paul VI unable to stem religious decline. The last year of his life was corroded by his ineffectual efforts to rescue from the Red Brigades' prison his friend Moro, a politician whose ideas certainly about openings to the left and perhaps about a generic anti-Fascism he shared. Then he had written disconsolately about 'the inhuman ferocity . . . again making bloody the streets of this city, once the teacher of civilisation, but now impotent witness to reborn barbarism'.[36] Not even the implied identification between himself, his Church and the city helped, and he died shortly after. As one friendly historian wrote in an obituary, Paul 'had been the Pope of Humility and Expiation. He had spoken openly of the historic faults of the Church. Ever since his election, perhaps he had prayed to God to fill the role of expiatory victim', whose death could signal revival.[37]

And, soon, papal melancholy was indeed to end. After the brief and, by most accounts, pitiable rule of Albino Luciani, who, in taking the name John Paul I, promised a Catholic historic compromise between the good-hearted populism of John XXIII and the agonised intellectuality of Paul VI, the Church passed into the more robust hands of Karol Wojtyla, John Paul II.[38] This Polish Cardinal-Archbishop of Cracow was elected pontiff on 16 October 1978 and served until his death on 2 April 2005, a term that was exceeded only by that of Pius IX.

John Paul II and his chief aide and successor, Joseph Ratzinger, who was to take the title of Benedict XVI, were the first non-Italian popes since the Dutchman, Hadrian VI, in 1522–3. Their origins marked them as separate certainly from Italian politics and perhaps from Italian society in a way that had not occurred since the Risorgimento, with its political invention of the Italian nation. These non-Italian popes signalled that the century-long battle between the Catholic and the Italian nationalist interpretation of Rome's meaning and purpose might at last be over, having largely faded into irrelevance. Rather than being made by Rome as Pius XII had once been, John Paul II bore an anti-communist and Polish nationalist history with him into the Vatican. Thus equipped, he became a major figure in the decline and fall of the Soviet Russian empire in Eastern Europe, backing the Solidarity movement in the Gdansk shipyards with funds and sympathy, and, in July 1985, calling on all Eastern Europeans to give fealty to their 'Christian faith' (especially if it was Catholic).

Recovering quickly from an assassination attempt in St Peter's Square by a lone Turkish gunman on 13 May 1981, John Paul was a restless figure, forever travelling from one country to another, fulsomely endorsing identities sprung from soil if not from blood by regularly kneeling to kiss the ground, in practice usually the airport tarmac, of whatever nation he was then visiting. He was similarly active in summoning aspects of Catholic tradition and history to his side, canonising 482 new saints from across the globe, a vaster number than any of his predecessors had approved. Typically 'universal' was 'World [Catholic] Youth Day', initiated in 1984 at the end of another supernumerary *Anno Santo* that the Church had found reason to celebrate on the fiftieth anniversary of Pius XI's Holy Year in 1933–4 (to muted enthusiasm from Romans).[39] To enhance their global momentum, Catholic Youth reassembled in Rome in 1985. Thereafter, however, except during the 'Jubilee of the Millennium' in 2000, they met in many diverse places – Buenos Aires (1987), Santiago de Compostela (1989), Czestochowa (1991), Denver (1993), Manila (1995), Paris (1997), Toronto (2002), Cologne (2005) and Sydney (2008). Here, these successive celebrations promised, stood resolute a universal Church, with an armour of global histories in past, present and future, an organisation that might have a home in the Vatican but whose ambit had far outgrown little Rome.

Critics of John Paul II nonetheless maintain that, despite his global span, under his pontificate the Roman Curia re-emerged with a power and self-confidence that it had renounced or hidden since the death of Pius XII. Now, once again, the papal bureaucracy was possessed of an authoritarian conviction that it was eternally right, openly demanding that there must be no relativist slippage of the view that the Church was the providentially guaranteed bearer of absolute truth and, on occasion, ready to privilege its presence in Rome over that of the Italian nation. In some eyes, this return to historic certainty was not a positive development. As a liberal commentator complained on John Paul II's death, never 'have Catholics been so divided, never has there been so much contempt and aggression between Catholics. Never has the local Church suffered so much at the hands of the Vatican and the papal centre.'[40]

As far as the city of Rome was concerned, the new confidence of the Church, its revived absolutism, was put on vivid display in the *Anno Santo* of 2000, the Holy Year of the Millennium, planned to be the most grandiose in the Church's history. It drew between 25 and 35 million pilgrims, more than double the total in 1975, and a hundred times more than the number who had come in 1750.[41] Yet these lavish celebrations were less centred than in the past on evoking a universal and Catholic Rome, being emphatic instead that the Church was a great, indeed the greatest, global organisation, the institution assigned by God with the task of spiritually carrying the whole world in its hands.

The ambition to control and harness human history to this end was scarcely concealed. As John Paul II explained in 1999 in announcing the 'Great Jubilee', the start of the third millennium was a good moment to reaffirm that 'Jesus is the genuine newness which surpasses all human expectations and such he remains for ever, from age to age'; the Saviour's life was 'the true criterion for evaluating all that happens in time and every effort to make life more human'.[42] For those who accepted the Church's mystery, the pope was stating, belief could overcome the effects of age and blunt history's sting. Equally, the pope preached, the Holy Year should be a time for reflection, a moment when the faithful could engage in a 'purification of memory'. Such dedication, he urged – in phrases that reflected the spreading contemporary view that heartfelt 'apology' could achieve 'closure' and wash away the stain of past ills – should be 'an act of courage and humility, in recognising the wrongs done by those who have borne or bear the name of Christians'.[43] Even while they were removing the sinful mote from their own eye, he added, Catholics should again denounce the greater evils of recent political times, saluting the numerous 'martyrs' of the twentieth century. They were very likely to have fallen victim to the Church's enemies, 'Nazism, communism, and racial or tribal conflict'. In this salutary remembering, the pious could be uplifted by extolling all those 'who suffered privation or worse because they refused to yield to an ideology which had become a pitiless dictatorial regime'.[44]

In this rendering of history, the pope's mixture contained little that was surprising. He duly took the occasion to warn against 'extreme' capitalism, preaching that the wealthier nations and 'the private sector' should take up the challenge to alleviate world poverty, so as to achieve social justice and general peace.[45] There was also a directly religious message: 'May the Jubilee serve to advance mutual dialogue until the day when all of us together – Jews, Christians and Muslims – will exchange the greeting of peace in Jerusalem', even if he avoided mention of 'Eastern religions', by now estimated to have 20,000 immigrant followers in Rome.[46] To emphasise the centrality of Israel/Palestine in Christian history (and, by implication, to hope for resolution of the interminable conflict there between Jews and Arabs), this Jubilee would be different from all the rest since it would be celebrated in Jerusalem as well as Rome.[47] Papal aides duly listed the Christian sites in Jerusalem, Bethlehem and Nazareth, where a visit would, in 2000, earn special indulgence as had long been the custom in Rome (there, the expected crowds were to be contented by adding to the familiar catalogue the lesser basilicas of San Lorenzo and Santa Croce in Gerusalemme, plus the Sanctuary of Divine Love and the catacombs).[48] During this *Anno Santo*, the pope did not cease his own roaming, spending Easter in the Holy Land and, in May, visiting Fatima in Portugal. (He had become convinced since his escape from the assassin's bullet that he was possessed of the 'Third Secret' of Fatima, infallible knowledge of the course of history allegedly granted by the Virgin to local peasant children in October 1917, just as the godless but eventually defeated Bolsheviks seized power in Russia.)[49] Once Pius XII had proclaimed Rome to be the new

Jerusalem. Now Jerusalem and other cities of the Holy Land shared the historical weight of Rome. Under John Paul II, the global was surpassing the urban.

Nonetheless, while the great days of jubilation approached, Catholic authorities did not forget to moralise about the city that housed the Vatican and its special history. As an Irish priest homilised: 'Going to Rome in the Holy Year is not a tour or a holiday. It is a religious exercise, a sort of travelling retreat and should be thought of in that light.' Catholics must avoid 'a too-ready indulgence in worldliness and material pleasure and . . . an unctuous, oozing spirituality and a religious ebullience which is apt to disturb everybody else'. 'When going to Rome,' he counselled, 'we are not doing it in order to admire the architecture, the works of art, the ancient ruins or the political institutions. . . . The pilgrim is there with a spirit of prayer and recollection, a certain penitential exercise and a happy relaxation, not at all incompatible with such a holy endeavour.'[50]

Such was the theory of the latest *Anno Santo* when, on 24 December 1999, John Paul broke open the Porta Santa at St Peter's, while 'dressed in a shimmering light-weight lurex and silk psychedelic cope' of a hundred colours. His every act was relayed to a world television audience of 1.5 billion, whose prayers, it was hoped, were supplementing those of the million pilgrims present in the city.[51] To meet this influx, the communal council, under Rutelli, had worked hard to make Rome pleasing to its visitors, whether their motives were religious or secular. Helped by a budget of 3,500 billion lire, officials boasted that their administration had launched almost 800 different public works initiatives in Rome and its surrounding towns, ranging from major exhibitions to practical road improvements.[52] Predictably, history was said to be on the side of every event. The city, it was announced, was primed by its centuries and even millennia of experience in proffering hospitality; this human generosity automatically showed through as visitors poured in, reaching their peak when the ordinary events of a jubilee were combined with World Youth Day.[53] There was even an effort to unite the short-term visitors with the immigrants from who knew where now living in Rome with a week-long festival in May, housed perhaps appropriately at that one-time triumph of Liberal planning, Piazza Vittorio Emanuele, on the Esquiline; the *festa* gloried in the city's past and future as 'a crossroads of multiethnic culture'.[54] Perhaps more excitingly and better reflective of the contemporary city, at the end of 1999 Romans could attend Pina Bausch's modern performance work, *O Dido*, which gave expression to a city that was 'Levantine, Middle Eastern and African; sweaty, jumbled, playful, aquatic, erotic, prostituted, caressing and malign'.[55]

Aiming at a more mainstream audience than that drawn to *O Dido*, the historical exhibitions that opened in the city over the next months were numerous and historically syncretic, like the purely religious feasts aiming at the global as much as the specifically Roman. True, classical times were not

35. Pope John Paul II in his lightweight lurex coat of many colours opens
St Peter's Holy Door and institutes the 'Jubilee of the Millennium', midnight on
24 December 1999.

forgotten, with a review of the culture of the Samnites in the refurbished Museo
Nazionale Romano, a display of female ornamentation and luxury in the Museo
Barracco and the inauguration of the splendidly modern 'Crypta Balbo', with its
technologised tour of ancient remains unearthed by excavations in the zone
abutting the Via delle Botteghe Oscure. The classics were bolstered by shows of
the paintings of Velázquez in the Borghese Gallery and of the culture of Yemen
(as 'the land of Sheba') at the Palazzo Ruspoli (backed by the Fondazione Pasolini
among others). During the first six months of the year, the Scuderie, once the
royal stables across the road from the Quirinal palace, hosted masterpieces from
the Hermitage in St Petersburg, while a selection of Monet's works were on show
in the ample space in the bowels of the Victor Emmanuel monument. Such
cheerful internationalism was at least partially matched by the Macchiaioli,
painters of the Risorgimento, who had some of their efforts patriotically hung

for public viewing in the Museo del Corso. Meanwhile, the general appearance of the city had been spruced up, with the purging from many of its finest buildings of the encrustation of the years and especially of the sullying by traffic pollution.[56] The car problem might have lessened in recent years, with public transport receiving lavish funding, but it had not been solved, as would become evident in the years after 2000, when the grime rapidly returned.

If many of the exhibitions were secular in character, Catholicism was not forgotten in the vast span of culture on display. From June to December, tourists could take in a display of 'Peter and Paul: History, Cult and Memory during the First Centuries' at the Palazzo della Cancelleria, while the Vatican Library offered examples of 'The Gospels of the People. The Word and Image of Christ in Culture and History'.[57] Elsewhere there was an exhibition of the pontificate of Boniface VIII, first sponsor of *Anni Santi*.[58] Fitting the moment, a collection illustrating 'women's appearance during jubilees' was opened, with the modish message that females had featured historically as 'entrepreneurs and traders', charitably organising hospitality for the social classes and, by implication, fans of the market throughout time.[59]

In this regard, the Vatican was not averse to more direct populism, sponsoring, as Holy Year commenced, an outdoor concert, televised globally. It mixed a cast of Italian performers with Tom Jones, Miriam Makeba and the children of the Harlem community choir.[60] To satisfy more basic appetites, in the summer the Church authorities endorsed a '*Giubileo Pizzaioli*', where the pope himself came to salute '2,000 pizza chefs from places as far flung as Australia, Spain and the United States. They made giant pizzas in the papal colours and distributed some 50,000 slices to pilgrims and beggars around Rome'.[61] More confrontingly for the Church, a rival convocation of homosexuals had been arranged in July, under a slogan ambiguously mocking American hegemony: 'In Pride We Trust'. Amid controversy, the gay march proceeded but was not allowed to penetrate the Via della Conciliazione. Newspaper reports described the Vatican area as deserted, battened down as once it had been during the inauguration of the statue of Giordano Bruno, with John Paul II upbraiding the demonstration as an 'insult to the Giubileo'.[62]

Such liberal Catholics as the historian Pietro Scoppola tried to put their own spin on Holy Year, approving Veltroni in his capacity as Minister of Culture when he hoped that Rome could acknowledge the poor and migrants from the periphery and favour the city's greening. For Scoppola and his friends, still Catholic anti-Fascists at heart, the fundamental purpose of the Jubilee was to celebrate equality, justice and freedom, through this multicultural process, they hoped, 'valorising' the city's past and artistic inheritance and 'revitalising' its contemporary architecture.[63] Yet such worthy aims were not central to John Paul II's Church which, beneath the festive sheen, was endeavouring to arm itself more strongly against its enemies. Just before the opening of the Porta Santa, Cardinal Camillo Ruini, Vicar General of the diocese of Rome and a staunch conservative, was unapologetic in asserting that from then on the Church would regard its intervention in daily political debate as a right and necessity.[64] Negative talk about clericalism, he stated, was dated and irrelevant. More instructive was the 'declaration' issued on 6 August by the Vatican under the name of Cardinal Ratzinger but with the approval of the pope. Heading its syllabus of deplorable errors were 'relativistic attitudes towards truth itself, according to which what is true for some would not be true for others; the radical opposition posited between the logical mentality of the West and the symbolic mentality of the East; the subjectivism which, by regarding reason as the only source of knowledge, becomes incapable of raising its "gaze to the heights, not daring to rise to the truth of being" '.[65]

Fortified by such trenchant words and their customary implication that the popes carried eternally and universally to the people the sole historical truth, the Church, into the new millennium, remained as viscerally opposed to many of the principles of the Enlightenment and the admission of democratic history wars as it had ever been. Its stance was regularly underlined in Rome where Ruini, by then aged seventy-seven, did not give up his vicariate until June 2008. As the leading spokesman of the Church in Rome he stood out against social reforms that might recognise gay marriage or more informal cohabitation, and refused to approve scientific experimentation which, in the religious view, infringed the sacrality of human life, with work on stem cells being specifically condemned. There were even hints that the Church had still not altogether rejected its hope in reinterpreting the Risorgimento, with the papal volunteers of 1870 now applauded as having evinced a 'real heroism and an uncommon faith'.[66] In similar vein, Cardinal Giacomo Biffi of Bologna suggested that national unification had demeaned Rome and Italy, creating 'a little second-rate kingdom, of no international importance, without ambitions, made bourgeois', whereas a better course (in his mind, ironically a more purely Italian national one) could have been achieved by continuing loyalty to the Church.[67]

But the most aggressive revisionism in Rome and Italy after the fall of the Berlin Wall came not from the Church but rather from the lay political right who were soon in business to demonstrate that the more strident and imperial aspects of Italian nationalism had not been cancelled out by the years of the Republic. What from the 1980s was celebrated in some places as a 'silent majority', dragooned during the previous two decades into kowtowing to the dominant anti-Fascist interpretation of the recent past, now found active spokespersons emphatic that Italians had been weighed down since 1945 by 'divided memory'.[68] A distortion of the history of the dictatorship and civil war, it was said, had blocked Italians from a properly passionate commitment and devotion to their nation and fostered a malign *partitocrazia* (rule by the political parties), at the potential cost of handing Italy over to non-national,

'totalitarian', communism. Ever since 8 September 1943, when King Victor
Emmanuel III and Marshal Badoglio fled Rome, the argument continued, Italy
had run along the wrong historical track.[69] The ritual blackening of everything
to do with Fascism must cease. In Rome itself, planners should stop harping
on the alleged errors of Fascist urbanisation and acknowledge instead that
then, as in every era, Rome expressed its eternal ability to possess 'new ways of
working, new ways of being read and a new rebirth', each of which was 'also
characterised by a partial destruction of the existing city and the denial of
virtue to the immediately preceding era'.[70]

This generic anti-anti-Fascism became the cultural sustenance of the
political career of entrepreneur Silvio Berlusconi, Prime Minister of Italy
in 1994–5, 2001–6, and since 2008, who also regularly sought historical
justification for his actions. Many foreigners and some Italians have found
Berlusconi a troubling figure, too rough and ready in his legal and financial
dealings and too crassly populist in his cultural and historical evocations, most
notably in his claim that 'Mussolini never killed anyone'.[71] It was predictable
that, in 2006, the American historian Alexander Stille should draw a familiar
parallel in condemnation of what Berlusconi's governance entailed with a book
entitled *The sack of Rome: how a beautiful European country with a fabled
history and a storied culture was taken over by a man named Silvio Berlusconi*.
Its cover displayed a bust of the politician as a modern Caesar, but with a sly
smile all his own, suggesting that here was a crook and not a conqueror. Stille
was appalled by Italy's retreat under the second Berlusconi government to 53rd
place in world listings of competitiveness and freedom of the press (in the
latter case behind Albania) and 41st in transparency (behind Namibia).[72]

Berlusconi's power base is in Milan, not Rome, and, despite his years in
government and the readiness of some to attach to him clichés about the
eternal corruption of Rome, he continues better to express the Lombard city's
business history than the complex weave of the national capital. His attitude to
the past and its use remains riveted to anti-communism as the only acceptable
moral stance on the travails of the twentieth century, as well as the cheapest
available interpretation of the recent past and the one likely to endear him to
neocon friends in the USA and such media colleagues or competitors as
Rupert Murdoch. Yet Berlusconi's more natural approach to history is that it is
a rich potential mine of happy events that can be commemorated to the
pleasure and financial advantage of all. This media magnate believes deeply in
'infotainment' and 'sellebration'. Nonetheless, he is adaptable, as he indicated
in his dealings with Gaddafi, noted in my introduction. Berlusconi wears most
history lightly and is ready to frame its interpretation according to the needs
and opportunities of the moment.

More rigid in their revisionism during these years were Italy's neo- or post-
Fascists, a not always united group who, however, had never renounced a

major presence in Rome. Their story went back to 1944–5, when survivors of Mussolini's regimes, both before July 1943 and in the *Repubblica Sociale*, soon rallied in the national capital. From the moment of liberation, there had been recalcitrants there, working under the leadership of Pino Romualdi, a close aide of Alessandro Pavolini, party secretary at Salò. Romualdi's influence was curiously enhanced by the rumour that he was another of Mussolini's bastard sons.[73]

In December 1946 the revival of Fascism became overtly political with the founding of the Movimento Sociale Italiano, where the word 'Sociale' endorsed the extreme and racist variety of Fascism practised or preached under the *Repubblica Sociale Italiana* from 1943 to 1945. The establishment of the MSI signalled a reading of history that saw little wrong with the Nazi alliance or anything else to do with the Fascist project. Soon, however, as had happened under the dictatorship, the fidelity of the MSI to violent Fascist revolution was conditioned by its opportunist appeal to bureaucrats, better-off people in Rome and further south, and its harmonious ties with the Vatican, all social forces unlikely to be enthusiasts of 'revolution', even of the Fascist kind. It was always likely, therefore, that neo-Fascists would temper their fundamentalism and accommodate to a more conservative world view. While these complications ran their course, in 1946 the anniversary of Mussolini's death was mourned in a mass at the Jesuit church of Sant'Ignazio and, in 1947, there were similar public ceremonies at Santa Maria del Popolo and Santa Maria in Aquiro in the city's historic centre.[74]

But any reverencing of the Duce's spirit mattered less than the MSI's rapid return as a factor in Roman communal politics: here, until the 1960s, party members and party sympathisers were able to join or otherwise back ruling coalitions in deals that remained unacceptable for national governments. For some decades after 1945, in local administration, business and sport, a Fascist background and/or a nostalgia for the good times of dictatorship retained a fundamental place in the belief systems of many Romans who mattered. So, too, did a refusal to confront the crimes committed by Italians during the war and, more generally, under the Fascist regime.[75] Fascist ideas about the 'triumph of the will' being capable of overcoming structural weakness or of the Great Man dominating history were equally omnipresent among 'moderate' or conservative voters, as a way to counter Marxist claims about economic determinism. Here a characteristic figure was the once Fascist and now radical conservative journalist, Indro Montanelli, who doubled as a popular historian, happily ready to argue that the empire of classical Rome had triumphed not because its citizens 'were the strongest, but because they were the most convinced that their country had been founded by the gods to fulfil a great destiny'.[76]

After 1960 changes in national politics symbolised in the 'Opening to the Left' presided over by Aldo Moro began to hem the MSI into greater isolation.[77] During the next decade Berlinguer's 'historic compromise' was rooted in the idea that all men and women of good will should unite in Italy, excluding only residual Fascists. Anti-Fascism seemed all the more correct a line at a time when an assortment of right-wing terrorists were creating as much mayhem as did the Red Brigades, with a preference for bombings in public places rather than targeted killings of what the BR judged 'enemies of the people'.[78] Now Rome's universities and high school campuses became battlegrounds for armed conflict between the extremes of left and right. In the suburbs, neo-Fascists aimed to create 'no-go areas', where thugs stood ready to prevent passage across a square of known leftists or any found carrying a newspaper friendly to their cause. One such zone was Piazza Euclide in the wealthy Parioli district around the church of Santo Cuore Immacolato di Maria, given its ugly Fascist design by Marcello Piacentini.[79]

By the 1990s, however, public violence moderated, with the focus switching to historical revision. One leading author was Carlo Mazzantini who had been a boy in 1930s Rome. Mazzantini endorsed the case, now common on the right, that anti-Fascism had crafted a pernicious and false history of the dictatorship, and especially of the Salò Republic, to the advantage only of the PCI, itself a viscerally Stalinist outfit, that, during the 1970s, had got too near power for comfort. Any opposition to this process had been hindered by the lack of public patriotism, a failure that sprang from 8 September. In Mazzantini's view: 'A nation could go on living after Sedan and after the fall of Berlin. But it could not survive 8 September 1943. On 8 September 1943, the country lost its soul.'[80] The only way to repair this damage, he maintained, was radically to recast the nation's understanding of its Second World War, and especially its interpretation of the civil conflict that stained its territory with blood during the RSI.

To some extent, a process whereby the MSI and its voters came in from the cold should not be regretted. Notably plausible was the adaptation of the neo-Fascist outlook on history by Gianfranco Fini, youthful successor to Almirante as leader of the MSI, and the party's guide towards a new brand-name (Alleanza Nazionale: National Alliance), government first in association and then fusion with Berlusconi and what was proclaimed 'post-Fascism'. Fini had been born in Bologna but was educated in Rome. The city became his political redoubt as was evident as early as 1993, when he narrowly lost a mayoral election to Rutelli, despite then still seeming fervent in his view that Mussolini, the 'greatest statesman of the twentieth century', should, one day, have 'squares and monuments' throughout the country named after him as did Cavour, Garibaldi and Mazzini.[81] A decade later, however, Fini, national Minister of Foreign Affairs 2004–6, had transmuted into an elegant grey-suited conservative politician, a potential Prime Minister in waiting. As spiritual preparation, in November 2003 he had travelled to Israel, respectfully visiting Yad Vashem, the museum in Jerusalem where the official Israeli interpretation of the

Holocaust is most graphically expressed, and there denounced Mussolini's racial laws. 'The Italian people', he stated, thus implying a merging of national history with that of Italy's Fascists and neo-Fascists, 'take responsibility for what happened in 1938, when the racial laws were adopted. There cannot be a condemnation without assuming responsibility.'[82] Fini was now convinced Mussolini's ideology had lost its historical lustre. Democracy, he urged, was always preferable to dictatorship.

Perhaps, even in that Rome where the architecture of the dictatorship was still omnipresent, the Fascist era had finally closed? Certainly, in the national capital, the Berlusconian coalition was slow to gain urban power, all the more because of the crucial role in it nationally of Umberto Bossi and the Lega Nord (Northern League). As was noted in Chapter 4 in recording their damning of Garibaldi, the *leghisti* based their political appeal on their hatred of 'Rome', once again readily made into a symbol of corruption and falsity, the deluding capital of an unjust and even irrelevant nation. '*Roma ladrona, La Lega non perdona*' (Fat thievish Rome, the League will never forgive you) became and remained the movement's chief slogan.

In these circumstances, it is not surprising to find that, as in the 1980s, Rome's city politics lagged behind the nation, with the sometime communist youth, Veltroni, succeeding Rutelli as mayor in 2001 and retaining office until 2008 with a leftist administration that had not quite abandoned the rhetoric of anti-Fascism. The city was also contented by its own prosperity. Now, for the first time certainly since 1870 and perhaps since the fall of the classical empire, Rome took a place either in or near the lead in the Italian peninsula in adapting to economic change, challenging Milan as the national centre of technological revolution. Its inhabitants' real wealth multiplied four times between 1951 and 1991 and thereafter continued to grow exponentially while the global boom continued.[83] To some eyes, the endless ranks of apartment blocks that constituted the city's newer suburbs were soulless, still 'barbarian' in their failure to express great history. But they, too, if not quite matching the luxury of the historic centre, were equipped with shops offering a rich range of products and, in the eyes of many immigrants, were a material paradise compared with the non-European world. In 2005 aides of Veltroni boasted that the city had achieved national primacy in 'services, trade and building' and was now the most economically prosperous urban centre in Italy, with an annual product almost equal to Singapore. Rome, it was announced, even stood second to Stockholm among European capitals in the relative availability of parks and other public space. It led the way in Italy's (modest) contribution to environmental awareness. Wise and humane rule by the moderate and realistic left had converted old Rome into 'the city of the future'.[84]

This achievement, Veltroni's administration claimed in words that Renato Nicolini, the PCI's cultural organiser a generation earlier, might have recognised, was based on cultural adaptation, and so on the use of what was good in Rome's multiple pasts and on the avoidance of the bad. The city, it was argued, no longer relied on 'the spent motor of the historic centre' but drew instead on its eternal international connections to rejoice in being 'polycentric'.[85] It was therefore able to enjoy, enliven and integrate the spreading quarters on its outskirts, potentially ready for a liberal nation that might itself eventually be arranged more federally than it had been since the triumph of Jacobin-style centralisation in the Risorgimento.[86] Rome, it was stated, as a happy part of united Europe had embraced all its citizens in a process that resulted in a synergy between past and present. Under Veltroni's heartening lead, it was successfully 'valorising' 'its extraordinary history, its exceptional accumulation [of pasts] and its cultural stratification, occurring across three thousand years' in order to achieve a model 'modernisation'.[87] The latest city plan, tabled in March 2003, endorsed the idea of 'continuous integration', defined as producing positive developments in 'urban infrastructure, the environment, the economy, finance, business, society and architecture'.[88] Even the graffiti that were so ubiquitous in the city, it was explained, might carry a positive message if read with subtle sociological understanding and with acknowledgement of their ancient origins.[89] As Veltroni himself declared, twenty-first-century Rome had leaped ahead in politics, economics, culture and society.[90] At last, he implied, the city had contented its rival histories by accepting each in its own glory. For a de-ideologised Roman left, identity politics were the best answer to the dilemma of friendly human cohabitation. Their skilled management was integrating Rome ever more effectively into the world. The tyranny and xenophobia of Fascism, it seemed, was dead and buried in Rome, just as other unlovely moments of human history were.

As if in academic proof, in 2007 in a review of Fascist building in the city, Emilio Gentile, Rome University's leading historian of the subject, concluded that only the stones of the dictatorship's roads and monuments survived; the words and myths that had once bloated them with totalitarian and imperial meaning had vanished.[91] Yet, less than a year after Gentile's book appeared, there was evidence that Fascism was alive in Rome. Its history was not, after all, buried.

In April 2008 Romans voted in as their mayor, Giovanni ('Gianni') Alemanno, a 'post-Fascist' from the National Alliance, who pledged decorously that he embodied a 'modern and tolerant right in an established two party democracy'.[92] There were reasons for doubt, however. In his youth, Alemanno had been a vigorous and unapologetic neo-Fascist, appointed in 1982 head of the MSI's youth organisation, the Fronte della Gioventù, in Rome. Then he was ready, it was said, to take charge of 'squadrist' attack on the party's enemies. Keeping to this pattern of Fascist fundamentalism, he married the daughter of Pino Rauti, an unrepentant ideologue who, in 1990–1, briefly ousted Fini from leadership of the MSI.[93] In 1989 Alemanno had been arrested while protesting against a visit by George H.W. Bush to Nettuno, pronouncing that this 'second landing' could only be tolerated by 'slaves of the occupiers' of the nation. The presence of the American President, he added, was an insult 'to the memory of the thousands of fallen [RSI] soldiers who fought for the dignity of the *patria*'.[94]

Thereafter, Alemanno did adapt himself to the course pursued by Fini. Shortly after his elevation to the mayor's office, he made a well-publicised trip to Rome's synagogue and honoured the Jewish wartime dead. A year later, he added that 'the Shoah had undoubtedly been one of the most tragic and aberrant events in human history', although he left some wriggle room by arguing that Fascist racial laws amounted to 'a yielding to Nazism'.[95] Alemanno may be honest when he contends that he, like his leader, has become a genuine post-Fascist. Perhaps the party chants and Fascist 'Roman' salutes that greeted the new mayor as he climbed the stairway past the statue of Cola di Rienzo to take office on the Campidoglio were mere window dressing and no more a political platform based on a serious reading of history than the similar or worse behaviour indulged in by Rome's football fans at every match. Yet, more worrying was the crude xenophobia that the new council (with the backing of Berlusconi's national government) displayed once in office, eliciting international press condemnation. One example occurred in July 2008 when arsonists attacked a gypsy camp on the city's periphery. Rather than deploring such violence and moving to prevent it in the future, Alemanno reiterated a statement that he had first made on obtaining office that he would 'purge' eighty-five camps in all.[96] Indeed he was soon celebrating a total of 6,216 expulsions during his first months in office and proclaiming that his firm action was allowing Rome to 'start again'.

Yet probably more significant was the fact that, along with prejudice, came (expensive) sport, that ultimate proof of capitalist modernity. In late 2009 Alemanno announced that Rome would become the venue of a Formula 1 Grand Prix motor race, and so really show that it was the capital of a modern economy. Perhaps to the satisfaction of the ghost of that sometime pensioner of the Duce, Oswald Mosley, or to Mussolini's own phantom (the dictator's image had been enhanced by his abilities as a pilot, motorcyclist and driver of fast cars), the race is to be contested around the perhaps modernist and certainly telegenic streets of EUR. At the same time, if more uneasily, Alemanno's Rome began to prepare for the 150th anniversary of the Risorgimento in 2011, when, as in past anniversaries, the capital had to fend off competition from leftist Turin. A multi-media patriotic exhibition on the history of national unification opened in the basement of the Victor Emmanuel monument in June 2009, to run until June 2011. In preparation for a shift in historical line in the city, Alemanno had commenced office by, for example, sacking Eugenio La Rocca, *Sovraintendente* of archaeological work in the city since 1993, while Berlusconi had simultaneously replaced the director of the national archives in EUR.

Meanwhile, controversy about a Fascist rather than a national heritage had broadened in September 2008, when AN Minister of Defence, Ignazio La Russa (a politician who bears a remarkable facial resemblance to 'The Master', evil enemy of Dr Who), recalling the events of 1943, took his chance publicly to applaud the patriotism of those who had opted for the RSI. A day earlier, Alemanno, on a visit to Israel, told *Il Corriere della Sera* that he 'did not and never has' seen Fascism as 'an absolute evil', even if he acknowledged the wickedness of the racial laws against the Jews. In reply, elderly anti-Fascist journalist Giorgio Bocca deplored Alemanno's efforts to separate a 'good' Fascism from a 'bad'.[97] Two days later, Bocca was joined by the historian Gentile who complained that 'de-fascistisation' had never got far in Italy, although he put the blame not on the right but instead on what he dismissed as the levity since 1945 of leftist accounts of the dictatorship.

His easy attribution of blame is arguable. Yet, Gentile did condemn the post-Fascist effort to reclaim patriotism for their cause. The Fascist version of the *patria*, he underlined, had never been for all and had always involved the killing of freedom. Worse, he added justly, was that the post-Fascists, Fini included, had only renounced the anti-Semitism of the racial laws, while by implication approving the many other tyrannies before 1938. All in all, Gentile feared, Rome and Italy were experiencing their own limp version of the 'end of history'. After the calming of the ideological disputes of the 1970s, Italians, he complained, had given up on serious readings of the past, viewing it instead with apathy and cynicism. Thus they were all the more exposed to the terrible simplifications of Alemanno and La Russa.[98] History, he seemed to be saying, had come to a full stop, and both his city and his country were the worse for it.

In his conclusions and his language, Gentile was repeating that formula, which has recurred in these pages, whereby the self-consciously enlightened fear that the masses have not been won over by the most recent reading of history, composed by their betters. Gentile is another Roman to assume that, in his city's streets, 'civilisation' is perennially under potential assault from 'barbarism'.[99] Yet if it is hard to see even the most extraordinary economic collapse prompting the rebirth of Fascism in Rome or Italy, placed as they are in a Europe where the clock has moved too far for its hands to be turned back to a world of racism, autarky and aggressive war, it may be sensible to continue to monitor the post-Fascist attempt to 'restore' history in Rome.

To give one national example: under Berlusconian impulse, Italy has acquired a third 'memory day' of its Second World War, 10 February. Then, in contrast to 25 April with its dedication to anti-Fascism and 27 January with its partially Italianised Holocaust, Italy, despite its record as the 'first ally' of Nazi

Germany, is presented as a 'victim'. Special focus is placed on the murders perpetrated by Yugoslavs and communists in the *foibe* or caves on the Carso above Trieste, as well as on the 'expulsion' of the national inhabitants of Istria, an Italian territory between the wars, but in 1945 seized by Yugoslavia. The twisting of wartime history evident here is not original. Most other ex-combatant nations are as anxious to compete for medals in the 'Olympics of victimhood' and as ready to wrench their history out of joint in relishing their own suffering and innocence. Dangers, however, lurk. Characteristically, on 10 February 2009 Alemanno was to the fore in demanding an Italian purge in interpreting the past. 'The Minister of Education', he argued, 'should check all history textbooks in such a way that ensures that those adopted in schools will deal fully with all aspects, with all the dramatic events of the twentieth century including the tragedy of the *foibe*.'[100] His language seemed moderate. But what he and his friends want and what they can plot to achieve while they hold urban power in Rome is 'equal time' for Fascist history, code for a totalitarian reading that, ideally, will exclude all others and, at a minimum, preach that imperial Rome is still, in its authoritarianism and rigour, the model for our times. Not far from the surface of their words, Alemanno (like Benedict XVI) has not renounced the hope that he might yet win Rome's history wars and impose one united memory on the people. Yet, rather than divided memory dampening Italian democracy as both right and many on the left maintain, it is Italy's many continuing limitations as a democracy that hamper the acceptance there of genuinely open historical debate (and an accepted division over the meanings of the past). As the twenty-first century continues, it is important to insist on the right of each citizen, each resident, each visitor in person or imagination, still to hymn their own Rome and, thereby, democratically contest the meaning of the city.

CONCLUSION

──────── ✳ ────────

With Alemanno and his friends armed, in the field and seeking again to impose a single history on Rome, should this book reach a pessimistic conclusion about the endurance and replenishment of debate about the past and its meaning, and turn out to be another account of decline and fall? Certainly, despite being studiously apolitical about Romans' ideological differences, the celebrated American anthropologist, Michael Herzfeld, when he assesses the fate of what he views as ordinary Romans, is pessimistic. Himself a frequent resident in the Monti area that runs up from the Colosseum to the Esquiline, Herzfeld fears that unchecked globalisation, gentrification and the 'heritage industry' are evicting the real histories of the people from the city centre. The matter, he complains, is 'a tragedy because it erases all alternatives to the neoliberal vision of the good life'.[1] In Herzfeld's eyes, the medley of 'pervasive corruption' and the popular skill in getting by were an ancient and natural result of the 'gnawing putrescence that strangely enhances the city's aging beauty, veining its robust surfaces with splinters and fractures that intimate the fragility and contingency of its social life'.[2] The 'long Roman conjuncture of corruption and civility', its 'generic model of original sin', he claims, until recent times blended to establish Rome as 'an architectural monument to . . . the capacity to thwart the arid admonitions of the law by generating in their place, sometimes out of uncompromising materials, a warmly sensual, inhabited and ecstatically illicit beauty'.[3] Now, however, Herzfeld laments, the poor who embodied this complex and vital humanity are to be ousted by 'hoteliers and other entrepreneurs with cosmopolitan pretensions and a cultivated sense of national identity'.[4] *Roma delenda est*, it might seem. Either that, or Herzfeld has proved another resuscitated Augustus Hare, one of those foreign commentators who, over the last two centuries, has seen 'their' Rome changing and decided therefore, from outraged and possessive love, that the city is dead and its meaning lost.

Yet in his last pages, Herzfeld pulls back from so vain, abrupt and despairing a conclusion. 'The irony', he remembers, 'of this all-too-human Eternal City is precisely that nothing is eternal; all is provisional, fixable, negotiable. . . . Here, eternally, eternity continues to fracture and to coalesce, repeatedly and without rest; for such, paradoxically, is the eternity of the Eternal City. It seems still that no bureaucratic hand can yet stay the corruption, at once and forever corrosive and creative, of time. When and if it succeeds, Rome will no longer be Rome.'[5]

Anthropology and history are different disciplines. Yet, at least if the monitory last sentence is ignored, Herzfeld does recognise that the city is too layered a place, with too many stories whispering through it, readily to have a final solution imposed on its meaning even by the seemingly all-powerful market. No doubt it can be agreed that, in the third millennium, Rome's myth and reality are on many counts less significant than they were in 1789. The Latin language and compelling yarns about the classical past no longer bear the loud message of once upon a time and even the Papacy has had to trim to modernity. Equally, it may be only honest to admit that, to quite a degree, the city of Rome is now composed of a 'galaxy' of settlements and 'communities', each with its own memory and meaning, all ironically globalised and doubtfully original.[6] At the same time, it may well be that, for many a visitor, the pap of the heritage and tourist industries is all that matters about the place, and a T-shirt with an image of St Peter's printed on it but made in China or Fiji is the chief token of remembrance to be taken home.

Yet it is important not to be too depressed or censorious about the present. When, after all, were there not many Romes in Rome? When were there not fraudsters at play in the pockets of gullible newcomers? When did the city not express multiple, frequently contradictory, messages? When were some of the histories located there not fading (and when were others not rising again)?

Rome is scarcely unique in this regard. Every city, every part of the world bearing human imprint, can be examined for lingering evidence of manifold pasts that matter or have mattered or will matter. Yet it is the contention of this book that Rome is an ideal site for listening to the whispers and the shouts of history. I began by noting the great sites – the classical ruins, the Vatican, the artistic glories of the Renaissance and baroque. Then, in the body of the book, my focus switched to less renowned but still significant parts of the city, zones where histories and memories wait to be identified and acknowledged. Since I am in great part a historian of Fascism and modern times, and my book is directed at the last two centuries of urban life and imagination, I have spent quite a bit of time recording Fascist echoes in a city that so expanded under Mussolini's dictatorship. As with all analysts, my background is a help and a hindrance; I see and I am blind. The itinerary of my book from the Napoleonic Museum to the plaque commemorating the deaths of Targhini and Montanari to the monuments to the Garibaldis, Giordano Bruno and King Victor Emmanuel II to the site of the Exhibition of the Fascist Revolution to the Villa Torlonia, Piazza Pio XII and the Foro italico and on to the Via Caetani and the recording of the life of Aldo Moro is therefore a special one; certainly many other tracks through Rome and its histories are possible and can prove as enlightening and illuminating as mine.

Pursuing them is one of the infinite pleasures of the city, a reason why Rome can be visited over and over again and an explanation why, in my conclusion, I am still dreaming of other paths through Rome, half ready to preach that an end is only a beginning. This book is the product of my senior years as a historian. Yet it began to stir in my imagination when I first stayed in the city as a callow PhD student from Cambridge in 1967. For the autumn and winter of that year, Michal and I subsisted happily in a tiny flat on the Via Tiburtina, then at the city's eastern periphery. A combination of thrift and recurrent public transport strikes meant that, as often or not, I made my own way on foot across Rome to the library where I worked, usually the Biblioteca di storia moderna e contemporanea in the Via Caetani. As yet this street lacked memorial to the murdered Moro (he was then Prime Minister of a coalition based on the 'opening to the left'). Nonetheless, when I traversed Rome, I walked through histories; the ghosts of Romans past were already nudging me to notice them and so I shall in these last of my pages that may read like another introduction.

Leaving our flat, I began my route west along the Via Tiburtina towards the Aurelian Walls and the historic centre of Rome. I soon passed the Verano cemetery, established in 1835 under Gregory XVI to modernise burial in the city, one of this pope's few gestures to the contemporary. If I strayed inside to admire the ornate tombs, among many others I could find those of Goffredo Mameli, 'heroic' martyr of 1849 and author of the national anthem, *Fratelli d'Italia*, and of Claretta Petacci, last lover of Benito Mussolini and the partner of his bathetic final moments. At the main entrance to the cemetery stood the sparely beautiful basilica of San Lorenzo, said to have been erected by the Emperor Constantine in 330 CE and updated by Pope Pelagius II in 579. From 1881 it had been the burial place of Pope Pius IX, enemy and/or victim of the Risorgimento. The still controversial pontiff lies in a mausoleum ornamented with the coats of arms of those members of the clerical aristocracy of the city who contributed to its cost. It was this church that was all but destroyed in the American bombing of 19 July 1943; the bombers were aiming at the nearby railway junctions of the Stazione Tiburtina.

If I did not delay too long at San Lorenzo, next I could breach the Aurelian Walls and contemplate briefly the soldier emperor of that name who ruled Rome from 270 to 275, warring successfully against the Goths and other 'barbarians' and destroying the independent state of Palmyra, which was ruled by the intrepid Queen Zenobia. A version of their story became the unlikely plot of an opera by Gioacchino Rossini, *Aureliano in Palmiro* (1813). In contemporary times, the Assad dictatorship in Syria, another regime to find meaning in Rome, has plotted a lavish restaging of the work amid the present-day ruins of Palmyra in the hope that, with such 'European' cultural display, Syria will lose its place in George Bush II's 'Axis of Evil'.

Once I was inside the walls, my path directed me past the Fascist buildings of Rome university to the modernist Termini station; it owed its name not to being a terminus but to its positioning near the Thermae or Baths of the Emperor Diocletian, 'restorer' of empire and persecutor of Christians (reigned 285–305). The Stazione Termini had begun its life in 1863 and had been completed between 1868 and 1874. In 1937, however, a project was launched to modernise it in time for the Fascist *Ventennio* in 1942, although, hindered by the war, it was not actually opened until the Holy Year of 1950. By then, with the usual adaptability or effrontery of the moment, it was read as an icon of the Republic and democracy.

After I had admired the station's stylish modernism, I turned briefly to the right to pass the Museo Nazionale Romano, since 1889 one of Rome's great depositories of archaeological digs, arranged with national or cosmopolitan purpose, and the Baths of Diocletian. Under the popes, this edifice had been converted into the church of Santa Maria degli Angeli, altered following Michelangelo's advice in the 1560s but now used for patriotic ceremony and unashamed in preserving positive records of Fascist empire. As an indication of historical continuity in this regard, across the road stood the monument to the '500' killed at Dogali in 1887, blocked by the stalls of second-hand book sellers from the lusciously sensual, plashing, fountain of the Naiads in Piazza dell'Esedra.

Now I swung left down the Via Nazionale, where the ugly Palazzo delle esposizioni jutted into my view about halfway along. This building was located near the opening of the Traforo or tunnel that led to the Via Rasella, in the 1920s site of Mussolini's bachelor flat and, in March 1944, the place where a partisan attack precipitated the massacre at the Ardeatine caves. If I did not turn to register this memory, soon I was descending towards the classical remains in and around the Via dei fori imperiali, with the intricately carved column of the Emperor Trajan (98–117), commander of the classical empire at its maximum extent, overseeing all. Since 1587 and at the order of Pope Sixtus V, a bronze statue of St Peter commands its summit, a replay of 'the triumph of the cross on the ruins of the Capitol' that intrigued Gibbon. Ahead now lay the white 'wedding cake' Victor Emmanuel monument, shining in the sun, while at its side stood the Renaissance Palazzo Venezia, from whose balcony the Duce had harangued 'oceanic' crowds. For the last stages of my morning walk I could choose either to go past the richly gilded baroque Jesuit Church of Gesù and, opposite it, the headquarters of the ruling Christian Democrat party, or down the Via delle botteghe oscure and the competing office of the Communist party with its Rinascita bookshop, promising in its name Marxist intellectual 'rebirth'. My objective, the Library of Modern and Contemporary History, was off to the left, occupying part of the Palazzo Caetani, at the edge of what was long the ghetto. In 1967 it remained a city quarter equipped with Jewish tailors, grocers, restaurants and other community stores.

If I could delay my yen for bookish research for another moment, just around the corner could be found the delightful sixteenth-century Fontana delle tartarughe, restored by Bernini a hundred years later, when the clambering tortoises from which the fountain draws its name were added. Furthermore, when past history palled, there was always the present, since, as the bus strikes suggested and with 1968, the 'Hot Autumn' and the *anni di piombo* of vicious political contestation approaching, already every space within reach in central Rome was filled with political posters and graffiti, each announcing battle over the ideal course to the future and attesting its virtue and justification from the past; each from one hour to the next slapped over with another claim.

Even back in our flat, histories entered our lives. Our neighbours were Calabrians, immigrants to Rome because of the processes of the 'economic miracle', and, although now permanent residents of the city, anchored in their own pasts and sites of memory. So, when we left Rome for Cambridge in January 1968, they gave us what we were assured were some ground bones of Santa Rita to see us through what they feared would be a long and imponderable journey. Thus sustained, we reached Britain safely, carrying as much of a Rome, 'our' Rome, as we could.

Yet our story was not finished. Thereafter, the saint's magic, that of the city and its histories, a nagging sense that more was to be known and discovered (and the humdrum opportunities of academic life) drew us back to Rome time and again. There was always reason for research in places like the Farnesina or Ministry of Foreign Affairs north near the Foro italico, or the Archivio centrale dello stato south-west at EUR, each a building planned under Mussolini's dictatorship. Everywhere, further Fascist and other Romes awaited our notice. Everywhere, pasts and their rival interpretations bustled through the city's streets and sought our attention. Everywhere and at any time, the same opportunity to find living histories exists for those willing to open their eyes, ears and minds to Rome. Salutary journeys through this city are without number or end.

Study the historian before you begin to study the facts, E.H. Carr long ago advised to the continuing dismay of more worthy practitioners of our discipline and many of its paymasters who are sure that objectivity is the prime task of all research and the uncontested and uncontestable answer its final purpose.[7] Yet the message that I have heard in Rome, have practised throughout my career as a historian and have inscribed in the pages of this book is a more nuanced one. It is a story of how it is 'the fate of humankind to live in mixed tenses' or, with amended metaphor, of how, wherever humankind gathers, multiple pasts jostle and heave, sometimes with injurious effect, sometimes beneficially.

Any society with aspirations to democracy should therefore acknowledge the resultant existence of very many histories in its ranks, and accept that these rival pasts will frequently battle against each other. Paradoxically, historians best serve society when they actively join the contests, when they are willing humbly to praise and to blame, to give their own firm interpretations in work that is always, by definition, selective and so simultaneously both right and wrong. In this deep irony, for the history profession, 'truth' may be the greatest threat to the survival of living, breathing and wrangling pasts, records that can be read in more than one way.

Certainly, it is not novel to be told by some authoritative force that Roman history should be accorded a single meaning and that political disputation about it should cease. As this book has illustrated, Catholics, before the Enlightenment but with equal determination after it and with further impulse following the Italian national takeover of the city in 1870, tried to impose on the faithful a story of a holy city that, in its beauty, its sins and their remission, was eternal and transcendental. They treasured a place centred on the Church, the Papacy and God, perpetually and providentially moving along a predetermined passage to the future. In the mind of Benedict XVI, this integral Catholic account of history survives, even if today it is more likely to be emphatic about the Church's universality than to put excessive weight on its urban role in Rome.

Nationality was another prompt to the view that the 'people' were possessed of a long and singular history. In the Mazzinian dream, the united nation meant that the Rome of the Caesars and that of the popes had been succeeded in due time by the Rome of the Italian people. They were the new God and Mazzini was their prophet. In 1870 there was still some generosity and flexibility in this project, as Quintino Sella and his colleagues sought to imprint on the national capital a universal, modern and scientific character, hoping that, in its new sectors, it could rise to express liberty and fraternity, if not equality. Soon, however, nationalism hardened into imperialism and, with Italian participation in the First World War, Fascism. From 1922 a dictatorship which proclaimed itself totalitarian sought more strenuously than had its liberal predecessors to impose a single understanding of history on its subjects, with Rome being the fount and origin of its usable past. Now, those histories deemed useless were ruthlessly demolished, both physically, in the massive Fascist reconstruction of the city, and spiritually.

Yet, however profound and lasting was the impact of Mussolini's regime on the Rome whose architecture is still so evidently Fascist, the ambition to achieve a cultural revolution failed, at least partially because national and, especially, Catholic comprehensions of the past, present and future were not cancelled by Fascism. Another factor contributing to this partial failure of totalitarian control over the masses can be seen in an enduring process, little remarked by Fascist, Liberal and Catholic spokesmen, whereby the populace of Rome had continued to defend and nourish histories or memories of their own. Such 'people's histories' could be local, suburban, familial and gendered or they could blend these concerns in a variety of combinations. They could also reflect the many pasts of different Italian regions that were being imported by immigrants into the city during its rapid population growth between the wars. For every public oration that armed a resuscitated Julius Caesar in a national and Fascist cause, a heartfelt private prayer evoked Rita or some other saint of the 'Italies' whose aura still gleamed in the urban periphery. Furthermore, despite its aggression and xenophobia, Mussolini's dictatorship was not so reckless and rich that it could turn back tourists from Rome or expel foreigners who lived there, ensuring that non-Italian readings of the city's historical meaning lingered beneath the regime's bluster about totalitarian unity at all costs.

With the defeat of Fascism and admitting that the 'restored' Church of Pius XII had scarcely surrendered its hope in primacy and authority, the urge to represent history in only one key became less compelling. By 1960, as was manifest in the many ambiguities of the representation of the urban past during the XVII modern Olympiad, a soft and diffuse 'anti-Fascist' reading became the official line of the Italian Republic, with the dictatorship written off as a 'parenthesis' in city life, politically or socially or both. In the Ardeatine Caves memorial, Rome acquired a national monument to an alleged wartime story of the people of the city and the nation being victimised by cruel and alien Nazis. With the Republic thus uneasily girded by a (false) claim to telling historical truth in its capital, a brutal challenge was launched in the 1970s, when left and right terrorists, each sure that they could read the past correctly and hopeful that they might, through spreading their gospels, win the power to build a better future, brought murder (back) to the heart of the State.

Once again, however, the ambition of these latest terrible simplifiers to control the course of history failed. Thereafter, paradoxically, Rome lost much of its profile in discussion of what mattered in the past. Already in the 1950s the end of the age of European imperialism cut into the fame of the Caesars. Soon Asterix or the detective Marcus Didius Falco the Finder[8] or the Russell Crowe version of a stout general turned gladiator in the reign of Commodus began to carry more evident 'historical' weight than did Cato, Augustus and Marcus Aurelius.[9] Moreover, after the killing of Aldo Moro in May 1978, the meaning of Rome lost ground in other fields, too; history wars about it have become more likely to be local and specialist than dramatically to express the grand ideologies of universal debate for worldwide consumption. This diminution of the city reflected the inexorable spread of globalisation, as well as the 'end of history' and the pervasive view since the 1980s that the market commands, infallibly rigged out with virtue and reality. Here, too, then, was another 'truth', one that aggressively sought hegemony, although its most immediate effect for Rome was to cast it as just another urban centre, if one where histories, strewn prolifically and charmingly around, could sustain cheerful tourist 'infotainment' and 'sellebration' more readily and profitably than could be achieved in more austere and 'newer' metropolises. In the comprehension of the ruling entrepreneurs embodied in Silvio Berlusconi, Fascism, the Risorgimento, the Baroque, the Renaissance, the Middle Ages and the classical age melded into a happy agglomeration, images of which locals, Italians and international tourists from who knows where could buy as memory trinkets like any other.

Nonetheless, historical disputation was not quite over. Suddenly, an increasing multitude of immigrants, some legal, many 'illegal', originating from well beyond Italy and implacably driven by the irruption of globalisation into their own societies, took up residence in Rome, adding further to the city's historical mix. Rome had long possessed English, French, German, American, gypsy and many other 'foreign' tourist and traveller histories, just as it housed histories from the Italies. Now it acquired pasts, presents and futures that

36. Multilingual and multicultural manifesto for immigrant strike against Roman racism and continued neo-Fascism of Berlusconi national and Alemanno communal governments, Esquiline, 1 March 2010.

were Chinese, Bangladeshi, Philippine, Eritrean, Polish, Romanian, Albanian and Iranian. To the Catholic, Jewish, Waldensian and other Protestant Roman histories were added Islamic, Hindu and Buddhist ones. 'Multiculturalism' was something that the city shared with every other urban centre of the developed world and, in any case, cities had always, even in classical times, been places of immigration. But until the 1980s the different pasts of the city ensured the Roman mix was peculiar and, therefore, Roman.

Presently, too, rival interpretations of historical meaning are now advocated in discussions that ring with Roman tones. Has the Church a special knowledge that passes all other understanding and will not fade away? Should the Italian nation impose a stronger national identity on its capital (and country) with a reworked and less critical national history syllabus and other didactic measures designed to suture its 'divided memory'? Do ex- or post-Fascists retain views on public order and the need to stifle ethnic cultural diversity that are again relevant? Can the left find any residual guidance in anti-Fascism or other humane interpretations of the course of recent or past events? In the present, too, arguments about the past and the future, and the relationship between the two, cry out for attention.

These conflicts, like all disputes, doubtless need scrutiny. Yet, as my charting of Rome and its histories over the last two centuries has time and again demonstrated, age has regularly refurbished and custom enlivened the city's infinite variety. No doubt, at first sight, Rome is anything but a redoubt of democracy. The city earned its initial fame as the fount of a republic and then empire that warred across its known world, enslaving its victims, where it did not perpetrate what today would be damned as genocide. This brutal state was replaced by an authoritarian Church, determined for ever to preach a mystical or irrational religion, which, even today, is no fan of democracy and free debate, whether in its administrative structures or its spiritual values. Eventually, the papal rulers of Rome were ousted by an Italian nation, itself by definition, like all nations, based on the historical lie that it was old and not new, and had fully united its in fact divergent peoples. In Italy's case, a liberal nation proved too difficult an oxymoron to be sustained and, after less than sweeping victory in the First World War, was replaced by a Fascist and 'totalitarian' dictatorship. In their different ways, ancient, Catholic, Italian and Fascist Romans, in other words, all sought to impose just one history on the city, and so to be 'terrible simplifiers' of successive contemporary understandings of the past. Thereafter, following Mussolini's defeat and death, the new Republic remained uncertain about what message to find in its capital city to a degree that was replicated by few other states. In response to this perceived weakness and confusion, the 'corruption' of the Republic, terrorists of the left, neo-Fascists and resurgent nationalists before long made new attempts to seize the city's meaning for themselves and only for themselves.

Yet, despite the repeated efforts over two millennia of history warriors of this or that crusading persuasion to arm themselves with a single 'true' history, the multiplicity of Roman pasts has frustrated and defeated them, whether these pasts are of the top people, makers of the cityscape and forgers of its official story, or of the (changing) ordinary peoples of the city, finding identity in their families or, if they are immigrants, in pasts imported into Rome. The city remains a wonderful site of memory and heritage, myth and histories, a place from where to understand that difference, mutability and political contestation are the beginning of wisdom and that, now more than ever, many pasts compete for good and ill with many presents and many futures in what a democracy prefers to be civil debate. In the highways and byways of this city, the ghosts of rich and poor, men and women, Jews and Christians, Muslims and Buddhists, anti-clericals and atheists, Roman-born and immigrant, Romulus and Remus, the brothers Gracchi, Augustus Caesar, Gallienus, Cola di Rienzo, Petrarch, Michelangelo, Queen Christina, Bernini, Pauline Bonaparte, Pope Leo XII, Anita Garibaldi, Ferdinand Gregorovius, Augustus Hare, Ernesto Nathan, Marcello Piacentini, Giuseppe Bottai, Pope Pius XII, Maria Goretti, the Rutelli family, and innumerable others still stir restlessly in the hope that their echoing stories may again be plumbed for contemporary lessons. The project to write, debate and reckon with the histories of the Romes remains an eternal one and Roman pasts still combine local, national, religious, lay and global import.

NOTES

———— ✳ ————

Preface

1. E. Gibbon, *Autobiography* (London: Oxford University Press, 1959), pp. 158–60.
2. P.B. Craddock, *Young Edward Gibbon: Gentleman of Letters* (Baltimore, MD: Johns Hopkins University Press, 1982), pp. 222–3.
3. C.I. Hemans, *Historic and Monumental Rome: A Handbook for the Students of Classical and Christian Antiquity in the Italian Capital* (London: Williams and Norgate, 1874), p. 251.
4. S. Hornblower and A. Spawforth (eds), *The Oxford Classical Dictionary*, rev. edn (Oxford University Press, 2003), p. 858.
5. M. Cima, 'Gli *Horti Liciani*: una residenza imperiale della tarda antichità' in M. Cima and E. La Rocca (eds), *Horti romani: atti del convegno internazionale, Rome, 4–6 maggio 1995* (Rome: 'L'Erma' di Bretschneider, 1998), p. 429.
6. For the origins and purpose of Pieter Geyl's aphorism, see R.J.B. Bosworth, *Explaining Auschwitz and Hiroshima: History Writing and the Second World War 1945–1990* (London: Routledge, 1993), p. 11.

Introduction

1. O. Pamuk, *Istanbul: Memories of a City* (London: Faber and Faber, 2005), p. 99.
2. M. Mazower, *Salonica: City of Ghosts: Christians, Muslims and Jews 1430–1950* (London: HarperCollins, 2004), p. 5.
3. G. Heiken, R. Funiciello and D. de Rita, *The Seven Hills of Rome: A Geological Tour of the Eternal City* (Princeton, NJ: Princeton University Press, 2005), pp. vii, 53.
4. A. Guidi, 'Nationalism without a nation: the Italian case' in M. Diaz-Andreu and T. Champion (eds), *Nationalism and Archaeology in Europe* (Boulder, CO: Westview Press, 1996), p. 109.
5. S. Freud, *Civilization and its Discontents* (New York: Dover, 1994), pp. 5–6. The familiar name of the sometime Flavian amphitheatre goes back not to classical times but to the venerable Bede. See M. Di Macco, *Il Colosseo: funzione simbolica, storica, urbana* (Rome: Bulzoni, 1971), p. 30.
6. S. Freud, *The interpretation of Dreams*, ed. J. Strachey, A. Tyson and A. Richards (Harmondsworth: Penguin, 1991), p. 633.
7. For the period use of this title, see J.C. Stobart, MA, *The Grandeur that was Rome: A Survey of Roman Culture and Civilisation* (London: Sidgwick and Jackson, 1912), a book that was many times republished.

8. E. Murray, *Fellini the Artist* (Bembridge: BCW Publishing, 1976), pp. 202–3.
9. E. Theodorakopoulos, 'The sites and sights of Rome in Fellini's films' in D.H.J. Larmour and D. Spencer (eds), *The Sites of Rome: Time, Space, Memory* (Oxford University Press, 2007), p. 353.
10. D. MacCannell, *The Tourist: A New Theory of the Leisure Class*, rev. edn (Berkeley: University of California Press, 1999), pp. 3, 8.
11. R.M. Dainotto, 'The Gubbio papers: historic centers in the age of the economic miracle', *Journal of Modern Italian Studies*, 8, 2003, pp. 68–9.
12. whc.unesco.org/en/list, accessed 14 July 2010.
13. D. Lowenthal, *Possessed by the Past: The Heritage Crusade and the Spoils of History* (New York: Free Press, 1996), p. 11.
14. Dainotto, 'The Gubbio papers', p. 76.
15. Lowenthal, *Possessed by the Past*, p. 121.
16. Ammianus Marcellinus, *The Later Roman Empire (AD 354–378)* (ed. A. Wallace-Hadrill) (Harmondsworth: Penguin, 2004), pp. 101–2.
17. P. Nora, 'Between memory and history: Les lieux de mémoire', *Representations*, 26, 1989, pp. 8–9. For his full version, see *Les lieux de mémoire* (Paris: Gallimard, 1984–6). It is available in English as *Realms of Memory: Rethinking the French Past*, 3 vols (New York: Columbia University Press, 1996–8).
18. For Italy more generally, see M. Isnenghi (ed.), *I luoghi della memoria*, 3 vols (Bari: Laterza, 1996–7).
19. A. Caracciolo, 'Roma' in M. Isnenghi (ed.), *I luoghi della memoria: simboli e miti dell'Italia unita* (Bari: Laterza, 1996), p. 172.
20. J.E. Young, *The Texture of Memory: Holocaust Memorials and Meanings* (New Haven, CT: Yale University Press, 1993), p. 2.
21. For special complaint, see E. Galli Della Loggia, *La morte della patria: la crisi dell'idea della nazione tra Resistenza, antifascismo e Repubblica* (Laterza: Bari, 1996). For more general placement, see J. Foot, *Fratture d'Italia: Da Caporetto al G8 di Genova. La memoria divisa del paese* (Milan: Rizzoli, 2009).
22. For this useful definition of the purpose of a professional historian, see S. Fitzpatrick, 'Afterword: revisionism revisited', *Russian Review*, 45, 1986, p. 412.
23. J.H.S. McGregor, *Rome from the Ground Up* (Cambridge, MA: Belknap Press, 2005), pp. 1–3.
24. T. Webb, ' "City of the soul": English romantic travellers in Rome' in M. Liversidge and C. Edwards (eds), *Imagining Rome: British Artists and Rome in the Nineteenth Century* (London: Bristol City Council in association with Merrell Holberton, 1996), p. 29.
25. P. Bondanella, *The Eternal City: Roman Images in the Modern World* (Chapel Hill: University of North Carolina Press, 1987), p. xiii.
26. C. Edwards, 'Introduction: shadows and fragments' in C. Edwards (ed.), *Roman Presences: Receptions of Rome in European Culture, 1789–1945* (Cambridge University Press, 1999), p. 3.
27. K. Tribe, 'Introduction' to R. Koselleck, *Futures Past: On the Semantics of Historical Time* (New York: Columbia University Press, 2004), p. xviii.
28. *La Repubblica*, 11, 12 June 2009.
29. For introduction, see A.R. Birley, *The African Emperor: Septimius Severus* (London: Batsford, 1988).
30. For a recent positive assessment of the architecture of the arch, see A. Claridge, *Rome: An Oxford Archaeological Guide* (Oxford University Press, 1998), pp. 75–6; Claridge notes 'artistically, the Arch's reputation is low. Actually, the carving was not at all bad.'
31. *Corriere della Sera*, 12 June 2009. Gaddafi also indicated that he was no unalloyed fan of liberal democracy, dismissing 'party rule', often associated in contemporary Italy with the corrupt dealings exposed in the 1990s during 'Tangentopoli', as 'democracy's abortion'.

1. Rome and the Romes across time

1. L. Sterne, *The Life and Opinions of Tristram Shandy: Gentleman* (London: Dent, 1912), p. 28.
2. Since the house was thought to have arrived by air, the Church in 1920 deemed it appropriate to make the Madonna of Loreto the patron saint of airmen. See M. Warner, *Alone of All Her Sex: The Myth and Cult of the Virgin Mary* (London: Vintage, 2000), p. 296.
3. S. Bing, *Rome, Inc. The Rise and Fall of the First Multinational Corporation* (New York: W.W. Norton, 2006), pp. xv; 9–10.
4. www.menudiroma.it/ita/locali/scheda.aspx?IDLocale=194, accessed 13 July 2010.
5. Ancient Romans may have consumed pizzas of some kind. However, the word is first recorded in medieval Latin just before the end of the first millennium CE, and the modern fast food probably originated in Naples in the nineteenth century. One of the food's commonest forms, the Pizza Margherita, was named in 1889 for Queen Margherita, wife of Umberto I, second king of Italy. See G. Riley, *The Oxford Companion to Italian Food* (Oxford University Press, 2007), pp. 410–11.
6. E. Hobsbawm and T. Ranger (eds), *The Invention of Tradition* (Cambridge University Press, 1983).
7. P. Vergilius Maro, *The Aeneid* (ed. W.F. Jackson Knight) (Harmondsworth: Penguin, 1956), p. 36.
8. J.C. Eustace, *A Tour Through Italy* (London: J. Mawman, 1813), vol. I, p. 455.
9. G. and V. Lattanzi and P. Isaja, *Pane e lavoro: storia di una colonia cooperativa: i braccianti romagnoli e la bonifica di Ostia* (Venice: Marsilio, 1986).
10. For introduction, see A. Birley, *Hadrian: The Restless Emperor* (London: Routledge, 1997). For our world, Hadrian's seemingly homosexual relationship with a beautiful young man named Antinous is of particular interest.
11. W.L. MacDonald and J.A. Pinto, *Hadrian's Villa and its Legacy* (New Haven, CT: Yale University Press, 1995), p. 322.
12. Despite trumpeted Fascist drainage work on the Pontine marshes, the curse of malaria was not overcome until the arrival of the Americans with DDT in and after 1944. See F.M. Snowden, ' "Fields of death": malaria in Italy, 1861–1962', *Modern Italy*, 4, 1999, pp. 25–57.
13. E. Sereni, *Il capitalismo nelle campagne (1860–1900)*, rev. edn (Turin: Einaudi, 1968), p. 172.
14. T. Ashby, *The Roman Campagna in Classical Times* (London: E. Benn, 1927), p. 20.
15. An English expert was delighted to report in 1930 that, although the Aurelian Walls were 'a real hindrance to traffic', the Fascist government had praiseworthily decided to preserve and restore them in grand part. 'The Wall is safe. It is breached, but not razed; and further decay is satisfactorily arrested.' I.A. Richmond, *The city walls of imperial Rome: An Account of its Architectural Development from Aurelian to Narses* (Oxford: Clarendon, 1930), p. 5.
16. J. Hook, *The Sack of Rome 1527*, rev. edn (Houndmills: Palgrave Macmillan, 2004), p. 27; cf. the brilliant, if self-boosting, period depiction in B. Cellini, *The Autobiography* (ed. G. Bull) (Harmondsworth: Penguin, 1999).
17. Hook, *The Sack of Rome*, pp. 186; 289.
18. W.L. Vance, *America's Rome: vol. I: Classical Rome* (New Haven, CT: Yale University Press, 1989), p. 155.
19. C. Jones, *Paris: Biography of a City* (London: Allen Lane, 2004), p. 27.
20. *Ibid.*, p. xvii.
21. M. Diaz-Andreu and T. Champion, 'Nationalism and archaeology in Europe: an introduction', in their *Nationalism and Archaeology in Europe* (Boulder, CO: Westview Press, 1996), pp. 7–8.
22. See, for example, the images made available in R. Coates-Stephens, *Immagini e memoria: Rome in the photographs of Father Peter Paul Mackey 1890–1901* (Rome: BSR, 2009), pp. 22; 132–5.

23. *Ibid.*, p. 22.
24. B. Painter, *Mussolini's Rome: Rebuilding the Eternal City* (New York: Palgrave Macmillan, 2005), pp. 132–3.
25. A. Claridge, *Rome: An Oxford Archaeological Guide* (Oxford University Press, 1998), pp. 294–6.
26. *The Protestant Cemetery in Rome: The Cemetery of Artists and Poets* (Rome: Grafica San Giovanni, 1986), p. 7.
27. H. Sienkiewicz, *Quo vadis?* (London: Dent, 1941).
28. Foodies may note that opposite the church of Domine Quo Vadis is the Trattoria Priscilla, which, like *Allo sbarco di Enea*, lures its customers with 'history'. Its website (www.diningcity.com/rome/ristorantetrattoriapriscilla21/index_eng.jsp, accessed 13 July 2010) notes that it is 'housed in a sixteenth century building which once was a place to exchange horses. This trattoria has been run by the same family for the past 120 years. It is attached to the monumental tomb of Priscilla, erected by her loving husband Tito Flavio Abascanto, a freed man from the time of the Roman Emperor Domitian. The tomb once was adorned with bronze statues which have long ago disappeared, but the tomb remains an impressive sight.'
29. For a review, see J.M.C. Toynbee, 'The shrine of St Peter and its setting', *Journal of Roman Studies*, 43, 1953, pp. 1–26.
30. For further introduction to the Constantinian church, see J. Lees-Milne, *Saint Peter's: The Story of Saint Peter's Basilica in Rome* (London: Hamish Hamilton, 1967), pp. 77–100.
31. *Ibid.*, p. 113.
32. *Ibid.*, p. 82.
33. P. Llewellyn, *Rome in the Dark Ages* (London: Constable, 1993), p. 192.
34. Cited *ibid.*, p. 175.
35. F.M. Nicholls (ed.), *Mirabilia Urbis Romae: The Marvels of Rome or a Picture of the Golden City: An English Version of the Medieval Guide-Book with a Supplement of Illustrative Material and Notes* (London: Ellis and Elvey, 1889), pp. 67; 125.
36. *ibid.*, pp. 139–40.
37. D. Marr (ed.), *Patrick White's Letters* (Sydney: Random House, 1994), p. 384. For a more positive view, see A. Blunt (ed.), *Guide to Baroque Rome* (London: Granada, 1982).
38. A. Giardina and A. Vauchez, *Il mito di Roma da Carlo Magno a Mussolini* (Bari: Laterza, 2000), p. 15.
39. C.T. Davis, 'Rome and Babylon in Dante' in P.A. Ramsay (ed.), *Rome in the Renaissance: The City and the Myth* (Binghamton, CT: Center for Medieval and Early Renaissance Studies, 1982), p. 20.
40. T.J. Dandelet, *Spanish Rome 1500–1700* (New Haven, CT: Yale University Press, 2001), p. 44.
41. J. Evelyn, *Diary* (ed. W. Bray) (London: J.M. Dent, 1911), p. 174.
42. R.J.B. Bosworth, *Mussolini* (London: Arnold, 2002), p. 332.
43. A.J.C. Hare, *Walks in Rome* (London: George Allen, n.d.), vol. II, p. 8.
44. P. Della Pergola, *The Borghese Gallery in Rome* (Rome: Istituto poligrafico dello stato, 1970), p. 3.
45. S. Pasquali, 'Roma antica: memorie materiali, storia e mito' in G. Ciucci (ed.), *Roma moderna* (Bari: Laterza, 2002), pp. 341–2.
46. For introduction, see H. Hibbard, *Bernini* (Harmondsworth: Penguin, 1965).
47. J.A. Pinto, *The Trevi Fountain* (New Haven, CT: Yale University Press, 1986), p. 237.
48. *Ibid.*, p. 1.
49. For background, see E. Bruscolini (ed.), *Rome in Cinema Between Reality and Fiction* (Rome: Centro sperimentale di cinematografia, 2000).
50. Fellini would claim that his purpose in the movie was a satirical study of the emptiness of life, although he may have been pleased that early screenings in 1959 already brought down papal anathemas on it. See P. Leprohon, *The Italian Cinema* (London: Secker and

Warburg, 1972), pp. 167–9. For further exploration, see E. Murray, *Fellini the Artist* (Bembridge: BCW Publishing, 1977), pp. 111–33.

51. Lucius Annaeus Seneca, *Dialogues and Letters* (ed. C.D.N. Costa) (Harmondsworth: Penguin, 1997), p. 8.
52. SVIMEZ, *Un secolo di statistiche italiane: Nord e Sud* (Rome: Istituto poligrafico dello stato, 1961), p. 1037.
53. J.S. Ackerman, 'The planning of Renaissance Rome, 1450–1580' in Ramsay (ed.), *Rome in the Renaissance*, p. 6.
54. L. Nussdorfer, *Civic Politics in the Rome of Urban VIII* (Princeton, NJ: Princeton University Press, 1992), p. 32.
55. C.M. Travaglini, 'Economia e finanza' in Ciucci (ed.), *Roma moderna*, p. 80.
56. Hook, *The sack of Rome*, p. 66.
57. A. Majanlahti, *The families who made Rome: A History and a Guide* (London: Chatto and Windus, 2005), p. 3.
58. C. Roth, *A History of the Jews of Italy* (Philadelphia, PA: Jewish Publication Society of America, 1946), p. 78.
59. *Ibid.*, p. 330.
60. *Ibid.*, p. 385.
61. For my own introduction to these matters, see R.J.B. Bosworth, *Nationalism* (Harlow: Pearson, 2007).

2. Rome, revolution and history

1. *Il Museo Napoleonico: guida alla visita* (Rome: Gangemi editore, 2004).
2. *Ibid.*, p. 10.
3. B. Mussolini, *Opera omnia* (ed. E. and D. Susmel) (Florence: La Fenice, 1956), vol. XXI, p. 433.
4. As did his French enemies. Chateaubriand concluded that 'he took after his Italian ancestors'. F.-R. de Chateaubriand, *The Memoirs* (ed. P. Baldrick) (Harmondsworth: Penguin, 1965), p. 327.
5. D. Mack Smith, *Mussolini* (London: Weidenfeld and Nicolson, 1981), p. 106.
6. For the English adaptation, see B. Mussolini and G. Forzano, *Napoleon: The Hundred Days* (London: Sidgwick and Jackson, 1932).
7. Mussolini, *Opera omnia*, vol. XXI, p. 425.
8. M. Caffiero, 'La construzione della religione repubblicana a Roma nel 1798–99: l'uso politico della storia antica', *Roma contemporanea*, 9, 2001, p. 48.
9. D.H.J. Larmour and D. Spencer, 'Introduction – Roma, Recepta: A Topography of the Imagination' in D.H.J. Larmour and D. Spencer (eds), *The Sites of Rome: Time, Space, Memory* (Oxford University Press, 2007), p. 57.
10. C.P. Murphy, *The Pope's Daughter* (London: Faber and Faber, 2004), p. 114.
11. J. Burckhardt, *The Civilization of the Renaissance in Italy: An Essay* (New York: Mentor, 1960), p. 149. Burckhardt's book was first published in 1860, coinciding with the Italian Risorgimento.
12. See B. Anderson, *Imagined Communities: Reflections on the Origin and Spread of Nationalism* (London: Verso, 1983); E.J. Hobsbawm, *Nations and Nationalism Since 1780: Programme, Myth, Reality* (Cambridge University Press, 1990); E. Hobsbawm and T. Ranger (eds), *The Invention of Tradition* (Cambridge University Press, 1983).
13. A. Grafton, *The Footnote: A Curious History* (Cambridge, MA: Harvard University Press, 1997), p. 121.
14. For exploration, see R. Bizzocchi, *Genealogie incredibili: scritti di storia nell'Europa moderna* (Bologna: il Mulino, 1995).
15. B.A. Naddeo, 'Cultural capitals and cosmopolitanism in eighteenth-century Italy: the historiography and Italy on the Grand Tour', *Journal of Modern Italian Studies*, 10, 2005, p. 184.

16. S. Pasquali, 'Roma antica: memorie materiale, storia e mito' in G. Ciucci (ed.), *Roma moderna* (Bari: Laterza, 2002), p. 332.

17. J. Black, *Italy and the Grand Tour* (New Haven, CT: Yale University Press, 2003), p. 157.

18. P. Ayres, *Classical Culture and the Idea of Rome in Eighteenth-Century England* (Cambridge University Press, 1997), pp. 64–8; 83.

19. For introduction, see J. Wilton-Ely, *The Mind and Art of Giovanni Battista Piranesi* (London: Thames and Hudson, 1978).

20. Black, *Italy and the Grand Tour*, p. 194.

21. O. Chadwick, *The Popes and the European Revolution* (Oxford: Clarendon, 1981), p. 27.

22. A. Grafton, 'The Renaissance' in R. Jenkyns (ed.), *The Legacy of Rome: A New Appraisal* (Oxford University Press, 1992), p. 106.

23. C.M.S. Johns, *Papal Art and Cultural Politics: Rome in the Age of Clement XI* (Cambridge University Press, 1993), pp. 117–21. He also promoted work on San Clemente. The first Pope Clement (*c.*91–*c.*101 CE) had been the third or fourth successor of St Peter and a figure with reasonable claims to historicity.

24. *Ibid.*, p. 37.

25. *Ibid.*, pp. 171–3.

26. S. Ditchfield, 'Leggere e vedere Roma come icona culturale (1500–1800 *circa*)' in L. Fiorani and A. Prosperi (eds), *Roma: la città del papa: vita civile e religiosa dal giubileo di Bonifacio VIII al giubileo di papa Wojtyla* (Turin: Einaudi, 2000), p. 49.

27. R.T. Ridley, *The Eagle and the Spade: Archaeology in Rome During the Napoleonic Era* (Cambridge University Press, 1992), pp. 31–7.

28. J.C. Eustace, *A tour through Italy exhibiting a view of its antiquities and monuments particularly as they are the objects of classical interest and elucidation with an account of the present state of its cities and towns and occasional observations on the recent spoliations of the French* (London: J. Mawman, 1813), vol. I, p. 218. Eustace estimated that the 'real' Forum lay 14 feet below the present site.

29. H. Marucchi, *The Roman Forum and the Palatine According to the Latest Discoveries* (Rome: Desclée-Lefebvre, 1906), pp. 14–20.

30. C. Pietrangeli (ed.), *Scavi e scoperte di antichità sotto il pontificato di Pio VI* (Rome: Studi Romani editore, 1983), p. 29.

31. Anon., *Monumenti antichi inediti ovvero notizie sulle antichità e belle arti di Roma per l'anno MDCLXXXIX* (Rome: Stamperia Pagliarini, 1789), pp. 29–30.

32. Pietrangeli (ed.), *Scavi e scoperte di antichità*, pp. 16; 29–30.

33. J.M. Robinson, *Cardinal Consalvi 1757–1824* (London: Bodley Head, 1987), p. 22.

34. H. Gross, *Rome in the Age of the Enlightenment: The Post-Tridentine Syndrome and the Ancien Regime* (Cambridge University Press, 1990), p. 311. Visconti was destined to be recorded in the city by the naming of a high school after him after the Italian occupation of Rome in 1870. The Visconti *liceo* was placed in the Collegio Romano, an edifice that had been built in the 1550s and reconstructed in the 1580s to train the first Jesuits. They were expelled from the place after their official suppression in Rome in 1773, as well as during the revolutionary era. The Jesuits only returned in 1824 under Pope Leo XII. There was another expulsion during the 1848–9 revolution, with the edifice being partially burned, but the Collegio resumed its teaching role in 1850. The building was again formally seized by the State in 1873, with room found in the vast structure for a 'national' library, an astronomical observatory and a museum, as well as the *liceo*. But the high school, expanded in 1890 to include a female section, gave the greatest lustre to the city, numbering among its pupils Pope Pius XII, the Jewish atomic physicist Enrico Fermi, the crafty and durable Catholic politician Giulio Andreotti, and the actor Claudia Koll.

35. *Ibid.*, p. 314.

36. See C. Roth, *The History of the Jews of Italy* (Philadelphia, PA: Jewish Publication Society of America, 1946), pp. 414–15; 418. D.I. Kertzer, *Unholy War: The Vatican's Role in the Rise of Modern Anti-Semitism* (Houndmills: Macmillan, 2001), p. 26.

37. J.W. Goethe, *Italian Journey* (Harmondsworth: Penguin, 1962), p. 128.
38. *Ibid.*, pp. 126; 137–8; 148.
39. *Ibid.*, pp. 133; 154.
40. G. Casanova, *History of My Life* (ed. W.R. Trask) (London: Longmans, 1967), vol. I, pp. 257; 260.
41. F. Bartolini, *Rivali d'Italia: Roma e Milano dal Settecento a oggi* (Bari: Laterza, 2006), p. 5.
42. C. Elling, *Rome: The Biography of its Architecture from Bernini to Thorvoldsen* (Tübingen: Ernst Wasmuth, 1975), pp. 489–90; A. Groppi, 'A matter of fact rather than principle: work and property in papal Rome (eighteenth–nineteenth centuries)', *Journal of Modern Italian Studies*, 7, 2002, pp. 37–55.
43. V.E. Giuntella, *Roma nel Settecento* (Bologna: Cappelli, 1971), pp. 68–9.
44. M. Andrieux, *Daily Life in Papal Rome in the Eighteenth Century* (London: George Allen and Unwin, 1968), pp. 81; 124.
45. *Ibid.*, pp. 70–1.
46. Gross, *Rome in the Age of the Enlightenment*, pp. 270–1.
47. O. Chadwick, *The Popes and the European Revolution*, p. 67.
48. P. Partner, 'Il mondo della curia e i suoi rapporti con la città' in Fiorani and Prosperi (eds), *Roma: la città del papa*, p. 226.
49. Gross, *Rome in the Age of the Enlightenment*, pp. 220; 228; Cardinal Wiseman, *Recollections of the Last Four Popes and of Rome in their Times* (London: Hurst and Blackett, 1858), pp. 6–7.
50. Andrieux, *Daily Life in Papal Rome*, p. 103.
51. Elling, *Rome*, p. 53.
52. Gross, *Rome in the Age of the Enlightenment*, p. 193.
53. Elling, *Rome*, p. 491.
54. *Ibid.*, pp. 39–40.
55. Cardinal Wiseman, *Recollections of the Last Four Popes*, pp. 92–3.
56. K. Marx, 'The Eighteenth Brumaire of Louis Bonaparte' in his *Surveys from Exile: Political Writings vol. 2* (ed. D. Fernbach) (Harmondsworth: Penguin, 1973), pp. 146–7.
57. Ridley, *The Eagle and the Spade*, p. 1.
58. A. Giardina and A. Vauchez, *Il mito di Roma da Carlo Magno a Mussolini* (Bari: Laterza, 2000).
59. Ridley, *The Eagle and the Spade*, p. 2.
60. Giardina and Vauchez, *Il mito di Roma*, p. 147.
61. C. Jones, *Paris: Biography of a City* (London: Allen Lane, 2004), p. 292.
62. C. von Metternich, *The Autobiography, 1773–1815* (Welwyn Garden City: Ravenhall Books, 2004), p. 133.
63. C. Springer, *The Marble Wilderness: Ruins and Representation in Italian Romanticism, 1775–1850* (Cambridge University Press, 1987), p. 17.
64. Robinson, *Cardinal Consalvi*, p. 35.
65. G. Pignatelli, *Aspetti della propaganda cattolica a Roma da Pio VI a Leone XII* (Rome: Istituto per la storia del Risorgimento italiano, 1974), p. 137.
66. *Ibid.*, pp. 174–6.
67. S. Foa, *Gli ebrei nel Risorgimento italiano* (Assisi: Beniamino Carucci Editore, 1978), p. 16.
68. R. De Felice, *Italia giacobina* (Naples: Edizioni Scientifiche Italiane, n.d.), p. 299. For a fuller account, see M. Cattaneo, *Gli occhi di Maria sulla rivoluzione: 'miracoli' a Roma e nello Stato della Chiesa (1796–1797)*, (Rome: Istituto nazionale di studi romani, 1995).
69. Pignatelli, *Aspetti della propaganda cattolica*, pp. 186–8.
70. A. Cretoni, *roma giacobina: storia della Repubblica romana del 1798–99* (Bari: Istituto di studi romani Edizioni Scientifiche Italiane), pp. 11–24.
71. *Ibid.*, pp. 24–5.
72. *Ibid.*, pp. 33–4.

73. G.A. Sala, *Diario romano degli anni 1798–99* (ed. V.E. Giuntella) (Rome: Biblioteca Vallicelliana, 1980), vol. I, p. 15.
74. For a modern edition, see Marcus Aurelius, *Meditations* (ed. M. Staniforth) (Harmondsworth: Penguin, 1964). Earlier, it had been claimed that he had foreseen the triumph of Christianity.
75. On 14 January 1900, Giacomo Puccini, the self-obsessed Tuscan composer, premiered *Tosca* at the Costanzi theatre in Rome, with a setting in the city one hundred years earlier and a politics of virtuous liberal anti-clericalism. By then scarcely linked to the preoccupations of contemporary Italians, *Tosca* was one of the few operas to be set in Rome. For a romantic recent evocation, mainly of 1799–1800, see S.V. Nicassio, *Tosca's Rome: The Play and the Opera in Historical Perspective* (University of Chicago Press, 1999).
76. Cretoni, *Roma giacobina*, pp. 45–9.
77. W. Doyle, *The Oxford History of the French Revolution* (Oxford University Press, 1990), p. 362.
78. Sala, *Diario romano*, vol. I, p. 39. They offered passers-by refreshments, catering thus for the body and the soul.
79. Cretoni, *Roma giacobina*, pp. 88–91. The ghetto was again assaulted in November 1798; Sala, *Diario romano*, vol. I, p. 22.
80. Robinson, *Cardinal Consalvi*, pp. 56–7.
81. Eustace, *A Tour Through Italy*, vol. I, p. 277.
82. Sala, *Diario romano*, vol. I, p. 116.
83. M.P. Donato, 'Roma in rivoluzione (1798, 1848, 1870)' in Fiorani and Prosperi (eds), *Roma: la città del papa*, pp. 910–11.
84. Sala, *Diario romano*, vol. I, pp. 43–4.
85. A. Galimberti, *Memorie dell'occupazione francese in Roma dal 1798 alla fine del 1802* (ed. L. Topi) (Rome: Istituto nazionale di studi romani, 2004), vol. I, p. 36.
86. R. De Felice (ed.), *I giornali giacobini italiani* (Milan: Feltrinelli, 1962), p. 24.
87. M.G. Sassoli, 'La città della rappresentazione: le feste e gli spettacoli', in Ciucci (ed.), *Roma moderna*, p. 212.
88. De Felice (ed.), *I giornali giacobini italiani*, p. 254.
89. Cretoni, *Roma giacobina*, p. 114. It was to be charged with the power of the archaeological discoveries. In the rhetoric of the moment, destined not to last, 'Rome' was treated as a 'Nation'.
90. *Ibid.*, pp. 333–44.
91. For some of the economic detail, see R. De Felice, *La rendita dei beni nazionali nella Repubblica romana del 1798–99* (Rome: Edizioni di Storia e Letteratura, 1960).
92. P.-L. Courier, *Lettere dall'Italia (1799–1812): aggiuntavi la polemica per la macchia d'inchiostro sul codice Laurenziano con un fac-simile della macchia* (Lanciano: R. Carabba editore, 1910), p. 31.
93. G. Ciucci, 'Introduzione' to Ciucci (ed), *Roma moderna*, p. xxii. It stayed at that level from 1800 to 1804.
94. Sala, *Diario romano*, vol. I, p. 127. He was talking about the sacking of the Villa Albani, great repository of the products of digs over the last half-century.
95. Cretoni, *Roma giacobina*, pp. 354–9.
96. Galimberti, *Memorie dell'occupazione francese*, vol. I, p. 392.
97. P.P. Racioppi, 'La Repubblica romana e le Belle Arti (1798–99): Disperzione e conservazione del patrimonio artistico', *Roma moderna e contemporanea*, 9, 2001, p. 207.
98. E. Vercesi, *Pio VII: Napoleone e la restaurazione* (Turin: Società Editrice Internazionale, 1933), p. 140.
99. For a contemporary account, see E. Guidoni, *L'urbanistica di Roma tra miti e progetti* (Bari: Laterza, 1990), pp. 210–17.
100. F. Bartoccini, *Roma nell'Ottocento: il tramonto della 'Città Santa', nascita di una capitale* (Bologna: Cappelli, 1985), p. 102; Ridley, *The Eagle and the Spade*, p. x. See

also P.-M.-C. de Tournon, *Études statistiques sur Rome et la partie occidentale des états romaines* (Paris: Libraire de Firmin Didot Frères, 1855).

101. C. Brice, 'La Roma dei "Francesi": una modernizzazione imposta' in Fiorani and Prosperi (eds), *Roma: la città del papa*, p. 368.
102. Springer, *The Marble Wilderness*, p. 84.
103. F. Lemmi, *Roma nell'impero napoleonico* (Florence: R. Deputazione di Storia Patria, 1916), pp. 13–14.
104. M.A. Finocchiaro, *Retrying Galileo 1663–1992* (Berkeley: University of California Press, 2005), p. 176.
105. Eustace, *A Tour Through Italy*, vol. II, p. 131.
106. M. Broers, *The Napoleonic Empire in Italy, 1796–1814: Cultural Imperialism in a European Context?* (Houndmills: Palgrave Macmillan, 2005), pp. 162; 298.
107. Madame de Staël, *Corinne, or Italy* (ed. S. Raphael) (Oxford University Press, 1998), p. 72.

3. A Holy City: its past and future restored?

1. For background, see M. Ozouf, *Festivals and the French Revolution* (Cambridge, MA: Harvard University Press, 1988), and R. Gildea, *The Past in French History* (New Haven, CT: Yale University Press, 1994).
2. Each was an immigrant to Rome, Targhini being a cook from Brescia and Montanari a Romagnole doctor. F. Bartoccini, *Roma nell'Ottocento: il tramonto della 'Città Santa', nascita di una capitale* (Bologna: Cappelli, 1985), p. 25.
3. M. D'Azeglio, *Things I Remember* (ed. E.R. Vincent) (London: Oxford University Press, 1966), p. 258. F. Dostoevsky would provide the most memorable portrait of revolutionary deviation in his novel *The Devils*.
4. J.N.D. Kelly, *The Oxford Dictionary of the Popes* (Oxford University Press, 1986), p. 306. There is no serious scholarly study of Leo's career.
5. See A. Caracciolo, *Roma capitale: dal Risorgimento alla crisi dello stato liberale* (Rome: Riuniti, 1974), pp. 92–7.
6. L. Pianciani, *La Roma dei papi* (Rome: Editore Edoardo Perino, 1891–2), vol. I, p. 248; vol. II, pp. 46; 96; 131–4.
7. Kelly, *The Oxford Dictionary of the Popes*, p. 209.
8. R.G. Musto, *Apocalypse in Rome: Cola di Rienzo and the Politics of the New Age* (Berkeley: University of California Press, 2003), p. 261.
9. For a introductory history, see L. Scaraffia, *Il Giubileo* (Bologna: il Mulino, 1999).
10. G. Parker, 'Introduction' to J. Burchard, *At the Court of the Borgias: Being an Account of the Reign of Pope Alexander VI Written by his Master of Ceremonies* (London: Folio Society, 1963), p. 28.
11. Burchard, *At the Court of the Borgias*, pp. 170–1.
12. D. Julia, 'L'accoglienza dei pellegrini a Roma' in L. Fiorani and A. Prosperi (eds), *Roma: la città del papa: vita civile e religiosa dal giubileo di Bonifacio VIII al giubileo di papa Wojtyla* (Turin: Einaudi, 2000), p. 833.
13. F. Sebastianelli, 'L'incendio della Basilica di S. Paolo fuori le Mura', *Roma moderna e contemporanea*, 12, 2000, pp. 544–7.
14. E. Vercesi, *Tre pontificate: Leone XII–Pio VIII–Gregorio XVI* (Turin: Società Editrice Internazionale, 1936), p. 44.
15. *Notificazione del Giubileo dell'Anno Santo della santità di N.S. Papa Leone XII esteso a tutto il mondo cattolico con omelia dell'eminentissimo sig. Card. Odescalchi Archivescovo* (Ferrara: Tipografia Archivescovile, 1826); Cardinal Wiseman, *Recollections of the Last Four Popes and of Rome in Their Times* (London: Hurst and Blackett, 1858), p. 272.
16. P. Boutry, 'La Restaurazione (1814–1848)' in G. Ciucci (ed.), *Roma moderna* (Bari: Laterza, 2002), p. 381.

17. Maybe his anal obsessions were encouraged by the fact that he suffered excruciatingly from piles. See N. Atkin and F. Tallett, *Priests, Prelates and People: A History of European Catholicism since 1750* (London: I.B. Tauris, 2003), p. 102.

18. P. Di Cori, 'Sacre misure. Spazio e tempo a Roma durante l'Anno Santo 1825' in S. Boesch Cajano and L. Scaraffia (eds), *Luoghi sacri e spazi della santità* (Turin: Rosenberg and Sellier, 1990), pp. 451–3.

19. Pianciani, *La Roma dei papi*, p. 133.

20. Wiseman, *Recollections of the Last Four Popes*, p. 257.

21. Di Cori, 'Sacre misure. Spazio e tempo a Roma durante l'Anno Santo 1825', p. 448.

22. V. Prinzivalli, *Gli Anni Santi (1300–1925): appunti storici con molte note inedite tratte dagli archivi di Roma* (Rome: Provenzani editore, [1925]), p. 197.

23. G. Orioli, 'Il secolo XIX' in L. Fiorani et al., *Riti, ceremonie, feste e vita di popolo nella Roma dei papi* (Bologna: Cappelli, 1970), p. 285.

24. Di Cori, 'Sacre misure. Spazio e tempo a Roma durante l'Anno Santo 1825', pp. 454–5.

25. Wiseman, *Recollections of the Last Four Popes*, p. 193.

26. See A. Gasbaroni (detto Gasperone), *La mia vita di brigante: redatta in prigione da Pietro Masi da Patrica, ergastolano, suo compagno di bando e di pena* (Rome: Atlante, 1952). He was still alive, to be released from his gaol by the Italians, in 1870. He did not die till 1882. See U. Pesci, *I primi anni di Roma capitale (1870–1878)* (Florence: Bemporad, 1907), pp. 699–700. For a milord, see C. Buxton, *The Memoirs of Sir Thomas Fowell Buxton* (London: Dent, 1925), pp. 217–22.

27. L.C. Farini, *Lo stato romano dall'anno 1815 al 1850* (ed. A. Patuelli) (Rome: Presidenza del Consiglio dei Ministri, Dipartimento per l'informazione e l'editoria, [1988]), pp. 12–14.

28. C. Roth, *The History of the Jews of Italy* (Philadelphia, PA: Jewish Publication Society of America, 1946), pp. 450–1.

29. G. Monsagrati, 'Roma nel crepuscolo del potere temporale' in Fiorani and Prosperi (eds), *Roma: la città del papa*, p. 1017.

30. P. Boutry, 'Espace du pélerinage, espace de la romainté: l'année sainte de la Restauration' in Boesch Cajano and Scaraffia (eds), *Luoghi sacri*, p. 424.

31. *Ibid.*, p. 420. Cf. D. Julia, 'L'accoglienza dei pellegrini a Roma' in Fiorani and Prosperi (eds), *Roma: la città del papa*, p. 839.

32. I. Fosi, 'Fasto e decadenza degli anni santi' in Fiorani and Prosperi (eds), *Roma: la città del papa*, p. 820.

33. *The Times*, 22 June 1825.

34. *The Times*, 20 January 1826.

35. Boutry, 'La Restaurazione (1814–1848)', p. 381.

36. Bartoccini, *Roma nell'Ottocento*, p. 152.

37. M. Petrocchi, *La restaurazione romana (1815–1823)* (Florence: Le Monnier, 1943), pp. 113–14.

38. A symbol was the failure to recover two-thirds of the abducted Inquisitional records, thousands of volumes of which had been lost, most sold as scrap paper. The surviving files were not to be released to historical scrutiny until the 1880s. See M.A. Finocchiaro, *Retrying Galileo 1663–1992* (Berkeley: University of California Press, 2005), p. 178.

39. J.M. Robinson, *Cardinal Consalvi 1757–1824* (London: Bodley Head, 1987), pp. 150–2. The motive may have been partially anti-Semitic, given the association of the Arch and the destruction of the Temple by Titus and his father Vespasian, and the 'traditional' ceremony forcing Rome's Jews to pass beneath it.

40. C. Pietrangeli (ed.), *Note storiche: la pontificia accademia romana di archeologia* (Rome: 'L'Erma' di Breitschneider, 1983), pp. 5–12.

41. C. Springer, *The Marble Wilderness: Ruins and Representation in Italian Romanticism 1775–1850* (Cambridge University Press, 1987), p. 86.

42. C. Castellaneta (ed.), *L'Opera completa di Hayez* (Milan: Rizzoli, 1971), p. 87.

43. Stendhal, *A Roman journal* (New York: Collier Books, 1961), p. 111.

44. R. Deakin, MD, *Flora of the Coliseum or, Illustrations and Descriptions of Four Hundred and Twenty Plants Growing Spontaneously upon the Ruins of the Coliseum of Rome* (London: Groombridge and Sons, 1873), pp. 152; 183; 193.
45. Orioli, 'Il secolo XIX', p. 282.
46. Boutry, 'La Restaurazione (1814–1848)', p. 393.
47. D. Mack Smith (ed.), *The Making of Italy 1796–1870* (New York: Harper and Row, 1968), pp. 64–6.
48. O. Chadwick, *A History of the Popes 1830–1914* (Oxford: Clarendon, 1998), p. 50.
49. See the work of G.B. De Rossi (1822–94). It began under Gregory XVI and culminated in his *La Roma sotteranea cristiana* (1877). It is still the basis of scholarship. See, for example, its updating (ed. G.B. De Rossi and A. Ferrua), *Inscriptiones Christianae urbis Romae: septimo saeculo antiquiores*, 2 vols (Vatican City: Pont. Institutum Archaeologiae Christianae, 1975–83). In 1849 De Rossi, ignoring the political excitement of that time and self-consciously a 'Christian archaeologist', 'rediscovered' the lost catacombs of San Callisto on the Via Appia Antica.
50. O. Niccoli, ' "Le donne biastemavano orazzioni": forma del consumo del sacro nella lunga Controriforma romana' in Fiorani and Prosperi (eds), *Roma, la città del papa*, pp. 624–5; 631.
51. F. Bartoccini, *Roma nell'Ottocento*, p. 166. SPQR and its ambiguities can still be contemplated on every Roman drain lid, sometimes adorned with fasces, sometimes not.
52. Springer, *The Marble Wilderness*, p. 110.
53. *Ibid.*, p. 111. By the 1980s Belli's work was being cosily updated as 'Roman, Italian and European' in its message. See R. Merolla, *G.G. Belli: romano, italiano ed europeo* (Rome: Bonacci, 1985).
54. In the early 1850s, Belli was for a while a severe papal censor and, as such, earned Verdi's disapprobation.
55. D'Azeglio, *Things I Remember*, pp. 258; 266–8.
56. *Ibid.*, p. 7.
57. *Ibid.*, pp. 74–5.
58. *Ibid.*, pp. 180–2.
59. *Ibid.*, pp. 200; 204.
60. *Ibid.*, p. 188.
61. See L. Riall, 'The politics of Italian romanticism: Mazzini and the making of a nationalist culture' in C.A. Bayly and E.F. Biagini (eds), *Giuseppe Mazzini and the Globalisation of Democratic Nationalism 1830–1920* (Oxford University Press, 2008), pp. 167–70.
62. F.-R. de Chateaubriand, *The Memoirs* (ed. R. Baldrick) (Harmondsworth: Penguin, 1965), pp. 378–81.
63. For introduction, see J. Rosselli, *The Opera Industry in Italy from Cimarosa to Verdi* (Cambridge University Press, 1984).
64. D. Kimbell, *Italian Opera* (Cambridge University Press, 1991), pp. 492–3.
65. Musto, *Apocalypse in Rome*, pp. 7–8.
66. Lord Lytton, *Rienzi* (London: Dent, 1911).
67. F. Gregorovius, *Rome and Medieval Culture: Selections from the 'History of the City of Rome in the Middle Ages'* (University of Chicago Press, 1971), p. 306.
68. V. Fleischer, *Rienzo: The Rise and Fall of a Dictator* (London: Aiglon Press, 1948).
69. See, for example, G. D'Annunzio, *Vita di uomini illustri e di uomini oscuri: la vita di Cola di Rienzo* (Milan: Treves, 1913).
70. Barzini may have been influenced in his ideas by Edmund Wilson. For his parallels between Mussolini and Cola di Rienzo, see E. Wilson, *Europe without Baedeker: Sketches Among the Ruins of Italy, Greece and England* (London: Hogarth Press, 1986), p. 66.
71. L. Barzini, *The Italians* (London: Hamish Hamilton, 1964), p. 138.
72. George Gordon, Lord Byron, *Poetical Works* (Oxford University Press, 1960), p. 233.

73. H. Chevalier, 'Editor's foreword' to Stendhal, *A Roman journal*, pp. 12–13; 210.
74. *Ibid.*, pp. 33; 104; 124. Under Gregory XVI the Corso did acquire a footpath, while the city cemetery at Campo Verano was systematised.
75. C.A. Eaton, *Rome in the Nineteenth Century Containing a Complete Account of the Ruins of the Ancient City, the Remains of the Middle Ages and the Monuments of Modern Times with Remarks on the Fine Arts, the Museum of Sculpture and Painting, the Manners, Customs, and Religious Ceremonies of Modern Romans*, 5th edn (London: Henry G. Bohn, 1852), vol. I, p. 339.
76. R. Jenkyns (ed.), *The Legacy of Rome: A New Appraisal* (Oxford University Press, 1992), p. 32.
77. F.J. Coppa, 'Pessimism and traditionalism in the personality and policies of Pio Nono', *Journal of Italian History*, 2, 1979, p. 211.
78. R.M. Johnston, *The Roman Theocracy and the Republic 1846–1849* (London: Macmillan, 1901), p. 38.
79. N. Roncalli, *Cronaca di Roma 1844–1870* (Roma: Istituto per la storia del Risorgimento, 1972), vol. I, pp. 209–10; 264–5.
80. Farini, *Lo Stato romano*, p. 114.
81. *Il Natalazio di Roma e Pio Nono: feste celebrate nell'Aprile 1847* (Rome: n.p., 1847), pp. 1–5.
82. J. Pemble, *The Mediterranean Passion: Victorians and Edwardians in the South* (Oxford: Clarendon, 1987), p. 7.
83. M. Fuller, *'These sad but glorious days': Dispatches from Europe, 1846–1850* (ed. L.J. Reynolds and S. Belasco Smith) (New Haven, CT: Yale University Press, 1991), pp. 137; 156. For the banquet, cf. a more disapproving description by Roncalli, *Cronaca di Roma 1844–1870*, vol. I, p. 254.
84. B. King, 'Introduction' to J. Mazzini, *The Duties of Man and Other Essays* (London: Dent, 1907), p. xxv.
85. V. Gioberti, *Del primato morale e civile degli italiani* (ed. G. Balsamo-Crivelli) (Turin: Tipografia Editrice Torinese, 1948), vol. I, pp. 23; 96.
86. *Ibid.*, pp. 110–14; 136.
87. V. Gioberti, *Il gesuita moderno* (Lausanne: S. Bonancini, 1847), vol. III, pp. 163–6.
88. *Ibid.*, vol. III, pp. 167–9; 183.
89. Pianciani, *La Roma dei papi*, p. 5.
90. For English-language introduction, see D. Mack Smith, *Mazzini* (New Haven, CT: Yale University Press, 1994).

4. Roman revolution, national revolution

1. G.M. Trevelyan, *Garibaldi's Defence of the Roman Republic 1848–9* (London: T. Nelson, 1924), pp. 11–12. In this post-war edition, Trevelyan maintained in a preface that 'Cavour and Garibaldi gave us Italy for an ally', just as Washington's and Lincoln's ghosts had brought the USA into the just cause of Britain and its allies. In the recent world war, Trevelyan remarked, 'The tombs were uncovered; the dead came to war' (p. 5).
2. *Ibid.*, p. 33.
3. For the manipulation, see L. Riall, *Garibaldi: Invention of a Hero* (New Haven, CT: Yale University Press, 2007).
4. C. Duggan, *Francesco Crispi 1818–1901: From Nation to Nationalism* (Oxford University Press, 2002), pp. 693–4.
5. Anathematised by the Church, the Freemasons were ubiquitous among the elite of Liberal Italy. For their story, see A.A. Mola, *Storia della Massoneria italiana dall'Unità alla Repubblica* (Milan: Bompiani, 1976).
6. M. Fabbri et al., *Il Palazzo di Giustizia di Roma* (Rome: Gangemi editore, n.d.).
7. For the embattled history of his corpse, see S. Luzzatto, *La mummia della Repubblica: storia di Mazzini imbalsamato 1872–1946* (Milan: Rizzoli, 2001).

8. See, as a recent example, A. Valerio, *Anita Garibaldi: A Biography* (Westport, CT: Praeger, 2001).
9. See C. Fogu, *The Historic Imaginary: Politics of History in Fascist Italy* (University of Toronto Press, 2003), p. 75.
10. For useful commentary on the link between the myth of Garibaldi and the interventionist cause in and after the First World War, see M. Jones, 'From Caporetto to *Garibaldiland*: interventionist war culture as a culture of defeat', *European Review of History*, 15, 2008, pp. 659–74.
11. Fogu, *The Historic Imaginary*, pp. 78–85.
12. F.P. Mulè, 'Garibaldi', *Capitolium*, 8, May 1932, p. 270.
13. B. Mussolini, *Opera omnia* (ed. E. and D. Susmel) (Florence: La Fenice, 1958), vol. XXV, p. 110.
14. See M. Isnenghi, 'Garibaldi' in M. Isnenghi (ed.), *I luoghi della memoria: personaggi e date dell'Italia unita* (Bari: Laterza, 1997), pp. 43–5.
15. L.C. Farini, *Lo stato romano dall'anno 1815 al 1850* (ed. A. Patuelli) (Rome: Presidenza del Consiglio dei Ministri. Dipartimento per l'informazione e l'editoria, 1988), p. 114.
16. Under the Fascist dictatorship, he was, however, sycophantically compared with Mussolini. See N. Naldoni-Cenenari, *Un romano: Angelo Brunetti* (Rome: Angelo Signorelli, 1940), pp. 3–4.
17. Farini, *Lo stato romano*, p. 182.
18. D. Mack Smith (ed.), *The Making of Italy 1796–1870* (New York: Harper and Row, 1968), pp. 151–2. Mack Smith is using William Ewart Gladstone's 1851 translation of Farini's diary, a source which illuminates the way that Roman events remained meaningful across Europe.
19. E. Fortini, *Solenne ricevimento della testa di Sant'Andrea Apostolo e Cappella presso al Ponte Milvio a lui consagrata: narrazione storica* (Rome: Tipografia Salviucci, 1848); A. Chigi, *Il tempo del Papa-Re: diario dell'anno 1830 al 1855* (Milan: Edizioni del Borghese, 1966), p. 230.
20. N. Roncalli, *Cronaca di Roma 1844–1870* (ed. M.L. Trebliani) (Rome: Istituto per la storia del Risorgimento, 1972), vol. I, p. 303.
21. O. Chadwick, *A History of the Popes 1830–1914* (Oxford: Clarendon, 1998), p. 130; Chigi, *Il tempo del Papa-Re*, p. 257 (for an account of a riot in the area of the ghetto on 24 October).
22. Roncalli, *Cronaca di Roma 1844–1870*, vol. II, p. 29.
23. G. Garibaldi, *My Life* (London: Hesperus Classics, 2004), p. 19.
24. L. Nasto, *Le feste civili a Roma nell'Ottocento* (Rome: Gruppo Editoriale Internazionale, 1994), p. 42.
25. Roncalli, *Cronaca di Roma 1844–1870*, vol. II, pp. 68–9.
26. L. Rodelli, *La Repubblica romana del 1849* (Pisa: Domus Mazziniana, 1955), p. 130.
27. The event has gained in irony, given the use by the Lega Nord as its favourite moment in history but with an anti-Roman message. For background in 1848–9, see D.R.B. Kimbell, *Verdi in the age of Italian romanticism* (Cambridge University Press, 1981), pp. 220–34.
28. Farini, *Lo stato romano*, p. 558.
29. E.E.Y. Hales, *Mazzini and the Secret Societies: The Making of a Myth* (London: Eyre and Spottiswoode, 1954), p. 29.
30. For an admirable summary of the extremity of Mazzini's nationalism, see C. Duggan, 'Giuseppe Mazzini in Britain and Italy: divergent legacies 1837–1915' in C.A. Bayly and E.F. Biagini (eds), *Giuseppe Mazzini and the Globalisation of Democratic Nationalism 1830–1920* (Oxford University Press, 2008), pp. 187–207.
31. Farini, *Lo stato romano*, pp. 596–7.
32. *Ibid.*, p. 598.
33. G. Beghelli, *La Repubblica romana del 1849* (Lodi: Società Cooperativa-Tipografica, 1874), p. 229.

34. Farini, *Lo stato romano*, p. 623.
35. Chigi, *Il tempo del Papa-Re*, p. 284.
36. F. Della Peruta, S.La Salvia and G. Monsagrati, 'Garibaldi, la dittatura e la propaganda della rivoluzione' in L. Rossi (ed.), *Fondare la Nazione: i repubblicani del 1849 e la difesa del Giancolo* (Rome: Fratelli Palombi Editori, 2001), p. 10.
37. Farini, *Lo stato romano*, p. 764.
38. G. Monsagrati, 'L'arte in guerra. Monumenti e politica a Roma al tempo dell'assedio del 1849', *Roma moderna e contemporanea*, 9, 2001, p. 227.
39. C. Capper, *Margaret Fuller: An American Romantic Life: The Public Years* (Oxford University Press, 2007), p. 421.
40. M. Fuller, '*These Sad but Glorious Days': Dispatches from Europe, 1846–1850* (ed. L.J. Reynolds and S. Belasco Smith) (New Haven, CT: Yale University Press, 1991), pp. 298; 303–4.
41. Rodelli, *La Repubblica romana*, p. 255.
42. C. Springer, *The Marble Wilderness: Ruins and Representation in Italian Romanticism 1775–1850* (Cambridge University Press, 1987), pp. 165–6. Predictably, the first site in Rome to be photographed was the Colosseum (1843).
43. R. Rinaldi, *Roma papale dalla repubblica alla monarchia 1849–1870* (Rome: Nuova Editrice Spada, 1992), p. 11.
44. R. De Cesare, *Roma e lo stato del Papa dal ritorno di Pio IX al xx settembre* (Rome: Forzani Editori, 1907), vol. I, pp. 17–18.
45. E.E.Y. Hales, *Pio Nono: A Study in European Politics and Religion in the Nineteenth Century* (London: Eyre and Spottiswoode, 1956), p. 150.
46. G. Pagnotta, 'L'economia' in V. Vidotto (ed.), *Roma capitale* (Bari: Laterza, 2002), pp. 209–10.
47. F. Bartoccini, *Roma nell'Ottocento: il tramonto della 'Città Santa', nascita di una capitale* (Bologna: Cappelli, 1985), p. 266.
48. De Cesare, *Roma e lo stato del papa*, vol. I, pp. 47; 63; 154; 181.
49. F. Bartoccini, *La 'Roma dei romani'* (Rome: Istituto per la storia del Risorgimento, 1972), pp. 523–4.
50. Cardinal Wiseman, *On the Perception of the Natural Beauty by the Ancients and the Modern. Rome, Ancient and Modern. Two Lectures Delivered on the 10th December 1855 and on the 31st of January 1856* (London: Burns and Lambert, 1856), pp. 37–8.
51. S. Carandini, 'L'effimero spirituale. Feste e manifestazioni religiose nella Roma dei papi in età moderna' in L. Fiorani and A. Prosperi (eds), *Roma, la città del papa: vita civile e religiosa dal giubileo di Bonifacio VIII al giubileo di papa Wojtyla* (Turin: Einaudi, 2000), p. 533.
52. D. Demarco, *Una rivoluzione sociale: la repubblica romana del 1849 (16 novembre 1848–3 luglio 1849)* (Naples: Mario Fiorentino Editore, 1944). The publication of this sympathetic social history of the revolution in 1944 was testimony of the need then seen for an anti-Fascist reworking of the Risorgimento.
53. M. Warner, *Alone of All Her Sex: The Myth and Cult of the Virgin Mary* (London: Vintage, 2000), p. 237. Pius continued to oppose the opening of Protestant churches in Rome and, until 1870, the sole one permitted was situated beyond Piazza del Popolo, at the city's periphery. De Cesare, *Roma e lo stato del papa*, vol. I, p. 299.
54. R. Lanciani, *Wanderings Through Ancient Roman Churches* (London: Constable, 1925), p. 59.
55. S. Negro, *Seconda Roma 1850–1870* (Milan: Hoepli, 1943), p. 263.
56. M.A. Tomei, *Scavi francesi sul Palatino: le indagine di Pietro Rosa per Napoleone III (1861–1870)*, (Rome: Ecole française de Rome, 1999), p. 21.
57. *Ibid.*, pp. 471–2.
58. S. Manning, 'Introduction' to N. Hawthorne, *The Marble Faun* (Oxford University Press, 2002), p. xviii.

59. Hawthorne, *The Marble Faun*, p. 4.
60. *Ibid.*, p. 8.
61. *Ibid.*, p. 58.
62. *Ibid.*, p. 86.
63. *Ibid.*, p. 301.
64. *Ibid.*, p. 316. Writing almost a century later in the aftermath of the Second World War, Edmund Wilson endorsed 'the perfect accuracy of Hawthorne's description of the effect of modern Rome on a Protestant Anglo-Saxon', a city that on every return visit seemed 'more fetid and corrupt than ever'. E. Wilson, *Europe without Baedeker: Sketches Among the Ruins of Italy, Greece and England* (London: Hogarth Press, 1986), pp. 200; 211–12.
65. A. Herzen, *My Past and Thoughts* (London: Chatto and Windus, 1968), vol. II, p. 703. For the same parallel in specific regard to the Roman people, see W.W. Story, *Roba di Roma* (Boston: Houghton Mifflin, 1893), vol. I, p. 39.
66. Another dismissive of papal Rome and ready to argue that any meaningful history in the city was lost was the French historian and writer, Hippolyte Taine. See his *Voyage en Italie*, vol. I: *Naples et Rome* (Paris: Hachette, 1910).
67. W.D. Howells, *Italian Journeys* (London: Heinemann, 1911), pp. 130–1.
68. *Ibid.*, p. 138.
69. *Ibid.*, p. 152.
70. F. Gregorovius, *Diari romani* (Milan: Hoepli, 1895), p. 3.
71. *Ibid.*, p. 34.
72. K.F. Morrison, 'Introduction' to F. Gregorovius, *Rome and Medieval Culture: Selections from the 'History of the City of Rome in the Middle Ages'* (University of Chicago Press, 1971), pp. xi–xii.
73. Gregorovius, *Rome and Medieval Culture*, p. 11.
74. *Ibid.*, p. 16.
75. Gregorovius, *Diari romani*, pp. 129; 139.
76. *Ibid.*, p. 158.
77. *Ibid.*, p. 460.
78. *Ibid.*, p. 541.
79. Rinaldi, *Roma papale*, p. 121.
80. D.I. Kertzer, *Prisoner of the Vatican: The Popes' Secret Plot to Capture Rome from the New Italian State* (Boston: Houghton Mifflin, 2004), pp. 11–49.
81. Rinaldi, *Roma papale*, p. 147.
82. F. Bartolini, *Rivali d'Italia: Roma e Milano dal Settecento a oggi* (Bari: Laterza, 2006), p. 89. Cavour's view continued to be opposed by D'Azeglio, who had not renounced his dislike of Roman history.
83. R. Cadorna, *La liberazione di Roma nell'anno 1870 ed il plebiscito* (ed. G. Talamo), (Milan: Mondadori, 1970), pp. 5; 11.
84. C. Balbo, *Le speranze d'Italia* (ed. A. Corbelli) (Turin: Unione Tipografico-Editrice Torinese, 1948), and his *Della monarchia rappresentativa in Italia: saggi politici* (Florence: Le Monnier, 1857), pp. 7–8; 17–19.
85. See www.papalencyclicals.net/Pius09/p9syll.htm, accessed 14 July 2010.
86. A. Stefanucci, *Roma ed i romani nel loro passato, nel presente e nell'avvenire* (Naples: Tipografia nazionale, 1865), pp. 1; 6.
87. *Ibid.*, pp. 47–9.
88. A Garibaldinian liturgy was published in 1866, blasphemously using the Hero's name instead of God. Its answer to the question 'How many persons are there in Garibaldi?', for example, was 'In Garibaldi there are three persons really distinct – the Father of his country, the son of the people, and the spirit of Liberty'. See J.T. Durkin, 'The early years of Italian unification as seen by an American diplomat', *Catholic Historical Review*, 30, 1944–5, p. 283 fn. 37.
89. Kertzer, *Prisoner of the Vatican*, p. 25.

90. Hales, *Pio Nono*, p. 278. For acute analysis of the papal effort to advance rather than retreat in face of the Risorgimento, see L. Riall, 'Martyr cults in nineteenth-century Italy', *Journal of Modern History*, 82, 2010, pp. 274-7.
91. Bartoccini, *La 'Roma dei romani'*, pp. 413-14.
92. *Ibid.*, p. 297.
93. F. Oakley, *The Conciliarist Tradition: Constitutionalism in the Catholic Church 1300-1870* (Oxford University Press, 2003), p. 207 fn. 100.
94. M. Caffiero, 'La maestà del Papa. Trasformazione dei rituali del potere a Roma tra XVIII e XIX secolo' in M.A. Visceglia and C. Brice (eds), *Cérémonial et rituel à Rome (XVIe-XIXe siècle)* (Rome: Ecole Française de Rome, 1997), pp. 294-5.
95. Bartoccini, *La 'Roma dei romani'*, p. 195.
96. De Cesare, *Roma e lo stato del Papa*, vol. I, pp. 449-50.

5. Italian Rome: rational and humanist

1. A.J.C. Hare, *Walks in Rome* (London: G. Allen, n.d.), vol. II, p. 181.
2. See, for example, A. Macadam (ed.), *The Blue Guide to Rome and Environs* (London: E. Benn, 1975), p. 77.
3. N. Paleario (1503), M. Serveto (1511), Luca Vanini (1585) and P. Romus (1515-62). Ironically, Jan Hus had a short biography written of him by the young anti-clerical and socialist Mussolini. See B. Mussolini, *Giovanni Huss: il veridico* (Rome: Edinac, 1948; first published 1913). An English translation was published in 1929, year of the Lateran Pacts and so of the Duce's reconciliation with clericalism. The purpose must have been malicious. See B. Mussolini, *John Huss* (New York: Albert and Charles Boni, 1929).
4. The sculptor was the mason Ettore Ferrari, noticed in the previous chapter as preparing the long-delayed monument to Mazzini.
5. *Civiltà cattolica*, f. 937, 26 June 1889; *L'Illustrazione italiana*, 16 June 1889.
6. *The Times*, 11 June 1889.
7. An official tabulation cut the number to 655 and estimated the crowd at 20,000. See C. Duggan, *Francesco Crispi 1818-1901: From Nation to Nationalism* (Oxford University Press, 2002), p. 561.
8. D.I. Kertzer, *Prisoner of the Vatican: The Popes' Secret Plot to Capture Rome from the New Italian State* (Boston: Houghton Mifflin, 2004), p. 267.
9. A. Guiccioli, *Diario di un conservatore* (Rome: Edizioni del Borghese, 1973), p. 161.
10. *Ibid.*, p. 162.
11. Duggan, *Francesco Crispi*, pp. 547-8; 561-2.
12. Pope Leo XIII et al., *The Pope and the People: Select Letters and Addresses on Social Questions* (London: Catholic Truth Society, 1943), pp. 78, 84.
13. *Civiltà cattolica*, f. 937, 26 June 1889.
14. P. d'Agostino, *Rome in America: Transnational Catholic Ideology from the Risorgimento to Fascism* (Chapel Hill, University of North Carolina Press), p. 70.
15. C. Manfroni (ed.), *Sulla soglia del Vaticano 1870-1901: dalle memorie di Giuseppe Manfroni* (Bologna: Zanichelli, 1920), vol. II, pp. 178-9.
16. *Ibid.*, vol. II, pp. 181-5.
17. *Documenti Diplomatici Italiani* [hereafter DDI], 2s XXII, 633, 18 July 1889, Crispi to ambassadors.
18. See, for example, DDI 2s XXII, 634, 18 July 1889, Nigra to Crispi; 636, 21 July 1889, Catalani to Crispi; 641, 21 July 1889, De Launay to Crispi.
19. G. De Sanctis, *Ricordi della mia vita* (ed. S. Accame) (Florence: Le Monnier, 1970), p. 11.
20. *New York Times*, 18 February 1898.
21. W.R. Thayer, *Italica: Studies in Italian Life and Letters* (London: A. Constable, 1908), p. 140.
22. For the pantheist memory of Bruno, see www.pantheism.net/paul/brunlife.htm, accessed 14 July 2010.

23. See www.Dr-Rath-Foundation.org, accessed 14 July 2010.
24. M.A. Finocchiaro, *Retrying Galileo 1663–1992* (Berkeley: University of California Press, 2005), p. 264. It was published in 1942.
25. A. Foa, '17 febbraio 1600. Il rogo di Giordano Bruno' in A. Carandini et al., *I giorni di Roma* (Bari: Laterza, 2007), p. 206.
26. Kertzer, *Prisoner of the Vatican*, p. 56.
27. R. Cadorna, *La liberazione di Roma nell'anno 1870 e il plebiscito* (ed. G. Talamo) (Milan: Mondadori, 1970), pp. 267–8.
28. B. Tobia, *L'altare della patria* (Bologna: il Mulino, 1998), p. 61.
29. F. Bartolini, 'Condizioni di vita e identità sociali: nascita di un metropoli' in V. Vidotto (ed.), *Roma capitale* (Bari: Laterza, 2002), p. 19.
30. A. Riccardi, 'La vita religiosa', *ibid.*, p. 273.
31. F. Bartoccini, *Roma nell'Ottocento: il tramonto della 'Città Santa', nascita di una capitale* (Bologna: Cappelli, 1985), p. 437.
32. W.E. Gladstone, *Rome and the Newest Fashions in Religion: Three Tracts* (London: J. Murray, 1875), pp. x; 155.
33. F. Gori, *Sullo splendido avvenire di Roma capitale d'Italia e del mondo cattolico e sul modo di migliorare l'interno della città e l'aria delle campagne: ragionamento* (Rome: Tipografia delle Belle Arti, 1870), p. 3.
34. *Ibid.*, pp. 9–12.
35. *Ibid.*, pp. 14–19; 28–9.
36. *Civiltà cattolica*, 8s, I, January 1871.
37. J. Mazzini, *The Duties of Man and Other Essays* (London: Dent, 1907), pp. 222–3.
38. D. Pick, *Rome or Death: The Obsessions of General Garibaldi* (London: J. Cape, 2005), p. 91.
39. *Ibid.*, p. 11.
40. O. Chadwick, *A History of the Popes 1830–1914* (Oxford University Press, 1998), p. 227.
41. R. Lanciani, *Notes from Rome* (ed. A.L. Cubberly) (British School at Rome, 1988), pp. 56–7.
42. M. Carcani, *Il Tevere, le sue inondazioni dalla origine di Roma ai giorni nostri: descrizione geografica e storica* (Rome: Tipografia Romana, 1875), pp. 27–8. Among the dates Carcani listed was the accession of Valerian in 253, destined to be abandoned to his terrible fate in Persia by his ungrateful son, Gallienus.
43. A. Grattarola, 'Introduzione' to G. Garibaldi, *Il progetto di deviazione del Tevere e di bonificazione dell'Agro Romano* (Rome: Tipografia Anzaloni, n.d.), p. 4.
44. U. Pesci, *I primi anni di Roma capitale (1870–1878)* (Florence: Bemporad, 1907), p. 565.
45. Garibaldi, *Il progetto di deviazione del Tevere*, pp. 11–12.
46. *Ibid.*, p. 45.
47. P. Romanelli, 'Giacomo Boni (nel centenario della nascita)', *Studi romani*, 7, 1959, p. 267.
48. For a description, see G. Tausig, *Le Climat romain: son influence sur la santé et les maladies: guide hygiènique* (Rome: Typographie Romaine, 1870), p. 56.
49. A.C. Jemolo, 'Prospettiva di un secolo' in A.C. Jemolo et al., *Un secolo da Porta Pia* (Naples: Guida, 1970), p. 16.
50. G. Talamo and G. Bonetta, *Roma nel novecento da Giolitti alla Repubblica* (Bologna: Cappelli, 1987), p. 50; J.R. Rodd, *Rome of the Renaissance and Today* (London: Macmillan, 1932), p. 4.
51. R. Morelli, 'Alla ricerca di un'identità: operai e sviluppo economico nella capitale (1870–1910)' in A. Caracciolo (ed.), *Il Lazio: storia d'Italia. Le regioni dall'Unità a oggi* (Turin: Einaudi, 1991), p. 52.
52. See D. Rizzo, 'Liberal decorum and men in conflict: Rome, 1871–90', *Journal of Modern Italian Studies*, 10, 2005, p. 284.
53. N. Nisco, *Roma prima e dopo del 1870* (Rome: Tipografia Barbera, 1878), pp. 22–4.
54. A. Herzen, *My Past and Thoughts: Memoirs* (London: Chatto and Windus, 1968), vol. III, p. 1459.

55. *Ibid.*, vol. III, p. 1462. The italics are in the original.
56. F. Gregorovius, *Diari romani* (Milan: Hoepli, 1895), pp. 459–60; 465.
57. *Ibid.*, p. 503.
58. DDI 2s, I, 13, 21 September 1870, Sella to Minghetti.
59. M. Manieri Elia, 'Roma capitale: strategie urbane e uso delle memorie' in Caracciolo (ed.), *Il Lazio*, p. 516.
60. M. Casciato, 'Lo sviluppo urbano e il disegno della città' in Vidotto (ed.), *Roma capitale*, p. 142; R. Ugolini, 'Luigi Pianciani: sindaco di Roma' in R. Ugolini et al. (eds), *Luigi Pianciani tra riforme e rivoluzione* (Università degli studi di Perugia, 1992), p. 23.
61. Bartoccini, *Roma nell'Ottocento*, pp. 499–500.
62. Cited by F. Chabod, *Storia della politica estera italiana dal 1870 al 1896* (Bari: Laterza, 1965), vol. I, p. 221.
63. *Ibid.*, vol. I, pp. 228–32.
64. P. and R. Della Seta, *I suoli di Roma: uso e abuso del territorio nei cento anni della capitale* (Rome: Riuniti, 1988), p. 18.
65. G. Pagnotta, 'L'economia' in Vidotto (ed.), *Roma capitale*, p. 214.
66. Pesci, *I primi anni di Roma capitale*, p. 202.
67. Bartoccini, *Roma nell'Ottocento*, p. 443.
68. P. and R. Della Seta, *I suoli di Roma*, p. 67.
69. Guiccioli, *Diario di un conservatore*, p. 40.
70. Bartoccini, *Roma nell'Ottocento*, p. 571.
71. M. Zocca, 'Roma, capitale d'Italia' in F. Castagnoli et al., *Topografia e urbanistica di Roma* (Bologna: Cappelli, 1958), p. 576.
72. G. Talamo, *Il 'Messaggero' e la sua città: cento anni di storia* (Florence: Le Monnier, 1979), vol. I, p. 94.
73. L. Rossi, 'Una capitale poco sportiva. Attività agonistica e luoghi di svago tra il 1870 e il 1940', *Roma moderna e contemporanea*, 7, 1999, pp. 233–8.
74. Guiccioli, *Diario di un conservatore*, pp. 132–3.
75. W.W. Story, *Roba di Roma* (Boston: Houghton Mifflin, 1893), vol. I, p. ix; M.K. Waddington, *Italian Letters of a Diplomat's Wife January–May 1880, February–April 1904* (London: Smith, Elder, 1905), p. 42.
76. Pesci, *I primi anni di Roma capitale*, pp. 199–200.
77. Lanciani, *Notes from Rome*, p. 1.
78. *Ibid.*, p. 51.
79. R. Lanciani, *Ancient Rome in the Light of Recent Discoveries* (New York: Benjamin Blom, 1888), pp. ix–x.
80. Lanciani, *Notes from Rome*, p. 71.
81. *Ibid.*, p. 143.
82. *Ibid.*, p. 193.
83. Lanciani, *Ancient Rome in the Light of Recent Discoveries*, p. 265.
84. *Ibid.*, p. xxv.
85. See especially T. Ashby, *The Aqueducts of Ancient Rome* (ed. I.A. Richmond) (Oxford: Clarendon, 1935).
86. Romanelli, 'Giacomo Boni', p. 270.
87. Lanciani, *Notes from Rome*, p. 108.
88. Pesci, *I primi anni di Roma capitale*, p. 1.
89. A. Gabelli, *Roma e i romani* (Rome: Tipografia Elzeviriana, 1881), pp. x–xiv.
90. F. Bartolini, *Rivali d'Italia: Roma e Milano dal Settecento a oggi* (Bari: Laterza, 2006), p. 137.
91. R. Drake, *Byzantium for Rome: The Politics of Nostalgia in Umbertian Italy, 1878–1900* (Chapel Hill: University of North Carolina Press, 1980), p. 5.
92. *Ibid.*, p. 11.
93. *Ibid.*, p. 20.

94. See Anon., 'La prima conferenza dantesca in Roma', *Nuova Antologia*, 13, 16 January 1888, pp. 340–5, for a description of Carducci's inauguration of a series of Dante lectures there.

95. G. Carducci, 'Introduzione' to U. Pesci, *Come siamo entrati in Roma* (Milan: Treves, 1911), pp. xx–xxi.

96. A. Oriani, *Viaggio in bicicletta ed altre pagine di viaggio e di paeasaggio* (Bologna: Massimiliano Boni editore, 1986), pp. 105–9.

97. A. Giardina and A. Vauchez, *Il mito di Roma da Carlo Magno a Mussolini* (Bari: Laterza, 2000), p. 197.

98. For the discovery in 1883, see Lanciani, *Notes from Rome*, p. 137.

99. A. Calza, *Roma moderna* (Milan: Fratelli Treves, 1911), pp. 115–16.

100. Cited by G. Finaldi, 'Italy's scramble for Africa from Dogali to Adua' in J. Dickie, J. Foot and F.M. Snowden (eds), *Disastro! Disasters in Italy since 1860: Culture, Politics, Society* (New York: Palgrave, 2002), p. 83 (and cf. pp. 82–8 on the context).

101. Manfroni (ed.), *Sulla soglia del Vaticano*, pp. 154–5.

102. For a biography, see M. Barnes, *Augustus Hare* (London: Allen and Unwin, 1984). Remarkably it is still possible to join the Augustus Hare Society.

103. Hare, *Walks in Rome*, vol. II, pp. 32–3.

104. *Ibid.*, vol. II, pp. 52; 141.

105. F.M. Crawford, *Ave Roma Immortalis: Studies from the Chronicles of Rome* (London: Macmillan, 1903), pp. 436–8; 566.

106. H. von Treitschke, *Politics* (ed. H. Kohn) (New York: Harcourt, Brace and World, 1963), pp. 33; 72.

107. K. Marx, *Surveys from Exile: Political Writings*, vol. II (ed. D. Fernbach) (Harmondsworth: Penguin, 1973), p. 299.

108. A. Giardina and A. Vauchez, *Il mito di Roma*, p. 163.

109. J. Joll, *The Second International 1889–1914* (New York: Praeger, 1956), p. 18.

110. M. Casella, *Roma fine Ottocento: forze politiche e religiose, lotte elettorali, fermenti sociali (1889–1900)* (Naples: ESI, 1995), p. 221.

111. Riccardi, 'La vita religiosa', p. 279.

112. L. Scaraffia, *Il Giubileo* (Bologna: il Mulino, 1999), p. 101; Kertzer, *Prisoner of the Vatican*, p. 291.

113. Chadwick, *A History of the Popes 1830–1914*, p. 280. Leo also sacked the last *castrati* to sing in the Sistine Chapel.

114. R. Moro, 'Religion and politics in the time of secularisation: the sacralisation of politics and the politicisation of religion', *Totalitarian Movements and Political Religions*, 6, 2005, p. 72.

115. Bartolini, *Rivali d'Italia*, p. 171.

116. R. De Cesare, 'L'Anno Santo', *Nuova Antologia*, f. 672, 16 December 1899, p. 729.

117. Manfroni (ed.), *Sulla soglia del Vaticano*, vol. II, pp. 268–9.

118. *M. Serao: The Conquest of Rome* (ed. A. Caesar) (New York University Press, 1992), p. 70.

119. N. Gallo, 'Roma e l'imperatore di Germania', *Nuova Antologia*, 1 October 1888, pp. 496; 503.

6. Italian Rome: national and imperialist

1. Foreshadowing this fate, in 1911 Zanelli had his biography written by Mario Lago, a Nationalist and later to be Fascist governor of the Dodecanese islands. See M. Lago, *Angelo Zanelli* (Rome: G. Romagna editore, 1911). His tale was a virtuous one of a worker turned patriot through his enthusiasm for Dante.

2. B. Tobia, 'Il Vittoriano' in M. Isnenghi (ed.), *I luoghi della memoria: simboli e miti dell'Italia unita* (Bari: Laterza, 1996), p. 253.

3. *The Times*, 5 June 1911.

4. A.J.C. Hare, *Walks in Rome* (London: G. Allen, n.d.), vol. II, p. 211.
5. M. Venturoli, *La Patria di marmo: tutta la storia del Vittoriano, il monumento più discusso dell'età umbertina, tra arte, spettacoli, invenzioni, scandali e duelli* (Rome: Newton Compton, 1995), p. 42.
6. *Ibid.*, pp. 47–8.
7. S. Bertelli (ed.), *La Chioma della Vittoria: scritti sull'identità degli italiani dall'unità alla seconda repubblica* (Florence: Ponte alle Grazie, 1997), p. 180.
8. B. Tobia, *L'Altare della Patria* (Bologna: il Mulino, 1998), p. 30.
9. *Ibid.*, p. 31.
10. C. Dossi, *I mattoidi al primo concorso pel monumento in Roma a Vittorio Emanuele II: note* (Rome: Sommaruga, 1884), pp. 43; 59.
11. For a period account, see P. Acciarese, *Giuseppe Sacconi e il suo monumento a Vittorio Emanuele II* (Rome: Società Tipografia A. Manuzio, 1926).
12. Tobia, *L'Altare della Patria*, pp. 39–42.
13. R. Lanciani, *Notes from Rome* (ed. A.L. Cubberly) (British School at Rome, 1988), pp. 126–7. Since, on his infrequent visits to Rome, Victor Emmanuel II liked to appear incognito at digs, his ghost may have been another to doubt the choice of terrain for his monument.
14. M. Casciato, 'Lo sviluppo urbano e il disegno della città' in V. Vidotto (ed.), *Roma capitale* (Bari: Laterza, 2002), p. 153.
15. Acciarese, *Giuseppe Sacconi*, pp. 17; 21.
16. Venturoli, *La Patria di marmo*, pp. 183–4.
17. *Ibid.*, pp. 115; 139.
18. *Ibid.*, pp. 336–8.
19. *Ibid.*, pp. 478–90. Ferrero had only recently completed his popularising work, *Greatness and decline of Rome* (5 vols) (London: Heinemann, 1909), which wrote off Julius Caesar as the ruin of a beneficent Roman republic. Betraying his many talents, Caesar became no more than 'a low-class demagogue, a persistent intriguer and unscrupulous man of business' (vol. I, p. 364).
20. *Il Messaggero*, 5 June 1911.
21. *Avanti!*, 5 June 1911.
22. Anon., 'Le commemorazioni patriottiche del 1911', *Civiltà cattolica*, f. 1460, 5 April 1911.
23. Anon., 'Il XX settembre: festa massonica', *Civiltà cattolica*, f. 1471, 27 September 1911.
24. G. Berghaus, *Italian Futurist Theatre, 1909–1944* (Oxford: Clarendon, 1998), p. 113.
25. *Ibid.*, p. 68.
26. *Ibid.*, pp. 233–4.
27. O. Chadwick, *A History of the Popes 1830–1914* (Oxford: Clarendon, 1998), pp. 365–6.
28. A. Riccardi, 'La vita religiosa' in Vidotto (ed.), *Roma capitale*, p. 285.
29. *Ibid.*, p. 284.
30. A. Calza, *Roma moderna* (Milan: Fratelli Treves, 1911), p. 72.
31. T. De Mauro and L. Lorenzetti, 'Dialetti e lingue nel Lazio' in A. Caracciolo (ed.), *Il Lazio: storia d'Italia. Le regioni dall'unità a oggi* (Turin: Einaudi, 1991), pp. 320–1.
32. See, for example, the case study, D.I. Kertzer, *The Kidnapping of Edgardo Mortara* (New York: Knopf, 1997).
33. Cited by S. Waagenaar, *The Pope's Jews* (London: Alcove Press, 1974), p. 281.
34. *Ibid.*, p. 282.
35. M.I. Macioti, *Ernesto Nathan: un sindaco che non ha fatto scuola* (Rome: Editrice Ianua, 1983), pp. 21–6.
36. A.A. Mola, *Storia della massoneria italiana dall'unità alla repubblica* (Milan: Bompiani, 1976), pp. 181; 194.
37. *Ibid.*, p. 229.
38. *Ibid.*, p. 251.
39. Macioti, *Ernesto Nathan*, pp. 57–8.

40. G. Barbalace, *Riforme e governo municipale a Roma in età giolittiana* (Naples: Liguori, 1994), pp. 22–3; 34; 57.

41. G. Montemartini, 'Un decennio di vita nei corpi consultivi della legislazione sociale in Italia (1903–1912)', *Nuova Antologia*, f. 998, 16 July 1913, pp. 294; 300.

42. Macioti, *Ernesto Nathan*, pp. 105–6.

43. Lanciani, *Notes from Rome*, pp. 410–11.

44. H. Ullrich, *Le elezioni del 1913 a Roma: i liberali fra massoneria e vaticano* (Milan: Società editrice Dante Alighieri, 1972), p. 11.

45. *Ibid.*, pp. 60; 72.

46. E. Nathan, *Roma papale e Roma italiana* (Rome: Tipografia F. Centenari, 1910), pp. 6–8.

47. *Ibid.*, pp. 12–14.

48. H.V. Morton, *A Traveller in Rome* (London: Methuen, 1957), pp. 43–4.

49. G. Talamo and G. Bonetta, *Roma nel novecento da Giolitti alla repubblica* (Bologna: Cappelli, 1987), pp. 49–51; 57; G. Talamo, *Il 'Messaggero' e la sua città: cento anni di storia* (Florence: LeMonnier, 1979), vol. I, p. 221.

50. D. Orano, *Come vive il popolo a Roma: saggio demografico sul quartiere Testaccio* (Pescara: Ettore Croce, 1912), p. 505.

51. M. Bertoletti et al. (eds), *Sculptures of Ancient Rome: The Collection of the Capitoline Museums at the Montemartini Power Plant* (Rome: Electa, 1999), p. 14.

52. Orano, *Come vive il popolo a Roma*, p. 508.

53. *Ibid.*, pp. 153–4; 201–3; 282–5; 370; 385; 434–6; 467; 508; 673.

54. G. Bertellini, 'Italian imageries, historical feature films and the fabrication of Italy's spectators in early 1900s New York' in M. Stokes and R. Maltby (eds), *American Movie Audiences: From the Turn of the Century to the Early Sound Era* (London: BFI Publishing, 1999), p. 34.

55. L. Piccioni, *San Lorenzo: un quartiere romano durante il fascismo* (Rome: Edizioni di Storia e Letteratura, 1984), pp. 15–16; 19–20.

56. *Ibid.*, pp. 21–2; 25.

57. A. Niceforo and S. Sighele, *La mala vita a Roma* (Sala Bolognese: A. Forni editore, 1987), pp. 79; 85; 165 (the book was first published in 1898); A. Staderini, *Combattenti senza divisa: Roma nella grande guerra* (Bologna: il Mulino, 1995), p. 244.

58. M. Sanfilippo, *San Lorenzo 1870–1945: storia e 'storie' di un quartiere romano* (Rome: Edilazio, 2003), p. 26.

59. Hare, *Walks in Rome*, vol. II, pp. 386–7.

60. Talamo and Bonetta, *Roma, nel novecento*, p. 137.

61. Orano, *Come vive il popolo a Roma*, p. 691.

62. A.C. Jemolo, *Anni di prova* (Florence: Passigli, 1991), pp. 44–6.

63. M. Baioni, *La 'religione della patria': musei e istituti del culto risorgimentale (1884–1918)* (Quinto di Treviso: Pagus Edizioni, 1994), pp. 39–40.

64. For a catalogue of the various events, see G. Piantoni (ed.), *Roma 1911* (Rome: De Luca editore, 1980).

65. For an account, see H. Petter, *Lutyens in Italy: The Building of the British School at Rome* (British School at Rome, 1992). Now, in the site to where it was transferred in 1911, the BSR, first opened in 1901 'on the model of Athens', is enigmatically set between the Via Gramsci and Piazza Winston Churchill.

66. E. Forcella, 'Roma 1911: quadri di una esposizione' in Piantoni (ed.), *Roma 1911*, pp. 33–4.

67. *La Tribuna*, 3 May 1911.

68. For some background, see R. Aldrich, *The Seduction of the Mediterranean: Writing, Art and Homosexual Fantasy* (London: Routledge, 1993), pp. 146–51.

69. Calza, *Roma moderna*, pp. 38–9. Sartorio's artistic *oeuvre* had focused on the Campagna, after he made his name with *Malaria* in 1882. After 1915, despite his age, Sartorio was a volunteer in the war, where he was wounded and then a POW.

70. *La Tribuna*, 24 April 1911.
71. E. Corradini, *Discorsi politici (1902–1924)*, (Florence: Vallecchi, 1925), p. 167.
72. E. Corradini, 'Nationalism and the syndicates' in A. Lyttelton (ed.), *Italian Fascisms from Pareto to Gentile* (London: J. Cape, 1970), p. 163.
73. E. Corradini, *Il nazionalismo italiano* (Milan: Fratelli Treves, 1914), p. 21.
74. Corradini, *Discorsi politici*, p. 176.
75. For their imperialist campaigns, see M. Petricioli, *Archeologia e Mare Nostrum: le missioni archeologiche nella politica mediterranea dell'Italia 1898–1943* (Rome: Valerio Levi editore, 1990).
76. See 'Contrasto tra l'aristocrazia e la plebea sulla guerra di Tripoli' in G. Vettori (ed.), *Canzoni italiane di protesta (1794–1974)* (Rome: Newton Compton editore, 1975), pp. 110–11.
77. B. Mussolini, *Opera omnia* (eds E. and D. Susmel) (Florence, 1951–63), vol. III, p. 190.
78. Macioti, *Ernesto Nathan*, p. 134. He worked as a liaison officer with a British medical unit. Nathan died in Rome in April 1921 in the bed that Mazzini had often used (p. 141).
79. 'G. De Frenzi' (L. Federzoni), *L'Italia nell'Egeo* (Rome: Gaetano Garzoni Provenzani, 1913), p. 113.
80. L. Federzoni, *La Dalmazia che aspetta* (Bologna: Zanichelli, 1915), pp. 67–9.
81. A. Staderini, 'L'interventismo romano 1914–1915', *Storia contemporanea*, 22, 1991, p. 265.
82. Staderini, *Combattenti senza divisa*, p. 22.
83. Berghaus, *Italian Futurist Theatre, 1909–1944*, p. 249.
84. C. Seton-Watson, *Italy from Liberalism to Fascism 1870–1925* (London: Methuen, 1967), pp. 446–7.
85. For the background, see R.J.B. Bosworth, *Mussolini's Italy: Life Under the Dictatorship* (London: Allen Lane, 2005), pp. 59–60.
86. R. Lanciani, *Ancient and Modern Rome* (London: G.G. Harrap, n.d.), p. 115.
87. *Ibid.*, pp. 135–8.
88. *Il Soldato*, 18 November 1917.
89. M. Moorman, *George Macaulay Trevelyan: A Memoir* (London: H. Hamilton, 1980), p. 159.
90. G.M. Trevelyan, *Scenes from Italy's War* (London: T.C. and E.C. Jack, 1919), pp. 30; 59. Stirred by his own reading of history, Trevelyan, despite his liberalism, saw some advantages, after the war, in Fascism, at least for Italians. See his *The Historical Causes of the Present State of Affairs in Italy* (Oxford University Press, 1923).
91. O. Spengler, *The Decline of the West* (London: George Allen and Unwin, 1961), pp. 29–42; 45–6.
92. *Ibid.*, p. 98.
93. For introduction, see J.F. Pollard, *Benedict XV: The Unknown Pope and the Pursuit of Peace* (London: Continuum, 1999).
94. E. Vercesi, *Il Vaticano, l'Italia e la guerra* (Milan: Mondadori, 1925), p. 31; 262–80.
95. Staderini, *Combattenti senza divisa*, p. 244.
96. G. Vettori (ed.), *Canti popolari italiani* (Rome: Newton Compton, 1974), pp. 192–3.
97. Staderini, *Combattenti senza divisa*, pp. 104–5; 375; 406.
98. *Ibid.*, p. 296.
99. *Ibid.*, pp. 80–92.
100. *Ibid.*, p. 412.
101. *Ibid.*, pp. 150; 166–7. The latter speaker was the later Fascist journalist, Nicola Pascazio. See, for example, his attack on British 'racial degeneration' during the next war in N. Pascazio, *La crisi sociale dell'impero britannico: studio compiuto in Inghilterra* (Milan: Garzanti, 1941).
102. Staderini, *Combattenti senza divisa*, p. 177.
103. See F. Martini, *Nell'Affrica italiana: impressioni e ricordi* (Milan: Fratelli Treves, 1925), where he philosophised about the power and natural purity of Affrica [*sic*] in liberating 'civilised man' from himself.

104. F. Martini, *Diario 1914–1918* (ed. G. de Rosa) (Milan: Mondadori, 1966), p. 1088.
105. Staderini, *Combattenti senza divisa*, pp. 431–2.
106. P. Bondanella, *The Eternal City: Roman Images in the Modern World* (Chapel Hill: University of North Carolina Press, 1987), p. 166.

7. Rome, its Histories and Fascist totalitarianism

1. S. Pasquarelli, 'Immagini per l'architettura di una capitale: via Nazionale e i concorsi alla fine dell'800', in Comune di Roma, *Il Palazzo delle esposizioni: urbanistica e architettura. L'Esposizione inaugurale del 1883. Le acquisizioni pubbliche. Le attività espositive* (Rome: Edizioni Carte Segrete, 1990), p. 22.
2. R. Siligato, 'L'edificio, senza eccedere in decorazioni, dovrà avere un'impronta speciale che caratterizza la sua decorazione' in *ibid.*, pp. 61–7.
3. See http://www.palazzoesposizioni.it/MEDIACENTER/FE/CategoriaMedia.aspx?idc=13, accessed 14 July 2010.
4. F. Gargano, *Italiani e stranieri alla Mostra della Rivoluzione Fascista* (Rome: SAIE, [1935]), p. i, notes the claim by Starace that 3,854,927 visitors came there between 28 October 1932 and 28 October 1934.
5. A. Giardina and A. Vauchez, *Il mito di Roma da Carlo Magno a Mussolini* (Bari: Laterza, 2000), p. 235.
6. D. Alfieri and L. Freddi (eds), *Mostra della Rivoluzione Fascista* (Bergamo: Istituto Italiano d'Arti Grafiche, 1933), pp. 45; 47.
7. *Ibid.*, p. 64.
8. M.S. Stone, *The Patron State: Culture and Politics in Fascist Italy* (Princeton, NJ: Princeton University Press, 1998), p. 143.
9. For an extreme evocation, see the poem by R.M. Stagi in his *Pellegrinaggio alla Mostra della Rivoluzione (liriche)* (Pisa: Nistri-Lischi editore, 1934).
10. For further introduction, see E. Braun, *Mario Sironi 1920–1945: Art and Politics in Fascist Italy* (Cambridge University Press, 1999).
11. Stone, *The patron state*, p. 152.
12. For description, see C. Fogu, *The Historic Imaginary: Politics of History in Fascist Italy* (University of Toronto Press, 2003), pp. 122–64.
13. Alfieri and Freddi (eds), *Mostra della Rivoluzione Fascista*, pp. 7–8.
14. *Ibid.*, pp. 9; 51.
15. Stone, *The Patron State*, p. 155.
16. E. Gentile, *Fascismo di pietra* (Bari: Laterza, 2007), p. 166.
17. R.G. Andrew, *Through Fascist Italy: An English Hiker's Pilgrimage* (London: G.G. Harrap, 1935), pp. 147–9. St Peter's similarly reminded him of 'the foyer of a cheap music-hall, decorated gorgeously to suit the taste of its ignorant patrons' (p. 153). In June 1934 the young Tory, R.A. Butler, wrote off the Palazzo delle esposizioni as 'a Daily Express building'. Butler papers, D48/1032–1038, Trinity College, Cambridge.
18. B. Mussolini, *Opera omnia* (eds E. and D. Susmel) (Florence, 1951–63), vol. XIII (hereafter BMOO). He rather defused the totality of his global intent by adding pretentiously that a modern man must have read Cervantes, Shakespeare, Goethe, Tolstoy and, of course best, Dante.
19. Gentile, *Fascismo di pietra*, p. 41.
20. BMOO X, p. 446.
21. BMOO X, p. 8
22. BMOO X, pp. 346; 349.
23. BMOO XI, p. 456.
24. BMOO XV, pp. 217–18.
25. BMOO XVI, p. 45.
26. BMOO XVI, p. 159.

27. The matter was underlined by the ex-nationalist Fascist, Luigi Federzoni, in his 'Introduzione' to B. Mussolini (ed.), *Italia-Roma e il Papato nelle discussioni parlamentari dal 1860 al 1871* (Rome: Libreria del Littorio, 1929), p. xiii. Federzoni added that, after his death, Cavour preserved 'a kind of posthumous dictatorship over the Nation' (p. xvii).
28. See, for example, L. Morpurgo (ed.), *Roma Mussolinea* (Rome: L. Morpurgo, 1932).
29. D.M. Leva, *Cronache del fascismo romano* (Perugia: Istituto dei 'Panorami di Realizzazioni del Fascismo' per la pubblicazione di opere sulla Rivoluzione, 1943), p. 179.
30. *Ibid.*, p. 58.
31. *Ibid.*, p. 197.
32. BMOO XVI, pp. 160–1 (cited by Gentile, *Fascismo di pietra*, p. 47).
33. L. Piccioni, *San Lorenzo: un quartiere romano durante il fascismo* (Rome: Edizioni di Storia e Letteratura, 1984), p. 34, reports that the first shots against the Fascists were fired by a local woman.
34. G. Talamo, *'Il Messaggero': un giornale durante il fascismo: cento anni di storia* (Florence: Le Monnier, 1984), vol. II, p. 180.
35. G. Bottai, 'Prefazio' to Leva, *Cronache del fascismo romano*, p. xii.
36. G.B. Guerri, *Giuseppe Bottai: un fascista critico* (Milan: Feltrinelli, 1976), pp. 19–25.
37. Piccioni, *San Lorenzo*, pp. 35; 89–90.
38. Leva, *Cronache del fascismo romano*, pp. 2–3.
39. Alfieri and Freddi (eds), *Mostra della Rivoluzione Fascista*, p. 9.
40. Piccioni, *San Lorenzo*, p. 87.
41. M. Sanfilippo, *San Lorenzo 1870–1945: storia e 'storie' di un quartiere romano* (Rome: Edilazio, 2003), pp. 73; 79–80.
42. A.G. Mackinnon, *Alma Roma: A Traveller's Companion to Rome* (London: Blackie and Son, 1926), pp. 213–14. For a case study of Fascist discipline on Rome's periphery, see M. Sinatra, *La Garbatella a Roma 1920–1940* (Milan: F. Angeli, 2006).
43. Sanfilippo, *San Lorenzo*, p. 94.
44. F. Mancini Lapenna, *In Campidoglio con Alberto Mancini: contributi alla cronistoria della vicenda municipale di Roma 1918–1926* (Florence: Vallecchi, 1958), p. 146.
45. G. Talamo and G. Bonetta, *Roma nel novecento da Giolitti alla repubblica* (Bologna: Cappelli, 1987), pp. 272–3.
46. For the situation among members of the Grand Council, see C. Ipsen, *Dictating Demography: The Problem of Population in Fascist Italy* (Cambridge University Press, 1996), p. 179. Mussolini had five legitimate children.
47. M. Sanfilippo, *La costruzione di una capitale: Roma 1911–1945* (Cinisello Balsamo: Silvana Editoriale, 1993), p. 27.
48. P. Salvatori, *Il governorato di Roma: l'amministrazione della capitale durante il fascismo* (Milan: F. Angeli, 2006), p. 58.
49. Piccioni, *San Lorenzo*, p. 81.
50. A. Aquarone, *L'organizzazione dello stato totalitario* (Turin: Einaudi, 1965), pp. 83–4. In September 1926 mayors throughout the country were replaced by *podestà* in one of the changes that legally underpinned the totalitarian state.
51. Salvatori, *Il governatorato di Roma*, p. 29. A visitor today can spot his name on the dome of the Rome opera house, restored during his time as *governatore* and, as the caption adds in Latin, when Mussolini was Duce and Victor Emmanuel king.
52. Archivio centrale dello stato (hereafter ACS), Mostra della Rivoluzione Fascista (hereafter MRF), 52, 5 October 1926 report.
53. ACS, MRF 53/123/16, February 1930 report.
54. ACS, *Partito Nazionale Fascista*, Situazione politica ed economica delle provincie (hereafter SPEP) 19, 19 May 1932.
55. SPEP 19, 25 March 1933.
56. BMOO XX, p. 229.
57. BMOO XX, p. 235.

58. For the classic denunciation of this aspect of Mussolini, see A. Cederna, *Mussolini urbanista: lo sventramento di Roma negli anni di consenso* (Bari: Laterza, 1979).
59. ACS Segreteria particolare del Duce, 5000019/I, 20 September 1931, Mussolini to Boncompagni Ludovisi.
60. A.B. Hawes, 'The new antiquarianism in Rome', *Classical Journal*, 27, 1932, p. 417; cf. D. Mustilli, *Il Museo Mussolini* (Rome: Max Bretschneider, 1939).
61. BMOO XXII, p. 48.
62. Gentile, *Fascismo di pietra*, p. 73.
63. G. Cuccia, *Urbanistica edilizia infrastruttura di Roma capitale 1870–1990: una cronologia* (Bari: Laterza, 1991), pp. 144–5.
64. For period exposition, see G. Ceroni, *Roma nei quartieri e nel suo suburbo* (Rome: Casa Editrice Fratelli Palombi, 1942), p. 125.
65. Mancini Lapenna, *In Campidoglio con Alberto Mancini*, p. 222.
66. B.W. Painter, *Mussolini's Rome: Rebuilding the Eternal City* (New York: Palgrave Macmillan, 2005), p. 18.
67. Cuccia, *Urbanistica edilizia infrastruttura di Roma capitale*, p. 155.
68. B. Tobia, *L'Altare della Patria* (Bologna: il Mulino, 1998), p. 87.
69. Anon., 'Vita Romana', *Roma*, 3, March 1925.
70. S. Kostof, *The Third Rome 1870–1950: Traffic and Glory* (Berkeley, CA: University Art Museum, 1973), p. 15.
71. I.S. Munro, *Beyond the Alps* (London: Alexander Maclehose, 1934), p. 92.
72. P. Baxa, 'Piacentini's Window: The Modernism of the Fascist Master Plan of Rome', *Journal of Contemporary History*, 39, 2004, pp. 3; 18.
73. C. Galassi Paluzzi, 'Roma nell'Ottocento', *Capitolium*, 8, January–February 1932, p. 3.
74. Kostof, *The Third Rome*, p. 32.
75. M. Piacentini, A. Prandi and B. Zambetti, *Tempio di Cristo Re* (Rome: Marietti, 1961), p. 18.
76. Fogu, *The Historic Imaginary*, pp. 10–11; 20.
77. See M. Conway, *Collaboration in Belgium: Léon Degrelle and the Rexist Movement 1940–1944* (New Haven, CT: Yale University Press, 1993). Degrelle relied on financial backing from the Italian regime.
78. G. Verucci, *La chiesa nella società contemporanea dal primo dopoguerra al Concilio Vaticano II* (Bari: Laterza, 1999), pp. 316–17.
79. For pious explanation, see E.J. Mahoney, *The Jubilee Year 1925: A Short Account of the Meaning and History of the Holy Year and the Conditions on which the Great Indulgence May Be Obtained* (London: Burns, Oates and Washburne, 1925).
80. E.V. Lucas, *A Wanderer in Rome* (London: Methuen, 1926), pp. 40–1.
81. A. O'H. McCormick, *Vatican journal 1921–1954* (New York: Farrar, Straus and Cudahy, 1957), p. 14.
82. F. Garafoli, *Anno Jubilaei Romae MCMXXV* (Milan: Ditta Raimondi di F. Pettinaroli e figli, 1925), p. 1.
83. Anon., 'L'Unione dei Cattolici e la divisione dei partiti in Italia', *Civiltà cattolica*, f. 1794, 21 March 1925.
84. Anon., 'Roma sacra', *Civiltà cattolica*, f. 1804, 15 August 1925.
85. *Civiltà cattolica*, f. 1801, 1 July 1925.
86. G. Seldes, *The Vatican: Yesterday – Today – Tomorrow* (London: Kegan Paul, Trench, Trübner, 1934), p. 7.
87. Cuccia, *Urbanistica edilizia infrastruttura di Roma capitale*, p. 141.
88. F. Colonna Di Stigliano, 'Il monumento del negro in Santa Maria Maggiore e l'ambasciata congolese a Roma del 1608', *Roma*, 3, March and April 1925.
89. See *Rivista illustrata della esposizione missionaria vaticana*, I, 15 December 1924.
90. Anon., 'Politica e Cattolicesimo', *Civiltà cattolica*, f. 1812, 19 December 1925.
91. Mazzini had ordered illumination during the tumultuous Easter of the Roman Republic. The matter was recalled in G. Ceccarelli, 'La Pasqua a Roma nel 1849', *Roma*, 3, June 1925.

92. *Il Messaggero*, 10 January 1933.
93. F.W. Ogilivie, *The Tourist Movement: An Economic Study* (London: Staples Press, [1933]), pp. 163; 167.
94. *Il Messaggero*, 23 May 1933.
95. *L'Illustrazione Vaticana*, 1–15 May 1933.
96. *Il Messaggero*, 26 May 1933; *Il Popolo d'Italia*, 26 May 1933.
97. *Il Messaggero*, 16 June 1933.
98. The term may not yet have acquired its full modern meaning. Pius XI himself told Mussolini that he favoured a totalitarian Church. See *Documenti diplomatici italiani* 7s, XI, 205, 11 February 1932, Mussolini to Victor Emmanuel III.
99. *Il Messaggero*, 8, 9 December 1933. Bernadette was elevated on the feast day of the Immaculate Conception.
100. M. Guasco, *Storia del clero in Italia dall'Ottocento a oggi* (Bari: Laterza, 1997), pp. 56–9.
101. *Il Popolo d'Italia*, 30 November 1933.
102. *Il Messaggero*, 1 April 1934.
103. *L'Illustrazione Italiana*, 8 April 1934.
104. *Il Popolo d'Italia*, 3 April 1934.
105. He joined those punished by *confino*. For his file, see ACS Ministero dell'Interno, Direzione Generale di Pubblica Sicurezza, Confinati Politici, b. 633. Martire had been arrested for insulting Mussolini's son-in-law, Galeazzo Ciano.
106. *Il Messaggero*, 1 April 1934.

8. The Rome of Mussolini and his history wars

1. L. Garibaldi (ed.), *Mussolini e il professore: vita e diari di Carlo Alberto Biggini* (Milan: Mursia, 1983), p. 362.
2. A.J.C. Hare, *Walks in Rome* (London: G. Allen, n.d.), vol. II, p. 23.
3. For introduction, see R.J.B. Bosworth, *Mussolini* (London: Arnold, 2002), pp. 209; 239–40.
4. See A. Del Boca, *I gas di Mussolini: il fascismo e la guerra d'Etiopia* (Rome: Riuniti, 1996).
5. A. Agati, 'La residenza di Mussolini a Villa Torlonia' in A. Campitelli (ed.), *Villa Torlonia: guida* (Rome: Electa, 2006), p. 184.
6. I. Silone, *Fontamara* (London: Methuen, 1934). Silone in recent times has provoked passionate debate over whether he was a paid informer of the Fascist secret police.
7. Campitelli (ed.), *Villa Torlonia*, p. 19.
8. For praise, see E. Gentile, *Renzo De Felice: lo storico e il personaggio* (Bari: Laterza, 2003); for criticism, cf. R.J.B. Bosworth, *The Italian Dictatorship: Problems and Perspectives in the Interpretation of Mussolini and Fascism* (London: Arnold, 1998), especially pp. 120–32.
9. Agati, 'La residenza di Mussolini a Villa Torlonia', p. 187.
10. P. Salvatori, *Il governatorato di Roma: l'amministrazione della capitale durante il fascismo* (Milan: F. Angeli, 2006), p. 54. For a case study, cf. E. Camarda, *Pietralata: Da campagna a isola di periferia* (Milan: F. Angeli, 2007).
11. G. Berlinguer and P. Della Seta, *Borgate di Roma* (Rome: Riuniti, 1960), p. 64.
12. Salvatori, *Il governatorato di Roma*, pp. 99–100.
13. For other post-war name changes, see *Dizionario topomastico di Roma*, March 1954.
14. See generally G. Cuccia, *Urbanistica edilizia infrastruttura di Roma capitale 1870–1990: una cronologia* (Bari: Laterza, 1991), pp. 150–75.
15. Salvatori, *Il governatorato di Roma*, p. 86.
16. G. Ghersi, *Mussolini: fabbro dello stato* (Milan: La Tradizione, 1937). Mussolini's socialist father, Alessandro, had, for a time, been the village blacksmith at Predappio. For regime version, see F. Bonavita, *Il padre del Duce* (Rome: Casa Pinciana, 1933).

17. See the hallucinatory A. Gravelli, *Uno e molti: interpretazioni spirituali di Mussolini* (Rome: Nuova Europa, 1938), p. 106.
18. L. Passerini, *Mussolini immaginario: storia di una biografia 1915–1939* (Bari: Laterza, 1991), pp. 156–7.
19. G. Viganoni, *Mussolini e i Cesari* (Milan: Edizioni 'Ultra', 1933), pp. 19–33; 237–9.
20. Gravelli, *Uno e molti*, p. 55.
21. *Ibid.*, p. 37.
22. Bosworth, *Mussolini*, p. 314.
23. B. Mussolini, *Opera omnia* (eds E. and D. Susmel) (Florence 1951–63), vol.XXVII, pp. 268–9.
24. E. Del Bufolo, *La Via Imperiale e il suo significato storico e politico* (Rome: Istituto di studi romani, 1940), p. 4.
25. E. Gentile, *Fascismo di pietra* (Bari: Laterza, 2007), p. 129 citing B. Baskerville, *What next, O Duce?* (London: Longmans, 1937), pp. 3–4.
26. G.L. Steer, *Caesar in Abyssinia* (London: Hodder and Stoughton, 1936).
27. G. Seldes, *Sawdust Caesar: The Untold History of Mussolini and Fascism* (London: A. Barker, 1936), p. 382.
28. See especially, Gentile, *Fascismo di pietra* and B. Painter, *Mussolini's Rome: rebuilding the Eternal City* (New York: Palgrave Macmillan, 2005).
29. See the reflection on the matter by *The Times* journalist, M.H.H. Macartney, *One Man Alone: The History of Mussolini and the Axis* (London: Chatto and Windus, 1944).
30. For a list, see A. Cederna, *Mussolini urbanista: lo sventramento di Roma negli anni di consenso* (Bari: Laterza, 1979), p. 258.
31. A. Riccardi, *Roma 'città sacra'? Dalla Conciliazione all'operazione Sturzo* (Milan: Vita e Pensiero, 1979), p. 98.
32. For his case, see L. Benevolo, *San Pietro e la città di Roma* (Bari: Laterza, 2004).
33. F. Sapori, *L'arte e il Duce* (Milan: Mondadori, 1932), p. 127.
34. L. Di Majo and I. Insolera, *L'EUR e Roma dagli anni trenta al duemila* (Bari: Laterza, 1986), pp. 47–8.
35. *Ibid.*, p. 1.
36. G.Q. Giglioli (ed.), *Mostra Augustea della romanità: catalogo* (Rome: Casa Editrice C. Colombo, 1938), p. viii.
37. G.Q. Giglioli, 'Il sepolcreto imperiale', *Capitolium*, 6, November 1930, p. 532; *Per il secondo millenario di Augusto* (Rome: Paolo Cremonese editore, 1931), p. 3.
38. 'Il Parrocco' (G.Q. Giglioli), *L'italianità della Corsica* (Livorno: Raffaele Giusti Editore, 1931); *Le glorie della lingua italiana a Malta* (Rome: Società Dante Alighieri, 1932).
39. Giglioli (ed.), *Mostra Augustea della romanità*, pp. vii–viii.
40. Archivio centrale dello stato, Segreteria particolare del Duce, Carteggio ordinario, b. 546254, 24 July 1943, Giglioli to Mussolini.
41. Cederna, *Mussolini urbanista*, p. 211.
42. See http://en.arapacis.it/sede/il_progetto_meier, accessed 13 October 2010.
43. *La Repubblica*, 2 June 2009.
44. Sapori, *L'arte e il Duce*, p. 145.
45. G. Giovannoni, 'Vecchie città ed edilizia nuova', *Nuova Antologia*, f. 995, 1 June 1913, pp. 449–72.
46. P. Nicoloso, *Gli architetti di Mussolini: scuole e sindacato, architetti e massoni, professori e politici negli anni del regime* (Milan: F. Angeli, 1999), pp. 33–8.
47. *Ibid.*, p. 94.
48. G. Giovannoni, *Vecchie città ed edilizia nuova* (Turin: Unione Tipografia-Editrice Torinese, 1931), p. 49.
49. *Ibid.*, pp. 113; 157.
50. *Ibid.*, pp. 209–10.
51. G. Giovannoni, *Lineamenti fondamentali del piano regolatore di Roma imperiale* (Rome: Istituto di studi romani, 1939), p. 5.

52. G. Giovannoni, 'L'espansione di Roma verso i colli e verso il mare' in G. Caffarelli et al., *Il piano regolatore provinciale di Roma* (Rome: Editore Cremonese, 1935), p. 145.

53. G. Giovannoni, *L'architettura come volontà costruttiva del genio romano e italico* (Rome: Istituto di studi romani, 1939), p. 4.

54. Nicoloso, *Gli architetti di Mussolini*, pp. 29–31.

55. M. Piacentini, *Sulla conservazione della bellezza di Roma e sullo sviluppo della città moderna* (Rome: Stabilimento Tipografico 'Aeternum' di Enrico Sabucchi, [1916]), p. 7.

56. *Ibid.*, pp. 14–15.

57. *Ibid.*, p. 19

58. *Ibid.*, pp. 8–9.

59. Nicoloso, *Gli architetti di Mussolini*, pp. 51; 67; 115; 166.

60. *Ibid.*, p. 166.

61. ACS Segreteria particolare del Duce, Carteggio Riservato, b. 103, file on Piacentini.

62. Nicoloso, *Gli architetti di Mussolini*, p. 204.

63. *Ibid.*, p. 213.

64. M. Piacentini, *Le vicende edilizia di Roma dal 1870 ad oggi* (Rome: Fratelli Palomba, [1952]), p. 3.

65. *Ibid.*, pp. 99–100.

66. *Ibid.*, p. 103.

67. For background, see R. Bosworth, 'Italy's Historians and the Myth of Fascism' in R. Langhorne (ed.), *Diplomacy and Intelligence During the Second World War: Essays in Honour of F.H. Hinsley* (Cambridge University Press, 1985), pp. 85–105.

68. M. Cagnetta, *Antichisti e impero fascista* (Bari: Dedalo, 1979), p. 37.

69. R. Paribeni, *Roma Aeterna* (Bologna: Zanichelli, 1932), pp. 2–3.

70. R. Paribeni, *L'Impero romano* (Rome: Istituto di studi romani, 1939), pp. 7; 72.

71. Cagnetta, *Antichisti e impero fascista*, p. 99.

72. *Ibid.*, pp. 87–8.

73. J. Gagé, *Gli studi francesi sulla figura e l'opera di Augusto e sulla fondazione dell'impero romano* (Rome: Istituto di Studi romani, 1938), p. 5.

74. M.P. Nilsson, *Imperial Rome* (London: G. Bell, 1926), pp. 247–9; 317–18.

75. *Capitolium*, 7, 1931.

76. K. Scott, 'Mussolini and the Roman Empire', *Classical Journal*, 27, 1932, pp. 648–9; 654.

77. C.B. Hershey, 'Rome. A Symbol?', *Classical Journal*, 27, 1931, pp. 126; 130.

78. E. Strong, *La legislazione sociale di Augusto e i fregi del recinto dell'Ara Pacis* (Rome: Istituto di studi romani, 1939), pp. 8–9; 17.

79. R. Syme, *The Roman Revolution* (Oxford University Press, 1939), p. 524.

80. *Journal of Roman Studies*, 30, 1940, pp. 75–80.

81. G. Bottai, *L'Italia di Augusto e l'Italia di oggi* (Rome: Istituto di studi romani, 1938), p. 23.

82. G. Bottai, *Roma nella scuola italiana* (Rome: Istituto di studi romani, 1939), pp. 4; 14.

83. G. Bottai, *La funzione di Roma nella vita culturale e scientifica della nazione* (Rome: Istituto di studi romani, 1940), pp. 3; 15.

84. Situazione politica ed economica delle provincie (SPEP hereafter) 19, reports of 24 January, 30 March 1939.

85. SPEP 19, 14 June 1940, report.

86. SPEP 19, 15 June 1940, report.

87. P. Cavallo, *Italiani in guerra: sentimenti e immagini dal 1940 al 1943* (Bologna: il Mulino, 1997), p. 344.

88. *Ibid.*

89. A. Ciampani, 'Municipio capitolino e governo nazionale da Pio IX a Umberto' in V. Vidotto (ed.), *Roma capitale* (Bari: Laterza, 2002), p. 105; P. Salvatori, 'L'Urbe va alla guerra', *Roma moderna e contemporanea*, 11, 2003, pp. 410–12.

90. M.L. D'Autilia, 'Caratteri strutturali: imprese, amministrazione pubblica, assistenza', *Roma moderna e contemporanea*, 11, 2003, p. 384.

91. Salvatori, *Il governatorato di Roma*, p. 116.
92. *Ibid.*, p. 136.
93. A. Milward, *War, Economy and Society 1939–1945* (Berkeley: University of California Press, 1977), p. 97.
94. G. Bottai, 'Latinità e Germanesimo', *Il Primato*, 1 January 1941; A. Grandi, *Gli eroi di Mussolini: Niccolò Giani e la scuola di mistica fascista* (Milan: BUR, 2004), p. 113.
95. Di Mayo and Insolera, *L'EUR e Roma*, p. 61.
96. L. Raganello, *Senza sapere da che parte stanno: ricordi dell'infanzia e 'diario' di Roma in guerra (1943–44)* (ed. L. Piccioni) (Rome: Bulzoni, 2000), p. 59.
97. A. Asor Rosa, *L'alba del mondo nuovo* (Turin: Einaudi, 2002), p. 138.
98. R. Giovagnoli, *Il Natale di Roma e la stirpe latina* (Rome: Tipografia 'Le Massime', 1925), p. 5.
99. A. Hitler, *Table Talk 1941–1944* (London: Weidenfeld and Nicolson, 1953), p. 80.
100. Gentile, *Fascismo di pietra*, p. 249.
101. G. Ciano, *Diary 1939–1943* (ed. M. Muggeridge) (London: Heinemann, 1947), p. 443.
102. A. Giardina and A. Vauchez, *Il mito di Roma da Carlo Magno a Mussolini* (Bari: Laterza, 2000), p. 263.
103. Salvatori, *Il governatorato di Roma*, p. 108.
104. See, for example, G. Colamarino, 'La Russia e l'Occidente', *Il Primato*, 15 August 1941, p. 6.

9. A Second Restoration? The Catholic and imperial Rome of Pius XII

1. For this number, see U. Gentiloni Silveri and M. Carli, *Bombardare Roma: gli Alleati e la 'città aperta' (1940–1944)* (Bologna: il Mulino, 2007), p. 103. Cf. also A. Portelli, *The Order Has Been Carried Out: History, Memory and Meaning of a Nazi Massacre in Rome* (New York: Palgrave Macmillan, 2003). Portelli (p. 77) reckons that there were up to 3,000 killed in the bombing and more than 10,000 injured.
2. For the most thorough study of an Italian city under such bombing, see G. Gribaudi, *Guerra totale: tra bombe alleate e violenze naziste Napoli e il fronte meridionale 1940–44* (Turin: Bollati Boringhieri, 2005).
3. A. Riccardi, 'La vita religiosa' in V. Vidotto (ed.), *Roma capitale* (Bari: Laterza, 2002), p. 312.
4. U. Giovannetti, *Roma: città aperta* (Milan: Editrice Ancora, 1962), p. 114.
5. R. Katz, *Fatal Silence: The Pope, the Resistance and the German Occupation of Rome* (London: Cassell, 2004), p. 15.
6. In 1962, Messina's overtly anti-Marxist statue of St Catherine of Siena, still to be seen on the Castel Sant'Angelo corner of the Via della Conciliazione, had been received in a lukewarm manner by John XXIII. See G. Parsons, 'A neglected sculpture: the monument to Catherine of Siena at Castel Sant'Angelo', *Papers of the British School at Rome*, 76, 2008, pp. 257–76.
7. The phrase, Defensor Civitatis, had been launched in *L'Osservatore romano* under German occupation in March 1944. The paper then compared the pope to Gregory the Great (590–604), who had resisted the Lombards and reasserted papal primacy. See Giovannetti, *Roma: città aperta*, p. 241.
8. O. Chadwick, *Catholicism and History: The Opening of the Vatican Archives* (Cambridge University Press, 1978), p. 100.
9. J. Cornwell, *Hitler's Pope: The Secret History of Pius XII* (Harmondsworth: Penguin, 2000).
10. D. Goldhagen, *A Moral Reckoning: The Role of the Catholic Church in the Holocaust and its Unfulfilled Duty of Repair* (New York: Knopf, 2002), pp. 47–8.
11. S. Zuccotti, *Under his very windows: the Vatican and the Holocaust in Italy* (New Haven, CT: Yale University Press, 2002).
12. R.J.B. Bosworth, *Italy: The Least of the Great Powers: Italian Foreign Policy Before the First World War* (Cambridge University Press, 1979), pp. 139–40.

13. Cornwell, *Hitler's pope*, pp. 13–20.
14. C. Galuzzi Paluzzi (ed.), *Roma nella parola di Pio XII* (Rome: Istituto di studi romani, 1943), pp. 11–12. The editor had had a distinguished career as a Fascist intellectual, if of a reactionary kind. See, for example, his *Per l'uso del Latino (i primi frutti di un rifiorire)* (Bologna: Cappelli, 1934), suggesting that Latin could be revived as the international scientific and diplomatic language and, more crassly, *Lo spirito di Roma e del Fascismo nella riforma della scuola* (Rome: Istituto di studi romani, 1939), summoning Mussolini to his side to advocate stiffer school discipline and the cancellation of the heretical freedoms that had misled the young since Rousseau.
15. Galuzzi Paluzzi (ed.), *Roma nella parola di Pio XII*, pp. 15–16.
16. *Ibid.*, p. 20.
17. *Ibid.*, p. 38.
18. J. Pollard, *Money and the Rise of the Modern Papacy: Financing the Vatican, 1850–1950* (Cambridge University Press, 2005), p. 187.
19. Galuzzi Paluzzi (ed.), *Roma nella parola di Pio XII*, p. 44.
20. Documenti diplomatici italiani 8s, VIII, 461, 7 April 1938, Pignatti to Ciano.
21. Galuzzi Paluzzi (ed.), *Roma nella parola di Pio XII*, p. 124.
22. Giovannetti, *Roma: città aperta*, pp. 7–8.
23. Cited by J. Whittam, 'The reluctant crusader: de Gasperi and the crisis of May 1947', *War and Society*, 2, 1984, p. 88.
24. L. Gedda, *18 Aprile 1948: memorie inedite dell' artefice della sconfitta del Fronte Popolare* (Milan: Mondadori, 1998), p. 123.
25. E. Di Nolfo, *Le paure e le speranze degli italiani (1943–1953)* (Milan: Mondadori, 1946), pp. 263–4.
26. F. Margiotto Broglio, 'Dalla Conciliazione al giubileo 2000', in L. Fiorani and A. Prosperi (eds), *Roma: la città del papa: vita civile e religiosa dal giubileo di Bonifacio VIII al giubileo di papa Wojtyla* (Turin: Einaudi, 2000), p. 1177.
27. A. Riccardi, 'Capitale del Cattolicesimo' in L. De Rosa (ed.), *Roma del duemila* (Bari: Laterza, 2000), p. 45.
28. Cited by P. Ginsborg, *A History of Contemporary Italy: Society and Politics 1943–1988* (Harmondsworth: Penguin, 1990), p. 158.
29. L. Lotti, 'Il Giubileo del 1950' in D. Sterpos (ed.), *I Giubilei: viaggio e incontro dei pellegrini* (Rome: Quaderni di Autostrade, 1975), p. 154.
30. Riccardi, 'Capitale del Cattolicesimo', pp. 47–8.
31. Pio XII, *Discorsi e radiomessaggi, vol. XI (2 marzo 1949–1 marzo 1950)* (Vatican City: Tipografia poliglotta Vaticana, 1950), pp. 11; 15.
32. *Ibid.*, pp. 162–3.
33. *Ibid.*, p. 299.
34. *Ibid.*, p. 327.
35. A. Brucculeri, 'Nello spirito dell'Anno Santo', *Civiltà cattolica*, vol. 101, 7 January 1950.
36. A. Messineo, 'Democrazia e religione', *Civiltà cattolica*, 101, 15 April 1950.
37. *L'Osservatore romano*, 19 January 1950.
38. S. Lener, 'I Patti Lateranensi e la nuova Italia', *Civiltà cattolica*, 101, 17 June 1950.
39. A. Oddone, 'Il fascino di Roma papale', *Civiltà cattolica*, 101, 16 December 1950.
40. D. Mondrone, 'La definizione dommatica dell'Assunta: messaggio di innovate speranze ai popoli', *Civiltà cattolica*, 101, 2 September 1950.
41. *L'Osservatore romano*, 2–3 January 1950.
42. I. Giordani, *Pio XII: un grande Papa* (Turin: Società Internazionale, 1961), p. 354.
43. *Il Messaggero*, 25 June 1950; Pio XII, *Discorsi e radiomessaggi (2 marzo 1950–1 marzo 1951* (Vatican City: Tipografia poliglotta Vaticana, 1951), p. 119.
44. M. Lizzani, 'La Romanità di alcuni santi del Giubileo', *Capitolium*, 25, 1950, pp. 267–76.
45. See S. Luzzatto, *Padre Pio: miracoli e politica nell'Italia del Novecento* (Turin: Einaudi, 2007), for a fine study of his career. There is nothing comparable on Maria Goretti.

46. M. Warner, *Alone of All Her Sex: the Myth and Cult of the Virgin Mary* (London: Vintage, 2000), p. 94.
47. *L'Osservatore romano*, 22 April 1950.
48. *L'Osservatore romano*, 8 December 1949; 12–13 June 1950.
49. J. More, *The Land of Italy* (London: Batsford, 1949), pp. 157–8.
50. C. Kininmonth, *Rome Alive: A Notebook* (London: John Lehmann, 1951), pp. 26; 29.
51. E. Clark, *Rome and a Villa* (London: M. Joseph, 1953), pp. 17–19.
52. *Ibid.*, p. 204.
53. E. Martire, 'Il Colosseo e l'Anno Santo', *Capitolium*, 25, 1950, p. 83.
54. A. Riccardi, *Roma 'città sacra'? Dalla Conciliazione all'operazione Sturzo* (Milan: Vita e Pensiero, 1979), pp. 273–4.
55. Cf. his participation in the lavish official publication, A. Giannini and G. Minozzi (eds), *Holy Year: The Jubilee of 1950* (Milan: Bompiani, 1950), which had pieces from a number of writers of conservative bent who had flourished under the dictatorship.
56. G. Prezzolini, 'Introduction' to H. Bittner and E. Nash (eds), *Rome* (Chicago: Henry Regnary, 1950), p. 7.
57. *Ibid.*, pp. 25–9.
58. *Ibid.*, pp. 17; 36.
59. *Ibid.*, p. 40.
60. G. Ceroni, *Roma intima (le note di un cronista)* (Roma: Editrice Nazionale, 1938); *Roma nei suoi quartieri e nel suo suburbio* (Rome: Fratelli Palombi, 1942).
61. *Il Messaggero*, 6 April 1950.
62. G. Ceroni, *Pietre di Roma: le case dove soggiornarono i santi, i preti, i genii* (Rome: Fratelli Palombi, 1945), p. 10.
63. G. Schwarz, *Ritrovano se stessi: gli ebrei nell'Italia postfascista* (Bari: Laterza, 2004), p. 5.
64. Giordani, *Pio XII*, p. 322.
65. R. di Segni, 'Spazi sacri e spazi maledetti nella Roma ebraica' in S. Boesch Cajano and L. Scaraffia (eds), *Luoghi sacri e spazi della santità* (Turin: Rosenberg and Sellier, 1990), p. 116.
66. E. Amidei, 'Gli ebrei in Roma', *Capitolium*, 8, May 1932, pp. 253–4.
67. For its story, see A. Stille, *Benevolence and Betrayal: Five Italian Jewish Families Under Fascism* (New York: Penguin, 1993).
68. E. Ovazza, *Sionismo bifronte* (Rome: Casa Editrice Pinciana, 1935), pp. 22–3; 31; 49; 95.
69. F. Wildvang, 'The enemy next door: Italian collaboration in deporting Jews during the German occupation of Rome', *Modern Italy*, 12, 2007, pp. 189; 200.
70. Schwarz, *Ritrovano se stessi*, pp. 10; 125.
71. *Ibid.*, p. 12.
72. R. De Felice, *Storia degli ebrei italiani sotto il fascismo* (Turin: Einaudi, 1961), pp. 286; 502.
73. Cornwell, *Hitler's pope*, p. 309.
74. See S. Ficacci, *Tor Pignattara: Fascismo e Resistenza di un quartiere romano* (Milan: F. Angeli, 2007).
75. F. Bartolini, *Rivali d'Italia: Roma e Milano dal Settecento a oggi* (Bari: Laterza, 2006), p. 247, and cf. G. Liguori, *Gramsci conteso: storia di un dibattito 1922–1996* (Rome: Riuniti, 1996).
76. *Dizionario toponomastico di Roma*, March 1954.
77. www.qscuole.it/lazio/roma/liceo-scientifico-primo-levi-di-roma, accessed 12 July 2010.
78. E. Piscitelli, *Storia della Resistenza romana* (Bari: Laterza, 1965), pp. v–vii.
79. *Ibid.*, p. 39.
80. M. de Wyss, *Rome Under the Terror* (London: Robert Hale, 1945), pp. 47–8.
81. Piscitelli, *Storia della Resistenza romana*, p. 155.
82. *Ibid.*, pp. 374; 379.
83. S. Gottlieb (ed.), *Roberto Rossellini's* Rome Open City (Cambridge University Press, 2004), p. 1.
84. For the parallel with 1922, see M. Landy, 'Diverting Clichés: Femininity, Masculinity, Melodrama and Neorealism in *Open City*', in Gottlieb (ed.), *Roberto Rossellini's* Rome Open City, p. 100.

85. For the French case, cf. H. Rousso, *The Vichy Syndrome: History and Memory in France since 1944* (Cambridge, MA: Harvard University Press, 1991).

86. J. Staron, *Fosse Ardeatine e Marzabotto: storia e memoria di due stragi tedesche* (Bologna: il Mulino, 2007), p. 100.

87. G. Lai, 'Ripresa', *Capitolium*, 19, July–September 1944.

88. Staron, *Fosse Ardeatine e Marzabotto*, pp. 100–2.

89. *Ibid.*, p. 103.

90. N. Ciampi and A. Ascarella, 'VI anniversario dell'eccidio alle Fosse Ardeatine', *Capitolium*, 25, 1950, pp. 91–8.

91. For a fuller list, see R.J.B. Bosworth, *Mussolini's Italy: Life Under the Dictatorship 1915–1945* (London: Allen Lane, 2005), pp. 498–9.

92. *L'Osservatore romano*, 11 June 1950. For Amendola, communist son of a liberal democrat (and imperialist Minister of Colonies), see G. Amendola, *Una scelta di vita* (Milan: Rizzoli, 1976); *Un'isola* (Milan: Rizzoli, 1980). For Pertini, cf. his explosively entitled G. Pertini, *Sei condanne, due evasioni* (Milan: Mondadori, 1970).

93. Staron, *Fosse Ardeatine e Marzabotto*, p. 205.

94. *Ibid.*, p. 241.

95. *Ibid.*, p. 346.

96. A. and E. Benzoni, *Attentato e rappresaglia: il PCI e via Rasella* (Venice: Marsilio, 1999), p. 49.

97. A. Portelli, 'Perché ci amazzano? Ambiguità e contraddizione nella memoria dei bombardamenti', *Roma moderna e contemporanea*, 11, 2003, pp. 658–9.

98. *Ibid.*, pp. 650–4.

99. The best source for such people is literature from the period, see the (patronising) A. Moravia, *The Woman of Rome* (Harmondsworth: Penguin, 1949). The book was first published in Italian. Cf. the less portentous C.E. Gadda, *Quer pasticciaccio brutto de Via Merulana* (Milan: Garzanti, 1957), translated into English as *That awful mess on the Via Merulana* (London: Quartet Books, 1985). Gadda, born in Milan and perhaps sharing the Milanese contempt for Rome, here offers a wondrous lexicon of terms of abuse of Mussolini and also avenges Rome on its archaeologists by having one of the potential killers in his murder story without end named Diomede Lanciani.

100. Riccardi, *Roma 'città sacra'?*, pp. 314; 322.

101. G. Talamo, 'Profilo politico', in L. De Rosa (ed.), *Roma del duemila* (Bari: Laterza, 2000), pp. 18–19.

102. *Ibid.*, p. 381.

103. L. Gedda, *18 Aprile 1848: memorie inedite dell'artefice della sconfitta del Fronte Popolare* (Milan: Mondadori, 1998), p. 162.

104. A. Riccardi, *Il 'Partito Romano' nel secondo dopoguerra (1945–1954)* (Brescia: Morcelliana, 1983), p. 222.

105. R. Montini, 'Romanità di Pio XII', *Capitolium*, 33, November 1958, p. 25.

106. L. Benevolo, *Roma oggi* (Bari: Laterza, 1977), p. 11.

107. Riccardi, 'Capitale del Cattolicesimo', p. 48.

108. M. Sanfilippo, *La costruzione di una capitale: Roma 1945–1991* (Cinisello Balsamo: Silvana Editoriale, 1994), p. 29.

109. Clark, *Rome and a Villa*, p. 197.

110. A. Natoli, *Il sacco di Roma: la speculazione edilizia all'ombra del Campidoglio* (Rome: Tipografia Lugli, 1954), pp. 10–11; 54; 95–8.

111. Riccardi, *Roma 'città sacra'?*, p. 404.

112. L. Canullo, *Taccuino di un militante: quarant'anni di lotta politica a Roma* (Rome: Riuniti, 1981), pp. 48–50.

113. G. Zizola, *Giovanni XXIII: la fede e la politica* (Bari: Laterza, 1988), p. 133; G. Andreotti, *Visti da vicino*, 3rd series (Milan: Rizzoli, 1985), p. 33.

10. Olympic Rome: sport, blood and histories

1. P. Avarello, 'L'urbanizzazione' in L. De Rosa (ed.), *Roma del duemila* (Bari: Laterza, 2000), p. 172.
2. G. Berlinguer and P. Della Seta, *Borgate di Roma* (Rome: Riuniti, 1960), p. 89.
3. I. Giordani, *Pio XII: un grande papa* (Turin: Società Editrice Internazionale, 1961), p. 702.
4. *Ibid.*, p. 295.
5. L. Gedda, *18 Aprile 1848: memorie inedite dell'artefice della sconfitta del Fronte Popolare* (Milan: Mondadori, 1998), pp. 207–8.
6. P. Blanshard, *Paul Blanshard on Vatican II* (London: George Allen and Unwin, 1967), p. 214.
7. F. Giannattasio, 'Olimpiadi a Roma', *Civiltà cattolica*, vol. 111, 1960.
8. Blanshard, *Paul Blanshard on Vatican II*, p. 23.
9. M. Manieri Elia, 'Roma capitale: strategie urbane e uso della memoria' in A. Caracciolo (ed.), *Il Lazio. Storia d'Italia. Le Regioni dall'Unità a oggi* (Turin: Einaudi, 1991), p. 547.
10. The ironies in this accommodation with the Fascist architectural past in Rome were numerous, and would remain so. One wry example of the management of history was evident at Christmas/New Year, 2007–8. Then, under a leftist administration, restoration work proceeded on the obelisk. Globalisation encouraged help from private enterprise in such action. The obelisk was for the duration of its repair covered with protective material. It bore the logo of the generous business sponsor – the Volkswagen company. Perhaps, somewhere beneath it, the ghost of A. Hitler twitched.
11. E. Clark, *Rome and a Villa* (London: M. Joseph, 1953), p. 115.
12. Banca Nazionale del Lavoro, *Guida Olimpica Roma 1960* (Rome: Banca Nazionale del Lavoro, 1960), p. 59.
13. *Ibid.*, p. 9.
14. *Ibid.*, p. 90.
15. S. Rebecchini, 'Il Comune di Roma da Michelangelo Caetani a Filippo Doria Pamphilj', *Studi romani*, X, May–June 1962, p. 279.
16. *Atti parlamentari*, CCII, session of 6 October 1959, p. 10612.
17. A. Agosti, *Palmiro Togliatti: A Biography* (London: I.B. Tauris, 2008), p. 200. This cynicism was matched by such prestigious US papers as the *New York Times* and *Los Angeles Times*, each of which thought any criticism of the Foro italico was simply another case of the PCI doing the Soviets' bidding. See E.M. Modrey, 'Architecture as a mode of self-representation at the Olympic Games in Rome (1960) and Munich (1972)', *European Review of History*, 15, 2008, p. 701.
18. *La Stampa*, 7 October 1959.
19. *Il Messaggero*, 10 August 1960.
20. *La Stampa*, 11 August 1960.
21. *Il Messaggero*, 11 August 1960.
22. *La Stampa*, 12 August 1960.
23. Puccini, a conservative anxious to deny a weakness for the Germanic powers, composed a memorial piece for this duke's father, Amedeo, sometime king of Spain (died 1890). For a patriotic obituary of Emanuele Filiberto, see E.M. Gray, *Il Duca d'Aosta: cittadino della riscossa italica* (Milan: Ente Autonomo Stampa, 1931).
24. For an example, see R. Lanciani, *New Tales from Old Rome* (London: Macmillan, 1901), p. 39, contrasting 'this unfortunate prince, Roman to the core' with that Constantine who soon moved the imperial capital to Constantinople.
25. Manieri Elia, 'Roma capitale', pp. 546–7.
26. C. Levi, *Fleeting Rome: In Search of La Dolce Vita* (Chichester: J. Wiley, 2005), p. 167.
27. P. de Coubertin, *Olympism: Selected Writings* (ed. N. Müller) (Lausanne: International Olympics Committee, 2000), pp. 270–1. For endorsement a century later by sometime Francoist José Antonio Samaranch, with his continued ambition that the modern

Games match the ancient, see M. Caporilli and F. Simeoni (eds), *Il Foro Italico e lo Stadio Olimpico: immagini dalla storia* (Rome: Tomo Edizioni, 1990), p. 15.

28. J.J. MacAloon, *This Great Symbol: Pierre de Coubertin and the Origins of the Modern Olympic Games* (Chicago: University of Chicago Press, 1981), pp. 8–12.

29. S. Rebecchini, 'I De Coubertin e Roma', *Capitolium*, 35, 1960, pp. 60–3; 'Pierre Fredy de Coubertin: le rinnovate Olimpiadi e Roma', *L'Urbe*, 23, July–August 1960, pp. 3–11.

30. In a later paradox, the Colosseum would appear on Olympic medals until the Sydney Games of 2004. However, this invocation of ancient Rome became the object of combined Greek–Australian attack and the image was converted to one of a victory flag flying over the stadium used at Athens in 1896. See K. Hopkins and M. Beard, *The Colosseum* (London: Profile Books, 2005).

31. De Coubertin, *Olympism*, p. 337.

32. *Ibid.*, p. 408.

33. *Ibid.*, pp. 409–10.

34. L. Rossi, 'Una capitale poco sportiva. Attività agonistica e luoghi di svago tra il 1870 e il 1940', *Roma moderna e contemporanea*, 7, 1999, pp. 245–6.

35. De Coubertin, *Olympism*, pp. 675–7; 681.

36. A. Mosso, *Mens sana in corpore sano* (Milan: Treves, [1903]), p. 73.

37. A. Mosso, 'I Giuochi Olimpici a Roma?', *Nuova Antologia*, 116, 1 April 1905, pp. 401–26.

38. Rossi, 'Una capitale poco sportiva', pp. 246–7.

39. L. Di Majo and I. Insolera, *L'EUR e Roma degli anni trenta al duemila* (Bari: Laterza, 1986), p. 78.

40. See, for example, V. Testa, 'Un quartiere modello nella Roma moderna', *Studi romani*, 1, January–Feburary 1953, pp. 50–7. Cf. a more grandiloquent justification of the area as signifying Rome's future, while, in its beauty, connecting fittingly with the Victor Emmanuel monument and St Peter's. I. Antonucci, 'Roma e il suo luminoso quartiere modello: l'EUR', *L'Urbe*, 33, 1960, pp. 34–9.

41. Pigorini lived between 1842 and 1925, rising to be nominated a Senator for life in 1912. For his collection, see B. Brizzi (ed.), *The Pigorini Museum* (Rome: Quasar, 1975).

42. Banca Nazionale del Lavoro, *Guida Olimpica*, p. 61.

43. *L'Osservatore romano*, 14, 21 August 1960.

44. M. De Nicolò, *La lente sul Campidoglio: amministrazione capitolina e storiografia* (Rome: Istituto nazionale di studi romani, 1996), pp. 19–20.

45. See, for example, D. Demarco, *Una rivoluzione sociale: la repubblica romana del 1849 (16 novembre 1848–3 luglio 1849)* (Naples: Mario Fiorentino editore, 1944); L. Rodelli, *La Repubblica romana del 1849* (Pisa: Domus Mazziniana, 1955), pp. 61–6.

46. S. Rebecchini, 'Roma nel 1848', *Capitolium*, 23, 1948, p. 29.

47. M. Lizzani, ' "1848" romano: il popolo', *Capitolium*, 23, 1948, pp. 67–72.

48. A. Caracciolo, *I sindaci di Roma* (Rome: Donzelli, 1993), p. 64.

49. M. De Nicolò, 'I problemi della Città: le scelte capitoline' in De Rosa (ed.), *Roma del duemila* p. 83. cf. also B. Bonomo, *Il quartiere delle valli: costruire Roma nel secondo dopoguerra* (Milan: F. Angeli, 2007).

50. *L'Unità d'Italia: mostra storica: Torino - Palazzo Carignano maggio–ottobre 1961* (Milan: A. Pizzi editore, 1961).

51. D. Mack Smith, *Italy: A Modern History* (Ann Arbor: University of Michigan Press, 1959).

52. For summary, see R. Romeo, *Risorgimento e capitalismo* (Bari: Laterza, 1974).

53. Comitato nazionale per la celebrazione del primo centenario dell'unità d'Italia, *La Celebrazione del Primo Centenario dell'Unità d'Italia: Italia '61* (Turin: Comitato nazionale per la celebrazione del primo centenario dell'unità d'Italia, 1961), p. 50.

54. In 1970, there were some half-hearted attempts to record the creation of Italian Rome but even *Capitolium* by then was possessed of enough of a social conscience to evoke the continuing history of *baracche* (shacks) in the city. See P.G. Liverani, 'Un inferno chiamato baracca', *Capitolium*, 45, January 1970, pp. 7–15.

55. Di Majo and Insolera, *L'EUR e Roma*, p. 111. When Pope John XXIII gave his offical welcome to athletes, he did so in French, then still the 'official language' of the Games. *La Stampa*, 23 August 1960.

56. G. Andreotti, 'L'anno dei giuochi olimpici', *Studi romani*, 8, January–February 1960, pp. 10–11. Andreotti would be the most durable and controversial politician of the Republic's history, a man whose life is still under debate, as is displayed in Paolo Sorrentino's film, *Il Divo*. It won the Jury prize at the Cannes festival in 2008 for its account of his alleged ties with the Mafia. The title reflects Andreotti's reputation as '*divo Giulio*', the modern version of '*Divus Julius Caesar*'.

57. *La Gazzetta dello Sport*, 23 August 1960.

58. U. Tupini, 'Turismo e Olimpiadi', *Capitolium*, 35, 1950, p. 7.

59. *The Italian News*, 8 July 1960.

60. H. Lechenperg (ed.), *Olympic Games 1960: Squaw Valley/Rome* (New York: T. Yoseloff, 1960), p. 114.

61. R. Vighi, 'Lo sport in Roma antica attraverso la documentazione artistica', *Capitolium*, 35, 1960, pp. 15–25.

62. A.M. Colini (ed.), *Il Fascio Littorio di Roma: ricercato negli antichi monumenti* (Rome: Libreria dello Stato, 1932).

63. A.M. Colini, 'Edifici sportivi di Roma antica', *Capitolium*, 35, pp. 26–36.

64. Tupini, 'Turismo e Olimpiadi', pp. 5–6.

65. R. De Gasperis, 'Competitizioni storiche alle XVII Olimpiadi', *Capitolium*, 35, p. 96.

66. G. Scalia, 'Gare e Giochi agonistici a Roma dal XIII al XVIII secolo', *Capitolium*, 35, 1950, pp. 37–44.

67. C. Baldassini, *L'ombra di Mussolini: l'Italia moderata e la memoria del fascismo (1945–1960)* (Soveria Mannelli: Rubettino, 2008), p. 113.

68. *L'Unità*, 11 September 1960. For a breathless account of American deeds at the Olympics (including those of the CIA), see D. Maraniss, *Rome 1960: The Olympics that Changed the World* (New York: Simon and Schuster, 2008). Cf. also the bland film version *La grande olimpiade*, directed by Romolo Marcellini (1961).

69. Berlinguer and Della Seta, *Borgate di Roma*, p. 165.

70. *L'Unità*, 21 August 1960.

71. In 1959 they were reckoned to originate 56% from Lazio and central Italy, 22% from southern Italy, 13% from the north and 9% from Sicily or Sardinia. M. Sanfilippo, *La costruzione di un capitale: Roma 1945–1991* (Cinisello Balsamo: Silvana Editoriale, 1994), p. 22.

72. A. Riccardi, 'Capitale del cattolicesimo' in L. De Rosa (ed.), *Roma del duemila* (Bari: Laterza, 2000), p. 49.

73. *Ibid.*, p. 59.

74. *Ibid.*, p. 57; G. Verucci, *La chiesa nella società contemporanea dal primo dopoguerra al Concilio Vaticano II* (Bari: Laterza, 1999), p. 369.

75. A. Ravaglioli, 'Giovanni XXIII ha salutato Roma del XX secolo', *Capitolium*, 38, January 1963, p. 4.

76. A. Ravaglioli, 'Giovanni XXIII: Vescovo di Roma', *Capitolium*, 38, June 1963, pp. 282–91.

77. M. Manzo, *Papa Giovanni vescovo a Roma: sinodo e pastorale diocesana nell'episcopato romano di Roncalli* (Milan: Edizioni Paoline, 1991), pp. 217; 238.

78. *Ibid.*, pp. 22–6; 34; 224.

79. Blanshard, *Paul Blanshard on Vatican II*, p. iii; 331.

80. *Concilio Ecumenico Vaticano II: costituzioni, decreti, dichiarazioni* (Rome: Edizioni "Domani", 1966), p. 26.

81. Blanshard, *Paul Blanshard on Vatican II*, p. 123.

82. *Concilio Ecumenico Vaticano II*, pp. 589–91.

83. Riccardi, 'Capitale del cattolicesimo', p. 42.

84. G.B. Montini, 'Roma e il Concilio', *Studi romani*, 10, 1962, pp. 505–6.

85. *Ibid.*, p. 504.
86. R.M. Dainotto, 'The Gubbio papers: historic centers in the age of the economic miracle', *Journal of Modern Italian Studies*, 8, 2003, pp. 68–71.
87. *Ibid.*, p. 73.
88. See, for example, C. Darida, 'Roma: la città della speranza', *Capitolium*, 49, January 1974, pp. 3–10.
89. Riccardi, 'Capitale del cattolicesimo', p. 66; V. Gorresio, *Roma: ieri e oggi* (Milan: Rizzoli, 1970), p. 104.
90. G.C. Argan, *Un'idea di Roma: intervista di Mino Monicelli* (Rome: Riuniti, 1979), p. 7.
91. *Ibid.*, p. 22.
92. *Ibid.*, p. 15.
93. *Ibid.*, pp. 46; 59–61.
94. P. and R. Della Seta, *I suoli di Roma: uso e abuso del territorio nei cento anni della capitale* (Rome: Riuniti, 1988), p. 165.
95. A. Samorè, 'Aspetti caratteristici degli Anni Santi: dalla documentazione dell'Archivio segreto vaticano', *Studi romani*, 23, October–December 1975, p. 441; E. Masina, 'Il Giubileo del 1975' in D. Sterpos (ed.), *Giubilei: viaggio e incontro dei pellegrini* (Rome: Quaderni di Autostrade, 1975), p. 169. Paul had renounced the traditional papal accoutrements including the *sedia gestatoria* in 1967.
96. G. Talamo, 'Profilo politico' in De Rosa (ed.), *Roma del duemila*, p. 33.
97. Riccardi, 'Capitale del cattolicesimo', p. 69.
98. R.N. Gardner, *Mission Italy: On the Front Line of the Cold War* (Lanham: Rowman and Littlefield, 2005), p. 35.
99. *Ibid.*, p. 73.
100. L. Benevolo, *Roma oggi* (Bari: Laterza, 1977), pp. 8–9.
101. The Caetani family, with popes in their past, provided the provisional governor of the city in 1870. The heir took office as Minister of Foreign Affairs in the aftermath of Adua in 1896 and later became mayor of Rome in the moderate clerical interest. For account of their world, see Duchess of Sermoneta, *Sparkle Distant Worlds* (London: Hutchinson, n.d.).

11. Eternity globalised

1. An edition of his speeches and writings was rushed out in 1979 with the friendly endorsement of George Mosse, the Jewish American historian of Fascist ideas, who had become close to Renzo De Felice and his school. See A. Moro, *L'intelligenza e gli avvenimenti: testi 1959-1978* (Milan: Garzanti, 1979). For typical criticisms that Moro could provoke, see A. Coppola, *Moro* (Milan: Feltrinelli, 1976), a work published before Moro's 'martyrdom' and anything but pious in its summation of the politician's character and intent.
2. G. Selva and E. Marcucci, *Aldo Moro: quei terribili 55 giorni* (Soveria Mannelli: Rubbettino, 2003), p. 148.
3. Cited by A. Jamieson, *The Heart Attacked: Terrorism and Conflict in the Italian State* (London: Marion Boyars, 1989), pp. 70–1.
4. G. Galli, *Storia del partito armato* (Milan: Rizzoli, 1986), p. 5.
5. *Ibid.*, p. 17.
6. *Ibid.*, p. 51.
7. R.C. Meade, *Red Brigades: The Story of Italian Terrorism* (Houndmills: Macmillan, 1990), p. 63.
8. Galli, *Storia del partito armato*, p. 13.
9. G. Spadolini, *Diario del drama Moro (marzo–maggio 1978): i cinquantaquattro giorni che hanno cambiato l'Italia* (Florence: Le Monnier, 1978), pp. 14; 18. In 1943-4 Spadolini had youthfully backed the RSI.
10. P. Togliatti, *Lectures on Fascism* (London: Lawrence and Wishart, 1976), p. 1.

11. Jamieson, *The Heart Attacked*, p. 15.
12. For description, see F. Focardi, *La guerra della memoria: la resistenza nel dibattito politico italiano dal 1945 a oggi* (Bari: Laterza, 2005), pp. 41–93.
13. F. Fukuyama, *The End of History and the Last Man* (London: Hamish Hamilton, 1992).
14. A. Caracciolo, *I sindaci di Roma* (Rome: Donzelli, 1993), p. 73.
15. I. Insolera and F. Perego, *Archeologia e città: storia moderna dei fori di Roma* (Bari: Laterza, 1983), p. 312.
16. *Ibid.*, pp. xvi–xvii.
17. P. and R. Della Seta, *I suoli di Roma: uso e abuso del territorio nei cento anni della capitale* (Rome: Riuniti, 1988), p. 250. After his sudden death in 1981, Petroselli had part of the ex-Via dei Monti, running from the Theatre of Marcellus to Santa Maria in Cosmedin, named after him.
18. R. Nicolini, 'L'introduzione' to C. Aymonino, *Progettare Roma capitale* (Bari: Laterza, 1990), pp. 8–9.
19. *Ibid.*, p. 7.
20. *Ibid.*, p. 9.
21. Aymonino, *Progettare Roma capitale*, p. 6.
22. F. Ferrarotti, *Roma madre matrigna* (Bari: Laterza, 1991), pp. 23–4.
23. *Ibid.*, p. 141.
24. Z. Ciuffoletti and M. Degl'Innocenti (eds), *L'emigrazione nella storia d'Italia 1868–1975: storia e documenti* (Florence: Vallecchi, 1978), p. 359.
25. For background, see R.J.B. Bosworth, *Italy and the Wider World 1860–1960* (London: Routledge, 1996), pp. 114–36.
26. A. Golini, 'La popolazione' in L. De Rosa (ed.), *Roma del duemila* (Bari: Laterza, 2000), pp. 140–2.
27. E. D'Elia and C. Rosati, 'I numeri di Roma', *Ufficio statistico del comune di Roma* January–February 2004.
28. M. Sanfilippo, *La construzione di una capitale: Roma 1945–1991* (Cinisello Balsamo: Silvana Editoriale, 1994), p. 68.
29. L. Fiorentino, *Il ghetto racconta Roma/The Ghetto Reveals Rome* (Rome: Gangemi, editore, 2005), p. 7.
30. *Ibid.*, p. 24.
31. *Ibid.*, pp. 111–13.
32. *Ibid.*, p. 25.
33. P. Portoghesi and V. Gigliotti, *Mosque and Islamic Cultural Centre under Construction in Rome* (Rome: n.p., 1989), p. 4.
34. I. Clough Marinaro, 'Integration or marginalisation? The failure of social policy for the Romi in Rome', *Modern Italy*, 8, 2003, was already warning about the failure then of left-wing urban administration to do anything that might end the gypsies' ancient 'marginalisation'.
35. G. Boursier, 'La persecuzione degli zingari nell'Italia fascista', *Studi storici*, 37, 1996, pp. 1067–70.
36. P. Macchi (ed.), *Paolo VI e la tragedia di Moro: 55 giorni di ansie, tentativi, speranze e assurda crudeltà* (Milan: Rusconi, 1998), pp. 14–15.
37. A.C. Jemolo, *Questa repubblica dal '68 alla crisi morale* (Florence: Le Monnier, 1981), p. 223.
38. On John Paul I, see the charges of English authors against either him or his entourage and the papal Curia, in D. Yallop, *In God's name* (New York: Bantam, 1984); J. Cornwell, *A Thief in the Night: The Death of John Paul I* (Harmondsworth: Penguin, 1990).
39. P. Avarello, 'L'urbanizzazione' in De Rosa (ed.), *Roma del duemila*, p. 189.
40. J. Cornwell, *The Pope in Winter: The Dark Face of John Paul II's Papacy* (London: Penguin, 2005), p. 297.
41. D. Julia, 'L'accoglienza dei pellegrini a Roma' in L. Fiorani and A. Prosperi (eds), *Roma: la città del papa: vita civile dal giubileo di Bonifacio VIII al giubileo di papa Woytyla* (Turin: Einaudi, 2000), p. 825.

42. John Paul II, *The Great Jubilee of the Year 2000: Bull of Indiction: 'Incarnationis Mysterium'* (London: Catholic Truth Society, 1999), p. 3.
43. *Ibid.*, p. 18.
44. *Ibid.*, p. 23.
45. *Ibid.*, pp. 21–2.
46. F. Pittau, 'Conoscere per accogliere', *Capitolium*, July 2000, pp. 12–15. According to his rough figures, they were supplemented by 50,000 'Orthodox and Protestants' and an equal number of Muslims. John Paul had already made official papal visits to the Rome synagogue in 1986, while the mosque had been backed by Paul VI.
47. For a more Jewish reading of the cities' allegedly twin histories, see M. Goodman, *Rome and Jerusalem: The Clash of Ancient Civilizations* (London: Allen Lane, 2007).
48. John Paul II, *The Great Jubilee of the Year 2000*, pp. 3; 29–30.
49. Cornwell, *The pope in winter*, pp. 171–4.
50. E. O'Gorman, *Towards the Great Millennium Jubilee 2000* (Leominister: Gracewing, [1998]), pp. 3; 7.
51. Cornwell, *The Pope in Winter*, p. 146. *La Repubblica*, 27 December 1999.
52. 'Lezioni di cantiere. Intervista a Guido Bertolaso, vice commissario straordinario di governo. Il bilancio ragionato su come sono stati utilizzati i finanziamenti per l'Anno Santo', *Capitolium*, March 2000, pp. 23–5.
53. *Capitolium*, editorial, July 2000.
54. L. Maiocco, 'Ricomincio da tre anni', *Capitolium*, July 2000, pp. 10–11.
55. *La Repubblica*, 24 November 1999.
56. For a massive list of government undertakings at this time, see *Capitolium*, December 2000, pp. 27–37.
57. For the list and a review, see *Studi romani*, January–February 2000.
58. P. Scoppola, 'Cenni storici: la tradizione giubilare' in P. Scoppola (ed.), *Piano di intervento del Giubileo dell'Anno 2000* (Rome: Fratelli Palombi Editori, 1998), p. 53.
59. L. Golfo, 'Presentazione' in A. Groppi and L. Scaraffia, *Le donne ai tempi del giubileo* (Milan: Skira editore, 2000), pp. 9–10.
60. *La Repubblica*, 19 December 1999.
61. Cornwell, *The Pope in Winter*, p. 178.
62. *La Repubblica*, 18 March, 9, 10 July 2000.
63. W. Veltroni, 'Prefazio' to Scoppola (ed.), *Piano di intervento del Giubileo*, pp. 7–9; Scoppola, 'Cenni storici', pp. 25–6. Scoppola also urged that events neither disdain nor forget Orthodox, Protestant, Jewish and Muslim sites in the city, or those of Eastern religions and paganism (p. 110).
64. *La Repubblica*, 23 December 1999.
65. Cornwell, *The Pope in Winter*, p. 195.
66. A. Bonetti, *In nome del Papa-Re* (Rome: Solfanelli, 2002).
67. Cited by D.I. Kertzer, *Prisoner of the Vatican: The Popes' Secret Plot to Capture Rome from the New Italian State* (Boston: Houghton Mifflin, 2004), pp. 294–5.
68. For an evocation of its strength in the 1950s, see C. Baldassini, *L'ombra di Mussolini: l'Italia moderata e la memoria del fascismo (1945–1960)* (Soveria Mannelli: Rubbettino, 2008).
69. For a typical statement of such views, see E. Galli Della Loggia, *La morte della patria: la crisi dell'idea della nazione tra resistenza, antifascismo e repubblica* (Bari: Laterza, 1996); *L'identità italiana* (Bologna: il Mulino, 1998).
70. E. Guidoni, *L'urbanistica di Roma tra miti e progetti* (Bari: Laterza, 1990), p. ix.
71. For the background, see R.J.B. Bosworth, 'A country split in two? Contemporary Italy and its usable pasts', *History Compass*, 4, August 2006.
72. A. Stille, *The Sack of Rome: How a Beautiful European Country with a Fabled History and a Storied Culture Was Taken Over by a Man Named Silvio Berlusconi* (New York: Penguin, 2006), pp. 287–8.
73. G. Parlato, *Fascisti senza Mussolini: le origini del neofascismo in Italia, 1943–1948* (Bologna: il Mulino, 2006), p. 79.

74. *Ibid.*, pp. 261–2.
75. Baldassini, *L'ombra di Mussolini*, pp. 34–55.
76. I. Montanelli, *Rome: The First Thousand Years* (London: Collins, 1962), p. 33.
77. For the theme, see P. Ignazi, *Il Polo escluso: profilo del Movimento Sociale Italiano* (Bologna: il Mulino, 1989).
78. According to one count, between 1967 and 1987 left terrorists killed 145 victims, the right 193. Jamieson, *The Heart Attacked*, p. 19.
79. For an autobiography from this world, see G. Salierno, *Autobiografia di un picchiatore fascista* (Turin: Einaudi, 1976).
80. C. Mazzantini, *I balilla andarono a Salò* (Venice: Marsilio, 1995), p. 60.
81. G. Locatelli and D. Martini, *Duce addio: la biografia di Gianfranco Fini* (Milan, 1994), pp. 216–17.
82. R. Ventresca, 'Mussolini's ghost: Italy's Duce in history and memory', *History and Memory*, 18, 2006, p. 103.
83. L. De Rosa, 'Conclusione' in his (ed.), *Roma del duemila*, p. 325.
84. R. Morassut, 'La città del futuro', in P. Salvagni (ed.), *Roma capitale nel XXI secolo: la città metropolitana policentrica* (Rome: Palombi editore, 2005), pp. 70–2.
85. *Ibid.*, p. 72.
85. P. Salvagni, 'La città metropolitana policentrica di Roma capitale' in Salvagni (ed.), *Roma capitale nel XXI secolo*, p. 15.
87. *Ibid.*, p. 13.
88. *Ibid.*, p. 10.
89. See E. La Rocca, 'Graffiti, un fenomeno antico' and L. Cardilli, 'La situazione romana: prospettive' in L. Cardilli (ed.), *Graffiti urbani: prevenzioni-interventi* (Rome: Atremide Edizioni, 2000).
90. Salvagni (ed.), *Roma capitale nel XXI secolo*, p. i.
91. E. Gentile, *Fascismo di pietra* (Rome: Laterza, 2007), p. 258.
92. *Il Messaggero*, 30 April 2008.
93. G. Rauti, *L'immane conflitto. Mussolini, Roosevelt, Stalin, Churchill, Hitler* (Rome: Centro editoriale nazionale, 1966), pp. 178; 190–1.
94. A. Giuli, *Il passo delle oche: l'identità irrisolta dei postfascisti* (Turin: Einaudi, 2007), pp. 37–8.
95. *Il Corriere della Sera*, 11 May 2009.
96. The *Independent*, 1 May 2008; *The Times*, 24 July 2008.
97. *La Repubblica*, 9 September 2008.
98. *La Repubblica*, 11 September 2008.
99. In fact, he is an immigrant from the Molise, in quite a few senses, a 'southern intellectual'.
100. *La Repubblica*, 11 February 2009.

Conclusion

1. M. Herzfeld, *Evicted from eternity: the restructuring of modern Rome* (University of Chicago Press, 2009), pp. 2; 23.
2. *Ibid.*, p. 7
3. *Ibid.*, pp. 54; 129–30.
4. *Ibid.*, p. 262.
5. *Ibid.*, pp. 308; 312.
6. P. Avarello, 'L'urbanizzazione' in L. De Rosa (ed.), *Roma del duemila* (Bari: Laterza, 2000), p. 201.
7. E.H. Carr, *What is history?* (Harmondsworth: Penguin, 1964), p. 23.
8. For his (fake) biography, see www.lindseydavis.co.uk/biography.MDF.htm, accessed 14 July 2010.
9. For the archaeological discovery of the tomb of Marcus Nonius Macrinus, sold as revealing the 'reality' behind *Gladiator*, see the *Guardian*, 17 October 2008.

INDEX

———— ✳ ————